A

BIBLIOGRAPHY

OF

REGIMENTAL HISTORIES

OF THE

BRITISH ARMY

Compiled by

ARTHUR S. WHITE, I.S.O., M.M., F.R.Hist.S.
late Librarian of the War Office

With a foreword by

FIELD MARSHAL SIR GERALD W. R. TEMPLER,
K.G., G.C.B., G.C.M.G., K.B.E., D.S.O., D.C.L.

WITH
ADDENDUM

Published by
THE NAVAL & MILITARY PRESS

First Published 1965 by The Society for Army Historical Research
in conjuction with The Army Museums Ogilby Trust

This Edition Published 1992 by

THE NAVAL & MILITARY PRESS Ltd.
The Military Book Specialists
DALLINGTON
EAST SUSSEX

Reprinted 1994

Additions Set by
LANGLANDS EDITION, LOUGHBOROUGH

Printed and bound in England by
ANTONY ROWE LTD, CHIPPENHAM

White, Arthur S.
A Bibliography of Regimental Histories of the British Army.
1. Great Britain. Army. Regiments. History. Bibliographies.
I. Title.
016.3553'1'0941

ISBN 1 897632 25 8

FOREWORD

by

FIELD MARSHAL SIR GERALD TEMPLER, K.G.

THIS is a bibliography for students of military history. It is not intended as a book for the general reader. There has never been anything like it before, though it has been badly wanted for years. For the author, or perhaps compiler would be the better word, it has been a labour of love stretching over a long period. For thirty-seven years, Mr. Arthur Sharpin White served in the War Office Library, and for eleven years he was its Librarian. Indeed his heart lay in his work and he, together with his predecessors and his successor, played a major part in building up this Library. Now known as the Ministry of Defence (Central and Army) Library, it contains some 360,000 separate items and is, I believe, the largest library in the United Kingdom devoted to a single subject.

The publication of this work will introduce to Librarians, both at home and abroad, the very considerable literature dealing with the Regiments and Corps of the British Army, information that has not previously been readily available. It has been sponsored by the Society for Army Historical Research of which Mr. White, now one of its Vice-Presidents, was a Founder-Member and for thirty-one years the Honorary Secretary.

It is right to record that the publication has been made possible by the provision of financial assistance by the Army Museums Ogilby Trust, which was set up by the late Colonel R. J. L. Ogilby, in 1954, to promote and foster Regimental Tradition. Colonel Ogilby was a Vice-President of the Society, and for many years Chairman of its Council.

The long and distinguished history of the British Army is an amalgam of its component parts—its Corps and Regiments—whether they have been disbanded or merged over the years, or whether they exist to-day in their original guise or in some new form.

Long may devotion to those Corps and Regiments continue. Without that devotion, the Army would lose something quite irreplaceable, as other Armies in the modern world have found.

The Publisher wishes to thank
The National Army Museum
Mr. Peter de Lotz
and others
for their assistance in the
preparation of the Addendum

PREFACE

WITH the large increase in the number of regimental histories that have appeared during the past half century the need for a bibliography has become more and more apparent. I began collecting material over thirty years ago, mainly for my own use. Now owing to the recent reorganization and amalgamations of regiments the time would seem appropriate for the production of such a work.

Mention should be made of two articles in the Journal of the Society for Army Historical Research which partly cover the field, *Militia Regiments of Great Britain; a Calendar of their Records and Histories* (1933) by the late Lt.-Col. J. H. Leslie and *A Bibliography of Volunteering* (1945) by Mr. Ernest J. Martin and the present compiler.

As with most bibliographies the problem has been what to include. In order to keep within reasonable limits autobiographies, recruiting brochures (largely advertisements), regimental journals, and items of more or less ephemeral interest have been excluded.

For the Regular Army the order adopted is roughly that in which the regiments are shewn in the Army List before the recent amalgamations, the pre-amalgamation titles being used. Current titles are given in the Appendix (the disbanded Irish regiments are included in their order of precedence). Then follow, in separate groups, Fencibles; Militia; Yeomanry; and Volunteers and Territorial Army units arranged under counties; Women's Corps; Disbanded Regiments and Corps; Colonials and Provincials; Foreign Corps in British Service; ending with the Royal Marines; and Body Guards.

In the text, square brackets [ ] are used to denote information not found on the title-page. The term 'plates' is used to describe illustrations inset on unnumbered pages and the size is given in inches. In a few cases where full details are not given, the item has been taken from a catalogue but I have been unable to see a copy. The usual abbreviations of military ranks have been used and all decorations omitted.

My grateful thanks are due to Mr. D. W. King, Librarian, Ministry of Defence (Central and Army) and Mr. R. T. Eldridge, Assistant Librarian, for their generous assistance and to the Army Museums Ogilby Trust for making publication possible.

August, 1965

A. S. WHITE

v

CONTENTS

Foreword   –   –   –   –   –   –   iii

Preface   –   –   –   –   –   –   –   v

SECTION I — GENERAL

General Works   –   –   –   –   –   –   2

General Works: Scottish –   –   –   –   –   3

SECTION II — REGULAR ARMY

Household Brigade   –   –   –   –   –   8

Household Cavalry   –   –   –   –   –   8

Royal Armoured Corps
     General   –   –   –   –   –   –   9
     Cavalry   –   –   –   –   –   –   10
     Royal Tank Regiment: Royal Tank Corps   –   –   25

Royal Regiment of Artillery
     General   –   –   –   –   –   –   27
     Royal Horse Artillery   –   –   –   –   30
     Royal Field Artillery   –   –   –   –   32
     Royal Garrison Artillery   –   –   –   –   32
     1914-1918 Formations : Divisions   –   –   –   33
     1914-1918 Formations : Brigades   –   –   –   33
     1914-1918 Formations : Batteries, R.F.A.   –   –   34
     1914-1918 Formations : Batteries, R.G.A.   –   –   34
     1939-1945 Formations : Royal Artillery   –   –   35

Corps of Royal Engineers
     General   –   –   –   –   –   –   36
     Regular Units   –   –   –   –   –   38
     1914-1918 Formations : Units   –   –   –   38
     1939-1945 Formations : Units   –   –   –   39

Royal Corps of Signals   –   –   –   –   –   40

Foot Guards   –   –   –   –   –   –   41

Infantry of the Line (in Army List order and including
     Disbanded Irish Regiments)   –   47

SECTION III — DEPARTMENTS: CORPS

Royal Army Chaplains' Department   –   –   –   138

Royal Army Service Corps   –   –   –   –   138

Royal Army Medical Corps   –   –   –   –   139

Royal Army Ordnance Corps   –   –   –   –   141

Royal Electrical and Mechanical Engineers   –   –   141

Corps of Royal Military Police   –   –   –   –   142

Royal Army Pay Corps –   –   –   –   –   142
Royal Army Veterinary Corps   –   –   –   –   142
Small Arms School Corps   –   –   –   –   142
Military Provost Staff Corps   –   –   –   –   142
Royal Army Educational Corps –   –   –   –   143
Royal Army Dental Corps   –   –   –   –   143
Royal Pioneer Corps   –   –   –   –   –   143
Army Physical Training Corps   –   –   –   –   143
Queen Alexandra's Royal Army Nursing Corps –   –   144

SECTION IV — AUXILIARY FORCES

Fencibles
      England and Wales –   –   –   –   –   146
      Scotland   –   –   –   –   –   –   147
Militia: Special Reserve
      England and Wales –   –   –   –   –   149
      Scotland   –   –   –   –   –   –   156
      Ireland   –   –   –   –   –   –   158
      Channel Islands   –   –   –   –   –   161
Yeomanry
      General   –   –   –   –   –   –   161
      England and Wales –   –   –   –   –   161
      Scotland   –   –   –   –   –   –   175
Volunteers : Territorial Force (later Army)
      General   –   –   –   –   –   –   178
      England and Wales –   –   –   –   –   179
      Scotland   –   –   –   –   –   –   223
      Ireland   –   –   –   –   –   –   234

SECTION V — MISCELLANEOUS

Women's Corps –   –   –   –   –   –   236
Disbanded Regiments and Corps
      General   –   –   –   –   –   –   236
      Section 1—Numbered   –   –   –   –   237
      Section 2—Named   –   –   –   –   –   242
Colonial
      Section 1—Regular –   –   –   –   –   246
      Section 2—Fencibles : Provincials   –   –   –   248
Foreign Corps in British Pay   –   –   –   –   250
Royal Marines –   –   –   –   –   –   253
Body Guards   –   –   –   –   –   –   255
Appendix showing present day titles of regiments   –   257

SECTION I

GENERAL

GENERAL WORKS

Note. For Cannon's Historical Records Series see under the separate regiments.

Famous Regiments of the British Army: their Origin and Services. With a Sketch of the Rise and Progress of the Military Establishment of England and Brief Memoirs of Eminent British Generals. By W. Davenport Adams. London: James Hogg and Sons [1864]. 320 pp., portraits, 1 coloured plate of uniform. 6½″

The Regiments of the British Army, chronologically arranged. Compiled by R. Trimen. London: W. H. Allen & Co., 1878. xii, 156 pp. 8½″

The British Army: its Regimental Records, Badges, Devices, etc. By Major J. H. Lawrence-Archer. London: George Bell and Sons, 1888. xxii, 623 pp., illustrations of badges. 8½″
   Contains Short Histories of all Regiments and Corps. 500 copies only printed.

Her Majesty's Army. A Descriptive Account of the various Regiments now comprising the Queen's Forces, from their first Establishment to the Present Time. By Walter Richards. London: J. S. Virtue & Co. Ltd. [1892]. 2 vols., with coloured illustrations. 11″
   Vol. 1 contains 16 and Vol. 2 15 coloured plates of uniform.

────── Another version. In 4 Divisions, each with separate titlepage.

The British Army and Auxiliary Forces. By Col. C. Cooper-King, R.M.A. With 90 [132] full-page plates from original photographs. London: Cassell & Co. Ltd. [1893]. 2 vols. 12¾″
   Short histories of each regiment and corps. Issued to subscribers.

The Records and Badges of Every Regiment and Corps in the British Army. By Henry Manners Chichester, late 85th Regiment, and George Burges-Short, late Major 3rd Battalion The Manchester Regiment. London: William Clowes and Sons Ltd., 1895. xiv, 568 pp., with 24 coloured plates and 230 illustrations in the text. 8½″
   20 coloured plates of uniform and 4 of colours.

────── 2nd edition. London: Gale & Polden Ltd. [1900]. xv, 942 pp., with 24 coloured plates and 240 illustrations in the text. 8½″
   Short histories of all Regiments and Corps.

The Regimental Records of the British Army. A Historical Resumé chronologically arranged of Titles, Campaigns, Honours, Uniforms, Facings, Badges, Nicknames etc. By John S. Farmer. London: Grant Richards, 1901. 238 pp., illustrations. 8½″

Famous British Regiments. By Major Arthur Griffiths. London: T. Fisher Unwin, 1900. 152 pp. 7½″

Famous Fighting Regiments. By G. Hood. London: Andrew Melrose, 1900.
121 pp. 7½"

Short Histories of the Territorial Regiments of the British Army, including the
Names of the Officers and Soldiers who have won the Victoria Cross, or, the
Distinguished Conduct Medal. Edited by R. de M. Rudolf, of the War Office.
London: His Majesty's Stationery Office [1905]. iv, 726 pp. 8½"
  These short histories of the 67 Infantry Regiments were also issued separately
  in pamphlet form. They were originally compiled and issued for recruiting
  purposes in 1894-95. Revised editions of the separate issues were published
  between 1910-1915.

British Regiments at the Front; the Story of their Battle Honours. By Reginald
Hodder. London: Hodder & Stoughton, 1914. 189 pp. (Daily Telegraph
War Books). 7½"

Our Regiments and their Glorious Records, with a History of the Territorials.
By Charles White. London: C. Arthur Pearson Ltd., 1915. 150 pp. 7½"

A Pocket History of the Regiments. By Charles Lamb. Edinburgh: Oliver &
Boyd, 1916. 95 pp. 6¾"

Regiments at a Glance. By E. T. Dorling. 2nd edition. London: G. Philip
& Son, Ltd., 1917. 127 pp., plates, illustrations. 7¼"
  4 coloured plates of colours.

GENERAL WORKS : SCOTTISH

Sketches of the Character, Manners, and Present State of the Highlanders of
Scotland; with details of the Military Service of the Highland Regiments. By
Col. David Stewart. Edinburgh: Archibald Constable & Co., 1822. 2 vols.
8½"
  Contains accounts of all Highland Regiments, past and present, including
  Fencibles. 2nd edition, 1822. 3rd edition, 1825.

A History of the Highlands and of the Highland Clans; with an extensive selection from the hitherto inedited Stuart Papers. By James Browne. New edition.
Edinburgh: A. Fullarton & Co. [1852-53]. 4 vols., portraits, plates, illustrations,
maps. 9¾"

———— 1st edition. Glasgow: 1838. 4 vols. (vols. 1-3 have 2nd tp. dated
1835-6).

———— Another edition. Glasgow: A. Fullarton & Co., 1840. 4 vols.

———— New edition. Edinburgh: A. Fullarton & Co., 1845. 4 vols.
  Contents similar to Stewart, above.

A History of the Scottish Highlands, Highland Clans and Highland Regiments, etc. Edited by John S. Keltie. Edinburgh: A. Fullarton & Co., 1875. 2 vols., portraits, illustrations, maps. 10½″
    An enlargement of the work by Browne, above.

────── New edition, with the Regimental Portion brought down to the present time from official sources by William Melven. Edinburgh: Jack, 1887. 2 vols., portraits, plates, illustrations. 10½″
    32 coloured plates of tartans and 8 of Regimental Colours.

────── Another edition. London, Edinburgh, Glasgow: William Mitchell, 1887. 2 vols. 10⅜″
    Copies are found bound in 5 or 6 volumes.

History of the Scottish Regiments in the British Army. By Arch. K. Murray, Major. Glasgow: Thomas Murray & Son, 1862. 416 pp., portraits, plates, plans. 8¼″
    36 coloured plates, including 14 of uniform and 7 of colours.

An Account of the Scottish Regiments, with the Statistics of each, from 1808 to March 1861. Compiled from old Regimental Record Books, and Monthly Returns of each Regiment, now rendered to the War Department. [By P. H. MacKerlie]. Edinburgh: William P. Nimmo, 1862. 48 pp. 8½″

Old Scottish Regimental Colours. By Andrew Ross, S.S.C., Hon. Sec., Old Scottish Regimental Colours Committee. With 28 coloured plates and other illustrations. Edinburgh: William Blackwood & Sons, 1885. x, 158 pp. 15″
    Items noted under separate regiments.

The Clans, Septs and Regiments of the Scottish Highlands. By Frank Adam. Edinburgh: W. & A. K. Johnston, Ltd., 1908. xxiii, 505 pp., portraits, plates, illustrations, maps. 8½″
    Sections on: The Highland Regiments, Past and Present; Scottish Lowland Regiments. Coloured plates of tartans.

────── 2nd edition. 1924. xxxiii, 523 pp.

────── 3rd edition, with Foreword by Thomas Innes of Learney. 1934. xxiv, 523 pp.

────── 4th edition, revised by Sir Thomas Innes of Learney. 1952. viii, 624 pp.

────── 6th edition. 1960. xii, 623 pp.

A Military History of Perthshire, 1660-1902. Edited by the Marchioness of Tullibardine. Perth: R. A. & J. Hay, 1908. xxiii, 634 pp., portraits, plates, maps. 9¾″
    Contains accounts of all Perthshire regiments, past and present which are noted separately.

A Military History of Perthshire, 1899-1902. Edited by the Marchioness of Tullibardine. With a Roll of the Perthshire men of the present day who have seen active service under the British Flag. Compiled by the Editor and Jane G. C. Macdonald. Perth: R. A. & J. Hay, 1908. Portraits, plates, maps. 9¾"

Territorial Soldiering in the North-East of Scotland, 1759-1814. By John Malcolm Bulloch. Aberdeen: The New Spalding Club, 1914. lxviii, 518 pp., portrait, plate, illustration. 10"
    Contains accounts of all Aberdeen and Banff regiments which are also recorded separately.

The Story of the Highland Regiments. By Frederick Watson. London: A. & C. Black, Ltd., 1915. xi, 317 pp., plates. 8½"
    8 coloured plates.

———— (1725-1925). [2nd edition]. London: A. & C. Black, Ltd., 1925. xi, 323 pp., plates. 8¼"
    8 coloured plates.

The Lowland Scots Regiments; their Origin, Character and Services previous to the Great War of 1914. Edited for the Association of Lowland Scots by the Rt. Hon. Sir Herbert Maxwell, Bt. Glasgow: James Maclehose & Sons, 1918. xii, 339 pp., portrait, plates. 10"
    12 coloured plates of uniform.
    Contents: The 2nd Dragoons-Royal Scots Greys, by Sir James Balfour Paul; The Scots Guards, by Capt. Charles B. Balfour of Newton Don; The Royal Scots (Lothian Regiment), by Major M. M. Haldane; The Royal Scots Fusiliers, by Lieut.-Col. Reginald Toogood; The King's Own Scottish Borderers, by Brig.-Gen. Montagu Grant Wilkinson; Notes on the Origin of the K.O.S.B., by Andrew Ross; The Cameronians (Scottish Rifles)-The 90th Perthshire Light Infantry, by Andrew Ross; Scottish Regiments disbanded, by Andrew Ross; Regimental Music.
    Each regiment was also issued separately.

The Scottish Regiments of the British Army. Edited with an Introduction by Major Ian H. Mackay Scobie. Edinburgh: Oliver & Boyd, Ltd., 1942. 112 pp. 7¼"
    Short Histories of all Scottish Regiments.

———— 2nd (corrected) impression. 1943.

The Regiments of Scotland; their histories, badges, tartans, etc. By J. B. Kirkwood. Edinburgh: The Moray Press, 1949. 142 pp., illustrations. 7¼"

The Highland Brigade and Regiments. With a Preface by Field-Marshal Earl Wavell. Glasgow: printed by R. E. Robertson Ltd., 1950. 132 pp., illustrations. 5½"
    Short histories of all Highland regiments.

The Highland Brigade and Regiments.   Another edition with title: Short History of the Highland Brigade and Regiments.   Glasgow: printed by R. E. Robertson, Ltd., 1952.   135 pp., illustrations. $5\frac{1}{2}''$

Scots of the Line.   By John Maclennan.   Foreword by Lieut.-Gen. Sir Colin Barber.   Edinburgh: W. & R. Chambers [1953].   183 pp. $8\frac{1}{2}''$
  Incidents in the history of Scottish regiments.

The Uniforms and History of the Scottish Regiments; Britain-Canada-Australia-New Zealand-South Africa, 1625 to the Present Day.   By Major R. Money Barnes, in collaboration with C. Kennedy Allen and Lieut. Thomas B. Beatty, Jnr.   Foreword by Gen. Sir Neil Methuen Ritchie.   London: Seeley Service & Co., 1956.   351 pp., plates, illustrations. $9\frac{5}{8}''$
  12 coloured plates of uniforms.

History of the Scottish Regiments.   By W. P. Paul.   Glasgow: McKenzie, Vincent & Co. Ltd., 1960.   189 pp., portraits, illustrations. $8''$

Scotland the Brave.   The Story of the Scottish Soldier.   By John Laffin. London: Cassell, 1963.   xiii, 191 pp., plates. $8\frac{1}{2}''$
  Short histories of the Scottish Regiments.   4 coloured plates of uniform.

The Sword of the North: Highland Memories of the Great War.   By Dugald MacEchern, Minister of Bower, Lieutenant, 5th Batt. The Seaforth Highlanders. Inverness: Robert Carruthers & Sons, " Courier " Office, 1923.   xvi, 672 pp., portraits, illustrations. $10''$
  Gives " a view of the general effort made by the Northern Highlands in the Great War " and includes chapters on the 51st (Highland) Division; Aberdeen Territorial Force Assoc.; Lovats Scouts; Scottish Horse; Inverness-shire R.H.A.; Argyll Mountain Battery; Ross & Cromarty Highland Mountain Battery; Black Watch, 6th and 7th Battalions; Seaforth Highlanders (each Battalion); Cameron Highlanders (each Battalion); Highland Mounted Brigade, T. & S. Column, R.A.S.C.; Highland Mounted Brigade Field Ambulance.

SECTION II

REGULAR ARMY

HOUSEHOLD BRIGADE

The Guards; or the Household Troops of England. By Captain Rafter. London: Clarke, Beeton & Co. [1852]. xix, 242 pp., plates. 6¼"

The Household Brigade Officer Cadet Battalion. History, Organization and Training. By Commanding Officer and Staff. London: W. Straker, Ltd., printers, 1918. 68 pp. 8½"

The King's Guards, Horse and Foot. By Henry Legge-Bourke. London: Macdonald & Co. [1952]. 169 pp., portraits, illustrations. 10½"
  Numerous coloured photographs. Each section also published separately.

———— New edition with title: The Queen's Guards, Horse and Foot. [By] Major Sir Henry Legge-Bourke. London: Macdonald & Co., 158 pp. 11"

HOUSEHOLD CAVALRY

The Story of the Household Cavalry. By Capt. Sir George Arthur, Bart., late Second Life Guards. London: Archibald Constable & Co. Ltd., 1909. 2 vols., portraits, plates. 10¼"
  1 coloured plate of uniform in vol. 1 and 4 in vol. 2.

———— Vol. 3. By Capt. Sir George Arthur, Bart., assisted by Capt. Shennan, Royal Horse Guards. London: William Heinemann Ltd., 1926. Plates. 10¼"

The Household Cavalry At War: First Household Cavalry Regiment. By Col. the Hon. Humphrey Wyndham. Aldershot: Gale & Polden, Ltd., 1952. xiii, 189 pp., portraits, plates, maps. 9½"

The Household Cavalry at War: the Story of the Second Household Cavalry Regiment. By Roden Orde. Aldershot: Gale & Polden Ltd., 1953. xxx, 624 pp., portraits, illustrations, maps, end-paper maps. 9½"

THE LIFE GUARDS

Historical Record of the Life Guards; containing an Account of the Formation of the Corps in the year 1660, and of its subsequent Services to 1835. Prepared for publication under the direction of the Adjutant General. London: printed by William Clowes and Sons, 1835. xii, x, 291 pp., plates. 8¾"
  6 coloured plates of uniform. Some copies have second engraved title-page Historical Records, of the British Army, 1837.

———— 2nd edition. To 1836. London: Longman, Orme & Co., 1840. [8], xvi, 299 pp., plates. (Cannon's Historical Records Series). 8¾"
  6 coloured plates of uniform.

A Short History of The Life Guards. By R. J. T. Hills, Squadron-Quartermaster-Corporal. Aldershot: Gale & Polden Ltd., 1933. 107 pp., maps. 7¼"

The Story of the First Life Guards. By Capt. C. W. Bell, A.E.C. London: George C. Harrap & Co. Ltd. [1922]. 80 pp. 7½″

War Diary of the 1st Life Guards. First Year, 1914-1915. By Capt. the Hon. E. H. Wyndham. No imprint. 80 pp., portraits, map. [1915]. 11¼″

———— Another edition. [London: Witherby & Co., printers, 1915]. 158 pp., portraits, map. 5½″×7½″

The Dress of the First Regiment of Life Guards in Three Centuries. By U. H. R. Broughton (late First Life Guards).   London: Halton & Truscott-Smith, Ltd., 1925. xxii, 36 pp., plates. 12½″
   80 plates, including 40 coloured. Limited to 300 numbered copies.

ROYAL HORSE GUARDS (THE BLUES)

An Historical Record of the Royal Regiment of Horse Guards or Oxford Blues, its Services, and the Transactions in which it has been engaged, from its first Establishment to the Present Time. By Edmund Packe, late Captain, Royal Horse Guards. London: William Clowes, 1834. x, 150 pp., portrait, plates. 8¾″
   6 coloured plates of uniform, coloured vignette on second title-page.

———— [Another edition]. London: Parker, Furnivall & Parker, 1847. xx, 152 pp., portrait, plates. (Cannon's Historical Records Series). 8¾″
   7 coloured plates of uniform, coloured vignette on second title-page.

Note. There is a re-issue of this edition in which the plates do not agree with the list given on p. xx. The plate of 1662 is omitted (it is not included in any edition) while two extra plates of 1815 and 1834 are included.

His Majesty's Royal Regiment of Horse Guards (The Blues). Colonel-in-Chief: His Majesty the King. [Short history]. Aldershot: Gale & Polden Ltd. [1947], 24 pp. 7¼″
   1 coloured plate of uniform.

ROYAL ARMOURED CORPS

The Royal Armoured Corps. By Captain J. R. W. Murland, 5th Royal Innis-killing Dragoon Guards. London: Methuen & Co. Ltd. [1943]. viii, 106 pp., plates, charts. 7¼″

With Pennants Flying. The Immortal Deeds of the Royal Armoured Corps. By David Masters. London: Eyre & Spottiswoode, 1943. 200 pp., plates. 8½″

The Royal Armoured Corps. Prepared for the War Office by Frank Owen and H. W. Atkins. [London: H.M. Stationery Office, 1945]. 72 pp., illustrations, maps. 9″
   Title on paper cover " The Official Account of the Royal Armoured Corps. Through Mud and Blood to the Green Fields Beyond."

The Italian Campaign, 3 Sept., 1943-2 May, 1945. Royal Armoured Corps. [A Series of sketches by Eric Manning and portraits by Grahame Drew]. No imprint [1945]. 97 pp., portraits, map. 11¾" × 15½"

1st KING'S DRAGOON GUARDS

Historical Record of the First, or King's Regiment of Dragoon Guards; containing an Account of the Formation of the Regiment in the year 1685, and of its subsequent Services to 1836. London: William Clowes and Sons, 1837. [8], xiv, 122 pp., plates. (Cannon's Historical Records Series). 8¾"
  4 coloured plates of uniform.

1st King's Dragoon Guards: Extracts from the Regimental Records, Army Despatches, and other papers connected with the History of the Regiment from the Formation in 1685 to 1912. [By Capt. I. O'Donnell]. London: William Clowes and Sons Ltd., 1913. [4], 60 pp., portraits. 8½"

────── Another edition. 1685 to 1920. [By Lieut.-Col. H. J. Williams]. [London: William Clowes and Sons Ltd., 1920]. [4], 42 pp., portrait. 8½"

A Short History of 1st King's Dragoon Guards, from the Regimental Records, Army Despatches, and other papers connected with the history of the Regiment from its formation in 1685 to 1929. Aldershot: Gale & Polden Ltd., 1929. 66 pp., portrait. 7¼"

History of the King's Dragoon Guards, 1938-1945. By Col. D. McCorquodale, Major B. L. B. Hutchings, Major A. D. Woozley. Edited by Major A. D. Woozley, with a Foreword by Gen. Sir Richard L. McCreery. [Glasgow: printed for the Regiment by McCorquodale & Co. Ltd., 1950]. xv, 403 pp., plates, maps. 8½"

1st King's Dragoon Guards. A Brief Pictorial Record of the Regiment, 1685-1958. [Aldershot: printed by Gale & Polden Ltd.], 1958. 32 pp., portraits, illustrations. 7½" × 9¾"
  5 coloured illustrations.

King's Dragoon Guards. 250th Anniversary of the Raising of the Regiment, 1685-1935. [Aldershot: Gale & Polden Ltd., 1935]. 24 pp., portraits, plates. 7¼" × 9¾"
  Souvenir album containing Roll, reproductions of photographs, standards, badge, etc.

Uniforms and Equipment of Cavalry Regiments, from 1685 to 1811. By the Rev. Percy Sumner. I.—Horse and Dragoon Guards Regiments. 1st Dragoon Guards. (In Society for Army Historical Research, Journal, vol. 13, 1934, pp. 82-106). Plates, illustrations. 9¼"

A Brief History of the Uniform of the King's Dragoon Guards. By Capt. R. G. Hollies-Smith. (In The K.D.G., 1958, pp. 302-312). Portraits, illustrations. 9½"

THE QUEEN'S BAYS (2ND DRAGOON GUARDS)

Historical Record of the Second, or Queen's Regiment of Dragoon Guards. (Queen's Bays): containing an Account of the Formation of the Regiment in 1685, and of its subsequent Services to 1837. London: William Clowes and Sons, 1837. viii, viii, viii, 100 pp., plates. (Cannon's Historical Records Series). 8¾"
    4 coloured plates of uniform.

A History of The Queen's Bays (The 2nd Dragoon Guards), 1685-1929. By Frederic Whyte and A. Hilliard Atteridge from Material collected by Major H. W. Hall. With a Foreword by Field-Marshal Viscount Allenby. London: Jonathan Cape, 1930. 525 pp., portraits, plates, maps, plans. 8¾"
    8 coloured plates of uniform.

A History of The Queen's Bays (The 2nd Dragoon Guards), 1929-1945. By Major Gen. W. R. Beddington, with a Foreword by Gen. Sir R. L. McCreery. Winchester: Warren & Son Ltd., 1954. xvi, 271 pp., portraits, plates, maps, end-paper maps. 8½"

A Short History of The Queen's Bays from the Outbreak of the Second World War, 3rd September, 1939, to the Capitulation of the German Armies in Italy, 2nd May, 1945. In three parts: I, France. II. North Africa. III. Italy. Aldershot: Gale & Polden Ltd. [1947]. [v], 49 pp., portraits, maps. 7¼"

3RD CARABINIERS (PRINCE OF WALES'S DRAGOON GUARDS)

3RD (PRINCE OF WALES'S) DRAGOON GUARDS

Historical Record of the Third, or Prince of Wales' Regiment of Dragoon Guards; containing an Account of the Formation of the Regiment in 1685, and of its subsequent Services to 1838. London: William Clowes and Sons, 1838. [8], viii, vi, 129 pp., plates. (Cannon's Historical Records Series). 8¾"
    2 coloured plates of uniform and 1 of Guidon.

The History of the Third (Prince of Wales's) Dragoon Guards, 1914-1918. [By Capt. H. P. Holt. Guildford: Billing and Sons Ltd.], 1937. xi, 112 pp., portraits, plates, maps. Privately printed. 8¾"

6TH DRAGOON GUARDS (THE CARABINIERS)

Historical Record of the Sixth Regiment of Dragoon Guards, or The Carabineers; containing an Account of the Formation of the Regiment in 1685, and of its subsequent Services to 1839. London: Longman, Orme & Co., 1839. [8], viii, vi, 104 pp., plates. (Cannon's Historical Records Series). 8¾"
    3 coloured plates of uniform (1 includes standard).

A Continuation of the Historical Records of the VI D. G. Carabineers. By Capt. A. Sprot. Chatham: Gale & Polden [1888]. xii, 76 pp. 7"

3rd Carabiniers (Prince of Wales's Dragoon Guards). 250th Anniversary of the Raising of the 3rd Dragoon Guards (Prince of Wales's) and The Carabineers (6th Dragoon Guards). Aldershot, July, 1935. [Aldershot: Gale & Polden Ltd., 1935]. 20 pp., portraits, plates. $7\frac{3}{4}'' \times 9\frac{3}{4}''$
   Souvenir Album containing Roll and reproductions of photographs, including standards, etc.

Regimental History, 3rd Carabiniers (Prince of Wales's Dragoon Guards). No imprint [1957]. 12 pp. $5'' \times 6\frac{1}{2}''$
   Coloured illustration of uniform on paper cover.

4TH/7TH ROYAL DRAGOON GUARDS

4TH ROYAL IRISH DRAGOON GUARDS

Historical Record of the Fourth, or Royal Irish Regiment of Dragoon Guards; containing an Account of the Formation of the Regiment in 1685, and of its subsequent Services to 1838. London: Longman, Orme & Co., 1839. [8], viii, vi, 94 pp., plates. (Cannon's Historical Records Series). $8\frac{3}{4}''$
   2 coloured plates of uniform, 1 of guidon.

Record of the 4th Royal Irish Dragoon Guards in the Great War, 1914-1918. By the Rev. Harold Gibb, Lieut., 4th R.I. Dragoon Guards, 1914-1915. Canterbury: [printed by Butler & Tanner, Frome], 1925. viii, 75 pp., portraits, plates. $8\frac{1}{2}''$
   Coloured plate of standard.

An Alphabetical List of the Officers of the Fourth (Royal Irish) Dragoon Guards, from 1800 to 1856. By Henry Stooks Smith. London: Longman, Brown, Green, Longman and Roberts, 1856. xvi, 32 pp. $8\frac{1}{2}''$

7TH DRAGOON GUARDS (PRINCESS ROYALS)

Historical Record of the Seventh, or Princess Royal's Regiment of Dragoon Guards; containing an Account of the Formation of the Regiment in 1688, and of its subsequent Services to 1839. London: Longman, Orme & Co., 1839. [8], viii, vi, 98 pp., plates. (Cannon's Historical Records Series). $8\frac{1}{2}''$
   2 coloured plates of uniform (1 includes standard).

Seventh (Princess Royal's) Dragoon Guards. The History of the Regiment (1688-1882). By Col. C. W. Thompson and With the Regiment in South Africa (1900-1902). By Major N. D. H. Campbell, Capt. W. S. Whetherly, Capt. J. E. D. Holland. Liverpool: The " Daily Post," Printers, 1913. Portraits, plates, maps, sketch maps. $11\frac{1}{4}''$
   1 coloured plate of standard.

Records of the Seventh Dragoon Guards (Princess Royal's) during the Great War. By Capt. F. J. Scott. Sherborne: F. Bennett & Co. Ltd., 1923. vii, 210 pp., portraits, plate, maps in end pocket. $8\frac{3}{4}''$

Actions of the 4th/7th Royal Dragoon Guards, May-June 1940. [Dorking: Rowe's, printers, 1941]. 55 pp., plate, maps. 8½″

The First and the Last. The Story of the 4th/7th Royal Dragoon Guards, 1939-1945. Compiled from the regimental war diary, squadron diaries, personal narratives and the unofficial "Actions of the 4th/7th Royal Dragoon Guards in France." By Major J. D. P. Stirling. London: Art & Educational Publishers Ltd. [1946]. xv, 192 pp., plates, maps. 8¼″

Short History of the 4th Royal Irish Dragoon Guards, 1685-1922; 7th (Princess Royal's) Dragoon Guards, 1688-1922; 4th/7th Royal Dragoon Guards, 1922-1939. [By Major J. A. d'Avigdor-Goldsmid]. Aldershot: Gale & Polden Ltd., 1943. [5], 66 pp., coloured plate. 7¼″

5TH ROYAL INNISKILLING DRAGOON GUARDS

5TH (PRINCESS CHARLOTTE OF WALES'S) DRAGOON GUARDS

Historical Record of the Fifth, or Princess Charlotte of Wales's Regiment of Dragoon Guards; containing an Account of the Formation of the Regiment in 1685, and of its subsequent Services to 1838. London: Longman, Orme & Co., 1839. [8], viii, vi, 99 pp., plates. (Cannon's Historical Records Series). 8¾″
  2 coloured plates of uniform and 1 of standard.

The Story of a Regiment of Horse, being the Regimental History from 1685 to 1922 of the 5th Princess Charlotte of Wales' Dragoon Guards. Compiled by Major the Hon. Ralph Legge Pomeroy, some time a Member of the Corps. Edinburgh: William Blackwood and Sons, 1924. 2 vols., portraits, plates, maps. 9¾″
  Vol. 1 contains 11 coloured plates, including 7 of uniform and 1 of standard; Vol. 2, 2 of uniform and 3 of standards.

The Green Horse in Ladysmith. Edited by Lieut.-Col. St. John Gore. London: Sampson Low, Marston & Co., 1901. xi, 171 pp., plates, map. Printed for private circulation. 7¼″

THE INNISKILLINGS (6TH DRAGOONS)

Historical Record of the Sixth, or Inniskilling Regiment of Dragoons; containing an Account of the Formation of the Regiment in 1689, and of its subsequent Services to 1846. Compiled by Richard Cannon, Esq., Adjutant-General's Office, Horse Guards. London: Parker, Furnivall, & Parker, 1847. xxiv, 108 pp., plates. 8¾″
  3 coloured plates of uniform and 1 of guidon.

———— Another edition . . . to 1843. London: John W. Parker. 1843. viii, viii, 116 pp., plates. 8¾″
  Plates as above.

The Inniskilling Dragoons.   The Records of an Old Heavy Cavalry Regiment.
By Major E. S. Jackson.   London: Arthur L. Humphreys, 1909.   xvi, 356 pp.,
portraits, plates, maps. $9\frac{1}{4}''$
   8 coloured plates including 7 of uniform and 1 of guidon.

Short History of the 6th (Inniskilling) Dragoons.   London: H.M. Stationery
Office [1908].   12 pp. $8\frac{1}{2}''$

With the Inniskilling Dragoons.   The Record of a Cavalry Regiment during the
Boer War, 1899-1902.   By Lieut.-Col. J. Watkins Yardley.   London: Longmans,
Green & Co., 1904.   xiv, 365 pp., portraits, plates, map. $9''$

The Story of the Fifth Royal Inniskilling Dragoon Guards together with a short
account of their illustrious parent regiments The Fifth Princess Charlotte of
Wales's Dragoon Guards and The Sixth Inniskilling Dragoons.   Compiled by
Roger Evans, Major-General.   Aldershot: Gale & Polden Ltd., 1951.   xiv,
44 pp., plates, end-paper maps. $8\frac{1}{2}''$
   2 coloured plates of uniform.

1st THE ROYAL DRAGOONS

Historical Record of the First, or The Royal Regiment of Dragoons; containing
an Account of the Formation in the reign of King Charles the Second, and of its
subsequent Services to 1839.   London: Longman, Orme & Co., 1840.   [8], viii,
viii, 133 pp., plates.   (Cannon's Historical Records Series). $8\frac{3}{4}''$
   2 coloured plates of uniform and 1 of guidon.

Historical Record of the First, or The Royal Regiment of Dragoons; containing
an Account of its Formation in the reign of King Charles the Second, and of its
subsequent Services to the Present Time.   By General De Ainslie, Colonel of
the Regiment.   London: Chapman & Hall Ltd., 1887.   xiv, 311 pp., plates. $9''$
   8 coloured plates of uniform and 1 of guidon.

History of the Royal Dragoons, 1661-1934.   By C. T. Atkinson.   With a Foreword by Brig.-Gen. E. Makins.   Glasgow: printed for the Regiment by Robert
Maclehose & Co. Ltd. [1934].   xx, 547 pp., portraits, plates, maps. $9\frac{3}{4}''$
   11 coloured plates including 6 of uniform and 3 of guidons.

A Short History of The Royal Dragoons.   Compiled by Lieut.-Col. E. Makins.
Potchefstroom, S. Africa: " Het Westen " Printing Works, 1914.   51 pp., plates.
$7''$

Short History of The Royal Dragoons.   [Aldershot: Gale & Polden Ltd., 1954].
31 pp. $7\frac{1}{4}''$
   Coloured plate of guidons.

The Story of the Royal Dragoons, 1938-1945; being the history of the Royal
Dragoons in the campaigns of North Africa, the Middle East, Italy and North-
West Europe.   By J. A. Pitt-Rivers.   London: William Clowes & Sons Ltd.,
1956.   xv, 160 pp., portraits, plates, maps, end-paper maps. $9\frac{1}{2}''$

The Royals in South Africa, 1899-1902. Edited by Lieut.-Col. E. Makins. [Potchefstroom, S. Africa]: published by The Editor of " The Eagle," The Royal Dragoons, 1914. xii, 199 pp., portraits, illustrations. 8½"

A Royal Dragoon in the Spanish Succession War. A contemporary narrative. Edited with Introduction and Notes by C. T. Atkinson. (Society for Army Historical Research, Special Publication No. 5). London: printed by Gale & Polden Ltd., 1938. 57 pp., maps. 9¼"

Uniform and Equipment of Cavalry Regiments, from 1685 to 1811. By the Rev. Percy Sumner. II. Dragoon Regiments. The 1st Royal Dragoons. (In *Society for Army Historical Research, Journal*, vol. 14, 1935, pp. 82-101, 125-142; vol. 16, 1937, pp. 100-108). Plates. 9¼"
    4 coloured plates of uniform.

THE ROYAL SCOTS GREYS (2ND DRAGOONS)

Historical Record of the Royal Regiment of Scots Dragoons now The Second, or Royal North British Dragoons, commonly called The Scots Greys; containing an Account of the Formation of the Regiment in the reign of King Charles II and of its subsequent Services to 1839. London: Longman, Orme & Co., 1840. [8], viii, viii, 137 pp., plates, (Cannon's Historical Records Series). 8¾"
    1 coloured plate of uniform and 1 of guidon.

History of the 2nd Dragoons—The Royal Scots Greys, 1678-1893. By Lieut.-Col. Percy Groves. Illustrated by Harry Payne. Edinburgh: W. & A. K. Johnstone, 1893. 30 pp., plates. (Illustrated Histories of Scottish Regiments, No. 2). 12¼"
    4 coloured plates of uniform.

The History of the Second Dragoons "Royal Scots Greys." By Edward Almack. London: Alexander Moring, Ltd., 1908. xx, 312 pp., portraits, plates. 12"
    3 coloured plates of uniform

"Royal Scots Greys." "Second to None." Extracts from Regimental History, 1678-1914. London: Sifton Praed & Co. Ltd., 1919. 80 pp., maps. 7¼"

The 2nd Dragoons—Royal Scots Greys. By Sir James Balfour Paul. Glasgow: James Maclehose and Sons, 1919. 32 pp. 9½"
    (Repr. from *The Lowland Scots Regiments;* edited by the Right Hon. Sir Herbert Maxwell, Bart.).
    Illustration of uniform on paper cover.

History of The Royal Scots Greys (The Second Dragoons), August 1914-March, 1919. Compiled by Major the Hon. Ralph Pomeroy, Col. W. F. Collins, Col. W. M. Duguid-McCombie, Lt.-Col. S. J. Hardy, Lt.-Col. A. I. Macdougall, Andrew Dewar Gibb, with a Foreword by Gen. Sir Philip W. Chetwode, Bt., Colonel, Royal Scots Greys. No imprint [1932], 216 pp. 9"

Second to None. The Royal Scots Greys, 1919-1945. By Lieut.-Col. R. M. P. Carver. With a Foreword by Field Marshal Viscount Montgomery of Alamein [Glasgow: printed for the Regiment by Messrs. McCorquodale & Co. Ltd., 1954]. xvi, 210 pp., portraits, plates, maps, end-paper maps. 8½″

The Scot Greys. An Address delivered in Princes Street, Edinburgh, on the 16th of November, 1906, by the Earl of Rosebery [at the Unveiling of a Memorial]. London: privately printed for E.C. and E.G. at the Chiswick Press, 1907.   10 pp. 8½″
    50 numbered copies printed.

Uniform and Equipment of the Royal Scots Greys (1678-1855). By the Rev. Percy Sumner. (In *Society for Army Historical Research, Journal*, vol. 15, 1936, pp. 115-170; vol. 16, 1937, pp. 124-146, 187-202). Plates, 3 coloured. 9¼″

3RD THE KING'S OWN HUSSARS

Historical Records of the Third, or King's Own Regiment of Light Dragoons, from the year 1685 to the present time. [By C. Stisted]. Glasgow: J. Starke, 1833. 87 pp. 8½″

Historical Record of the Third, or The King's Own Regiment of Light Dragoons; containing an Account of the Formation of the Regiment in 1685, and of its subsequent Services to 1846. Compiled by Richard Cannon, Esq., Adjutant-General's Office, Horse Guards. London: Parker, Furnivall & Parker, 1847. xvi, 14, xxxi-xl, 121 pp., plates. 8¾″
    2 coloured plates of uniform.

———— Appendix, pp. 123-138. No title page. 1 coloured plate. Sometimes found issued together with previous item.

———— to 1857. Revised from the Edition published by authority in 1847 by the late Richard Cannon by George E. F. Kauntze, Captain. London: printed by B. D. Cousins [1857]. xvi, 288 pp., plates. 8½″
    4 coloured plates of uniform.

———— [Revised edition with title] Historical Record of the Third (King's Own) Hussars . . . services to 1903. London: W. P. Griffith & Sons Ltd., 1903. xx, 349 pp., plates 8½″
    8 coloured plates of uniform.

———— [Revised edition with title] Historical Record of 3rd The King's Own Hussars . . . to 1927. Aldershot: Gale & Polden Ltd., 1927. viii, 191 pp. No plates. 8½″

The 3rd (King's Own) Hussars in the Great War (1914-1919). By Lieut.-Col. Walter Temple Willcox. London: John Murray, 1925. xx, 387 pp., portraits, plates, maps. 8½″

The Galloping Third; the Story of the 3rd The King's Own Hussars. By Hector Bolitho. London: John Murray, 1963. xiii, 341 pp. Portraits, plates, maps, end-paper maps. 8½″

A Short History of 3rd The King's Own Hussars, 1685-1939. [By Lt.-Col. F. R. Burnside]. Aldershot: Gale & Polden Ltd. [1939]. vii, 30 pp., portrait, plates. 7¼"
    4 coloured plates, including 3 of uniform.

——— Another edition, 1685-1945. Aldershot: Gale & Polden Ltd. [1947]. [x], 46 pp., portraits, plates. 7¼"
    6 coloured plates including 4 of uniform.

4TH QUEEN'S OWN HUSSARS

Historical Record of the Fourth, or The Queen's Own Regiment of Light Dragoons; containing an Account of the Formation of the Regiment in 1685, and of its subsequent Services to 1842. London: John W. Parker, 1843. viii, 115 pp., plates. (Cannon's Historical Records Series). 8¾"
    Coloured plate of uniform.

The 4th (Queen's Own) Hussars in the Great War. By Capt. H. K. D. Evans and Chapters ix and x by Major N. O. Laing. With a Foreword by Right Hon. Winston Churchill. Aldershot: printed for the Regimental Committee by Gale & Polden Ltd., 1920. xv, 199 pp., portraits, plates, maps. 9½"

4th Hussar; the story of the 4th Queen's Own Hussars, 1685-1958. By D. Scott Daniell, with a foreword by Sir Winston Churchill, Colonel of the Regiment. Aldershot: Gale & Polden Ltd., 1959. xvi, 416 pp., portraits, plates, maps. 9"
    11 coloured portraits and uniform plates.

A Short History of the IV. Queen's Own Hussars. [By Lt.-Col. T. W. Pragnell]. [Meerut: The Pathak Machine Printing Press, 1923]. 77 pp. 5½"
    Written up to 1909 only, by Major H. Watkin.

A Short History of the 4th Queen's Own Hussars. By Major T. J. Edwards. Canterbury: Gibbs & Sons, 1935. 56 pp. 7¼"

Correspondence relative to the stationing of a troop of the Fourth Regiment of Dragoons in the County of Carnarvon. [Edited by Edward Griffith]. 3rd edition. London: J. Johnson, 1806-07. 143 pp. 8vo.

7TH QUEEN'S OWN HUSSARS

Historical Record of the Seventh, or The Queen's Own Regiment of Hussars; containing an Account of the Origin of the Regiment in 1690, and of its subsequent Services to 1842. London: John W. Parker, 1842. viii, 102 pp. (Cannon's Historical Records Series). 8¾"
    Coloured plate of uniform.

The 7th (Queen's Own) Hussars. By C. R. B. Barrett. London: Royal United Services Institution, 1914. 2 vols. Portraits, plates, illustrations, maps. 9½"
    Vol. 1 has 4 coloured plates of uniform and Vol. 2, 6.

A Short History of the Seventh Queen's Own Hussars from 1689 to 1932. Aldershot: Gale & Polden Ltd., 1932. ix, 58 pp., portraits, plates. 7¼"

The Seventh and Three Enemies. The Story of World War II and the 7th Queen's Own Hussars. By Brig. G. M. O. Davy. Cambridge: W. Heffer & Sons Ltd., 1953. xiv, 468 pp., portraits, plates, maps. 8¾"

The Years Between. The Story of the 7th Queen's Own Hussars, 1911-1937. Compiled by Major-Gen. Roger Evans. With a Foreword by Gen. Sir James Cassels. Aldershot: Gale & Polden Ltd., 1965. xv, 112 pp. Portraits, plates, maps. 9½"

The Life of a Light Cavalry Regiment; a report on the Anglesey Papers dealing with the 7th Light Dragoons (Hussars). By T. H. McGuffie. (In *Society for Army Historical Research, Journal*, vol. 38, 1960, pp. 69-74, 127-134, 175-183; vol. 39, 1961, pp. 20-26, 75-85, 113-125, 198-204). 9¼"

8TH KING'S ROYAL IRISH HUSSARS

Historical Record of the Eighth, or The King's Royal Irish Regiment of Hussars; containing an Account of the Formation of the Regiment in 1693, and of its subsequent Services to 1843. London: John W. Parker, 1844. viii, 134 pp., plates. (Cannon's Historical Records Series). 8¾"
    2 coloured plates of uniform.

Historical Record of the Eighth King's Royal Irish Hussars, from its being raised, to 1803. Drawn up by John Francis Smet, late Surgeon of the 8th Hussars. London: W. Mitchell & Co., 1874. viii, 86 pp. 8"

The History of the VIII King's Royal Irish Hussars, 1693-1927. By the Rev. Robert H. Murray. With a Foreword by Gen. the Right Hon. Sir Bryan T. Mahon. Cambridge: W. Heffer & Sons Ltd., 1928. 2 vols. Portraits, maps, plates. 9¾"
    Vol. 1 contains 10 coloured plates including 5 of uniform and 4 coloured portraits.
    Vol. 2, 5 coloured plates including 4 of uniform.
    Limited to 200 copies. There was a remainder issue without plates.

Men of Valour: the third volume of the history of the VIII King's Royal Irish Hussars, 1927-1958. By Olivia Fitzroy, with a foreword by H.R.H. The Duke of Edinburgh, Colonel of the Regiment. Liverpool: printed by C. Tinling & Co., Ltd., 1961. xx, 375 pp., portraits, plates, maps, end-paper maps. 9½"
    Coloured portrait.

8th (King's Royal Irish) Hussars. Diary of the South African War, 1900-1902. By J. W. Morton, Squadron-Sergeant-Major. Aldershot; Gale & Polden Ltd., 1905. xv, 159 pp., portraits, plate. 8½"

Korean Campaign Supplement [&] 2nd Supplement to "The Crossbelts,"
1950/51; 1951/52. Journal of the VIII King's Royal Irish Hussars. 1st
Supplement. Aldershot: Gale & Polden Ltd.; 2nd Supplement printed at
Luneberg, Germany, by Druck- und Verlagshaus Hoppe & Co., 1951-52. 42,
39 pp., portraits, illustrations, maps. 10¾"

9TH QUEEN'S ROYAL LANCERS

Historical Record of the Ninth, or The Queen's Royal Regiment of Light
Dragoons; Lancers: containing an Account of the Formation of the Regiment
in 1715, and of its subsequent Services to 1841. London: John W. Parker, 1841.
viii, 72 pp. (Cannon's Historical Records Series). 8¾"
  Coloured plate of uniform.

The Ninth (Queen's Royal) Lancers, 1715-1903. By Frank H. Reynard, late
Captain Ninth Lancers. Edinburgh: William Blackwood and Sons, 1904.
xv, 258 pp., portraits, plates. 9"
  11 coloured plates, including 8 of uniform, 2 of medals and 1 of guidons.

The Ninth Queen's Royal Lancers, 1715-1936. By Major E. W. Sheppard.
Aldershot: Gale & Polden Ltd., 1939. xxiii, 439 pp., portraits, plates, maps,
plans. 9¾"
  10 coloured plates of uniform.

The Ninth Queen's Royal Lancers, 1936-1945. The Story of an Armoured
Regiment in Battle. Edited by Joan Bright. Aldershot: Gale & Polden Ltd.,
1951. xxxi, 359 pp., portraits, plates, maps, end-paper maps. 9¾"

A Short History of the 9th Queen's Royal Lancers, 1715-1949. [By Major W.
Hanwell]. Aldershot: Gale & Polden Ltd., 1949. xiii, 71 pp., portraits,
plates. 8½"
  4 coloured plates of uniform.

The Ninth Lancers in Afghanistan, 1878-1879-1880. The Second Afghan War.
The First Squadron in the Koorum Valley; the Attack in the Shutergarden Pass;
the Taking of Cabul; the Battle of Charasia; the Defence of Sherpur; the Battle
of Kandahar; and the Famous March from Cabul to Candahar under Major-Gen.
Sir Frederick Roberts, Bart. . . ., being a Diary kept daily by Private B. P. Crane.
[Part II. The Return to Old England. A Diary of Journey in India, by rail from
Umballa to Bombay, etc., November, 1883 to January 16, 1884]. 2nd edition.
London: D. Collins, printer, n.d. 92 pp. 7"

Diary of the 9th (Q.R.) Lancers during the South African Campaign, 1899 to 1902.
By Bt.-Lieut.-Col. F. F. Colvin and Capt. E. R. Gordon. London: Cecil Roy,
1904. xv, 304 pp., portraits, illustrations, map in end-pocket. 7¾"

10TH ROYAL HUSSARS (PRINCE OF WALES'S OWN)

Historical Record of the Tenth, or The Prince of Wales's Own Royal Regiment of Hussars; containing an Account of the Formation of the Regiment in 1715 and of its subsequent Services to 1842.   London: John W. Parker, 1843.   viii, viii, 92 pp.   (Cannon's Historical Records Series).   8¾"
   1 coloured plate of uniform.

Historical Records of the Services of the Tenth or Prince of Wales's Own Royal Regiment of Hussars.   [In *The United Services Magazine*, 1874-76].   250 pp.   8½"

The Memoirs of the Tenth Royal Hussars (Prince of Wales's Own).   Historical and Social.   Collected and arranged by Col. R. S. Liddell.   With Illustrations by Oscar Norie.   London: Longmans, Green and Co., 1891.   xvii, 566 pp., portraits, plates.   10"
   12 coloured plates of uniform.   There was a remainder issue without plates.

The 10th (P.W.O.) Royal Hussars and The Essex Yeomanry, during the European War, 1914-1918.   By Lt.-Col. F. H. D. C. Whitmore.   Colchester: Benham and Company Ltd., 1920.   viii, 326 pp., plates, maps.   10"

The 10th Royal Hussars in the Second World War, 1939-1945.   Aldershot: Gale & Polden Ltd., 1948.   xiii, 212 pp., portraits, plates, maps.   8½"

11TH HUSSARS (PRINCE ALBERT'S OWN)

Historical Record of the Eleventh, or The Prince Albert's Own, Regiment of Hussars; containing an Account of the Formation of the Regiment in 1715, and of its subsequent Services to 1842.   London: John W. Parker, 1843.   viii, viii, 107 pp.   (Cannon's Historical Records Series).   8¾"
   1 coloured plate of uniform.

The Historical Records of the Eleventh Hussars Prince Albert's Own.   By Capt. Trevelyan Williams.   London: George Newnes, Ltd., 1908.   xii, 417 pp., portraits, plates, maps, plans.   11½"
   12 coloured plates of uniform and 1 of guidons.

History of the Eleventh Hussars (Prince Albert's Own), 1908-1934.   By Capt. L. R. Lumley, M.P.   London: The Royal United Service Institution, 1936.   xvi, 544 pp., portraits, plates, maps, plans.   9¾"

Regimental History of the 11th Hussars (Prince Albert's Own).   Aldershot: Gale & Polden Ltd. [1925].   v, 57 pp., portraits [2 coloured], plates.   7¼"

———— Another edition with title: A Short History of the XI Hussars (Prince Albert's Own).   Aldershot.   1930.   [v], 59 pp.   7¼"

An Alphabetical List of the Officers of the Eleventh, or Prince Albert's Own, Regiment of Hussars, from 1800 to 1850.   By Henry Stooks Smith.   London: Simpkin, Marshall & Co., 1850.   [iv], 32 pp.   8½"

A History of the Uniform of the Eleventh Hussars.   By A. A. Nesbitt.   (In *XI Hussars Journal*, 1960, pp. 177-187).   Illustrations.   10¾"

12TH ROYAL LANCERS (PRINCE OF WALES'S)

Historical Record of the Twelfth, or The Prince of Wales's Own Royal Regiment of Lancers; containing an Account of the Formation of the Regiment in 1715, and of its subsequent Services to 1842. London: John W. Parker, 1842. viii, viii, 84 pp. (Cannon's Historical Records Series). 8¾"
    1 coloured plate of uniform.

The Story of the XII Royal Lancers from 1715 to 1918. By Lt.-Col. G. W. Hobson. [Northampton: Xpress Printers Ltd.], 1945. 315 pp., portraits. 9¾" For private circulation only. [24 copies only printed—Author].

The History of the XII Royal Lancers (Prince of Wales's). By Capt. P. T. Stewart. London: Oxford University Press, 1950. xvi, 516 pp., portrait, plates, maps. 8¾"
    4 coloured plates, including 3 of uniform.

The 12th Royal Lancers in France, August 17th, 1914-November 11th, 1918. By Major H. V. S. Charrington. Aldershot: Gale & Polden Ltd., 1921. [v], 50 pp., portraits, plates. 7½"

Some XII Royal Lancers. Stories collected by Lt.-Col. G. W. Hobson. Long Compton, Shipston-on-Stour: The 'King's Stone' Press. [viii], 272 pp., portraits, plates. 8¾"

13TH/18TH ROYAL HUSSARS (QUEEN MARY'S OWN)

13TH HUSSARS

Historical Record of the Thirteenth Regiment of Light Dragoons; containing an Account of the Formation of the Regiment in 1715, and of its subsequent Services to 1842. London: John W. Parker, 1842. viii, 96 pp. (Cannon's Historical Records Series). 8¾"
    1 coloured plate of uniform.

History of The XIII Hussars. By C. R. B. Barrett. Edinburgh: William Blackwood & Sons, 1911. 2 vols., portraits, plates, illustrations, maps, plans. 10"
    5 coloured plates of uniform in vol. 1 and 1 in vol. 2.

The Thirteenth Hussars in the Great War. By the Right Hon. Sir H. Mortimer Durand. Edinburgh: William Blackwood & Sons, 1921. xiii, 392 pp. Portraits, plates, sketch maps in text. 10"
    10 coloured plates including 4 of early uniform.

A Short History of the 13th Hussars. (Preface signed J.P.R.). Aldershot: Gale & Polden Ltd. [1923]. viii, 63 pp., plates (1 coloured). 7¼"

———— Another edition. [1932]. iv, 67 pp., plates (1 coloured). 7¼"

XIII Hussars. South African War, October, 1899-October, 1902. Aldershot: May & Co., printers [1902]. 202 pp. 7"

18TH ROYAL HUSSARS (QUEEN MARY'S OWN)

Historical Record of the Eighteenth Hussars. By Capt. Harold Malet. London: William Clowes and Sons, 1869. xii, 68 pp., portraits, plates. 8½"
2 coloured plates of uniform.

The Historical Memoirs of the XVIIIth Hussars (Princess of Wales's Own). Collected and arranged by Col. Harold Malet. London: Simpkin & Co. Ltd., 1907. xii, 345 pp., portraits, plates, illustrations. 8½"
7 coloured plates of uniform.

The Memoirs of the 18th (Queen Mary's Own) Royal Hussars, 1906-1922, including Operations in the Great War. By Brig. Gen. Charles Burnett. Winchester: Warren and Son, 1926. [ix], 215 pp., portraits, plates, maps, plans. 8½"

The 18th Hussars in South Africa. The Records of a Cavalry Regiment during the Boer War, 1899-1902. By Major Charles Burnett. Winchester: Warren & Son, 1905. [viii], 319 pp., portraits, plates, maps. 8½"

History of the 13th/18th Royal Hussars (Queen Mary's Own), 1922-1947. By Major-Gen. Charles H. Miller. London: Chisman & Bradshaw Ltd. [1949]. xviii, 227 pp., portraits, plates, maps. 9½"

A Brief History of the 13th/18th Hussars (Queen Mary's Own). No imprint, 1951. 24 pp. 7¼"

XIII/XVIII Hussars. Sialkot 1934. [Aldershot: Gale & Polden Ltd., 1934]. 32 pp. Portraits, plates. 9¾" × 13"
Souvenir album containing reproduction of photographs, including drum banners. No text.

14TH/20TH KING'S HUSSARS

14TH KING'S HUSSARS

Historical Record of the Fourteenth, or the King's Regiment of Light Dragoons; containing an Account of the Formation of the Regiment and of its subsequent Services. Compiled by Richard Cannon, Esq., Adjutant-General's Office, Horse Guards. London: Parker, Furnivall, & Parker, 1847. xxxix, 83 pp., plates. 8¾"
3 coloured plates, including 1 of uniform and 2 of guidons.

Historical Record of the 14th (King's) Hussars from A.D. 1715 to A.D. 1900. By Col. Henry Blackburne Hamilton. London: Longmans, Green & Co., 1901. xxxi, 632 pp., portraits, plates, maps. 9¼"
15 coloured plates, including 12 of uniform and 2 of guidons.

———— 1900-1922. Vol. 2. By Brig. J. Gilbert Browne and Lieut.-Col. E. J. Bridges. Edited by Major J. A. T. Millet. London: Royal United Service Institution, 1932. xvi, 568 pp., portraits, maps, plans. 9¼"
1 coloured plate. Maps in end-pocket.

20TH HUSSARS

20th Hussars in the Great War.   By Major J. C. Darling.   Published privately by the Author, Homeland, Lyndhurst, Hampshire, 1923.   [ix], 131 pp., portraits, maps.   9″

A Short History of the 14th/20th Hussars.   Aldershot: Gale and Polden Ltd, [1923].   48 pp.   7¼″

A Short History of 14th/20th King's Hussars, 1715-1950.   [Aldershot: Gale & Polden Ltd., 1950].   viii, 54 pp., portraits, plates, maps.   8½″
    4 coloured plates, including 2 portraits in uniform.

15TH/19TH THE KING'S ROYAL HUSSARS

15TH THE KING'S HUSSARS

Historical Record of the Fifteenth, or, The King's Regiment of Light Dragoons, Hussars; containing an Account of the Formation of the Regiment in 1759, and of its subsequent Services to 1841.   London: John W. Parker, 1841.   viii, viii, 118 pp.   (Cannon's Historical Records Series).   8¾″
    1 coloured plate of uniform.

Historical Record of the Fifteenth, or, the King's, Regiment of Light Dragoons, Hussars.   Meerut: printed at the XV " The King's " Hussars Press, 1877 [1879]. vi, 187 pp.   7½″
    9 coloured plates, including 8 of uniform and 1 of guidons.

XVth (The King's) Hussars, 1759 to 1913.   By Col. H. C. Wylly.   London: Caxton Publishing Company Ltd., 1914.   x, 564 pp., portraits, plates, illustrations, plans.   9½″
    12 coloured plates of uniform.   Large paper edition 11½″.

The History of the 15th The King's Hussars, 1914-1922.   By Lord Carnock. With a Foreword by Brig.-Gen. A. Courage.   Gloucester: The Crypt House Press Ltd., 1932.   xii, 270 pp., portrait, illustrations, maps.   9¾″

19TH ROYAL HUSSARS (QUEEN ALEXANDRA'S OWN)

The Nineteenth and their Times; being an Account of the Four Cavalry Regiments in the British Army that have borne the number Nineteen and of the Campaigns in which they served.   By Col. John Biddulph.   London: John Murray, 1899.   xxi, 330 pp., portraits, plates, maps, illustrations.   8¾″
    3 coloured plates of uniform and 1 of guidon.

The History of 15/19 The King's Royal Hussars, 1939-1945.   By Major G. Courage.   With a Foreword by Brig. Sir Henry Floyd, Bt.   Aldershot: Gale & Polden Ltd., 1949.   xiii, 329 pp., portraits, plates, maps.   9¾″

A Short History of Your Regiment. XV. XIX The King's Royal Hussars. Aldershot: Gale & Polden Ltd. [1935]. [vi], 66 pp., portrait, plates. 7¼"
   3 coloured plates of uniform.

16TH/5TH THE QUEEN'S LANCERS

16TH THE QUEEN'S LANCERS

Historical Record of the Sixteenth, or The Queen's Regiment of Light Dragoons, Lancers; containing an Account of the Formation of the Regiment in 1759, and of its subsequent Services to 1841. London: John W. Parker, 1842. viii, 120 pp. (Cannon's Historical Records Series). 8¾"
   Coloured plate of uniform.

History of the Sixteenth, The Queen's Light Dragoons (Lancers), 1759 to 1912. By Col. Henry Graham. Devizes: George Simpson, privately printed, 1912. xvi, 334 pp., portraits, plates, maps. 11"
   8 coloured plates of uniform, including 6 portraits.

——— 1912 to 1925. By Col. Henry Graham. Devizes: George Simpson, privately printed, 1926. xi, 148 pp., portraits, plates, maps, maps in end-pocket. 11"

5TH ROYAL IRISH LANCERS

The Historical Records of the Fifth (Royal Irish) Lancers from their Foundation as Wynne's Dragoons (in 1689) to the Present Day. By Walter Temple Willcox, Major. London: Arthur Doubleday & Company Ltd., 1908. xxiii, 287, lxvi pp., portraits, plates, maps, plans. 11¾"
   8 coloured plates, including 7 of uniform and 1 of drum-banners.

The History of the 5th (Royal Irish) Regiment of Dragoons from 1689 to 1799, afterwards The 5th Royal Irish Lancers from 1858 to 1921. By Col. J. R. Harvey, completed to 1921 by Lieut.-Col. H. A. Cape. Aldershot: Gale & Polden Ltd., for private circulation only, 1923. xxiii, 460 pp., portraits, plates, maps, plans. 11"
   11 coloured plates including 7 of uniform and 3 of guidons.

———————

History of the 16th/5th The Queen's Royal Lancers, 1925-1961. By Brig. C. N. Barclay. Aldershot: Gale & Polden Ltd., 1963. xvi, 235 pp., portraits (1 coloured), plates, maps. 11"

A Short History of the 16th/5th Lancers. By Major H. G. Parkyn. Aldershot: Gale & Polden Ltd. [1934]. ix, 72 pp., maps. 7⅛"
   4 coloured plates of uniform.

17TH/21ST LANCERS

17TH LANCERS (DUKE OF CAMBRIDGE'S OWN)

Historical Record of the Seventeenth Regiment of Light Dragoons: Lancers; containing an Account of the Formation of the Regiment in 1759, and of its subsequent Services to 1841. London: John W. Parker, 1841. viii, 84 pp., plates. (Cannon's Historical Records Series). 8½″
   7 coloured plates of uniform.

A History of the 17th Lancers (Duke of Cambridge's Own). By Hon. J. W. Fortescue. London: Macmillan and Co., 1895. xv, 246 pp., portraits, plates. 10″
   13 coloured plates of uniform.

—————— Vol. 2. 1895-1924. By Major Gilbert Micholls. London: Macmillan & Co. Ltd., 1931. ix, 250 pp., portraits, plates, maps (maps in end-pocket). 10″

"The Death or Glory Boys." The Story of the 17th Lancers. By D. H. Parry. London: Cassell and Company Ltd., 1899. viii, 308 pp., plate. 8″

A History of the 17th/21st Lancers, 1922-1959; with a Foreword by Field-Marshal Lord Harding of Petherton. By Lt.-Col. R. L. V. ffrench Blake. London: Macmillan & Co. Ltd., 1962. xvi, 284 pp., portraits, plates, maps, end-paper maps. 9¼″

Death or Glory; a short history of the 17th/21st Lancers. By Major R. L. C. Tamplin. Nairobi: The Regiment, [1959]. viii, 92 pp., plates. 9¾″
   2 coloured plates of uniform.

ROYAL TANK REGIMENT: ROYAL TANK CORPS.

The Tank Corps. By Major Clough Williams-Ellis and A. Williams-Ellis. With an Introduction by Major-Gen. H. J. Elles. London: "Country Life" Ltd. [1919]. xvi, 288 pp., portrait, plates, maps. ("Country Life" Series of Military Histories). 9″

The Tank Corps Book of Honour. Compiled from Official Records and edited by Major R. F. G. Maurice (late 13th Battalion, Tank Corps). London: Spottiswoode, Ballantyne & Co. Ltd., 1919. [6], 460, iv pp., portrait, plates. 8½″

Fighting Tanks. An Account of the Royal Tank Corps in action 1916-1919. Written, or from material supplied, by Major-Gen. Sir Hugh Elles; Major-Gen. Sir John Ponsonby; Col. J. F. C. Fuller; Col. J. Uzielli; Col. Le Q. Martel; Commander Locker-Lampson; Lt.-Col. E. Hotblack; Capt. Thomas Reginald Price; Capt. J. L. Cottle; Sergeant E. Hearn; and other Officers and N.C.O.'s. Edited by G. Murray Wilson, late Senior Chaplain to the Royal Tank Corps. London: Seeley Service & Co., Ltd., 1929. 250 pp., portraits, plates. 8½″

A Brief History of the Royal Tank Corps. By F. G. Woolnough, Army Educational Corps. Aldershot: Gale & Polden Ltd., 1925. 2nd edition. v., 41 pp., plates, maps. $7\frac{1}{4}''$

A Short History of the Royal Tank Corps.   Aldershot: Gale & Polden Ltd., 1930. ix, 112 pp., portraits, plates. $7\frac{1}{4}''$

———— 2nd edition.   ix, 124 pp., 1931; 3rd edition.   xii, 134 pp., 1934;   4th edition.   xii, 139 pp., 1936;   5th edition.   xii, 168 pp., 1938.

Tanks in the Great War, 1914-1918.   By Brev.-Col. J. F. C. Fuller.   London: John Murray, 1920.   xxiv, 321 pp., plates, diagrams, maps. $8\frac{3}{4}''$

The Tanks.   The History of the Royal Tank Regiment and its predecessors: Heavy Branch Machine Gun Corps, Tank Corps and Royal Tank Corps, 1914-1945.   By Capt. B. H. Liddell Hart, with a Foreword by Field Marshal Viscount Montgomery of Alamein.   London: Cassell, [1959].   2 vols., portraits, plates, maps. $8\frac{1}{2}''$

Historical Record of the 4th Battalion Royal Tank Corps.   [By Lt.-Col. H. G. R. Burges-Short].   Aldershot: Gale & Polden Ltd., [1925].   viii, 77 pp., maps. $8''$

Memories.   Hazeley Down Camp, Winchester.   Jan. 1918-May 1919.   [A Brief History of No. 24 (Tank Corps) Officer Cadet Battalion].   [Winchester: printed by Warren & Son Ltd., 1919].   67 pp. $8\frac{1}{4}''$

The War History of the Sixth Tank Battalion [By A. H. T., 6th Lord Somers]. [Edinburgh: R. & R. Clark, Ltd.], Privately printed, 1919.   viii, 247 pp., portraits, plate. $8\frac{1}{2}''$

Narrative History of "G" and 7th Tank Battalion.   Aldershot: Gale & Polden Ltd., 1919.   vii, 35 pp., plate, maps. $7\frac{1}{4}''$

Operations of the 17th (Armoured Car) Tank Battalion during the Battle of 1918.   Compiled from Original Notes and Accounts, May, 1919.   Aldershot: Gale & Polden Ltd., 1920.   vii, 87 pp., plates, maps. $7\frac{1}{4}''$

Blue Flash.   The Story of an Armoured Regiment [4th Royal Tank Regt.].   By Alan Jolly.   With a Foreword by Gen. Sir John T. Crocker.   [London: printed for the author by The Solicitors' Law Stationery Soc., Ltd., 1952].   xii, 168 pp., portraits, plates, maps. $9''$

"A" Squadron Diary, 7th Royal Tank Regiment.   [By Major R. A. Jocelyne. Krefeld, Germany: printed by Scherpe, 1946].   72 pp., portraits, illustrations. $8\frac{1}{4}''$

9th Battalion, Royal Tank Regiment, June 1941-May 1945.   [Printing & Stationery Services, B.A.O.R., 1945].   [20], pp. $7''$
   Badges in colour on paper cover.

The First Royal Tank Regiment in Hong Kong, 1957-58.   [Hong Kong: Cathay Press].   1958.   12 pp., plates. $8\frac{1}{2}''$

ROYAL REGIMENT OF ARTILLERY

Englands Artillerymen. An Historical Narrative of the Services of the Royal Artillery, from the Formation of the Regiment to the Amalgamation of the Royal and Indian Artilleries in 1862. By James Alex. Browne, Royal Artillery. London: Hall, Smart and Allen, 1865. xiii, 330 pp., portraits, plate. 6¾″

History of the Royal Regiment of Artillery. Compiled from the Original Records by Capt. Francis Duncan . . . Superintendent of the Royal Artillery Regimental Records, etc. London: John Murray, 1872-73. 2 vols., portraits. 8¾″

———— 3rd edition. 1879. 2 vols. 8¾″

Notes on the Early History of the Royal Regiment of Artillery (to 1757). By the late Colonel Cleaveland, R.A. [Edited, with Notes by Lieut.-Col. W. L. Yonge]. No titlepage or imprint. [1892]. 271 pp. 9½″

History of the Royal Regiment of Artillery, 1815-1853. By Lieut.-Col. Henry W. L. Hime. London: Longmans, Green and Co., 1908. x, 148 pp. 8¾″

The History of the Royal Artillery (Crimean Period). By Col. Julian R. J. Jocelyn. London: John Murray, 1911. xxviii, 508 pp., portraits, plates, illustrations, maps. 8¾″

The History of the Royal and Indian Artillery in the Mutiny of 1857. By Col. Julian R. J. Jocelyn. London: John Murray, 1915. xxvi, 520 pp., portrait, plates, illustrations, maps. 8¾″

The History of the Royal Artillery from the Indian Mutiny to the Great War. Woolwich: Royal Artillery Institution. [1931]; 37; 40. Portraits. 8¾″
    Vol. 1. 1860-1899. By Major-Gen. Sir Charles Callwell and Major-Gen. Sir John Headlam.
    Vol. 2. 1899-1914. By Major-Gen. Sir John Headlam.
    Vol. 3. Campaigns, 1860-1914. By Major-Gen. Sir John Headlam. Separate case of maps.

A Short History of the Royal Regiment of Artillery. Aldershot: Gale & Polden Ltd. [1923]. 24 pp., portrait, plates. 8½″
    2 coloured plates of uniform.

A Short History of the Royal Regiment of Artillery. By W. O. J. Loughlin, A. E. C. With a Foreword by Major-Gen. W. H. Kay. Aldershot: Gale & Polden Ltd. [1927]. ix, 69 pp., portrait, plates. 7″

The Story of the Royal Regiment of Artillery. By Lieut.-Col. C. A. L. Graham, assisted by Officers of the Regiment. Woolwich: Royal Artillery Institution. 1928. [6], 94 pp., plates. 7¼″

The Story of the Royal Regiment of Artillery.   5th edition.   1944.   vi, 108 pp.

────── 6th edition, revised.   1962.   vi, 88 pp.

Outline History of the Development and Organization of the Royal Artillery, 1716-1950.   By Lieut.-Col. M. E. S. Laws.   Woolwich: Royal Artillery Institution, 1950.   20 pp. $9\frac{3}{4}''$

English Artillery, 1326-1716.   By Brig. O. F. G. Hogg.   Woolwich: Royal Artillery Institution.   1963.   x, 310 pp., portraits, plates. $8\frac{1}{2}''$
   Chapter on formation of the Regiment.

The History of Coast Artillery in the British Army.   By Col. K. W. Maurice-Jones, with a Foreword by Gen. Sir Cameron Nicholson.   London: Royal Artillery Institution.   1959.   xvi, 234 pp., illustration, sketch maps and maps in pocket. $8\frac{1}{2}''$

History of the Royal Irish Artillery.   By J. J. Crooks (Major)   Dublin: Browne and Nolan Ltd., 1914.   viii, 368 pp., portraits. $7\frac{1}{4}''$

Battery Records of the Royal Artillery, 1716-1859.   Compiled by Lieut.-Col. M. E. S. Laws.   Woolwich: Royal Artillery Institution.   1952.   xx, 313 pp. $8\frac{1}{2}'' \times 11''$

Famous Batteries of the Royal Artillery.   By Ubique.   Portsmouth: W. H. Barrell Ltd., 1930.   [10], 106 pp., portraits, illustrations. $7\frac{1}{4}''$

The Right of the Line; being some stories from the history of the Royal Regiment of Artillery.   By R. Power Berrey.   London: James Nisbet & Co., Ltd., 1904. 236 pp. $7\frac{3}{4}''$

Some Outstanding Episodes of Regimental History.   Written at the request of the Regimental Historical Committee.   Woolwich: The Royal Artillery Institution [1954].   72 pp., plans. $9\frac{1}{2}''$

The Services of the Royal Regiment of Artillery in the Peninsular War, 1808 to 1814.   By Major John H. Leslie.   London: Hugh Rees Ltd., 1908. $8\frac{3}{4}''$
Chapter I.   Pp. 1-18.
Chapter II.   The Coruna Campaign (October, 1808, to January, 1809) with which is incorporated The Diary of 2nd Captain Richard Bogue, R.H.A. Pp. 17-70, portraits, plates, maps.
Chapter III.   (November, 1808 to end of 1809).   Woolwich: Royal Artillery Institution.   Pp. 71-100.
   Each chapter issued separately, with titlepage, in paper cover.   Chapters 4 and 5 (1810-11) were published in the *Journal of the Royal Artillery*, vols. 51 (1924), 53 (1926), and 67 (1940).

The Royal Regiment of Artillery at Le Cateau, Wednesday, 26th August, 1914. By Major A. F. Becke.   Woolwich: Royal Artillery Institution, 1919.   viii, 87 pp., maps in end-pocket. $9\frac{1}{2}''$

The Royal Artillery War Commemoration Book. A Regimental Record written and illustrated for the most part by Artillerymen while serving in the Line during the Great War. London: published on behalf of the R.A. War Commemoration Fund by G. Bell & Sons Ltd., 1920. xxiv, 408 pp., portraits, plates, illustrations. 12½"
    25 coloured plates.

The Royal Artillery Commemoration Book, 1939-1945. Published on behalf of The Royal Artillery Benevolent Fund by G. Bell & Sons Ltd., 1950. xi, 790 pp., portraits, plates, illustrations, maps. 12½"

List of Officers of the Royal Regiment of Artillery, as they stood in the year 1763, with a continuation to the Present Time: containing the date of their regimental and Brevet Promotions, . . . also a Succession of Master Generals, Lieutenant Generals, Colonels Commandant, Commanding Officers of the Garrison of Woolwich, Regimental and Battalion Staff, etc. With a List of Officers of the Corps of Royal Artillery Drivers . . . and of the Officers of the Military Medical Department of the Ordnance, since 1763; with a List of the . . . Field Train Department of the Ordnance, since 1793; to which is added an Appendix: containing several Tables relative to the gradual increase and Establishments of the Regiment . . . Extracts and Memoranda relative to the Dress of the Officers and Men, etc. [Compiled by John Kane, Lieut. and Adjt., Royal Invalid Artillery]. Greenwich: printed by Elizabeth Delahoy, Albion Printing Office, 1815. [12], 99 pp. 12½"

—— Revised edition, with title; List of Officers of the Royal Regiment of Artillery from the year 1716 to the present time. Woolwich: Royal Artillery Institution, 1869. [ix], 200 pp. 10¾"

—— Revised edition, with title List of Officers . . . Present Date. Woolwich: Royal Artillery Institution, 1891. [9], 285 pp. 10¾"

—— 4th edition, with title, List . . . to the year 1899. To which are added the Notes on Officers' Services collected by General W. H. Askwith. London: printed by William Clowes & Sons Ltd. for the Royal Artillery Institution, 1900. [13], 274 pp. 11"
    Pp. 1-164 have also an 'A' page.

—— New edition, Vol. 2. List . . . from June, 1862 to June, 1914, with Appendices. Sheffield: printed by Sir W. C. Leng & Co. (Sheffield Telegraph), Ltd. for the Royal Artillery Institution, 1914. ix, 405 pp. 11¼"
    Vol. 1 not published.

Alphabetical List of the Officers of the Royal Artillery, from 1800 to 1851. By Henry Stooks Smith. London: Simpkin, Marshall & Co. [1851]. No. 1, pp. 1-8; no more published. 8¾"

Memoirs of the Royal Artillery Band, its origin, history and progress. An Account of the Rise of Military Music in England. By Henry George Farmer. London: Boosey & Co., 1904. 189 [10] pp., portraits, plates. 8"

History of the Royal Artillery Band, 1762-1953. By Henry George Farmer. London: Royal Artillery Institution, 1954. xiv, 485 pp., portraits, plates, illustrations. $8\frac{1}{2}''$

The History of the Dress of the Royal Regiment of Artillery, 1625-1897. Compiled and illustrated by Captain R. J. Macdonald. London: Henry Sotheran & Co., 1899. xx, 131 pp., plates, illustrations. $12\frac{3}{4}''$
   25 coloured plates of uniform. Limited to 1500 copies.

The Dress of the Royal Artillery from 1898-1956. By Major D. A. Campbell. Woolwich: Royal Artillery Institution, 1960. viii, 66 pp., illustrations. $9\frac{5}{8}''$

Tradition in the Royal Regiment of Artillery and how it can best be preserved. By Major J. H. Leslie. A Lecture delivered at the Royal Artillery Institution, Woolwich, on 17 October, 1912. Woolwich: Royal Artillery Institution, 1913. 42 pp., portraits, illustrations. $9\frac{1}{4}''$
   Reprinted (with some amendments and additional illustrations) from vol. 39 of the *Journal of the Royal Artillery.*

———— (Another edition). Bicentenary Commemoration. Sheffield: Sir W. C. Leng & Co. (Sheffield Telegraph) Ltd., 1916. 36 pp., portraits, illustrations. $10\frac{1}{2}''$

The History and Traditions of the Royal Artillery. A Lecture delivered at the Royal Artillery Institution on 20 March 1918, by Col. E. A. P. Hobday. Woolwich: Royal Artillery Institution, 1918. 23 pp. $9\frac{1}{4}''$
   Reprinted from *The Journal of the Royal Artillery.*

The Royal Artillery Mess, Woolwich and its Surroundings. By Lieut. Col. A. H. Burne. Portsmouth: W. H. Barrell, Ltd., 1935. [8], 248 pp., portraits, plates, plans. $8''$

The Woolwich Mess. An abridgement and revision of " The Royal Artillery Mess, Woolwich and its Surroundings." By Lieut.-Col. Alfred H. Burne. Aldershot: Gale & Polden Ltd., 1954. x, 94 pp., plates, plans. $8''$

The History of the Royal Artillery War Memorial, 1939-45. Woolwich: Royal Artillery Institution [1953]. 24 pp. $9\frac{1}{2}''$

ROYAL HORSE ARTILLERY

Records of the Horse Brigade from its formation to the present time. [By Lt.-Col. J. E. Michell]. Woolwich: Boddy, 1874. 20 pp., tables. $11\frac{1}{4}''$

———— Revised edition with title: Records of the Royal Horse Artillery from its Formation to the Present Time, being the revised edition of " The Records of the Horse Brigade." London: W. Mitchell & Co., 1888. [20], 279 pp. $11\frac{1}{4}''$

Some Brief Reference Notes on the Royal Horse Artillery. Collected by Lt.-Col. R. H. C. Probert. Woolwich: Royal Artillery Institution, 1956. 28 pp., chart. $9\frac{1}{2}''$

From Coruña to Sebastopol. The History of 'C' Battery, 'A' Brigade (late 'C' Troop), Royal Horse Artillery. With Succession of Officers from its Formation to the Present Time. By Col. F. A. Whinyates. London: W. H. Allen & Co., 1884. viii, 308 pp., maps in end-pocket. 8¾″

Records of 'D' Battery, 'C' Brigade, Royal Horse Artillery, originally 3rd Troop, Bombay Horse Artillery. Compiled by Lieut.-Col. [T. N.] Holberton. Woolwich: printed by F. J. Cattermole, 1878. xxxvi, 29 pp. 9½″

History of the E. Battery, D Brigade Royal Horse Artillery from 1820 to 1876. [By Major H. Le Cocq. Coventry: Curtis & Beamish, printers, 1876]. 19 pp. 8½″

Records of 'E' Battery, 'E' Brigade, Royal Horse Artillery (originally 4th Troop, Bombay Horse Artillery). Compiled by Major [T. N.] Holberton, R.H.A. Woolwich: printed by F. J. Cattermole, 1876. iv, 44 pp. 9½″

The Story of " F " Troop, Royal Horse Artillery. First compiled in 1905 by Major A. S. Tyndale-Biscoe. New edition to date in 1932. Aldershot: printed by Wm. May & Co. Ltd., 1932. [iv], 84 pp., portraits, plates, maps. 8¼″

The Story of " G " Troop, Royal Horse Artillery. By Major H. M. Davson. Woolwich: Royal Artillery Institution, 1914. viii, 106 pp., portraits, plate, maps. 8½″
    Introduction dated Feb. 1919.

Narrative of the Crimean Services of " I " Troop, now " O " Battery, R.H.A. By Assistant Surgeon R. Thornton. Woolwich: Royal Artillery Institution, 1892. 19 pp. (reprinted from Proceedings of the Royal Artillery Institution, vol. 19). 9¼″

The History of " J " Battery, Royal Horse Artillery (formerly A Troop, Madras Horse Artillery). Compiled from Private and Official Records by Major Guilbert E. Wyndham Malet, Captain of the Battery, 1875-79. London: printed by Charles Good & Co. [1898]. viii, 73 pp., plate. 7″

Some Pages from the History of "Q" Battery, R.H.A. in the Great War. Strung together by A. H. B[urne], [Woolwich]: Royal Artillery Institution, 1922. 51 pp., plates, maps. 8¼″

A Short History of the Eagle Troop, R.H.A. No imprint. [Printed in Germany], 1955. 40 pp. 8″

Record of the History of "U" Battery, Royal Horse Artillery. Manchester; 1902. 39 pp.

History of D.D.(Jerboa) Battery, Royal Horse Artillery from October, 1941, to May, 1945. Aldershot: Gale & Polden Ltd. [1946]. 96 pp. 7¼″

ROYAL FIELD ARTILLERY

Battery History of 12th (Minden) Field Battery, R.A., 1747-1959.   By Major Walter Bull.   Colchester: duplicated, 1959.   viii, 32 pp.   13″.

The History of the 13th Battery, Royal Field Artillery, from 1759 to 1913.   By Major H. Marriott Smith.   Written for the Soldiers of the Battery, Past, Present and Future.   [Edinburgh: printed by Hugh Paton and Sons], 1913.   55 pp., plate.   8½″

History of the 22nd (The Residency) Field Battery, Royal Artillery.   By Capt. P. A. Brooke.   Allahabad: The Pioneer Press, 1931.   [10], 47 pp., plates, maps. 7½″

A Short History of the 27th Battery, R.F.A.   With special reference to the European War, 1914-1919.   Compiled by Capt. C. M. Vallentin.   Woolwich: Royal Artillery Institution, 1919.   [6], 49 pp., illustrations.   9¾″

History of 28 Field Battery, R.A., 1755-1960.   By Lieut. A. A. McDowell, 1962. Duplicated.   147 pp.   13″

A Brief Account of the War Services of the 67th Field Battery, R.A.   Woolwich: Royal Artillery Institution [1927].   [4], 20 pp.   9¾″

69th Battery, R.F.A.   Diary of the Boer War, 1899-1900-1901.   Multan: Blooming Press [1902].   84 pp.   8½″

Diary of 70th Battery, 34th Brigade, Royal Field Artillery from 4th August, 1914, to 3rd March, 1915, kept by Major H. C. Stanley Clarke.   Woolwich: Royal Artillery Institution, 1920.   13 pp.   9½″

The History of Strange's Royal Artillery, 1848-1958.   Hong Kong: Ye Olde Printerie, Ltd., 1958.   69 pp.   Portrait.   8½″

Royal Artillery.   Extracts from the Digest of Service of "W" Field Battery and its predecessors, 1807 to 1938.   Compiled by Lt.-Col. J. H. McGuinness, 1957.   47 pp.   Duplicated.   7½″ × 12¾″

ROYAL GARRISON ARTILLERY

Diary of Eleventh Siege Battery, R.G.A., now Eleventh Howitzer Battery, R.G.A. [Birmingham: E. C. Osborne, Ltd., 1922].   57 pp.   9¾″

Digest of Services of No. 18 Company, Eastern Division, Royal Artillery. No imprint [1897].   35 leaves printed one side.   13″

With the Heavies in Flanders, 1914-'15-'16-'17-'18-'19.   A Record of the Active Service of the 24th Heavy Battery, R.G.A.   By Harold F. Berdinner.   London: The Botolph Printing Works, 1922.   143 pp., portraits, plates.   8½″

History of 81 Siege Battery, R.G.A.   By Major H. J. G. Gale, R.G.A., O.C. 81 Siege Battery, from August 4th, 1914, to December 31st, 1918.   London: J. & E. Bumpus, Ltd. [1919].   27 pp., plate.   8½″

1914-18 FORMATIONS: DIVISIONS

Narrative of the 5th Divisional Artillery, 1914-1918. By Brig.-Gen. A. H. Hussey. Woolwich: Royal Artillery Institution, 1919. 55 pp. 9¾″

History of the 20th Divisional Artillery, 1914-1919. Compiled by Capt. E. G. Earle. Woolwich: Royal Artillery Institution, 1919. [4], 40 pp., portraits. 9½″

29th Divisional Artillery. War Record and Honours Book, 1915-1918. By Lieut. Col. R. M. Johnson. Woolwich: Royal Artillery Institution, 1921. vii, 235 pp., plate. 9¼″

Artillery and Trench Mortar Memories. 32nd Division. Diaries by A. B. Scott, R. E. Grice-Hutchinson, L. Heathcote-Amory—Memories, etc., by S. Reed, J. E. Prince, S. A. Cooper, V. H. Laar, W. E. English, T. Slane. Epilogue by S. Reed. London: printed by Unwin Brothers Ltd. [1932]. 687 pp. 8½″

The History of the 33rd Divisional Artillery in the War, 1914-1918. By J. Macartney-Filgate, late Major. With a Foreword by General Lord Horne. London: Vacher & Sons Ltd. [1921]. xii, 212 pp., maps. 9¾″

A Short History of the 39th (Deptford) Divisional Artillery, 1915-1918. By Lt.-Col. H. W. Wiebkin. London: E. G. Berryman & Sons Ltd., 1923. 80 pp. portrait. 8½″

BRIGADES

The XV Brigade Group, R.F.A., at Le Cateau, 26th August, 1914. By Martin Gale [i.e., Brig. E. G. Earle]. No imprint [1964]. 11 pp., plan. 9½″

The City of Aberdeen Royal Field Artillery (157th Brigade). The Story of the Raising, compiled by Col. the Rev. James Smith. [Aberdeen: " Daily Journal" Office]. 1917. 123 pp., portraits. 9½″

The History of the locally raised 160th (Wearside) Brigade, Royal Field Artillery. [Sunderland: Robert Youll, printer]. 1921. 41 pp., portraits, plate. 9¾″

The 25th Army Brigade, R.G.A., on the Western Front in 1918. By C. S. B. Buckland, sometime Capt. and Adjt. Oxford: Basil Blackwell, 1940. xi, 110 pp., maps. 7½″

61 How some Wheels went round. By Brig.-Gen. O. C. Williamson Oswald. London: Henry J. Drane [1929]. 218, [8] pp., map. 8½″

History of the 77th Brigade, R.G.A. Compiled by the Brigade Commander Lt.-Col. H. de L. Walters and illustrated by Capt. F. W. Walter. London: Spottiswoode, Ballantyne & Co. Ltd., 1919. 75 pp., portrait, plates. 8½″

Nine Days. Adventures of a Heavy Artillery Brigade 90th of the Third Army during the German Offensive of March 21-29, 1918. By Arthur F. Behrend (late Capt. and Adjutant, 90th Brigade, R.G.A.). Cambridge: W. Heffer & Sons Ltd., 1921. xvi, 115 pp., portraits, plates, maps. 7½″

1914-1918: BATTERIES. R.F.A.

The War Diary of the 84th Battery, R.F.A., 1914-1919. [London: Forster Groom & Co. Ltd.], *n.d.* 94 pp. 4¾″

The Diary of "C" Battery, 62nd Brigade, R.F.A., in the European War, 1914-1918. [Edited by Lt.-Col. J. C. Dundas]. Woolwich: Royal Artillery Institution, 1921. [6], 72 pp., plate. 9¼″

The History of ' A ' Battery, 84th Army Brigade, Royal Field Artillery, 1914-1919. By D. F. Grant (late Major). London: Marshall Brothers Ltd. [1922]. 96 pp. 7¼″

The Diary of "B " Battery, R.F.A., 84th Army Brigade, 1914 to 1918. [London: Canada Newspaper Co. Ltd.], *n.d.* 80 pp. 7¼″

History of the Scarborough Pals' Battery, "C" Battery, 161st (Yorks.) Brigade, Royal Field Artillery. Compiled by Sydney Foord and Thomas Northern. No imprint. Scarborough, 1961. 41 pp., map. 10″
   1915-1919 on cover.

1914-1918: BATTERIES. R.G.A.

14th Heavy Battery R.G.A. War Diary, List of Honours and Awards to Officers, N.C.O.'s and Men whilst serving with the Battery, List of Officers who have served with the Battery, Roll of Honour. London: Robert Scott, 1919. 108 pp., portraits, plates, map. 9¾″

27th Siege Battery, Royal Garrison Artillery: B.E.F. France and Flanders, 5th September, 1915 to 15th April, 1919. Nominal Roll—Roll of Honour. [Aldershot: Gale & Polden Ltd.], 1919. 12 pp. 8″

The History of 76 Siege Battery, R.G.A. By L. F. Penstone. [London: S. Tinsley & Co. Ltd., 1937]. 112 pp. 8½″

History of the 91st (Siege) Battery, R.G.A., December, 1915 to 11 November, 1918. By Major W. F. Christian. Woolwich: Royal Artillery Institution, 1920. [4], 55 pp., map. 9½″

Siege Battery 94 during the World War, 1914-1918. Compiled by Major Charles E. Berkeley Lowe. With an Introduction by Lieut.-Col. D. A. Sandford. London: T. Werner Laurie Ltd. [1919]. 160 pp., plates, map. 8½″

126 Heavy Battery, R.G.A., 1915-1919. [London: W. P. Griffith & Sons Ltd., 1919]. 83 pp., portraits. 6″

The History of the 135th Siege Battery, R.G.A. Compiled by Lieut. D. J. Walters and Lieut. C. R. Curle Hobbs. With a Foreword by Lieut.-Col. C. S. S. Curteis. London: A. Hartley Robinson, 1921. 197 pp., portrait, plates, maps. 9¾″

The Hampstead Heavies (138th Heavy Battery, R.G.A.). A Narrative of a 60 Pounder Battery in France and Belgium during the Great War. By Walter Wright. [London]: published at 14 Mackeson Road, Hampstead, N.W.3, 1926. [7], 40 pp. 7¾″

A History of 154 Siege Battery, Royal Garrison Artillery. By Capt. Maurice C. Walker. Dublin: printed by John T. Drought [1919]. [11], 84 pp., portraits, plates. 8½″

178 Siege Battery, R.G.A. B.E.F. France, 1916-1918. [Edited by J. J. Webber]. Leeds: Chorley & Pickersgill, Ltd., 1919. viii, 127 pp., portraits, maps. 8½″

The Itinerary of 211 Seige (sic) Battery, Royal Garrison Artillery. Compiled by the Members who served in it. Norton, Malton, Yorks.: T. Baker, printer. [c. 1920]. 11 pp. 6½″

" Two Eleven," being the History of 211 Siege Battery, R.G.A., on the Western Front. Compiled and privately printed for those who served in it. Portsmouth: W. H. Barrell, Ltd., 1925. 86 pp., plates. 8″

" 228." The History of a Siege Battery during the Great War. [By Major C. E. Hare]. [Portsmouth: W. H. Barrell, Ltd., 1922]. 45 pp., plates, maps. 7¾″

With a Siege Battery in France. 303 Siege Battery, R.G.A., 1916-1919. Woolwich: Royal Artillery Institution, 1919. iv, 90 pp., plates. 9½″

The Record of 355 Siege Battery. Compiled and published under the auspices of 355 Siege Battery Old Comrades Association. [London: Sutherin & Co., printers, 1920]. 48 pp., portraits, plate. 8¼″

ROYAL ARTILLERY, 1939-1945

A Short History of 3rd Field Regiment, Royal Artillery, from the Outbreak of War. [By Lt.-Col. G. R. Brocklebank]. Duplicated, prepared in Italy at end of the War, 1945. ii, 83 pp., portraits, maps. 12⅞″

15 Field Regiment Royal Artillery. Regimental Record of War Service, 1939-1945. Altrincham: John Sherrat & Son [1948]. 110 pp., portraits, plates, sketch maps. 8½″

24th Field Regiment, R.A. 1939-1945. [By Major J. M. A. Lumsden, assisted by Major L. F. Robinson]. [Manchester: James Galt & Co. Ltd., 1947]. 67 pp., plates, maps. 8½″

25th Field Regiment Royal Artillery (w.e.f. 1 May, 1947, changed to 29 Field Regiment, R.A.); 12/25 Battery—31 (Kirkee) Battery—58 (Maiwand) Battery (now 8/79 (Kirkee) and 145 (Maiwand) Field Batteries, North-West Europe, 1944-1945. [Aldershot: Gale & Polden Ltd., 1948]. [5], 33 pp., maps. 8½″

This is the Story of 2 Medium Regiment Royal Artillery in Italy from December 21st 1943 to May 8th 1945. [By Lieut. J. T. Plume]. Torino: Vincenzo Bona [1945]. 90 pp., illustrations, maps. 9⅜″

The History of 3rd Medium Regiment Royal Artillery, 1939-1945. Foreword by Major-Gen. F. W. H. Pratt. Liverpool: printed by The Northern Publishing Co. Ltd., 1946. 381 pp., plates, maps. 8½″

The History of the 7th Medium Regiment, Royal Artillery (now 32nd Medium Regiment, R.A.) during World War II, 1939-1945. [Edited by Capt. J. A. C. Monk]. [Sheffield: privately printed, Loxley Brothers Ltd., 1951]. ix, 222 pp., plates, maps. 8½″

The History of 11th (Essex) Medium Regiment, Royal Artillery. Winterswijk: Drukkerii Helders, *n.d.* 75 pp., sketch maps. 8½″

Short History of 70 Medium Regt., R.A. By J. M. Bannerman. No imprint, 1945. 30 pp. 8½″

The History of the 61st Medium Regiment, R.A. London: 1950, 132 pp. 8vo

A Short History of 7th Heavy A.A. Regiment, 3rd September, 1939-5th March, 1944, in the Defence of Malta. [Aldershot: Gale & Polden Ltd., 1947]. [7], 35 pp., plates, maps. 7¼″

1st Air Landing Light Regiment, R.A. Regimental History, 1941-1945. [London: Gale & Polden Ltd., 1945]. 40 pp. 10″

Coast Artillery in Sicily and Italy, 1943-1945. [203 Fixed Defences]. By Col. S. C. Tomlin. [Rome: printed by Failli Fauste]. 1945. 167 pp., plates, diagrams, sketch maps. 7½″

CORPS OF ROYAL ENGINEERS

The History of the Corps of Royal Sappers and Miners. By T. W. J. Connolly, Quartermaster Serjeant of the Corps. London: Longman, Brown, Green & Longmans, 1855. 2 vols. 8¼″
    17 coloured plates of uniform.

History of the Royal Sappers and Miners, from the Formation of the Corps in March 1772, to the date when its designation was changed to that of Royal Engineers, in October 1856. By T. W. J. Connolly, Quartermaster of the Royal Engineers. London: Longman, Brown, Green, Longmans, and Roberts, 1857. 2 vols. 2nd edition, with considerable additions. 8¼″
    17 coloured plates of uniform.

History of the Corps of Royal Engineers.   By Whitworth Porter, Major General, Royal Engineers.   London: Longmans, Green & Co., 1889.   2 vols., portraits, plans.   8½″
   4 coloured plates of uniform in vol. 1.

────── Vol. 3.   By Col. Sir Charles M. Watson.   Chatham: The Royal Engineers Institute, 1915.   vii, 409 pp., portrait.   8¼″

────── Vol. 4.   By Brig.-Gen. W. Baker Brown.   1952.   xvii, 434 pp., portrait, maps.   (Reprinted 1954).

────── Vol. 5.   The Home Front, France, Flanders and Italy in the First World War.   1952.   xxi, 728 pp., portraits, plate, maps in end-pocket.

────── Vol. 6.   Gallipoli, Macedonia, Egypt and Palestine, 1914-1918.   1952. xvii, 444 pp., portraits, sketch maps, maps in end-pocket.

────── Vol. 7.   Campaigns in Mesopotamia and East Africa and the Inter-War Period, 1919-38.   1952.   xv, 351 pp., portraits, maps, map in end-pocket.

────── Vol. 8.   1938-1948.   Campaigns in France and Belgium, 1939-40. Norway.   Middle East.   East Africa.   Western Desert, North West Africa, and activities in the U.K.   By Major-Gen. R. P. Pakenham-Walsh.   xv, 488 pp., portraits, plates, maps.

────── Vol. 9.   1938-1948.   Campaigns in Sicily and Italy; the War against Japan; North-West Europe, 1944-45; minor and non-operational areas; post-war, 1945-48.   By Major-Gen. R. P. Pakenham-Walsh.   xviii, 644 pp., portraits, plates, maps.
   Vols. 4-9 Chatham: The Institution of Royal Engineers.   8¾″

The Royal Engineers in Egypt and the Sudan.   By Lieut.-Col. E. W. C. Sandes. Chatham: The Institution of Royal Engineers, 1937.   xxxii, 571 pp., portraits, plates, maps, plans.   9½″

The Military Engineer in India.   By Lieut.-Col. E. W. C. Sandes.   Chatham: The Institution of Royal Engineers, 1933-35.   2 vols., portraits, plates, illustrations, maps.   9½″

Roll of Officers of the Corps of Royal Engineers, from 1660 to 1898.   Compiled from the MS. Rolls of the late Capt. T. W. J. Connolly, R.E. and brought up to date in the Office of the R.E. Institute, Chatham.   Edited by Capt. R. F. Edwards, R.E., Secretary R.E. Institute.   Chatham: printed by W. & J. Mackay & Co. Ltd., and published by the Royal Engineer Institute, 1898.   viii, 130 pp.   9½″ × 12¼″

Biographical Notices of Officers of the Royal (Bengal) Engineers.   Arranged and compiled by Col. Sir Edward T. Thackeray.   London: Smith, Elder & Co., 1900.   xii, 278 pp., portraits.   8¾″

The Uniforms of the Corps of Royal Engineers up to 1914.   By Lieut.-Col. P. H. Kealy.   (In *The Royal Engineers Journal*, vol. 48, 1934, pp. 186-208, 505-513; vol. 49, 1935, pp. 402-418).   Portraits, plates.   9¼″

The Pictures and Plate of the R.E. Headquarters Mess, Chatham. By Col. B. R. Ward. Chatham: Institution of Royal Engineers, 1909. iv, 82 pp., portraits, plates. 9¾″

The Portraits & Silver of the R.E. Headquarters Mess, Chatham. By J. M. Lambert. Chatham: Institution of Royal Engineers, 1963. 134 pp., portraits, illustrations. 9¾″
Coloured frontispiece of The Queen.

The R.E. Headquarters Mess. By Col. J. M. Lambert. (In *The Royal Engineers Journal*, 1957). 22 pp., plates. 9¼″

A History of Royal Engineers Cricket, 1862-1924. By Capt. R. S. Rait-Kerr. Chatham: Institution of Royal Engineers, 1925. 96 pp., portraits. 9¾″

The Corps of Royal Engineers. A Handbook for the Use of Candidates for Third Class Certificate of Education. Compiled in the Education Office, Training Battalion, R.E. Chatham: Institution of Royal Engineers, 1943. 52 pp. 5¼″

REGULAR UNITS

History of the 7th Field Company, R.E., during the War 1914-1918. By Capt. H. A. Baker. [Chatham: Institution of Royal Engineers, 1932]. 68 pp., portraits, maps. 9¾″

History of the 12th Company Royal Engineers. By Lieut. M. R. Caldwell. Reproduced with additions from *The Royal Engineers Journal*. Chatham: Institution of Royal Engineers, 1925. 79 pp., plates, maps. 9¾″

38 Field Squadron, Royal Engineers, 1861-1957. [By Lt.-Col. Ronald J. G. Begbie, edited by 2/Lt. N. Whittington]. [Dortmund: Fritz Brandt Druck], 1957. 77 pp., portraits, illustrations. 8¼″

The " Four-Two." Scraps from the History of the 42nd Field Company, R.E. Edited by A. H. M. Morris. Aldershot: Gale & Polden Ltd., 1952. xii, 69 pp., portraits, plates. 7¼″

1914-1918 WAR FORMATIONS. UNITS

5th Signal Company, Royal Engineers; Summary of War History, 1914-1919. [Aldershot: Gale & Polden Ltd.], 1919. 8 pp. 8¼″

65 R.E. A Short Record of the Service of the 65th Field Company Royal Engineers. Cambridge: W. Heffer & Sons Ltd., 1920. xii, 156 pp., portraits, plates. 7¼″

Collections and Recollections of 107th Field Company, R.E. [Edited by Lieut. N. Bateman and Lieut. M. J. Rattray]. Darlington: Wm. Dresser & Sons, 1918. 146 pp., illustrations. 8″

Further Recollections of 107th Field Coy., R.E. [Edited by Lieut. M. J. Rattray]. Darlington: Wm. Dresser & Sons, 1920. 228 pp., plates, maps. 8"

History of the 206th Field Company (1st Glasgow) Royal Engineers, 14th Infantry Brigade, 32nd Division, British Expeditionary Force, France: Belgium: Germany: 1915-1919. By James Smith. [Paisley: W. A. Lochhead], printed for private circulation [1932]. 110 pp., portraits, illustrations, maps. 8¼"

Chronicles of the 20th Light Railway Train Crews Co., Royal Engineers. With the British Expeditionary Force, 1917-1919. [Edited by Sapper J. Helliwell Laytham]. Bath: Coward & Gradwell. 52 pp., portraits, illustrations. 10½"

The 111th Railway Company Royal Engineers or " The Three Ones." By A. F. Westcott. Bristol: printed by Edward Everard, Ltd., n.d. 72 pp., map, diagrams. 8¾"

Tunnellers. The Story of the Tunnelling Companies, Royal Engineers, during the World War. By Capt. W. Grant Grieve and Bernard Newman. London: Herbert Jenkins, Ltd. [1936]. 334 pp., portraits, plates, maps, sketch maps. 8½"

The Life of a Tunnelling Company, being an intimate Story of the Life of the 185th Tunnelling Company Royal Engineers, in France, during the Great War, 1914-1918. By Capt. H. W. Graham. With an Introduction by Lt.-Col. R. G. Stokes. Illustrated from sketches mainly by Lieut. F. C. B. Cadell. Hexham: J. Catherall & Co. (Printers), Ltd., 1927. xv, 180 pp., portraits, illustrations, map. 8¼"

With the Special Brigade, R.E.; a brief story of 186 Company, R.E. and ' C ' Special Company, R.E., 1915-1919. By Martin S. Fox. [Privately published: M. S. Fox, 6 Willingdon Park Drive, Eastbourne], 1957. 136 pp., portraits, plates, maps. 8"

1939-1945 WAR FORMATIONS. UNITS

The Royal Engineers, Sixth Armoured Division. Padova: Tipografia Antoniana, 1946 [for private circulation]. 132, xxxi pp., illustrations, maps. 9¼"

5 Armoured Engineer Regiment. H Hour D Day—VE Day. No imprint [1945]. 51 pp. 8¼"

19th Field Survey Company Royal Engineers. Overseas Service, 1939-1946. [Sketch map of the Routes and Stations, with brief history]. [Printed by 19th Field Survey Coy., R.E.], 1946. Single sheet folded 8" × 6"

The Story of 92 Company Royal Engineers.   Part I, by Cpl. Bond, W., being a somewhat incomplete, and wholly inadequate account of the wanderings of just one unit of the Royal Engineers that came into being during the World War of 1939-1945.   Part 2, by Sgt. Wilson, E.   With a Tailpiece by Major K. C. Brown. [Northampton: Stenton & Son, printers, 1946].   54 pp., illustrations. $7\frac{1}{4}''$

The Circus.   Diary of 234 Field Company R.E.   " D " Day—" VE " Day. [By Lieut. H. H. Campbell].   No imprint [Dortmund, 1945].   36 pp., illustrations, map. $8\frac{1}{4}''$

The Desert.   By 517 Corps Field Survey Coy. Royal Engineers.   [Written, edited, drawn and printed by members of 517 Field Survey Coy. R.E., 1944]. 72 pp., illustrations. $8\frac{7}{8}''$

That White Horse.   A Brief History The 629 (9th) Field Squadron Royal Engineers.   By B. Douglas Arnot.   Aldershot: Gale & Polden Ltd., 1947. viii, 69 pp., portraits, illustrations. $8\frac{1}{2}''$

Our Part; being the Story of 756 Field Company Royal Engineers from Formation to Victory, Nov. 1940-May 1945.   No imprint.   175 pp., illustrations. $7\frac{1}{4}''$

" Go to it."   The Story of the 3rd Parachute Squadron, Royal Engineers.   By Major J. S. R. Shave.   [Extracted from *The Royal Engineers Journal*, 1949-50]. 94 pp., portraits, maps.   9″

The History of 5 Engineer (Base) Workshop, Royal Engineers.   [By Major J. C. G. Richardson].   [Hannover, 1948].   [28] pp. $10\frac{1}{4}''$

ROYAL CORPS OF SIGNALS

The Royal Corps of Signals.   A Short History of Signals in the Army.   London: The Royal Corps of Signals Association, 1927.   58 pp. $7\frac{3}{4}''$

——— Part 2: The British Expeditionary Force, 1939-40.   *n.d.*   72 pp., maps, diagrams.

——— Part 2: Addition.   *n.d.*   14 pp., map, diagram.

The Royal Corps of Signals.   A History of its Antecedents and Development (*circa* 1800-1955).   By Major-Gen. R. F. H. Nalder.   London: Royal Signals Institution, 1958.   xvi, 672 pp., portraits, plates, maps. $9\frac{1}{2}''$

Royal Signals.   [London: Royal Signals Institution], 1957.   52 pp., portraits, illustrations. $9\frac{3}{4}''$
Booklet for new entrants, mainly historical.

History of 2nd Divisional Signals. [Aldershot: Mays, printers, 1939]. 42 pp. 7″

12 Air Formation Signals. The Story of our Campaign. Edited by Capt. C. M. Arman, with contributions from Capt. I. McKinnon, Lieut. H. V. Crabtree and Cpl. F. R. Smith. [Bückeburg, Germany: printed by Grimmesche Hofbuch-druckerei, 1945]. 100 pp., portraits, illustrations. 8″

150 Officer Cadet Training Unit, Royal Corps of Signals. Coventry, no title-page, 1945. Typescript. Unnumbered pp. Photographs gummed in. 4to

FOOT GUARDS

The Foot Guards. By the Hon. John W. Fortescue. London: Macmillan & Co. Ltd., 1915. 31 pp. 8¼″

A History of the Foot Guards to 1856. By Major H. L. Aubrey-Fletcher. London: Constable & Co. Ltd., 1927. xiv, 463 pp., maps, plans. 9¼″

A Short History of the Brigade of Guards. Aldershot: Gale & Polden Ltd., 1944. 95 pp., maps. 8½″
  Originally embodied in a booklet " Notes for Lecture to Recruits of the Brigade of Guards." Compiled in 1898 by Major (afterwards Major-Gen.) Hon. A. H. Henniker.

The Official Records of the Guards Brigade in South Africa. London: J. J. Keliher & Co. Ltd., 1904. 344 pp., portraits, map. 8½″

6th Guards Tank Brigade. The Story of the Guardsmen in Churchill Tanks. By Patrick Forbes. London: Sampson Low, Marston & Co. Ltd. [1946]. xii, 244 pp., portraits, plates, maps, end-paper maps. 9¾″

The British Foot Guards; a bibliography. By L. C. Silverthorne and W. D. Gaskin. Cornwallville, N.Y.: Hope Farm Press, 1960. iv, 67 pp. 9½″

Fighting with the Guards. By Keith Briant. London: Evans Brothers Ltd. [1960]. 244 pp., portraits, plates, end-paper maps. 8¼″

——— Cadet edition. [1960]. 191 pp., plates. 7¾″

GRENADIER GUARDS

The Origin and History of the First or Grenadier Guards. From Documents in the State Paper Office, War Office, Horse Guards, contemporary history, regi-mental records, etc. By Lieut.-Gen. Sir. F. W. Hamilton. London: John Murray, 1874. 3 vols., portraits, plates, maps. 9″
  4 coloured plates of uniform, 3 of colours.

——— Corrigenda and Addenda; with portrait of Thomas, Lord Wentworth. London: John Murray. xxxiv pp. 1877.

History of the Grenadier Guards, 1656-1949.   [Abridged; by Capt. F. Martin].
Aldershot: Gale & Polden Ltd.   [1951].   [vi], 66 pp., portrait. $7\frac{1}{4}$"

The Grenadier Guards in the Great War of 1914-1918.   By Lieut.-Col. the Right
Hon. Sir Frederick Ponsonby, with an Introduction by Lieut.-Gen. The Earl
of Cavan.   London: Macmillan & Co. Ltd., 1920.   3 vols., portraits, plates,
maps.   9"

The Grenadier Guards in the War of 1939-1945.   By Capt. Nigel Nicolson and
Patrick Forbes.   Aldershot: Gale & Polden Ltd., 1949.   2 vols., portraits,
plates, maps. $9\frac{1}{2}$"
   Vol. 1.   The Campaigns in North-West Europe; by Patrick Forbes.
   Vol. 2.   The Mediterranean Campaigns; by Capt. N. Nicolson.

The Grenadier Guards, 1939-1945.   Aldershot: Gale & Polden Ltd. [1946].
[8], 79 pp., portraits, illustrations, maps. $9\frac{1}{2}$"

First or Grenadier Guards in South Africa, 1899-1902.   Records of the Second
Battalion; compiled by Brig.-Gen. F. Lloyd.—Records of the Third Battalion;
compiled by Brevet-Major Hon. A. Russell.   London: J. Keliher & Co. Ltd.,
1907.   114, 138 pp., plates, plans. $8\frac{1}{2}$"

The Grenadier Guards.   A tercentenary exhibition held by gracious permission of
Her Majesty the Queen at St. James's Palace, 30 May-23 June 1956.   [London:
Vail & Co. Ltd., printers], 1956.   30 pp., portraits, plates. $9\frac{3}{4}$"
   4 coloured plates of uniform and 1 coloured portrait.

The Grenadier Guards.   Tercentenary Year, 1656-1956; a pictorial record of
the historic celebrations of 1956.   Birdcage Walk, London, S.W.1.   Private
circulation, Dec., 1956.   [89] pp., portraits, illustrations (some coloured).   11"

The Colours of the British Army; comprising the Standards, Guidons and Flags
of every regiment in Her Majesty's Service.   By Robert French McNair.   London:
Day and Son Ltd., 1867.   xii, 56 pp., plates.   11"
   17 coloured plates, including 14 of the Grenadier Guards, the only regiment
   dealt with.   Parts 1-3 no more published.

The Colours of the Grenadier Guards.   [Colchester: Benham and Co. Ltd.,
privately printed, 1937].   40 pp., plates. $8\frac{1}{2}$"
   17 coloured plates.

The Colours of the First or Grenadier Regiment of Foot Guards. Ipswich: printed by W. S. Cowell, Ltd., 1958. 48 pp., plates. 8½"
  18 coloured plates.

First Battalion Grenadier Guards, 4th Oct.-8th Nov., 1914. [By Capt. H. L. Aubrey-Fletcher]. Westminster: Metchim & Son [1915]. 28 pp., maps. (Confidential). 8¼"

Household Brigade Magazine. 3rd Battalion Grenadier Guards Number. Aldershot: Gale & Polden Ltd., 1961. 102 pp., portraits, illustrations, maps. 9½"

The First or Grenadier Guards Club, 1917. [List of Members, Rules, proceedings of Annual Meeting, Historical Precis, etc.] [Colchester: Benham & Co. Ltd., 1917]. 108 pp. 7¼"

COLDSTREAM GUARDS

Origin and Services of the Coldstream Guards. By Col. [Daniel] MacKinnon. London: Richard Bentley, 1835. 2 vols., plates. 8½"

The Early History of the Coldstream Guards. By G. Davies. Oxford: Clarendon Press, 1924. xxxviii, 160 pp., portraits, plates, plan. 10"

A History of the Coldstream Guards, from 1815 to 1895. By Lt.-Col. Ross of Bladensburg. Illustrated by Lieut. Nevile R. Wilkinson. London: A. D. Innes & Co., 1896. xxi, 492 pp., portrait, plates, maps. 10"
  6 coloured plates of uniform and 2 of colours.

The Coldstream Guards, 1885-1914. By Col. Sir John Hall, Bart. Oxford: Clarendon Press, 1929. xi, 394 pp., maps, 10"

The Coldstream Guards, 1914-1918. By Lieut.-Col. Sir John Ross-of-Bladensburg. Oxford: University Press, 1928. 2 vols. and separate vol. of maps. 10"

The Coldstream Guards, 1920-1946. By Michael Howard and John Sparrow. London: Oxford University Press, 1951. xvii, 593 pp., maps. 9⅞"

Nulli Secundus. The Record of the Coldstream Guards, 1650-1950. [By Col. R. J. Marker, Major-Gen. A. G. C. Dawnay & Col. E. R. Hill; edited by Col. the Earl of Lucan]. No imprint [1950]. xii, 91 pp., end-paper, map. 7½"
  Earlier editions: Chiswick Press, 1907; 1916, and London: Vacher & Sons, Ltd., 1923.

The Coldstream Guards in the Crimea. By Lt.-Col. Ross-of-Bladensburg. London: A. D. Innes & Co., 1897. xii, 312 pp., maps. 7½"

History of the First Battalion Coldstream Guards during the Eastern Campaign, from February, 1854, to June, 1856. By John Wyatt, Battalion Surgeon. [London: S. Straker's Steam Printing Works], 1858. [8], 138 pp., plate. 8½"

"No Dishonourable Name." The 2nd and 3rd Battalions Coldstream Guards in France, North Africa and Italy, 1939-1946. Compiled and edited by D. C. Quilter. London: William Clowes & Sons, Ltd. [1947]. 334 pp., portraits, illustrations, maps. 11"

Household Brigade Magazine. 3rd Battalion Coldstream Guards Number, 1897-1959. Aldershot: Gale & Polden Ltd., 1959. 84 pp., portraits, illustrations. 9½"

A Distant Drum. War Memories of the Intelligence Officer of the 5th Bn. Coldstream Guards, 1944-45. By Capt. J. Pereira, with a Foreword by Gen. Sir Charles Loyd. Aldershot: Gale & Polden Ltd., 1948. xiii, 213 pp., portraits, plates, maps. 8½"

" Clothed all in Green-o," being an account in narrative and pictorial form of the activities of 2nd Battalion Coldstream Guards in Malaya in 1948 and 1949. With a Foreword by Gen. Sir John Harding. [Ipoh, Perak; printed by Charles Grenier & Co. Ltd., 1950]. 54 pp., portraits, plates, maps. 10⅞"

The Great Deeds of the Coldstream Guards. By F. W. Walker. London: J. M. Dent & Sons Ltd. [1916]. 176 pp., coloured plate of uniform. (The Story of the Regiments). 7"

Coldstream Guards. The Colours and Customs. London: Headquarters Coldstream Guards [printed by Harrison & Sons Ltd., 1921]. 40 pp. 6½"

SCOTS GUARDS

The Scots Guards. By Capt. Charles B. Balfour of Newton Don. Glasgow: James Maclehose and Sons, 1919. 53 pp. (Reprinted from *The Lowland Scots Regiments*, edited by the Right Hon. Sir Herbert Maxwell, Bart.). 9½"
    Illustration of uniform on paper cover.

The History of the Scots Guards from the Creation of the Regiment to the Eve of the Great War. By Major-Gen. Sir F. Maurice. London: Chatto & Windus, 1934. 2 vols., portraits, plates, maps. 10"
    3 coloured plates of uniform and 1 of colours in each volume.
    Also a special edition signed by H.R.H. The Duke of York as Colonel of the Regiment with additional plates hand-coloured by C. C. P. Lawson.

The Scots Guards in the Great War, 1914-1918. By F. Loraine Petre. Wilfred Ewart and Major-Gen. Sir Cecil Lowther. London: John Murray, 1925. xiii, 349 pp., maps. 8½"

The Scots Guards, 1919-1945. Compiled by David Erskine. London: Publ. for the Scots Guards by William Clowes & Sons Ltd., 1956. xx, 624 pp., portraits, plates, maps. 9¾"

Scots Guards, their Story in a Few Words. Compiled by Viscount Bury, from James Grant's *"The Scots Fusilier Guards,"* and from other Sources. [London: printed by Hamilton Bros., Ltd., 1942]. 14 pp. 7½"

A Loan Exhibition depicting the History of the Scots Guards, 39, Grosvenor Square, S.W.1. December 1st-23rd, 1934. Aldershot: Gale & Polden Ltd., 1934. 60 pp., portraits, plates. 9¾"
  Title on paper cover: Scots Guards, 1642-1934; The History of a Scottish Regiment.
  1 coloured plate of uniform.

The 1st Battalion Scots Guards in South Africa, 1899-1902. Edited by Capt. J. H. Cuthbert. London: Harrison & Sons [1903]. [8], 259 pp., portraits, illustrations. 12¼"×9¾"

2nd Battalion Scots Guards. Malaya, 1948-1951. [Kuala Lumpur: Caxton Press Ltd., 1951] [v], 90 pp., portraits, plates, maps. 9½"

A Short History of the Scots Guards. Aldershot: printed by Gale & Polden Ltd., 1925. 16 pp. 7⅛"

IRISH GUARDS

A Short History of the Irish Guards. By Lieut. T. H. H. Grayson. Colchester: printed by Benham & Co. Ltd., 1931, 95 pp., portrait, maps. 7½"
  Title on cover reads: A Short History of the Irish Guards, 1900-1927 (including Chapters on the History of the Brigade of Guards and the Irish Regiments that fought in the South African War).

The Irish Guards in the Great War. Edited and compiled from their Diaries and Papers by Rudyard Kipling. London: Macmillan & Co. Ltd., 1923. 2 vols, maps. 9"

History of the Irish Guards in the Second World War. By Major D. J. L. Fitzgerald. With a Foreword by Field Marshal The Viscount Alexander of Tunis. Aldershot: Gale & Polden Ltd., 1949. xv, 615 pp., portraits, illustrations, maps. 8½"

WELSH GUARDS

History of the Welsh Guards. By C. H. Dudley Ward. With an Introduction by Lieut.-Gen. Sir Francis Lloyd. London: John Murray, 1920. x, 505 pp., portraits, plates, maps. 9"
  3 coloured plates of uniform.

The Welsh Regiment of Foot Guards, 1915-1918. By Major C. Dudley Ward. London: John Murray, 1936. vii, 147 pp., maps. 8½"

Welsh Guards: an account of the Battle Honours awarded to the Regiment; the Great War, 1915-1918. Colchester: Benham & Co. Ltd., 1934, viii, 52 pp., map. $7\frac{1}{4}''$

Welsh Guards at War. By Major L. F. Ellis. Aldershot: Gale & Polden Ltd., 1946. xv, 386 pp., portraits, plates, illustrations, maps. $8\frac{1}{2}''$
  10 coloured plates.

Wales and the Welsh Guards. By Major H. M. C. Jones-Mortimer. [Cardiff: Western Mail & Echo Ltd.], 1948. 48 pp., plates. $7\frac{1}{4}''$
  Illustrations of colours.

Welsh Guards: a short account of their achievements. Colchester: Benham & Co. Ltd. [1946]. 80 pp., maps. $7\frac{1}{8}''$

Welsh Guards. An Informal Account of the Fifty Years, 1915-1965. [Devonport: printed by Hiorns & Miller Ltd.] 1965. 150, [14] pp., portraits (1 coloured), illustrations. $9\frac{1}{2}''$

INFANTRY OF THE LINE
(in Army List order and including
Disbanded Irish Regiments)

LIST OF REGIMENTS

including Disbanded Irish, arranged in order of precedence, the numbers
indicating their old numerical titles.

The Royal Scots (The Royal Regiment)   [1]
The Queen's Royal Regiment (West Surrey)   [2]
The Buffs (Royal East Kent Regiment)   [3]
The King's Own Royal Regiment (Lancaster)   [4]
The Royal Northumberland Fusiliers   [5]
The Royal Warwickshire Regiment   [6]
The Royal Fusiliers (City of London Regiment)   [7]
The King's Regiment (Liverpool)   [8]
The Royal Norfolk Regiment   [9]
The Royal Lincolnshire Regiment   [10]
The Devonshire Regiment   [11]
The Suffolk Regiment   [12]
The Somerset Light Infantry (Prince Albert's)   [13]
The West Yorkshire Regiment (The Prince of Wales's Own)   [14]
The East Yorkshire Regiment (The Duke of York's Own)   [15]
The Bedfordshire and Hertfordshire Regiment   [16]
The Royal Leicestershire Regiment   [17]
The Royal Irish Regiment   [18]
The Green Howards (Alexandra, Princess of Wales's Own Yorkshire
                                           Regiment)   [19]

The Lancashire Fusiliers   [20]
The Royal Scots Fusiliers   [21]
The Cheshire Regiment   [22]
The Royal Welch Fusiliers   [23]
The South Wales Borderers   [24]
The King's Own Scottish Borderers   [25]
The Cameronians (Scottish Rifles)   [26 and 90]
The Royal Inniskilling Fusiliers   [27 and 108]
The Gloucestershire Regiment   [28 and 61]
The Worcestershire Regiment   [29 and 36]
The East Lancashire Regiment   [30 and 59]
The East Surrey Regiment   [31 and 70]
The Duke of Cornwall's Light Infantry   [32 and 46]
The Duke of Wellington's Regiment (West Riding)   [33 and 76]
The Border Regiment   [34 and 55]
The Royal Sussex Regiment   [35 and 107]
The Royal Hampshire Regiment   [37 and 67]
The South Staffordshire Regiment   [38 and 80]
The Dorset Regiment   [39 and 54]
The South Lancashire Regiment (The Prince of Wales's Volunteers)   [40 and 82]
The Welch Regiment   [41 and 69]

The Black Watch (Royal Highland Regiment)   [42 and 73]
The Oxfordshire and Buckinghamshire Light Infantry   [43 and 52]
The Essex Regiment   [44 and 56]
The Sherwood Foresters (Nottinghamshire and Derbyshire Regiment)
                                                    [45 and 95]
The Loyal Regiment (North Lancashire)   [47 and 81]
The Northamptonshire Regiment   [48 and 58]
The Royal Berkshire Regiment (Princess Charlotte of Wales's)   [49 and 66]
The Queen's Own Royal West Kent Regiment   [50 and 97]
The King's Own Yorkshire Light Infantry   [51 and 105]
The King's Shropshire Light Infantry   [53 and 85]
The Middlesex Regiment (Duke of Cambridge's Own)   [57 and 77]
The King's Royal Rifle Corps   [60]
The Wiltshire Regiment (Duke of Edinburgh's)   [62 and 99]
The Manchester Regiment   [63 and 96]
The North Staffordshire Regiment (The Prince of Wales's)   [64 and 98]
The York and Lancaster Regiment   [65 and 84]
The Durham Light Infantry   [68 and 106]
The Highland Light Infantry (City of Glasgow Regiment)   [71 and 74]
Seaforth Highlanders (Ross-shire Buffs, The Duke of Albany's)   [72 and 78]
The Gordon Highlanders   [75 and 92]
The Queen's Own Cameron Highlanders   [79]
The Royal Ulster Rifles   [83 and 86]
The Royal Irish Fusiliers (Princess Victoria's)   [87 and 89]
The Connaught Rangers   [88 and 94]
The Argyll and Sutherland Highlanders (Princess Louise's)   [91 and 93]
The Prince of Wales's Leinster Regiment (Royal Canadians)   [100 and 109]
The Royal Munster Fusiliers   [101 and 104]
The Royal Dublin Fusiliers   [102 and 103]
The Parachute Regiment
The Rifle Brigade (Prince Consort's Own)

THE ROYAL SCOTS (THE ROYAL REGIMENT)   [1]

An Historical Account of His Majesty's First, or The Royal Regiment of Foot: General George, Duke of Gordon, Colonel. Compiled by Major Joseph Wetherall. London: printed by W. Clowes, 1832. [vi], 226 pp. 8¼″

Historical Record of The First, or Royal Regiment of Foot; containing an Account of the Origin of the Regiment in the reign of King James VI of Scotland and of its subsequent Services to 1846. Compiled by Richard Cannon, Esq., Adjutant-General's Office, Horse Guards. London: Parker, Furnivall & Parker, 1847. xxxii, 289 pp., plates. 8¾″
   3 coloured plates, including 1 of uniform and 1 of colours.

The Story of The Royal Scots (The Lothian Regiment) formerly The First or The Royal Regiment of Foot. By Lawrence Weaver. With a Preface by the Earl of Rosebery. London: " Country Life " [1915]. xii, 272 pp., portraits, plates, illustrations, maps. (" Country Life " Series of Military Histories) 9½″
   1 coloured plate of uniform.

The Regimental Records of The Royal Scots (The First or The Royal Regiment of Foot). Compiled by J. C. Leask and H. M. McCance, Capt., late The Royal Scots. Dublin: Alexander Thom & Co., Ltd., 1915. xxiv, 787 pp., portraits, plates, illustrations. 10″
   12 coloured plates of uniform, 2 of colours and 12 plates of badges.

The Royal Scots. By Lauchlan Maclean Watt. Edinburgh: W. P. Nimmo, Hay & Mitchell [1916]. 63 pp., plates. 6¼″
   3 coloured plates of uniform and 1 of colours.

The Royal Scots (Lothian Regiment). By Major M. M. Haldane. Glasgow: James Maclehose and Sons, 1919. 42 pp. (Reprinted from *The Lowland Scots Regiments;* edited by the Right Hon. Sir Herbert Maxwell, Bart.). 9½″
   Illustration of uniform on paper cover.

The Royal Scots, 1914-1919. By Major John Ewing. With a Foreword by the Right Hon. Lord Salvesen. Edinburgh: Published for the Association of Lowland Scots by Oliver and Boyd, 1925. 2 vols., portraits, plates, maps. 9″

A Short History of the Royal Scots. By D. T. H. McLennan. Poona: printed by the Scottish Mission Industries Co. Ltd., 1924. iv, 48 pp.
   Specially designed for young soldiers.

Three Hundred Years. The Royal Scots (The Royal Regiment). By Col. H. J. Simson. Edinburgh: printed by J. Skinner & Co. Ltd., 1935. 143 pp. 8½″

The Royal Scots (The Royal Regiment). A short history of the First or Royal Regiment of Foot. By the Colonel of the Regiment [Brig. N. R. Crockatt]. Aldershot: Gale & Polden Ltd., 1952. 12 pp. 7⅛″

The First of Foot; the History of The Royal Scots (The Royal Regiment).   By Augustus Muir; foreword by H.R.H. The Princess Royal.   Edinburgh: The Royal Scots History Committee, 1961.   xvi, 504 pp., portrait, plates, maps.   8½″

The Royal Scots (The Royal Regiment), 1633-1933.   Tercentenary Souvenir. [Aldershot: Gale & Polden Ltd., 1933].   28 pp., portrait, plates.   9″
   11 coloured plates of uniform.

Diary of Services of the First Battalion Royal Scots during the Boer War, South Africa, 1899-1902.   London: Burt & Sons, printed for private circulation, 1904. 83 pp., plates.   8½″

Freemasonry in The Royal Scots (The Royal Regiment).   By T. F. Henderson, Lieut.   With a Foreword by Sir Iain Colquhoun of Colquhoun and Luss, Bart. Aldershot: printed by Gale & Polden Ltd., 1934.   xv, 100 pp., plate.   8½″

Mackay's Regiment: a Narrative of the Principal Services of the Regiment from its Formation in 1626, to the Battle of Nordlingen, in 1634; and of its subsequent Incorporation with the Corps now known as The Royal Scots or First Regiment of Foot of the British Army.   A Paper read before the Gaelic Society of Inverness by John Mackay of Ben Reay.   (Reprinted from the Society's Transactions, for private circulation).   Inverness: Free Press Printing Company, 1879.   63 pp. 8½″

An Old Scots Brigade, being the History of Mackay's Regiment now incorporated with The Royal Scots.   With an Appendix containing copies of many original documents connected with the history of the Regiment.   By John Mackay (late) of Herriesdale.   Edinburgh: William Blackwood and Sons, 1885.   xv, 260 pp., plate.   6¾″

THE QUEEN'S ROYAL REGIMENT
(WEST SURREY)   [2]

Historical Record of The Second, or Queen's Royal Regiment of Foot; containing an Account of the Formation of the Regiment in the year 1661, and of its subsequent Services to 1837.   London: printed by Clowes and Sons, 1838.   [x], 95 pp., plates.   (Cannon's Historical Records Series).   8¾″
   2 coloured plates of uniform and 1 of colours.

The History of the Second, Queen's Royal Regiment, now The Queen's (Royal West Surrey) Regiment.   By Lieut. Col. John Davis.   London: vols. 1-3, Richard Bentley & Son; vols. 4-6, Eyre & Spottiswoode, 1887-95; 1902-06. Portraits, plates, maps, plans.   10″
   Coloured plates: vol. 2 contains 1 of colours; vol. 3, 4 of uniform, 1 of colours and 1 of badge; vol. 5, 3 of uniform, 1 of colours and 1 of badge.
   Vol. 6.   Officers' Services, 1661 to 1904.

History of The Queen's Royal Regiment.   Vol. 7.   Compiled by Col. H. C. Wylly.   Aldershot: Gale & Polden Ltd., for the Regimental Committee [1925]. xvi, 308 pp., portrait, plates, maps.   9½″
   With Separate Case of Maps.

————— ————— Vol. 8.   1924-1948.   Compiled by Major R. C. G. Foster. Aldershot: Gale & Polden Ltd., 1953.   xix, 595 pp., portraits, plates, maps.   9¾″

————— ————— Vol. 9.   Part 1.   1948-1959.   Part 2.   Summary, 1661-1959. Compiled by Major R. C. G. Foster.   Aldershot: Gale & Polden Ltd., 1961. viii, 86 pp., portraits, plates, maps.   9¾″
   2 coloured plates of colours.

The History of The Queen's (Royal West Surrey Regiment) in the form of a Lantern Lecture with Supplementary Notes.   By the Rev. H. J. Burkitt . . . Chaplain to the Depot . . . With an Introduction by Major-Gen. Sir E. O. F. Hamilton, Colonel-in-Chief of the Regiment.   Guildford: A. C. Curtis & Co. Ltd. 1917.   96 pp., plates.   8¼″
   1 coloured plate of colours.

A Short History of The Queen's Royal Regiment.   Aldershot: Gale & Polden Ltd. [1939].   54 pp.   7¼″

——— Another edition.   1953.   56 pp.   7¼″

Some Notes on the Queen's Royal West Surrey Regiment, together with an Account of the 2nd and 3rd Battalions in the late South African Campaign and Guildford's aid to the troops during peace and war.   With a preface by Canon Grant.   Guildford: Frank Lasham, 1904.   94 pp., illustrations.   8vo

An Infantry Company in Arakan and Kohima.   By Major M. A. Lowry.   With a Foreword by Gen. Sir George Giffard.   Aldershot: Gale & Polden Ltd., 1950. xiv, 132 pp., maps, end-paper maps.   7¼″
   " B " Company, 1st Battalion The Queen's Royal Regiment.

———————————

History of the 11th Battalion, " The Queen's."   Compiled by Capt. E. W. J. Neave.   With a Foreword by Lieut.-Gen. Sir Sydney Lawford.   [London: Brixton " Free Press " Printing & Advertising Co. Ltd.], 1931.   xii, 123 pp., portraits, plates, maps.   9¾″

THE BUFFS (ROYAL EAST KENT REGIMENT) [3]

Historical Record of the Third Regiment of Foot, or The Buffs; formerly designated The Holland Regiment; containing an Account of its Origin in the Reign of Queen Elizabeth, and of its subsequent Services to 1838. London: Longman, Orme and Co., 1839. [6], 12, xiv, 281 pp., plates. (Cannon's Regimental Records Series). 8¾"
4 coloured plates, including 1 of uniform and 1 of colours.

Historical Record of The Buffs, from 1838 to 1864. [London: W. Clowes and Sons], 1864. Printed for Regimental Use only and not published. 47 pp. 8¼"

Historical Records of The Buffs, East Kent Regiment, 3rd Foot, formerly designated The Holland Regiment and Prince George of Denmark's Regiment. Vol. 1. 1572-1704. By Capt. H. R. Knight. London: Gale & Polden Ltd., 1905. Maps, plans. 8½"

[Vol. 2]. 1704-1914. By Capt. C. R. B. Knight. London: The Medici Society Ltd., 1935. 2 parts. Portraits, plates, maps, plans 8¾"

[Vol. 3]. 1914-1919. By Col. R. S. Moody. London: The Medici Society, Ltd., 1922. Plates, maps. 8¾"

[Vol. 4]. 1919-1948. By Col. C. R. B. Knight. London: The Medici Society Ltd., 1951. Portraits, plates, maps, plans. 8¾"

The Buffs, East Kent Regiment. By J. G. Ives. Canterbury, 1891. 60 pp. 8vo.

Brief Digest of the Services of The Buffs (East Kent Regiment). Compiled by Capt. H. R. Knight for the occasion of the Presentation of Colours to the First Battalion by the Right Honourable The Lord Mayor of the City of London on the ninety-fifth Anniversary of the Battle of Albuhera, 16th May, 1906. London: Gale & Polden Ltd., 1906. vii, 45 pp. 8½"

A Short History of The Buffs, East Kent Regiment (3rd Foot); formerly designated The Holland Regiment and Prince George of Denmark's Regiment. By Eric Foster Hall, a Captain in the Regiment. London: The Medici Society Ltd., 1929. 80 pp., portraits, plates, maps. 5½"

——— 2nd edition. 1950. 128 pp.

Paa Felttog med The Buffs gennen Italien. [By] Aage Juel. Kobenhavn: Chr. Erichsens Forlag, 1947. 167 pp. 8"

Late 7th Battalion

The History of "A" Squadron, 141st Regiment R.A.C. (The Buffs), June, 1940-November, 1945. [By Major G. A. Storrar]. [Cupar-Fife: printed by J. & G. Innes Ltd., 1946]. [8], 86 pp., portraits, plates. 8"

"Playboys." ["B" Squadron, 141st Regiment R.A.C. (The Buffs)], 1944-45. [By Capt. H Bailey]. [Leeds: J. H. Davenport & Sons Ltd., printers], *n.d.* 136 pp., plates, maps.   8½″
    Late 7th Battalion.

THE KING'S OWN ROYAL REGIMENT
(LANCASTER)   [4]

Historical Record of the Fourth, or The King's Own, Regiment of Foot; containing an Account of the Formation of the Regiment in 1680 and of its subsequent Services to 1839.   London: Longman, Orme & Co., 1839.   [viii], 12, x, 152 pp., plates.   (Cannon's Historical Records Series).   8¾″
    3 coloured plates, including 1 of uniform and 1 of colours.

The King's Own.   The Story of a Royal Regiment.   Edited by Col. L. I. Cowper from material supplied by the Members of the Regimental Historical Sub-Committee.   Oxford: University Press, printed for the Regiment, 1939.   2 vols. portraits, plates, maps.   9″
    Vol. 1. 1680-1814.   Vol. 2. 1814-1914.
    Contains a chronological table of changes of clothing, arms and equipment.

———— Vol. 3. 1914-1950.   Compiled by Col. J. M. Cowper.   Aldershot: Gale & Polden Ltd., 1957.   xvi, 527 pp., plates, maps.   9″

A Gallant Regiment.   A Short History of the King's Own.   Reprinted from the *Lancaster Observer*, etc.   Lancaster: Thos. Bell [1914].   8 pp. 16mo.

A Record of Articles and Monuments of Historical Interest placed in The King's Own Memorial Chapel, Lancaster, since its dedication by the Right Rev. the Lord Bishop of Manchester on 24th July, 1904.   [By Lt.-Col. A. D. Thorne]. [London: W. H. Smith and Son, 1924].   23 pp., plates.   9¼″   '

Record of the War Memorial of The King's Own Royal Lancaster Regiment, 1914-1918.   [London: W. H. Smith and Son, 1924].   31 pp., plates.   8¼″

THE ROYAL NORTHUMBERLAND FUSILIERS   [5]

Historical Record of the Fifth Regiment of Foot, or Northumberland Fusiliers; containing an Account of the Formation of the Regiment in the year 1674, and of its subsequent Services to 1837.   London: W. Clowes and Sons, 1838.   [8], x, 117 pp., plates.   (Cannon's Historical Records Series).   8¾″
    4 coloured plates, including 3 of uniforms (1 of which includes colours). The re-issue has 5 coloured plates, 3 of uniform, 1 of colours and 1 of badge.

The Northumberland Fusiliers. By Walter Wood. London: Grant Richards, [1901]. xxv, 236 pp., portraits, plate. (British Regiments in War and Peace, II). 7½"

A History of the Northumberland Fusiliers, 1674-1902. By H. M. Walker. London: John Murray, 1919. xx, 502 pp., portraits, plates, maps. 8½"
  2 coloured plates of uniform

The Fifth in the Great War. A History of the 1st & 2nd Northumberland Fusiliers, 1914-1918. By Brig. H. R. Sandilands. Dover: G. W. Grigg and Son, 1938. xiv, 310 pp., portraits, plates, maps. 11"
  Separate volume of maps.

The History of the Royal Northumberland Fusiliers in the Second World War. By Brig. C. N. Barclay. London: published for the Regimental History Committee by William Clowes & Son Ltd. [1952]. xxii, 241 pp., portraits, plates, maps. 9¾"

A Short Narrative of the Fifth Regiment of Foot, or Northumberland Fusiliers; with a Chronological Table and Succession List of the Officers, from 1st January 1754 to 1st May, 1873. By One who has spent many happy years in the Regiment. London: Howard, Jones & Parkes, printed for private circulation, 1873, 86 pp. plates. 8½"
  6 coloured plates, including 5 of uniform (1 of which shows colours).

Summary of the History and Traditions of "The Fifth" The Royal Northumberland Fusiliers. Compiled by Major R. M. Pratt. [Newcastle-upon-Tyne: J. & P. Bealls, Ltd., 1950], 16 pp. 6½"

The Northumberland Fusiliers ("The Fighting Fifth"). By Alfred Brewis. Privately printed for presentation to the Non-Commissioned Officers and Men of the 16th, 18th and 19th Service Battalions. Newcastle-upon-Tyne [Andrew Reid & Co. Ltd.], 1915, 22 pp., illustrations. 8¾"

A Short History of the 5th Fusiliers from 1674 to 1911. [By Serjt.-Major G. Wooll]. [Newcastle-upon-Tyne: J. & P. Bealls, Ltd., printers], 1934. 63 pp. Reprinted from the 1911 Ghariel edition. 5½"

Catalogue of the Regimental and Foster Collection of Medals in the Regimental Museum of the Royal Northumberland Fusiliers. Fenham Barracks, Newcastle-upon-Tyne. Compiled by G. N. Farrier. No imprint, 1956. 32 pp., illustrations. 11"

What the Fusiliers did. An Account of the part taken by the 1st Battalion, 5th Northumberland Fusiliers in the Afghan Campaigns of 1878-79 and 1879-80. By Private H. Cooper. Lahore: printed by Ram Das, at the "Civil and Military Gazette" Press, 1880. 137 pp. 5⅞″

2nd Battalion Fifth Fusiliers. Fyzabad, 1924. [Aldershot: Gale & Polden Ltd., 1934]. 18 pp., portraits, plates. 7¼″×9¾″
  Souvenir album containing reproductions of photographs.

Historical Records of the 9th (Service) Battalion Northumberland Fusiliers. By Capt. C. H. Cooke. Newcastle-upon-Tyne, 1928. xix, 193 pp., portraits, plates, maps. (Histories of the Northumberland Fusiliers. Hon. General Editor: Alfred Brewis, vol. 1). 9¼″

Historical Records of the 16th (Service) Battalion, Northumberland Fusiliers. By Capt. C. H. Cooke. Newcastle-upon-Tyne, 1923. xx, 235 pp., portraits, plates, maps. (Histories of the Northumberland Fusiliers. Hon. Gen. Editor: Alfred Brewis, vol. 2). 9¼″

Historical Records of the 18th (Service) Battalion Northumberland Fusiliers (Pioneers). By Lieut.-Col. John Shakespear. Newcastle-upon-Tyne: 1920. xv, 211 pp., portraits, plates, maps. (Histories of the Northumberland Fusiliers. Hon. Gen. Editor: Alfred Brewis, vol. 3). 9¼″

Historical Records of the 19th (Service) Battalion Northumberland Fusiliers (Pioneers). By Capt. C. H. Cooke. Newcastle-upon-Tyne: 1920. xvi, 306 pp., portraits, plates, maps. (Histories of the Northumberland Fusiliers. Hon. Gen. Editor: Alfred Brewis, vol. 4). 9¼″
  The 4 volumes above were published for private distribution by the Council of the Newcastle and Gateshead Incorporated Chamber of Commerce.

A Record of the 17th and 32nd Service Battalions Northumberland Fusiliers (N.E.R.) Pioneers, 1914-1919. By Lt.-Col. Shakespear. Edited by Major H. Shenton Cole. Newcastle-upon-Tyne: Northumberland Press Ltd., 1926. xv, 183 pp., portraits, plates, maps. 9¾″

The Story of The Tyneside Scottish. By Brig.-Gen. Trevor Ternan. 20th, 21st, 22nd and 23rd (S.) Battns. Newcastle-upon-Tyne: Northumberland Press, [1919]. 160 pp., portraits, plates. 7½″

Irish Heroes in the War. Foreword by John E. Redmond, M.P. . . . The Tyneside Irish Brigade; by Joseph Keating. Compiled by Felix Lavery. London: Everett & Co. Ltd., 1917. 336 pp., portraits. 8½″
  24th, 25th, 26th, 27th (Service) and 30th (Reserve) Battalions.

THE ROYAL WARWICKSHIRE REGIMENT [6]

Historical Record of The Sixth, or Royal First Warwickshire Regiment of Foot, containing an Account of the Formation of the Regiment in the year 1674, and of its subsequent Services to 1838. London: Longman, Orme and Co., 1839. viii, 12, viii, 115 pp. (Cannon's Historical Records Series). 8¾"
   1 coloured plate of uniform and 1 of colours.

The Story of the Royal Warwickshire Regiment (formerly the Sixth Foot). By Charles Lethbridge Kingsford. London: "Country Life," Ltd., 1921. x, 235 pp., portraits, plates, illustrations, maps. (" Country Life " Series of Military Histories). 8¾"
   1 coloured plate of uniform.

History of the Royal Warwickshire Regiment, 1919-1955. By Marcus Cunliffe. Foreword by Field Marshal the Viscount Montgomery of Alamein. London: William Clowes & Sons Ltd., 1956. xii, 200 pp., portraits, plates, maps. 8½"

Extracts from the Digest of Services of the Royal Warwickshire Regiment, late 6th Foot. Compiled for the use of the 2nd Battalion. Colombo: printed by authority, 1894. 13 pp. 8vo

A Short History of the Royal Warwickshire Regiment. London: Gale & Polden Ltd. [1921]. 24 pp. 7¼"
   1 coloured plate of uniform and colours and badge on paper covers.

——— [Another edition]. Aldershot [1938]. 24 pp. No plates. 7¼"

The Royal Warwickshire Regiment in France and Flanders, 1939-1940. (Supplement to *The Antelope*). [Weston-super-Mare: printed by Lawrence Bros. Ltd.], 1940. 11 pp., maps. 9¼"

The 11th Royal Warwicks in France, 1915-16. From the Personal Diary of its Commanding Officer. By Brevet-Col. C. S. Collison. With a Foreword by Major-Gen. Lord Edward Gleichen. Birmingham: Cornish Brothers Ltd., 1928. 134 pp., maps, plans. 7¼"

The First Birmingham Battalion in the Great War, 1914-1919; being a History of the 14th (Service) Battalion of the Royal Warwickshire Regiment. By J. E. B. Fairclough. With Forewords by Gen. Sir R. B. Stephens and Col. G. White Lewis. Birmingham: Cornish Brothers Ltd., 1933. xvi, 210 pp., portraits, plates, maps. 7¼"

The 15th Battalion Royal Warwickshire Regiment (2nd Birmingham Battalion) in the Great War. By Major C. A. Bill, with a Foreword by Lieut.-Col. Colin Harding. Birmingham: Cornish Brothers Ltd., 1932. [x], 151 pp., portrait, plates, maps. 7¼"

Birmingham City Battalions Book of Honour. Edited by Sir William H. Bowater. London: Sherratt & Hughes. 1919. [iv], 424 pp. Portraits. 9¾"
   14th, 15th, and 16th Battalions.

THE ROYAL FUSILIERS
(CITY OF LONDON REGIMENT)   [7]

Historical Record of the Seventh Regiment or The Royal Fusiliers; containing an Account of the Formation of the Regiment in 1685, and of its subsequent Services to 1846. Compiled by Richard Cannon, Esq., Adjutant-General's Office, Horse Guards. London: Parker, Furnivall, & Parker, 1847. xxviii, 114 pp., plates. $8\frac{3}{4}''$
  2 coloured plates of uniform and 1 of colours.

Historical Record of the Seventh or Royal Regiment of Fusiliers. Compiled at the request and with the assistance of the Officers of the Regiment by W. Wheater. Leeds: printed for private circulation, 1875.   232, [72] pp. $12\frac{1}{2}''$
  A Special Edition, very few copies, with 21 coloured plates of uniform, was also issued.

Historical Records of the 7th or Royal Regiment of Fusiliers, now known as The Royal Fusiliers (The City of London Regiment), 1685-1903. Compiled from histories of the Royal Fusiliers by the late Mr. Cannon . . . and the late Col. G. H. Waller (afterwards Maj.-Gen. Sir G. H. Waller, Bt.) and from MS. Records and Journals supplied by the Officers of the Regiment by Lieut.-Col. Percy Groves, Royal Guernsey Artillery. Guernsey: Frederick B. Guerin, 1903. viii, 454, [2] pp., portraits, plates, plans. $9\frac{1}{4}''$
  15 coloured plates of uniform and 1 of colours.

The Royal Fusiliers in the Great War. By H. C. O'Neill. London: William Heinemann, 1922.   xiv. 436 pp., portraits, plates, maps. $8\frac{1}{2}''$

Always a Fusilier. The War History of The Royal Fusiliers (City of London Regiment), 1939-1945. By C. Northcote Parkinson. London: Sampson Low, 1949.   xvi, 320 pp., portraits, plates, maps, end-paper maps. $8\frac{1}{2}''$

The Royal Fusiliers in an Outline of Military History, 1685-1926. Aldershot: printed by Gale & Polden Ltd., 1926.   xv, 88 pp., portraits, plates. $9\frac{3}{4}''$

———— [2nd edition].   1685-1932.   xv, 88 pp.   1932.

———— [3rd edition].   1685-1938.   xv, 90 pp.   1938.
  11 coloured plates, including 5 of uniform, 1 of colours and 1 of badge.

A Short History of the Royal Fusiliers (City of London Regiment), 1685-1960. 4th edition. London: Regimental Office, H.M. Tower of London, 1960.   24 pp. $7\frac{1}{4}''$
  1st edition, 1949; 2nd, 1951; 3rd, 1953.

1st Battalion Royal Fusiliers in B.A.O.R. Aldershot: Gale & Polden Ltd. 1948. $7\frac{1}{4}''$

A Short History of the 2nd Battalion Royal Fusiliers (City of London Regiment) during the First Year of the War. [Aldershot: Gale & Polden Ltd., 1941]. 26 pp., map, chart. 8½″

The Royal Fusiliers (City of London Regiment). History of the 2nd Battalion in North Africa; Italy and Greece, March 1943-May 1945. [By Lt.-Col. C. A. L. Shipley]. Aldershot: Gale & Polden Ltd., 1946. [vi], 89 pp., portraits, plates, maps. 8½″

An Empire-Building Battalion; being a history, with reminiscences of the 3rd Battalion Royal Fusiliers, formed 1898, disbanded 1922. By Lt.-Col. E. C. Packe. Leicester: privately published for the author by Edgar Backus [1957]. ix, 258 pp., maps. 9¾″

The 17th (S.) Battalion Royal Fusiliers, 1914-1919. By Everard Wyrall. With a Foreword by Major-Gen. Sir C. E. Pereira. London: Methuen & Co. Ltd. [1930]. viii, 312 pp., map. 7½″

The History of the Royal Fusiliers " U.P.S." University and Public Schools Brigade (Formation and Training) [18th-21st Battalions]. London: " The Times " [1917]. 128 pp., portraits, plates, illustrations. 9¾″

A History of the 22nd (Service) Battalion Royal Fusiliers (Kensington). Edited by Major Christopher Stone. Privately printed for the Old Comrades Association of the Battalion. [London: H. Rosewarne], 1923. 79 pp., portraits, map. 7¼″

The 23rd (Service) Battalion Royal Fusiliers (First Sportsman's). A Record of its Services in the Great War, 1914-1919. By Fred W. Ward, Captain R.E., formerly No. 662 First Sportsman's Battalion. London: Sidgwick & Jackson Ltd., 1920. vii, 168 pp., portraits, plates. 8½″

With the Judaeans in the Palestine Campaign. By Lieut.-Col. J. H. Patterson. London: Hutchinson & Co. [1922]. 279 pp., portraits, plates, map. 8½″
    38th-42nd Battns. Royal Fusiliers.

With the Zionists in Gallipoli. By Lt.-Col. J. H. Patterson. London: Hutchinson & Co., 1916. viii, 316 pp., maps. 7½″

British Jewry Book of Honour. Edited by Rev. Michael Adler. Organizer: Max R. G. Freeman. London: Caxton Publishing Company Ltd., 1922. xix, 636, 364 pp., portraits, plates. 11″
    Contains Accounts of Jewish Units raised during the War, 1914-1918.

The Story of the Jewish Legion. By Vladimir Jabotinsky. Translated by Samuel Katz. With a Foreword by Col. John Henry Patterson. New York: Bernard Askeman, Inc., 1945. 191 pp., portraits, plates. 8¾″
    38th-40th Battns, Royal Fusiliers.
    Originally published in Paris, 1925, in Russian.

THE KING'S REGIMENT (LIVERPOOL)   [8]

Historical Record of The Eighth, or, The King's Regiment of Foot; containing an Account of the Formation of the Regiment in 1685, and of its subsequent Services to 1844.   London: Parker, Furnivall & Parker, 1844.   viii, 118 pp., plates.   (Cannon's Historical Records Series). $8\frac{3}{4}''$
    3 coloured plates of uniform and 1 of colours.

——— 2nd edition, with title Historical Record of The King's, or Liverpool Regiment of Foot, containing . . . . to 1881, also Succession Lists of the Officers who served in each of the regimental ranks, with Biographical Notices and Summaries of their War Services.   London: Harrison & Sons, 1883.   xl, 361 pp., portraits, plates, plans. $8\frac{1}{2}''$
    4 coloured plates of uniform and 1 of colours.

——— 3rd edition . . . to 1903; including Affiliated Militia and Volunteer Battalions.   Enniskillen: William Trimble, 1904.   xlvii, 555 pp., portraits, plates, plans, map. $8\frac{1}{2}''$
    Preface dated Nov. 1905.   9 coloured plates of uniform, 1 of colours and 1 of badge.

The Story of The King's (Liverpool Regiment) formerly the Eighth Foot.   By T. R. Threlfall.   With a Preface by the Earl of Derby.   London: Offices of " Country Life" [1917].   xviii, 215 pp., portraits, plates, plans, map. ("Country Life" Series of Military Histories). $9''$
    1 coloured plate of uniform.

The History of the King's Regiment (Liverpool), 1914-1919.   By Everard Wyrall.   London: Edward Arnold & Co. [1928-35].   3 vols., portraits, plates, maps. $9\frac{3}{4}''$

The Story of the King's Regiment, 1914-1948.   By Lt.-Col. J. J. Burke Gaffney. Liverpool: printed by Sharpe & Kellet Ltd., 1954.   xiii, 203 pp., portraits, plates, maps. $8\frac{1}{2}''$

A Short History of The King's Regiment (Liverpool).   Aldershot: Gale & Polden Ltd. [1925].   31 pp., plates. $7''$
    3 coloured plates of uniform and 1 of colours, badge in colour on paper cover.

2nd Battalion The King's Regiment.   250th Anniversary Celebration, 1685-1935. [Aldershot: Gale & Polden Ltd., 1935].   24 pp., portraits, plates. $7\frac{1}{4}'' \times 9\frac{3}{4}''$
    Souvenir Album containing reproductions of photographs and 2 coloured plates of colours.

The Record of the 11th Battalion of the King's (Liverpool) Regiment subsequently the 15th Battalion of the Loyal North Lancs. Regiment, Pioneers, 14th Light Division. August, 1914-March, 1919. London: R. E. Thomas and Co., printers, 1920. 46 pp., map. 7"

The History of the 89th Brigade, 1914-1918. [17th-20th Battalions The King's]. By Brig.-Gen. F. G. Stanley. Liverpool: "Daily Post," Printers, 1919. 295 pp., portraits. 7¼"

THE ROYAL NORFOLK REGIMENT   [9]

Historical Record of the Ninth, or The East Norfolk, Regiment of Foot; containing an Account of the Formation of the Regiment in 1685, and of its subsequent Services to 1847. Compiled by Richard Cannon, Esq., Adjutant-General's Office, Horse Guards. London: Parker, Furnivall, & Parker, 1848. Plates, xxxi, 135 pp. 8¾"
   1 coloured plate of uniform and 1 of colours.

The History of The Norfolk Regiment, 1685-1918. By F. Loraine Petre. Norwich: Jarrold & Sons Ltd. [1924]. 2 vols., portraits, plates, maps.   9¾"
   14 coloured plates, including 5 of uniform and 3 of colours in vol. 2.

──────── Vol. 3. History of the Royal Norfolk Regiment, 1919-1951. By Lieut.-Commdr. P. K. Kemp. Foreword by Brig. W. J. O'B. Daunt. Norwich: Regimental Association of The Royal Norfolk Regiment, 1953. 192 pp., portraits, illustrations, maps, end-paper maps. 9¾"
   Coloured plate of arm badges.

A Brief History of the Norfolk Regiment. Compiled by Corpl. F. W. Loads. [Devonport: Hiorns & Miller, printers, 1935]. 27 pp. 8½"

The History of the 1st Battalion The Royal Norfolk Regiment during the World War, 1939-45. By the Battalion [Major H. M. Wilson and others]. Norwich: Jarrold & Sons Ltd. [1947]. 111 pp., portraits, plates, end-paper maps.   9¾"

The Britannia. Journal of The Royal Norfolk Regiment. First Battalion, Special Korea Issue, July, 1952. Norwich: The Soman-Wherry Press Ltd., 1952. 49 pp. Portraits, illustrations, maps. 9¾"

Historical Records of The 2nd Battalion of Her Majesty's Ninth Regiment of Foot, now the 2nd Battalion, Norfolk Regiment. Compiled by Col. C. H. Shepherd. Cork: printed by Guy and Co. Ltd., 1898, 91 pp., portraits, illustrations. 8½"

THE ROYAL LINCOLNSHIRE REGIMENT   [10]

Historical Record of The Tenth, or The North Lincolnshire, Regiment of Foot, containing an Account of the Formation of the Regiment in 1685, and of its subsequent Services to 1847. Compiled by Richard Cannon, Esq., Adjutant-General's Office, Horse Guards. London: Parker, Furnivall, & Parker, 1847. xxxi, 84 pp., plates. 8¾"
4 coloured plates, including 2 of uniform and 1 of colours.

The History of the Tenth Foot (The Lincolnshire Regiment). By Albert Lee. Aldershot: Published for the Regimental Committee by Gale & Polden Ltd., 1911, 2 vols., portraits, plates. 8½"
5 coloured plates of colours in vol. 1

The History of the Lincolnshire Regiment, 1914-1918. Compiled from Diaries, Despatches, Officers' Notes and other sources. Edited by Major-Gen. C. R. Simpson, Colonel of the Regiment. With a Foreword by the Earl of Yarborough. Illustrated by Charles Simpson, R.I. London: The Medici Society Ltd., 1931. xvi, 511 pp., illustrations, maps, plans. 9¾"

The History of the Tenth Foot, 1919-1915. Compiled from War Diaries, Officers' Narratives and other sources by Major L. C. Gates. Edited by Major-Gen. J. A. A. Griffin, Colonel of the Regiment. Aldershot: Gale & Polden Ltd., 1953. xii, 355 pp., portraits, plates, maps. 9½"

A Short History of the Lincolnshire Regiment (The 10th Foot). Aldershot: Gale & Polden Ltd., 1926. 72 pp., plates. 7¼"

A Short History of the Royal Lincolnshire Regiment. Goslar: Germany: Heinrich Winkelhagen, 1954. 98 pp., plates. 7½"

1st Battalion (X Foot) The Lincolnshire Regiment. London, Wellington Barracks, 14th August to 19th September, 1929. [Aldershot: Gale & Polden Ltd., 1929]. 32 pp., portraits, plates. 7¼"×9¾"
Souvenir album containing Roll and reproductions of photographs.

The History of the First Battalion The Lincolnshire Regiment in India, Arakan, Burma and Sumatra, September 1939 to October 1946. [Compiled by Major L. C. Gates from documents supplied by Lieut.-Col. C. A. C. Sinker and Lieut.-Col. D. P. St. C. Rissier]. [Lincoln: Keyworth & Sons, printers, 1949]. 75 pp., portraits, illustrations, maps. 9¾"

Second Battalion The Lincolnshire Regiment. On Special Service in Malta and Palestine, 19th September, 1935-20th December, 1936, n.p. [Printed by N.A.A.F.I., 1937], 52 pp., plates, map. 9¾"

The History of the Second Battalion The Lincolnshire Regiment in North-West Europe. Hermanville-sur-Mer 6 June 1944 to Lengerich 8 May, 1945. No imprint [printed in Germany]. 79 pp. 10"

The Lincolnshire Regiment X Foot. 250 Anniversaries, 1185-1935. [Hong Kong: Ye Olde Printerie, Ltd, 1935]. [32 pp.] Portraits, illustrations. $7\frac{1}{4}'' \times 9\frac{3}{4}''$

8th (S.) Battalion, Lincolnshire Regiment, 1914-1919. [Aldershot: Gale & Polden Ltd., 1919]. 12 pp., portraits. 8"

THE DEVONSHIRE REGIMENT [11]

Historical Record of The Eleventh, or The North Devon Regiment of Foot; containing an Account of the Formation of the Regiment in 1685, and of its subsequent Services to 1845. London: Parker, Furnivall, & Parker, 1845. viii, 88 pp., plates. (Cannon's Historical Records Series). $8\frac{3}{4}''$
  2 coloured plates of uniform and 1 of colours.

The Bloody Eleventh. The Story of the Devonshire Regiment. London: Hutchinson & Co. (Publishers) Ltd., 1941. 96 pp. $7\frac{1}{4}''$
  (The Roll of the Drum Histories of the Regiments of the British Army; edited by Wolmer Whyte).

The Devons. A History of The Devonshire Regiment, 1685-1945. By Jeremy Taylor, with a Preface by Arthur Bryant. Bristol: The White Swan Press, 1951. xii, 339 pp., plates, maps. $8\frac{1}{2}''$

The Devonshire Regiment, 1914-1918. Compiled by C. T. Atkinson, late Capt., Oxford University O.T.C. Exeter: Eland Brothers, 1926. xxv, 742 pp., plates, maps, plans. $8\frac{1}{2}''$

A Short History of the Devonshire Regiment. Aldershot: Gale & Polden Ltd. [1922], 39 pp. 7"
  1 coloured plate of uniform and coloured reproduction of badge and colours on paper covers. Reprinted 1925 and 1940.

The Record of a Regiment of the Line, being A Regimental History of the 1st Battalion Devonshire Regiment during the Boer War, 1899-1902. By Col. M. Jacson. London: Hutchinson & Co., 1908. xv, 226 pp., plates, maps. $7\frac{1}{2}''$

Through Hell to Victory, from Passchendaele to Mons with the 2nd Devons in 1918. By Reginald A. Colwill who was with the Battalion during the period. Torquay: Published by Reginald A. Colwill at 33 Thurlow Rd. [1927]. 272 pp. $7\frac{1}{4}''$

We landed in Sicily and Italy. A Story of the Devons. By Lieut.-Col. A. W. Valentine. Aldershot: Gale & Polden Ltd. [1944]. [8], 55 pp., plates, maps. $7\frac{1}{4}''$
  [2nd Battalion].

First Battalion the Devonshire Regiment, 1953-1955; the Mau-Mau Emergency, Kenya, 1962. [Duplicated typescript]. ii, 80 pp., plan. $11\frac{1}{2}''$

THE SUFFOLK REGIMENT   [12]

Historical Record of The Twelfth, or The East Suffolk Regiment of Foot; containing an Account of the Formation of the Regiment in 1685, and of its subsequent Services to 1847.   Compiled by Richard Cannon, Esq., Adjutant-General's Office, Horse Guards.   London: Parker, Furnivall, & Parker, 1848. xxxi, 103 pp., plates.   8¾"
   4 coloured plates including 1 of uniforms and 1 of colours.

History of the 12th (The Suffolk) Regiment, 1685-1913.   By Lieut.-Col. E. A. H. Webb.   Including a Brief History of the East and West Suffolk Militia, the latter being now the 3rd Battalion Suffolk Regiment.   London: Spottiswoode & Co. Ltd., 1914.   xxii, 505 pp., portraits, plates, plans.   9¾"
   17 coloured plates, including 12 of uniform and 2 of colours.

The History of the Suffolk Regiment, 1914-1927.   By Lieut.-Col. C. C. R. Murphy.   London: Hutchinson & Co. (Publishers) Ltd. [1928].   431 pp., portraits, plates, map, end-paper map.   9"

The Suffolk Regiment, 1928-1946.   By Col. W. N. Nicholson.   Ipswich: The East Anglian Magazine Ltd. [1948].   376 pp., portraits, plates, maps.   9"

A Short History of the Suffolk Regiment (12th Regiment of Foot).   London: Gale & Polden Ltd. [1921].   23 pp., portrait, plates.   7"
   Coloured reproduction of colours on paper cover.

——— [Another edition].   The Suffolk Regiment.   XII Foot.   Aldershot: Gale & Polden Ltd., 1933.   48 pp., portrait, plates.   7¼"
   Title on cover: A Short History of the Suffolk Regiment.

The Annals of the Twelfth East Suffolk Regiment.   By C. H. G. [Lt.-Col. C. H. Gardiner].   Bury St. Edmunds: " Free Press " Works, 1908.   9¾"

——— Another edition.   Calcutta: Wyman Bros.   n.d.   [vi], 104 pp.   9½"
   Reprinted from the " Bury Free Press."

Centurions of a Century, among which are many who have soldiered in The Twelfth, or The Suffolk Regiment of Foot, distinguished by its services at Dettingen, June 27th, 1743 . . . South Africa, 1899-1902.   [Edited by Lt.-Col. C. H. Gardiner].   [Brighton: F. V. Hadlow and Sons, printers, 1911].   xi, 500 pp., plates, map.   8½"

An Illustrated Record of The 12th Foot for 250 years, 23 June 1685-23 June 1935. [Bury St. Edmunds: The Suffolk Regimental Gazette, printed by The Bury Free Press], 1935.   28 pp., portraits, plates.   9¾"

1st Battalion Suffolk Regiment, Malta, 1909.   Paris: phototypie P. G. Evrard, 1909.   36 pp.   8½" × 10¾"
   An album of photographs.

The Record of the Foreign Service Tour of 1st Battalion The Suffolk Regiment, 1907-1926. Compiled from the Digest of Service of 1st Battalion and The Suffolk Regimental Gazette. Published by Capt. J. S. D. Lloyd, 1st Battalion Suffolk Regiment. No imprint [1926]. 100 pp., portraits, plates. $9\frac{3}{4}''$

The March of the 1st Bn. Suffolk Regiment through the County of Suffolk, 16th to 23rd August, 1927. Arranged by Lieut. W. M. Lummis. No imprint, 1927. 32 pp., portraits, illustrations. 11"

The Story of the Colours, 1685 to 1954. By Lt.-Col. H. B. Monier-Williams. [Inset to The Suffolk Regimental Gazette]. Bury St. Edmunds: The Editor, 1954. 32 pp., illustrations. 10"

The 2nd Battalion Suffolk Regiment illustrated; with a Brief Historical Account of the Services of the Regiment. Quetta, Baluchistan, 1899. 50 pp. $9\frac{3}{4}'' \times 12\frac{1}{2}''$
   38 photographs by Frederick Bremner.

THE SOMERSET LIGHT INFANTRY (PRINCE ALBERT'S) [13]

Historical Record of The Thirteenth, First Somerset, or The Prince Albert's Regiment of Light Infantry; containing an Account of the Formation of the Regiment in 1685, and of its subsequent Services to 1848. Compiled by Richard Cannon, Esq., Adjutant-General's Office, Horse Guards. London: Parker, Furnivall & Parker, 1848. xxxvi, 128 pp., plates. $8\frac{1}{2}''$
   3 coloured plates, including 1 of uniform and 1 of colours.

Historical Record of The Thirteenth, First Somersetshire, or Prince Albert's Regiment of Light Infantry. Edited by Thomas Carter, Adjutant-General's Office, Horse Guards. London: W. O. Mitchell, 1867. xv, 200 pp., portraits, plates. $8\frac{1}{4}''$
   4 coloured plates, including 2 of uniform and 1 of colours.

The History of The Somerset Light Infantry (Prince Albert's), 1685-1914. By Major-Gen. Sir Henry Everett. With a Foreword by H.R.H. The Duke of York, Colonel-in-Chief. London: Methuen & Co. Ltd. [1934]. xvi, 421 pp., portraits, plates, maps, plans. $9\frac{3}{4}''$
   5 coloured plates, including 3 of uniform and 1 of colours.

The History of The Somerset Light Infantry (Prince Albert's), 1914-1919. By Everard Wyrall. With a Foreword by H.R.H. The Duke of York. London: Methuen & Co. Ltd., 1927. xvi, 419 pp., portraits, plates, maps. $9\frac{3}{4}''$

The History of The Somerset Light Infantry (Prince Albert's), 1919-1945. Compiled by George Molesworth. Regimental Committee Somerset Light Infantry. [Frome: printed by Butler & Tanner Ltd., 1951]. xvi, 286 pp., portraits, maps. $9\frac{3}{4}''$

History of The Somerset Light Infantry (Prince Albert's), 1946-1960. By Kenneth Whitehead. With a Foreword by Field Marshal The Lord Harding of Petherton. Taunton: The Somerset Light Infantry, 1961. xvi, 167 pp., portraits, plates, maps. $8\frac{1}{2}''$

A Short History of The Somerset Light Infantry (Prince Albert's). Compiled from the full text of Volume I and II of The History of The Somerset Light Infantry (Prince Albert's). Aldershot: Gale & Polden Ltd. [1931]. 46 pp. $7\frac{1}{4}''$
    1 coloured plate of colours. First edition, 1922. 29 pp.

A Brief History of the 13th Regiment (P.A.L.I.) in South Africa during the Transvaal and Zulu Difficulties, 1877-8-9. By Edward D. McToy, 1st Battalion 13th Light Infantry. Devonport: A. H. Swiss, 1880. [vii], 109 pp. $7''$

A History of the 1st Battalion The Somerset Light Infantry (Prince Albert's), July 1st, 1916 to the end of the War. By Major V. H. B. Majendie. Taunton: Goodman and Son, 1921. xii, 127 pp., maps. $7\frac{1}{4}''$

2nd Bn. The Somerset Light Infantry (Prince Albert's). Tour of Duty at Chelsea Barracks, Wellington Barracks, H.M. Tower of London, 1936. [Aldershot: Gale & Polden Ltd., 1936]. 28 pp., portraits, plates. $7\frac{1}{4}'' \times 9\frac{3}{4}''$
    Souvenir album containing Roll and reproduction of photographs.

Scrap Book of the 7th Bn. Somerset Light Infantry (13th Foot), being a Chronicle of their experiences in the Great War, 1914-1918, contributed by Officers and other ranks of the 7th (Service) Battalion The Somerset Light Infantry (Prince Albert's), with a Foreword by Col. C. J. Troyte-Bullock . . . No imprint [1932]. 156 pp., plate, maps. $9\frac{3}{4}''$

———- Supplement: Cambrai. By Lieut.-Col. R. P. Preston-Whyte. 1933. 3 pp., map.

The Story of the Seventh Battalion The Somerset Light Infantry (Prince Consort's). Collected and told by Capt. J. L. J. Meredith. Designs and illustrations by L. R. Stokes. No imprint [printed in Germany, 1945]. 216 pp., illustrations, maps. $10\frac{5}{8}''$
    Title on cover: From Normandy to Hanover, June, 1944-May, 1945.

Incidents with the Seventh Battalion, The Somerset Light Infantry in France and Germany from June 1944 to June 1945. No imprint. *n.d.* 74 pp. $8''$

THE WEST YORKSHIRE REGIMENT
(THE PRINCE OF WALES'S OWN)   [14]

Historical Record of The Fourteenth, or, The Buckinghamshire Regiment of Foot; containing an Account of the Formation of the Regiment in 1685, and of its subsequent Services to 1845.   London: Parker, Furnivall, & Parker, 1845. viii, 106 pp., plates.   (Cannon's Historical Records Series).   8½"
 1 coloured plate of uniform and 1 of colours.

Historical Records of the 14th Regiment, now The Prince of Wales's Own (West Yorkshire Regiment), from its Formation, in 1685 to 1892.   Edited by Capt. H. O'Donnell.   Devonport: A. H. Swiss.   [1893].   xxii, 415 pp., Portraits, plates, illustrations.   8½"
 13 coloured plates, including 12 of uniform and 1 of colours.

The West Yorkshire Regiment in the War, 1914-1918.   A History of the 14th, The Prince of Wales's Own (West Yorkshire Regt.) and of its Special Reserve, Territorial and Service Battns. in the Great War of 1914-1918.   By Everard Wyrall.   London: John Lane, The Bodley Head Ltd., 2 vols.   [1924-27]. Plates, maps, plans.   9½"

From Pyramid to Pagoda; the Story of the West Yorkshire Regiment (The Prince of Wales's Own) in the War 1939-45 and afterwards.   By Lieut.-Col. E. W. C. Sandes.   [London: printed by F. J. Parsons Ltd., 1952].   xv, 306 pp., portraits, maps.   11"

A Short History of The West Yorkshire Regiment (The Prince of Wales's Own). London: Gale & Polden Ltd., 1921.   25 pp.   7"
 Coloured plate of uniform and coloured reproduction of colours and badge on paper covers.

History of the West Yorkshire Regiment.   [By Capt. E. V. Tempest].   [Bradford: printed by Lund, Humphries & Co. Ltd.], 1941.   64 pp., portrait.   8½"

The West Yorkshire Regiment (The Prince of Wales's Own).   1685-1935. 250th Anniversary Souvenir.   [Aldershot: printed by Gale & Polden Ltd.], 1935. 36 pp., portraits, plates, illustrations.   9¼"
 12 coloured plates of uniform and coloured reproduction of colours and badge on paper covers.

Extract from Digest of Services of the 2nd Battalion, The Prince of Wales's Own (West Yorkshire Regt.) in South Africa from October 30th, 1899, to August 4th, 1902.   [York: The Yorkshire Herald Newspaper Co. Ltd.], 1903.   106 pp.   8¼"

History of the Prince of Wales's Own West Yorkshire Regiment.   11th (Service) Battalion.   [By Major C. L. Armstrong].   Sunderland: Jas. D. Todd & Sons, 1919.   100 pp.   7¼"

THE EAST YORKSHIRE REGIMENT
(THE DUKE OF YORK'S OWN) [15]

Historical Record of The Fifteenth, or The Yorkshire East Riding Regiment of Foot, containing an Account of the Formation of the Regiment in 1685, and of its subsequent Services to 1848. Compiled by Richard Cannon, Esq., Adjutant-General's Office, Horse Guards. London: Parker, Furnivall, & Parker, 1848. xxxi, 96 pp., plates. 8½″
   1 coloured plate of uniform and 1 of colours.

A History of The 15th (East Yorkshire) Regiment (The Duke of York's Own) 1685 to 1914. By Robert J. Jones. Beverley: The Regiment, 1958. iv, 575 pp., portraits, plates. 9½″

The East Yorkshire Regiment in the Great War, 1914-1918. By Everard Wyrall. London: Harrison & Sons Ltd., 1928. xx, 486 pp., portraits, plates maps. 9½″

A History of the East Yorkshire Regiment (Duke of York's Own) in the War of 1939-45. By P. R. Nightingale, Lt.-Col. York: William Sessions Ltd., 1952. xvii, 348 pp., portraits, plates, maps. 8½″

A Short History of the East Yorkshire Regiment. Compiled by Lieut.-Col. Starke, for the Rank and File of its First Battalion. Londonderry: no imprint, 1882. 41 pp. 7½″

——— A Continuation from 1881-1913 of Lieutenant-Colonel William Starke's Short History of the East Yorkshire Regiment. Compiled by Capt. E. L. P. Edwards, 1st Battalion. [Aldershot: Gale & Polden Ltd., 1913]. 60 pp.   7½″

A Short History of The East Yorkshire Regiment (The "Snappers"), 1685 to 1933. [By Col. D. F. Anderson]. [Aldershot: Gale & Polden Ltd., 1933]. 37 pp., coloured plate of colours.   8½″

——— [Another edition] . . . 1685 to 1949. No imprint. [1950]. [ii], 46 pp. 8½″

The East Yorkshire Regiment (The Duke of York's Own) 250th Anniversary, 1685-1935. [Aldershot: Gale & Polden Ltd., 1935]. 40 pp., portraits, plates. 8½″

With the Second Battalion East Yorkshire Regt. in South Africa, 1900-1901-1902. By C. W. Lazenby. [Aldershot: Gale & Polden Ltd., 1902]. 41 pp.   7″

Regimental History of 2nd Battalion The East Yorkshire Regiment, 6th June, 1944, to 8th May, 1945. [Liverpool: William Potter, printer, 1945]. 31 pp. 7¼″

The East Yorkshire Regiment in the Bermudas 1819 to 1821, 1868 to 1870, 1916-1919. Compiled from the History of the East Yorkshire Regt. by R. Jones, The East Yorkshire Regt. in the Great War 1914/18, by Everard Wyrall, and other sources, by Major H. A. K. McGonigal. No imprint, *n.d.* 17 pp.   6¾″

A ·History of the 10th (Service) Battalion The East Yorkshire Regiment (Hull Commercials), 1914-1919. London: A. Brown & Sons, Ltd., 1937. xix, 204 pp., portrait, plates, maps. 8½″

A Short Diary of the 11th Service Battalion, East Yorkshire Regiment, 1914-1919. Compiled by "Some of Them." Hull: Goddard, Walker & Brown, Ltd., 1921. [vii], 105 pp., portraits, plates. 8½″
    Coloured plate of divisional and regimental patches.

Record of Service of the 4th (Hull) or 13th (Service) Battalion East Yorkshire Regiment. Compiled by Townley Truman, Capt. [Hull: Richard Johnson and Sons], *n.d.* 52 pp., illustrations. 8½″

THE BEDFORDSHIRE AND HERTFORDSHIRE REGIMENT [16]

Historical Record of The Sixteenth, or, The Bedfordshire Regiment of Foot: containing an Account of the Formation of the Regiment in 1688, and of its subsequent Services to 1848. Compiled by Richard Cannon, Esq., Adjutant-General's Office, Horse Guards. London: Parker, Furnivall, & Parker, 1848. xxviii, 45 pp., plates. 8½″
    1 coloured plate of uniform and 1 of colours.

The 16th Foot. A History of The Bedfordshire and Hertfordshire Regiment. By Major-Gen. Sir F. Maurice. With a Foreword by Gen. The Earl of Cavan, Colonel of the Regiment. London: Constable & Company Ltd., 1931. xi, 240 pp., sketch maps. 8¾″

Notes on the History of the 16th Foot. 1931.

Additional Notes on the History of the 16th Bedfordshire & Hertfordshire Regiment. Compiled by Major E. G. Fanning. By request of Her Majesty Queen Marie of Yugoslavia. No imprint. [1931]. 10 pp. 5¼″

THE ROYAL LEICESTERSHIRE REGIMENT [17]

Historical Record of The Seventeenth, or The Leicestershire Regiment of Foot; containing an Account of the Formation of the Regiment in 1688, and of its subsequent Services to 1848. Compiled by Richard Cannon, Esq., Adjutant-General's Office, Horse Guards. London: Parker, Furnivall, & Parker, 1848. xxxii, 56 pp., plates. 8½″
    1 coloured plate of uniform and 1 of colours.

A History of the Services of The 17th (The Leicestershire) Regiment, containing an Account of the Formation of the Regiment in 1688, and of its subsequent Services. Revised and continued to 1910. By Lt.-Col. E. A. H. Webb. London: Vacher & Sons Ltd., 1911. xxvii, 322 pp., portraits, plates, illustrations. 9″
    ·11 coloured plates, including 9 of uniform and 2 of colours.
    ——— 2nd edition. London: Vacher & Sons Ltd., 1912. xxvii, 336 pp. 9″

History of the 1st & 2nd Battalions The Leicestershire Regiment in the Great War. By Col. H. C. Wylly. Aldershot: printed and published for Regimental Committee by Gale & Polden Ltd. [1928]. vii, 215 pp., portraits, plates, maps. 9¾″

The Royal Leicestershire Regiment, 17th Foot; a history of the years 1928 to 1956. Editor, Brig. W. E. Underhill. Leicester; The Regiment [printed by Underhill (Plymouth) Ltd., 1958]. x, 277 pp., portraits, plates, maps. 9½″

Notes on the History of The Leicestershire Regiment. Jhansi: Albion Press, 1923. 20 pp. 8½″

A Short History of the Royal Leicestershire Regiment, 1688-1955. [Morecombe: The Morecombe Bay Printers Ltd.], 1955. 16 pp. 5½″

The Colours of the 17th or The Leicestershire Regiment of Foot. [By Lieut. P. D. S. Palmer]. Aldershot: Gale & Polden Ltd. [1930]. vii, 48 pp., plates. 8½″

Freemasonry in The Leicestershire (17th) Regiment of Foot. By Bro. Capt. William Thomas. [Paper read at the 197th Meeting of the Lodge of Research, Leicester, 28-3-1927]. No imprint. 24 pp., 2 plates. 8½″

History and Traditions of The Leicestershire Regiment (17th Foot). Aldershot: Gale & Polden Ltd. [1939]. 16 pp. 5½″

"Come on Tigers," being the Story of The Royal Leicestershire Regiment, 1688-1955. Compiled by Major A. D. Chilton, edited by Lt.-Col. S. D. Field. Morecombe: The Morecombe Bay Printers Ltd., 1955. 154 pp., portraits, illustrations. 9½″
  A recruiting brochure, largely advertisements.

THE ROYAL IRISH REGIMENT   [18]

Historical Record of The Eighteenth, or The Royal Irish Regiment of Foot; containing an Account of the Formation of the Regiment in 1684, and of its subsequent Services to 1848. Compiled by Richard Cannon, Esq., Adjutant-General's Office, Horse Guards. London: Parker, Furnivall, & Parker, 1848. xxxvi, 91 pp., plates. 8½″
  3 coloured plates, including 1 of uniform and 1 of colours.

The Campaigns and History of the Royal Irish Regiment from 1684 to 1902. By Lieut.-Col. G. le M. Gretton. Edinburgh: William Blackwood and Sons, 1911. xiv, 462 pp., plates, maps. 10″

——— Vol. 2. From 1910 to 1922. By Br.-Gen. Stannus Geoghegan. Edinburgh: William Blackwood and Sons, 1927. xiii, 207 pp., portraits, plates, maps. 10″

A Short History of the Royal Irish Regiment. London: Gale & Polden Ltd., 1921. 24 pp. 7¼"
1 coloured plate of uniform, and colours and badge in colour on paper covers.

THE GREEN HOWARDS
(ALEXANDRA, PRINCESS OF WALES'S OWN YORKSHIRE REGIMENT) [19]

Historical Record of The Nineteenth, or The First Yorkshire North Riding Regiment of Foot; containing an Account of the Formation of the Regiment in 1688, and of its subsequent Services to 1848. Compiled by Richard Cannon, Esq., Adjutant-General's Office, Horse Guards. London: Parker, Furnivall, & Parker, 1848. xxxi, 40 pp., plates. 8½"
1 coloured plate of uniform and 1 of colours.

A History of the Services of the 19th Regiment, now Alexandra, Princess of Wales's Own (Yorkshire Regiment), from its Formation in 1688 to 1911. By Major M. L. Ferrar. London: Eden Fisher & Company Ltd. [1911]. [viii], 451 pp., portraits, plates, maps. 9½"
9 coloured plates, including 8 of uniform and 1 of colours.

The Green Howards in the Great War, 1914-1919. By Col. H. C. Wylly. Richmond, Yorks; [printed by Butler & Tanner Ltd., Frome & London], 1926. xvi, 420 pp., portraits, plates, maps. 9¾"

The Story of The Green Howards, 1939-1945. By Capt. W. A. T. Synge. Richmond, Yorks; The Green Howards, 1952. xxviii, 428 pp., portrait, map. 8½"

The History of The Green Howards. A Series of Short Lectures. Aldershot: Gale & Polden Ltd. [1940]. 47 pp., plate, plan. 7¼"
1 coloured plate of colours.

——— [Another edition]. 1954. 56 pp.

With the Green Howards in South Africa, 1899-1902. By Major M. L. Ferrar. London: Eden Fisher & Co. Ltd., 1904. [vi], 199 pp., portraits, plate, plan. 7¼"

1st Battalion The Green Howards (Alexandra, Princess of Wales's Own Yorkshire Regiment). London, Wellington Barracks, 8th August to 1st September, 1930. [Aldershot: Gale & Polden Ltd., 1930]. 32 pp., portraits, plates. 7¼"×9¾"
Souvenir Album cont. Roll and reproductions of photographs.

The Green Howards in Malaya (1949-1952). The Story of a Post-War Tour of Duty by a Battalion of the Line. By Major J. B. Oldfield. Aldershot: Gale & Polden Ltd., 1953. xxvi, 191 pp., portraits, plates, maps. 8½"

The Green Howards (Alexandra, Princess of Wales's Own Yorkshire Regiment). For Valour, 1914-1918. Richmond, Yorks.: no imprint. 16 pp., portraits, illustrations. 9¾"

Officers of The Green Howards, Alexandra, Princess of Wales's Own (Yorkshire Regiment), (formerly the 19th Foot), 1688 to 1920. By Major M. L. Ferrar. London: Eden Fisher & Co. Ltd., 1920. xv, 349 pp., plate. 8¾"

——— [Another edition]. 1688-1931. Belfast: W. & G. Baird, Ltd. xv, 350 pp., plate. 8½"

THE LANCASHIRE FUSILIERS [20]

Historical Record of The Twentieth, or The East Devonshire Regiment of Foot; containing an Account of the Formation of the Regiment in 1688, and of its subsequent Services to 1848. Compiled by Richard Cannon, Esq., Adjutant-General's Office, Horse Guards. London: Parker, Furnivall, & Parker, 1848. xxxv, 79 pp., plates. 8½"
1 coloured plate of uniform and 1 of colours.

History of the XX Regiment, 1688-1888. Compiled by B. Smyth, Lieut., Quartermaster. London: Simpkin, Marshall & Co., 1889. xv, 427 pp., portraits, plates, maps, plans. 8¾"
11 coloured plates of uniform.

——— Another edition. 2 vols. Dublin: Sackville Press, 1903-04. Portrait, plates, maps. 8½"
13 coloured plates of uniform (3 in vol. 1; 10 in vol. 2).

The History of the Lancashire Fusiliers, 1914-1918. By Major-Gen. J. C. Latter. Aldershot: Gale & Polden Ltd., 1949. 2 vols., illustrations, maps. 9½"

Regiment of the Line. The Story of XX The Lancashire Fusiliers. [By] Cyril Ray. London: B. T. Batsford Ltd., 1963. xiii, 194 pp., portraits, plates. 8¾"

XX The Lancashire Fusiliers Handbook. Compiled and edited by Major-Gen. G. Surtees, Colonel. [London: Malcolm Page Ltd.], 1952. 184 pp. (1-20, 164-184 adverts.), portraits, illustrations. 8½"
Contains short histories of all units. Recruiting handbook. 1 coloured plate of colour.

Orders, Memoirs, Anecdotes, etc. connected with the XX Regiment. [Edited by Lieut. F. W. Barlow]. Printed at the " Minden Press " by Frederick Watkins Barlow, Lieutenant, 1868. [8], 60 pp. 8"
100 copies printed for private circulation.

Mis-statements in the Historical Records of the XXth Regiment in regard to the Services of the late Lieut.-Colonel Philip Bainbrigge in the Expedition to Holland in 1794, corrected. [By Lt.-Gen. Philip Bainbrigge]. London: Ford & Tilt [1860]. 18 pp. $8\frac{1}{4}''$

The Lancashire Fusiliers. The Roll of Honour of the Salford Brigade (15th, 16th, 19th, 20th and 21st Lancashire Fusiliers). Edited by Sir C. A. Montague Barlow. London: Sherratt & Hughes, 1919. 85, 183, 96, 18 pp., portraits, plates. $9\frac{1}{2}''$

The Lancashire Fusiliers Annual. Nos. 1-36, 1891-1926. Compiled and edited by Major B. Smyth. (Nos. 5-8 by C. M. Hutton). Nos. 1, 2, Manchester: The Manchester Examiner Ltd.; No. 3, Richard Gill; Nos. 4, 5, Minden Press, Curragh & Athlone; Nos. 6-9, Dublin: Corrigan & Wilson; Nos. 10-12, Dublin: The Irish Wheelman Pr. & Publ. Co. Ltd.; Nos. 13-26, Dublin: Sackville Press. 1891-1926. Portraits, illustrations, maps, diagrams. $8\frac{1}{2}''$
Discontinued and replaced by a quarterly *The Gallipoli Gazette* (First issue Jan., 1926).

THE ROYAL SCOTS FUSILIERS [21]

Historical Record of the Twenty-First Regiment, or The Royal North British Fusiliers; containing an Account of the Formation of the Regiment in 1678, and of its subsequent Services to 1849. Compiled by Richard Cannon, Esq., Adjutant-General's Office, Horse Guards. London: Parker, Furnivall, & Parker, 1849. xxxvii, 64 pp., plates. $8\frac{1}{2}''$
  2 coloured plates of uniform and 1 of colours.

Historical Record and Regimental Memoir of The Royal Scots Fusiliers, formerly known as the 21st Royal North British Fusiliers; containing an Account of the Formation of the Regiment in 1678 and its subsequent Services until June 1885. Compiled from various authentic sources by James Clark, late Sergeant. Edinburgh: Banks & Co., 1885. xxiv, 185 pp., plates. $8\frac{1}{2}''$
  5 coloured plates of uniform and 1 of colours.

History of the 21st Royal Scots Fusiliers (formerly The 21st Royal North British Fusiliers), now known as the Royal Scots Fusiliers, 1678-1895. By Lieut.-Col. Percy Groves. Edinburgh: W. & A. K. Johnston, 1895. 72 pp., plates. $10''$
  9 coloured plates of uniform. 530 copies only.

The Royal Scots Fusiliers. By Lieut.-Col. Reginald Toogood. (Reprinted from *The Lowland Scots Regiments;* edited by the Right Hon. Sir Herbert Maxwell, Bart.). Glasgow: James Maclehose and Sons, 1919. 38 pp. $9\frac{1}{2}''$
  Illustration of uniform on paper cover.

The History of The Royal Scots Fusiliers (1678-1918). By John Buchan. With a Preface by H.R.H. The Prince of Wales, Colonel-in-Chief. London: Thomas Nelson & Sons Ltd. [1925]. xvi, 502 pp., portrait, plates, maps, plans. 9″
  2 coloured plates of colours and 2 of uniform.

The History of the Royal Scots Fusiliers, 1919-1939. By Col. J. C. Kemp, with a Foreword by Field Marshal Sir Francis Festing. Glasgow: privately printed by Robert Maclehose & Co. Ltd., 1963. xvi, 423 pp., portraits, plates, maps. 8½″

A Short History of the Royal Scots Fusiliers. [By Lieut.-Col. A. G. Baird Smith]. Aldershot: Gale & Polden Ltd. [1933]. 63 pp., portraits, plates. 7¼″

A Short History of the Royal Scots Fusiliers. Ayr: Observer Printing Works [1948]. 8 pp., illustrations. 8¼″

The Royal Scots Fusiliers. By Major-Gen. J. E. Utterson-Kelso. [Ayr: "Advertiser" Office, 1958]. 16 pp., portrait, illustrations. 8¼″
  Reprinted from the *Ayr Advertiser*.

THE CHESHIRE REGIMENT [22]

Historical Record of The Twenty-Second, or The Cheshire Regiment of Foot; containing an Account of the Formation of the Regiment in 1689, and of its subsequent Services to 1849. Compiled by Richard Cannon, Esq., Adjutant-General's Office, Horse Guards. London: Parker, Furnivall, & Parker, 1849. xxxv, 64 pp., plates. 8½″
  3 coloured plates, including 1 of uniform and 1 of colours.

The History of the Twenty-Second Cheshire Regiment, 1689-1849. By Major-Gen. W. H. Anderson. London: Hugh Rees [1920]. xv, 164 pp. 7¼″

Twenty-Second Footsteps, 1849-1914; an account of life in the 22nd (Cheshire) Regiment in those years. By Arthur Crookenden, some time Colonel. Chester: W. H. Evans, Sons & Co. Ltd., printer, 1956. ix, 102 pp., portraits, illustrations, map. 9½″

The History of the Cheshire Regiment in the Great War. By Arthur Crookenden, Colonel of the Regiment. [Chester: printed by W. H. Evans, Sons & Co., Ltd., 1938]. 2nd edition. xiii, 358 pp., portraits, plates, maps, plans. 9¾″

The History of the Cheshire Regiment in the Second World War. By Arthur Crookenden, sometime Colonel of the Regiment. [Chester: W. H. Evans, Sons & Co. Ltd., 1949]. ix, 371 pp., portraits, plates, maps. 9¾″

The Cheshire Regiment or 22nd Regiment of Foot. A Lecture delivered before the Chester Archaeological Society on December 15th, 1903. By Frank Simpson. Chester: G. R. Griffith, printer, 1903. 40 pp., portrait, plates. (Reprinted from Chester Archaeological Society, Journal, vol. 11). 8½"
  2 coloured plates of colours.

A Short History of the Twenty-Second or Cheshire Regiment. By Arthur Crookenden, sometime Colonel of the Regiment. [Chester: The Regiment, 1958]. 64 pp., plate. 7½"

The 22nd (Cheshire Regiment). A Pocket History. [By Col. A. Crookenden]. [Chester: printed by W. H. Evans, Sons & Co. Ltd., 1958]. 10 pp. 5½"

The Cheshire Regiment or 22nd Regiment of Foot. The First Battalion at Mons and The Miniature Colour. By Frank Simpson. [Chester: printed by W. H. Evans, Sons & Co., 1929]. 75 pp., portraits, plates, plan. 8½"

The Jungle War. With the First Battalion the Cheshire Regiment in Malaya. By John Gleave. Chester: The Chester Chronicle and Associated Newspapers, Ltd., 1958. 31 pp., portraits, illustrations. 8½"

Extracts from an Officer's Diary, 1914-18, being the Story of the 15th and 16th Service Battalions The Cheshire Regiment (originally Bantams). By Lt.-Col. Harrison Johnston. Manchester: Geo. Falkner & Sons, 1919. 156 pp. 8½"

THE ROYAL WELCH FUSILIERS [23]

Historical Record of The Twenty-Third Regiment or The Royal Welsh Fusiliers; containing an Account of the Formation of the Regiment in 1689, and of its subsequent Services to 1850. Compiled by Richard Cannon, Esq., Adjutant-General's Office, Horse Guards. London: Parker, Furnivall, & Parker, 1850. xlvi, 187 pp., plates. 8½"
  2 coloured plates of uniform and 1 of colours.

Historical Record of the Royal Welch Fusiliers late The Twenty-Third Regiment, or Royal Welsh Fusiliers (The Prince of Wales's Own Royal Regiment of Welsh Fuzeliers; containing an Account of the Formation of the Regiment in 1689, and of its subsequent Services to 1889. Arranged by Major Rowland Broughton-Mainwaring, in continuation of the compilation published in 1850 by Richard Cannon . . . London: Hatchards, 1889. lviii, 372 pp., plates. 8¾"
  24 coloured plates, including 15 of uniform and 1 of colours.

The Story of The Royal Welsh Fusiliers. By H. Avray Tipping. London: "Country Life" [1915]. xii, 281 pp., portraits, plates, illustrations, maps. ("Country Life" Military Histories Series). 9"
  1 coloured plate of uniform.

A History of the Royal Welsh Fusiliers late The Twenty-Third Regiment. By Howel Thomas. London: T. Fisher Unwin Ltd. [1916]. 288 pp., plates. 7¼"
    1 coloured plate of uniform.

Regimental Records of the Royal Welch Fusiliers (late the the 23rd Foot). London: Forster, Groom & Co. Ltd., 1921, 23, 28, 29. Portraits, plates, maps, plans. 9¾".
    Vol. 1. 1689-1815. Vol. 2. 1816-1914 (July). Compiled by A. D. L. Cary & Stouppe McCance, Capt.
    Vol. 3. 1914-1918. France and Flanders. Compiled by Major C. H. Dudley Ward.
    Vol. 4. 1915-1918. Turkey, Bulgaria, Austria. Compiled by Major C. H. Dudley Ward.
    Vol. 1 contains 7 coloured plates of uniform and 1 of colours.
    Vol. 2 contains 6 coloured plates of uniform and 1 of colours.

The Red Dragon; the Story of The Royal Welch Fusiliers, 1919-1945, by Lt.-Commdr. P. K. Kemp and J. Graves, with a Foreword by Gen. Sir Hugh Stockwell. Aldershot: Gale & Polden Ltd., 1960. xvi, 414 pp., portraits, plates, maps. 8½"

A Short History of the Royal Welch Fusiliers. By Col. E. O. Skaife. [3rd edition]. Aldershot: Gale & Polden Ltd., 1940. [ix,] 78 pp., portraits, plates. 9¼"
    10 coloured plates, including 8 of uniform, 1 of colours and 1 of badges.
    The 2nd edition (72 pp.) was published in 1925; 1st edition, 1913.

Royal Welch Fusiliers Battle Honours. [Aldershot: Gale & Polden Ltd., printers, 1913]. 62 pp., plates, illustrations. 8½"
    13 coloured plates of uniform.

The War the Infantry Knew, 1914-1919. A Chronicle of Service in France and Belgium with The Second Battalion His Majesty's Twenty-Third Foot, The Royal Welch Fusiliers: founded on personal records, recollections and reflections, assembled, edited and partly written by One of their Medical Officers. London: P. S. King & Son, Ltd., 1938. xvi, 613 pp., maps. 8½"

The War Diary (1914-1918) of 10th (Service) Battalion Royal Welch Fusiliers. Edited by Lieut.-Col. F. N. Burton, assisted by Lieut. A. P. Comyns. Plymouth: William Brendon & Sons, Ltd., 1926. 100 pp. 8½"

14th (Service) Batt. Royal Welsh Fusiliers War Diary, 1914-1918. [Aldershot: Gale & Polden Ltd.], 1920. 17 pp., illustrations. 7½"
    Badge and colours in colour on paper covers.

THE SOUTH WALES BORDERERS   [24]

Historical Records of the 24th Regiment, from its Formation in 1689.   Edited by Col. George Paton, Col. Farquhar Glennie, Col. William Penn Symons, Lieut.-Col. H. B. Moffat.   London: Simpkin, Marshall, Hamilton, Kent & Co., 1892.   xi, 371 pp., portraits, plates, illustrations.   8½"
  6 coloured plates of uniform.

The History of the South Wales Borderers, 1914-1918.   By C. T. Atkinson. London: The Medici Society, 1931.   xi, 614 pp., maps, sketch maps.   10"

The South Wales Borderers, 24th Foot, 1689-1937.   By C. T. Atkinson. Cambridge: printed for the Regimental History Committee at the University Press, 1937.   xxi, 601 pp., portraits, plates, illustrations, maps.   10"
  23 coloured plates, including 12 of uniform and 1 of colours.

History of the South Wales Borderers and The Monmouthshire Regiment, 1937-1952.   5 parts.   Pontypool: Hughes and Son Ltd., 1953-56.   Portraits, plates, maps.   8½"
  Part I.   By Lt.-Col. G. A. Brett.   132 pp.   1953.
  Part II.   The 2nd Battalion, the South Wales Borderers.   D Day, 1944 to 1945. By Major J. T. Boon.   146 pp. 1955.
  Part III.   The 2nd Battalion The Monmouthshire Regiment, 1933-1952.   By Lt.-Col. G. A. Brett.   126 pp.   1953.
  Part IV.   The 3rd Battalion The Monmouthshire Regiment.   By Major J. J. How.   134 pp.   1954.
  Part V.   The 6th Battalion the South Wales Borderers, 1940-1945.   By Lieut.-Col. G. A. Brett.   86 pp.   1956.

A Short History of The South Wales Borderers (The 24th Regiment of Foot). By Capt. Richard J. Pakenham.   London: Gale & Polden Ltd. [1919]. 23 pp. 7"
  1 coloured plate of uniform and coloured reproduction of colours and badge on paper covers.

A Short History of the South Wales Borderers, 24th Foot and The Monmouthshire Regiment.   Compiled by direction of the Regimental Committee. [Cardiff: printed by Western Mail & Echo, Ltd., 1940].   83 pp.   8½"

Rambling Reminiscences of the Punjaub Campaign, 1848-49, with a Brief History of the 24th Regiment from 1689-1889.   By Lieut.-Col. Andrew John Macpherson. Chatham: Mackay & Co., 1889.   viii, 104 pp. 8vo.

Historical Records of the 2nd Battalion, 24th Regiment, for the Kaffir War of 1877-8.   [Pietermaritzburg: printed at the Office of the 1-24th by Sergeant M. Hornibrook.   1878] for private circulation.   27 pp.   6½"

THE KING'S OWN SCOTTISH BORDERERS   [25]

The Records of The King's Own Borderers, or Old Edinburgh Regiment. Edited by Capt. R. T. Higgins. London: Chapman and Hall, 1873. xvi, 382 pp. 8¾″

The King's Own Scottish Borderers. By Brig.-Gen. Montagu Grant Wilkinson [&] Note on the Origin of the K.O.S.B. by Andrew Ross, Ross Herald. (Repr. from *The Lowland Scots Regiments;* edited by the Right Hon. Sir Herbert Maxwell, Bart.). Glasgow: James Maclehose and Sons, 1919. 57 pp. 9½″
  Illustration of uniform on paper cover.

The K.O.S.B. in the Great War. By Capt. Stair Gillon. London: Thomas Nelson and Sons Ltd. [1930]. xiv, 488 pp., portraits, plates, plans, maps in end-pocket. 8¾″

Borderers in Battle. The War Story of The King's Own Scottish Borderers, 1939-1945. By Capt. Hugh Gunning. [Berwick-upon-Tweed: Martin's Printing Works, Ltd., 1948]. 287 pp., portraits, plates, maps. 8½″
  1 coloured plate of colours.

A Short History of The King's Own Scottish Borderers (25th Foot). Aldershot: Gale & Polden Ltd. [1923]. xiii, 42 pp., plates. 7¼″
  3 coloured plates, including 1 of uniform and 1 of colours, and coloured repro-
  duction of badge on paper cover.

——— Reprint. 1930. xiii, 42 pp., plates. 7¼″

" Blue Bonnets o'er the Border." A Short History of The King's Own Scottish Borderers, 1689 to 1951. By the Colonel of the Regiment (Major-Gen. E. G. Miles). [Aldershot: Gale & Polden Ltd., 1951]. 20 pp. 7¼″
  1 coloured plate of colours.

——— [Another edition] . . . 1689 to 1953. 1953. 24 pp. 7½″

A Border Battalion. The History of the 7/8th (Service) Battalion King's Own Scottish Borderers. [Compiled by Capt. J. Goss]. Edinburgh: [T. N. Foulis], privately printed, 1920. xx, 367 pp., portraits, maps. 7½″

THE CAMERONIANS (SCOTTISH RIFLES)   [26 and 90]

Some Account of the Twenty-Sixth, or Cameronian Regiment, From its Formation to the present Period. London: printed by Gunnell and Shearman, for
G. Mills, 1828. 107 pp. 8½″

Historical Record of the Twenty-Sixth, or Cameronian Regiment. Edited by Thomas Carter, Adjutant-General's Office, Horse Guards. London: Byfield, Stanford & Co., 1867. xvi, 265 pp., plates. 8¼"
  2 coloured plates of uniform and 1 of colours. A few copies contain 24 coloured plates of uniform by R. Simkin.

Records of the 90th Regiment (Perthshire Light Infantry), with Roll of Officers from 1795 to 1880. By Alex. M. Delavoye, Captain. London: Richardson & Co., 1880. iv, 260, lxvi pp., plans. 10"

The Cameronians (Scottish Rifles)—The 90th Perthshire Light Infantry. By Andrew Ross, Ross Herald. (Reprinted from *The Lowland Scots Regiments;* edited by the Right Hon. Sir Herbert Maxwell, Bart.). Glasgow: James Maclehose & Sons, 1919. 58 pp. 9¾"
  Illustration of uniform on paper cover.

The Cameronians. The Story of the Scottish Rifles. London: Hutchinson & Co. (Publishers) Ltd., 1941. 95 pp. 7"
  (The Roll of the Drum Histories of the Regiments of the British Army; edited by Wolmer Whyte).

The History of the Cameronians (Scottish Rifles), 26th and 90th.
  Vol. 1. 1689-1910. By S. H. F. Johnston. Aldershot: Gale & Polden Ltd., 1957. Portraits, maps. 8½"
  Vol. 2. 1910-1933. By Col. H. H. Story. [Lanark: Regimental Secretary; printed by Hazell, Watson & Viney Ltd.], 1961. Portraits, plates (1 coloured), maps, map in end-pocket. 9¾"
  Vol. 3. 1933-1946. By Brig. C. N. Barclay. London: Sifton Praed [1949]. Portraits, plates, maps. 8½"

A Short History of The Cameronians (Scottish Rifles). By Col. H. C. Wylly. With a Foreword by Major-Gen. Sir Philip R. Robertson. Aldershot: printed by Gale & Polden Ltd., 1924. [viii], 64 pp., plates, maps. 8½"
  10 coloured plates of uniform.

——— 2nd edition. 1939. x, 105 pp. 8½"

The Cameronians (Scottish Rifles). The Story of the Regiment. By Douglas Ferrier. [Hamilton]: printed by The Hamilton Advertiser Ltd. [1918]. 16 pp. 5¼"

The Cameronians in Sicily. An Account of a Battalion [2nd] of The Cameronians (Scottish Rifles) in the Sicilian Campaign of 1943. Foreword by Gen. Sir Bernard L. Montgomery. [Hamilton: printed by The Hamilton Advertiser, Ltd., 1944]. 38 pp., plates, map. 7¼"

Regimental Roll of Honour of the Officers, Warrant Officers, N.C.O.s & Men of The Cameronians (Scottish Rifles) who, to uphold Liberty and Justice in the World, laid down their lives in the Great War, 1914-1918. Aldershot: Gale & Polden Ltd. *n.d.* 188 pp. 5½"×8"

The Tenth Battalion The Cameronians (Scottish Rifles). A Record and a Memorial, 1914-1918. Edinburgh: printed for private circulation by The Edinburgh Press, 1923. xiv, 168 pp., portraits. 9½"

THE ROYAL INNISKILLING FUSILIERS [27 and 108]

The Historical Record of the 27th Inniskilling Regiment, from the period of its Institution as a Volunteer Corps till the present Time; with an Appendix, Roll of Colonels, Roll of Present Officers, etc.   By W. Copeland Trimble.   London: Wm. Clowes and Sons, 1876.   xx, 160 pp., plates, map.   8¾″
    3 coloured plates, including 2 of uniform.

The Royal Inniskilling Fusiliers, being the History of the Regiment from December 1688 to July 1914.   Compiled under the direction of a Regimental Historical Records Committee.   London: Constable & Co. Ltd., 1928.   xxv, 673 pp., portraits, plates, illustrations.   8½″
    17 coloured plates, including 16 of uniform and 1 of colours.

———— [Revised edition, no plates].   London: Constable & Co., 1934.   xx, 673 pp.   8½″

The Royal Inniskilling Fusiliers in the World War.   A Record of the War as seen by The Royal Inniskilling Fusiliers Regiment, thirteen Battalions of which served.   By Sir Frank Fox.   London: Constable & Co. Ltd. [1928].   xiv, 318 pp., portraits, plates, maps.   8½″

The Royal Inniskilling Fusiliers in the Second World War.   A Record of the War as seen by The Royal Inniskilling Fusiliers, three Battalions of which served.   By Sir Frank Fox.   Aldershot: Gale & Polden Ltd., 1951.   xv, 204 pp., portraits, plates, maps and end-paper maps.   8½″

A Short History of The Royal Inniskilling Fusiliers, the 27th Inniskilling Regiment.   [Aldershot: Gale & Polden Ltd., 1949].   [26 pp.].   6¼″
    Coloured representation of uniform, colours and badge on paper covers.

———— [Another edition].   [1957].   26 pp.   6¼″

The Story of the 27th Regiment of Foot, the Royal Inniskilling Fusiliers. Belfast: British Broadcasting Corporation, Northern Ireland, 1952.   41 pp. Duplicated.   13″

A Short Account of the part played by the First Battalion The Royal Inniskilling Fusiliers during the South African Campaign, October 1899-May, 1902.   Published by the Regiment as a Memento of the Campaign.   Enniskillen: printed at the Impartial Reporter Office, by Wm. Trimble, 1903.   ·109 pp.   8½″

The Royal Inniskilling Fusiliers at the Battle of Inniskilling Hill, fought in South Africa, February 23 and 24, 1900, as told in verse by W. Copeland Trimble. Enniskillen: " Impartial Reporter " Office, 1900.   24 pp., portraits, illustrations. 10″ × 15″

With the 2nd Battalion The Royal Inniskilling Fusiliers in France, 1914-16. Compiled from Official Records [by Major C. A. M. Alexander]. [Omagh: " Tyrone Constitution " Ltd., 1928]. 80 pp., illustrations. 7″

The Story of the 6th Service Battalion of the Royal Inniskilling Fusiliers. Enniskillen: printed at the " Impartial Reporter " Office, by Wm. Trimble [1919]. 63 pp. 7¼″

The Book of the Seventh Service Battalion The Royal Inniskilling Fusiliers from Tipperary to Ypres. By C. A. Cooper Walker. Dublin: Brindley & Son, printer [1920]. xvi, 141 pp., portraits, plates, maps. For private circulation. 8¾″

THE GLOUCESTERSHIRE REGIMENT [28 and 61]

Narrative of the Campaigns of the Twenty-Eighth Regiment since their Return from Egypt in 1802. By Lieut.-Col. Charles Cadell. London: printed for Whittaker & Co., 1835. xx, 281 pp. 8″

Historical Records of the Twenty-Eighth North Gloucestershire Regiment, from 1692 to 1882. Edited by Lieut.-Col. F. Brodigan. London: Blackfriars Printing and Publishing Co. Ltd., 1884. v, 232 pp. 8½″

An Alphabetical List of the Officers of the 28th, or North Gloucestershire Regiment, from 1800 to 1850. By Henry Stooks Smith. London: Simpkin, Marshall & Co., 1851. 8½″

Infantry. An Account of the 1st Gloucestershire Regiment during the War 1914-1918. By Brig.-Gen. A. W. Pagan. Aldershot: Gale & Polden Ltd., 1951. xi, 211 pp. Separate case of maps. 8½″

Now Thrive the Armourers. A Story of Action with the Gloucesters in Korea (November 1950-April 1951). By Robert O. Holles. London: George C. Harrap & Co. Ltd. [1952]. 176 pp., plate. 7¾″

The Gloucesters. An Account of the Epic Stand of the First Battalion The Gloucestershire Regiment in Korea. The Story written by E. J. Kahn, junior, as published in the American magazine *The New Yorker* of May 26th 1951. London: H.M. Stationery Office, 1951. 16 pp. 7¼″

Historical Record of The Sixty-First, or, The South Gloucestershire Regiment of Foot; containing An Account of the Formation of the Regiment in 1758 and of its subsequent Services to 1844. London: Parker, Furnivall & Parker, 1844. viii, vi, 68 pp., plates. (Cannon's Historical Records Series). 8½″
   1 coloured plate of uniform and colours.

The Gloucestershire Regiment in the War, 1914-1918.   The Records of the 1st (28th), 2nd (61st), 3rd (Special Reserve) and 4th, 5th and 6th (First Line T.A.) Battalions.   By Everard Wyrall, with a Foreword by Field Marshal Sir G. F. Milne.   London: Methuen & Co. Ltd. [1931].   ix, 357 pp., portraits, maps. $8\frac{3}{4}''$

The Gloucestershire Regiment.   War Narratives, 1914-1915.   [1st and 2nd Battalions].   Compiled by Capt. R. M. Grazebrook.   [Bristol: The Gloucestershire Regimental Association, 1927].   84 pp., maps. $9\frac{1}{2}''$

Cap of Honour; The Story of The Gloucestershire Regiment (The 28th/61st Foot), 1694-1950.   By David Scott Daniell from Material provided by Col. R. M. Grazebrook, with a Foreword by H.R.H. The Duke of Gloucester.   London: George G. Harrap & Co. Ltd. [1951].   344 pp., plates, illustrations, maps. $8\frac{1}{2}''$
  4 coloured plates, including 2 of uniform.

A Short History of The Gloucestershire Regiment, for the use of the newly-raised battalions.   Published by and for the Gloucestershire Regimental Association.   Bristol: printed by Buckle, 1918.   12 pp. $7\frac{1}{4}''$

A Short History of The Gloucestershire Regiment.   Aldershot: Gale & Polden Ltd. [1920].   30 [10] pp., plate. $7\frac{1}{2}''$

——— [Another edition without Appendices.].   1923.   33 pp.

_____

12th (Service) Battalion Gloucestershire Regiment, " Bristol's Own."   Souvenir . . . containing 39 illustrations.   Compiled and edited by Howard Rankin and Albert G. Wain etc.   Bristol: Colston Publ. Co. 1915.   32 pp.   Fo.

THE WORCESTERSHIRE REGIMENT   [29 and 36]

History of Thos. Farrington's Regiment, subsequently designated The 29th (Worcestershire) Foot, 1694 to 1891.   By Major H. Everard.   Worcester: Littlebury and Company, 1891.   xvii, 598 pp., portraits, illustrations. $9\frac{3}{4}''$

The First Battalion The Worcestershire Regiment in North West Europe.   Told by Major D. Y. Watson.   [Worcester: Ebenezer Baylis and Son Ltd., 1948].   136 pp., illustrations, sketch maps, end-paper maps. $9\frac{1}{2}''$

Historical Record of The Thirty-Sixth, or The Herefordshire Regiment of Foot; containing an Account of the Formation of the Regiment in 1701, and of its subsequent Services to 1852.   Compiled by Richard Cannon, Esq., Adjutant-General's Office, Horse Guards.   London: printed by George E. Eyre and William Spottiswoode, for Her Majesty's Stationery Office.   Published by Parker, Furnivall, & Parker, 1853.   xix, xii, 135 pp., plates. $8\frac{1}{2}''$
  3 coloured plates, including 1 of uniform and 1 of colours.

Historical Records of The Thirty-Sixth. Re-issue, with continuation with separate titlepage: Historical Records of The Thirty-Sixth Regiment, from 1852 to 1881. Compiled from the Official Digest of Services of the Regiment. London: Mitchell & Co., 1883. xix, xii, 135, 123 pp., plates. 8½″
    4 coloured plates in Part 1, including 2 of uniform and 1 of colours; 1 coloured uniform plate in Part 2. Different plates from those in original edition. The 2nd Part is sometimes found bound separately.

The Worcestershire Regiment in the Great War. By Capt. H. Fitz-M. Stacke. With a Foreword by Field Marshal Sir Claud Jacob, Colonel of the Regiment. Forming part of the Worcestershire County War Memorial. Kidderminster: G. T. Cheshire & Sons Ltd., 1929. xxx, 667 pp., portraits, plates, maps, plans. 11″

The Worcestershire Regiment, 1922-1950. By Lieut.-Col. Lord Birdwood. Aldershot: Gale & Polden Ltd., 1952. xv, 302 pp., portraits, plates, maps. 8½″

The Worcestershire Regiment. Regimental History. No imprint, 1930. 12 pp. 8½″

The History of the Worcestershire Regiment: a lecture to recruits. By Capt. K. M. Mylne. Worcester: Littlebury & Co. 1918. 32 pp. 7¼″

The Worcestershire Regiment; an historical note. Bromsgrove: " Messenger " Co., 1946. 26 pp., illustrations. 8½″

The Worcestershire Regiment. The Action of Gheluvelt, fought on October 31st, 1914. Devonport: Hiorns & Miller [1917]. 14 pp., folding plan. 7″

THE EAST LANCASHIRE REGIMENT [30 and 59]

Historical Records of the XXX Regiment. London: William Clowes and Sons Ltd., 1887, ix, 283 pp. 9¾″

History of The Thirtieth Regiment, now the First Battalion East Lancashire Regiment, 1689-1881. By Lieut.-Col. Neil Bannatyne. Liverpool: Littlebury Bros., 1923. ix, 474 pp., portraits, plates, maps. 9½″
    14 coloured plates of uniform.

Spectamur Agendo. 1st Battalion, The East Lancashire Regiment, August and September 1914. By Capt. E. C. Hopkinson. [Cambridge: Heffer & Sons Ltd., privately printed, 1926]. vii, 73 pp., portraits, maps. 8½″

1st Battalion The East Lancashire Regiment. Saar Plebiscite, 1935. [Aldershot: Gale & Polden Ltd., 1935]. 32 pp., portraits, plates. 7¼″×9¾″
    Souvenir album containing Roll and reproductions of photographs.

1st Battalion, The East Lancashire Regiment; France, 1940. [By Brig. J. W. Pendlebury]. 2nd edition. [Ringwood: Brown & Son (Ringwood) Ltd., printers, 1946]. 16 pp., map. 8″

Annals of the " Five and Nine "; being the History of H.M. 59th Regiment (2nd Nottinghamshire), now the Second Battalion East Lancashire Regiment. By Second Lieut. F. M. James. Poona: S. Shalom & Bros., 1906. 135 pp. 8½″

History of The East Lancashire Regiment in the Great War, 1914-1918. [Compiled by Maj.-Gen. Sir Lothian Nicholson and Major H. T. McMullen]. Liverpool: Littlebury Bros. Ltd., 1936. xvi, 568 pp., portraits, plates, maps, plans. 9½″

History of The East Lancashire Regiment in the War, 1939-1945. [Edited by Brig. G. W. P. N. Burden]. Manchester: H. Rawson & Co. Ltd., 1953. xv, 331 pp., portraits, illustrations, maps. 9⅜″

The East Lancashire Regiment. A Short History of the Regiment. By Sgt.-Instructor F. W. Wood, with Additions for the Great War by Capt. R. E. D. Green. Preston: T. Snape & Co. Ltd., 1938. 52 pp., sketch maps. 5½″

A Short History of the East Lancashire Regiment. Preston: T. Snape & Co. Ltd., 1952. iv, 23 pp., plate. 5½″

THE EAST SURREY REGIMENT [31 and 70]

Historical Record of The Thirty-First, or, The Huntingdonshire Regiment of Foot; containing an Account of the Formation of the Regiment in 1702, and of its subsequent Services to 1850; to which is appended An Account of the Services of the Marine Corps, from 1664 to 1748; The Thirtieth, Thirty-First, and Thirty-Second Regiments having been formed in 1702 as *Marine Corps*, and retained from 1714 on the Establishment of the Army as Regiments of Regular Infantry. Compiled by Richard Cannon, Esq., Adjutant-General's Office, Horse Guards. London: Parker, Furnivall & Parker, 1850. xliv, 213 pp. App*., x, 56 pp., plates. 8½″
    5 coloured plates, including 2 of colours; 1 coloured plate of uniform and 1 of colours in Appendix which was also issued as a separate publication.

Historical Record of The Seventieth, or The Surrey Regiment of Foot; containing an Account of the Formation of the Regiment in 1758, and of its subsequent Services to 1848. Compiled by Richard Cannon, Esq., Adjutant-General's Office, Horse Guards. London: Parker, Furnivall, & Parker, 1849. xxvii, 21 pp. 8½″
    1 coloured plate of uniform and colours.

History of the 31st Foot, Huntingdonshire Regt.--70th Foot, Surrey Regt., subsequently 1st & 2nd Battalions The East Surrey Regiment.
Vol. 1.   1702-1914.   By Col.   Hugh W.   Pearse.   London: Spottiswoode, Ballantyne & Co. Ltd., 1916.   Portraits, plates, maps, 2 coloured plates of uniform. $9\frac{1}{2}''$
Vols. 2, 3 [1914-1919] with title: History of the East Surrey Regiment.   By Col. H. W. Pearse and Brig.-Gen. H. S. Sloman.   London: The Medici Society Ltd., 1933-34.   Plates, maps. $9\frac{1}{2}''$
Vol. 4.   1920-1952,   By David Scott Daniell.   With a Foreword by Brig. G. R. P. Roupell.   London: Ernest Benn Ltd., 1957.   Plates, maps. $8\frac{1}{2}''$

A Short History of the East Surrey Regiment.   [Aldershot: Gale & Polden Ltd., 1950].   24 pp. $7\frac{1}{4}''$

_____

The History of the 12th (Bermondsey) Battalion East Surrey Regiment.   Written and compiled by John Aston, and L. M. Duggan.   With Letters from Lieut.-Gen. Sir Sydney T. B. Lawford and Brig.-Gen. F. W. Towsey.   London: The Union Press, 1936.   Portraits, plates, illustrations, maps.   [10], 331 pp. $9\frac{1}{2}''$

THE DUKE OF CORNWALL'S LIGHT INFANTRY
[32 and 46]

Historical Records of the 32nd (Cornwall) Light Infantry, now the 1st Battalion Duke of Cornwall's Light Infantry, from the Formation of the Regiment in 1702 down to 1892.   Compiled and edited by Col. G. C. Swiney, from the Orderly Room Records and other Sources.   London: Simpkin, Marshall, Hamilton, Kent, & Co., Ltd., 1893.   xii., 388 pp., portraits, plates, illustrations. $8\frac{1}{2}''$
    10 coloured plates of uniform.

The Story of The First Battalion The Duke of Cornwall's Light Infantry (32nd Foot).   [By Lieut. H. N. Newey].   Aldershot: Gale & Polden Ltd. [1924]. vii, 46 pp., portrait, plates, plan. $7''$
    1 coloured plate of uniform and coloured reproduction of colours and badge on paper covers.   Cover reads "A Short History of The Duke of Cornwall's Light Infantry", but it deals only with the 1st Battalion.

History of The 1st D.C.L.I., 1914.   Compiled from Official Records and other Sources.   By E. M. Channing-Renton, Lieutenant.   Illustrated by Viscount French, John Hassall, R.I., Major T. A. Kendall and others.   [Alexandria]; Studies Publications, 1924.   [x], 43, v pp., portrait, plates, maps.   (The Duke of Cornwall's Light Infantry Great War History Series) $9''$

Notes on the History of The Duke of Cornwall's Light Infantry.   Compiled by Major J. H. T. Cornish-Bowden.   Devonport: Hiorns and Miller.   [1913-14].   7″

No. 1.   The Raising of the Regiment and the Meaning of its name.   64 pp.

No. 2.   Early War Services.   55 pp.

The History of The Duke of Cornwall's Light Infantry, 1914-1919.   By Everard Wyrall.   With a Foreword by H.R.H. The Prince of Wales and Duke of Cornwall, Colonel-in-Chief.   London: Methuen & Co. Ltd., 1932.   xix, 514 pp., portraits, plates, maps, plans.   9″

Historical Record of The Forty-Sixth, or The South Devonshire, Regiment of Foot; containing an Account of the Formation of the Regiment in 1741 and of its subsequent Services to 1851.   Compiled by Richard Cannon, Esq., Adjutant-General's Office, Horse Guards.   London: Parker, Furnivall, & Parker, 1851.   xxxv, 76 pp., plates.   8½″
   1 coloured plate of uniform and 1 of colours.

A Short History of The Duke of Cornwall's Light Infantry; its Formation and Services, 1702-1928.   Devonport: Swiss & Co., 1929.   xvi, 63 pp.   Coloured plate of colours.   6½″

—— [Another edition] . . . 1702-1938.   Plymouth: Underhill (Plymouth) Ltd., printers, 1939.   xvi, 63 pp., plate.   6⅜″

A Short History of the Duke of Cornwall's Light Infantry, 1702-1945.   Compiled by Lawrence S. Snell.   Aldershot: Gale & Polden Ltd., 1945.   [7], 54 pp., plates.   7¼″
   1 coloured plate of uniform and 1 of colours.

THE DUKE OF WELLINGTON'S REGIMENT
(WEST RIDING) [33 and 76]

History of the Thirty-Third Foot, Duke of Wellington's (West Riding) Regiment.   By Albert Lee.   Norwich: printed by Jarrold & Sons Ltd., 1922.   ix, 471 pp., portraits, plates, plans.   8¾″
   11 coloured plates, including 10 of uniform.

Historical Record of the 76th "Hindoostan" Regiment from its Formation in 1787 to 30th June, 1881.   Compiled by Lieut.-Col. F. A. Hayden.   Lichfield: A. C. Lomax's Successors.   1908.   xix, 275 pp., portraits (1 coloured), plans, coloured plate of colours.   8½″

History of The Duke of Wellington's Regiment [1st & 2nd Battalions], 1881-1923.   By Brig.-Gen. C. D. Bruce.   London: The Medici Society Ltd. [1927].   xv, 263 pp., portraits, plates, maps.   10″

The History of The Duke of Wellington's Regiment, 1919-1952. Produced under the direction of the Regimental Council. Edited by Brig. C. N. Barclay. London: William Clowes and Sons Ltd. [1953]. xxi, 398 pp., portraits (1 coloured), plates, maps. $9\frac{3}{4}''$

History of the Duke of Wellington's West Riding Regiment (The Iron Duke's Own) during the First Three Years of the Great War from August 1914 to December 1917. By J. J. Fisher (Military Correspondent). [Halifax: Exors. of Geo. T. Whitehead, printer, 1917]. 152 pp., illustrations. $9\frac{3}{4}''$

A Short History of the Duke of Wellington's Regiment. Compiled by Brevet Lt.-Col. M. V. le Poer Trench. Aldershot: Gale & Polden Ltd. [1922]. 30 pp. $7\frac{1}{4}''$
    1 coloured plate of uniform.

——— [Another edition]. 1940. 32 pp. $7\frac{1}{4}''$

——— [Another edition]. Newcastle-upon-Tyne. Printed for the Regiment by J. & P. Bealls Ltd., 1944. 32 pp. $7\frac{1}{4}''$
    1 coloured plate of colours.

The War Memorials of The Duke of Wellington's Regiment (West Riding). No imprint. 7 pp., plate. 12''

1st Battalion The Duke of Wellington's Regiment (West Riding). Presentation of Colours. [30th July, 1925]. [Aldershot: Gale & Polden Ltd., 1925]. 36 pp., portraits, plates. $7\frac{1}{4}''\times9\frac{3}{4}''$
    Souvenir album containing reproductions of photographs.

2nd Battalion The Duke of Wellington's Regiment. Egypt, 1922-26. [Aldershot: Gale & Polden Ltd., 1926]. 44 pp., portraits, illustrations. $6\frac{1}{2}''\times8''$
    Souvenir album containing reproductions of photographs.

THE BORDER REGIMENT [34 and 55]

Historical Record of The Thirty-Fourth, or, The Cumberland Regiment of Foot; containing an Account of the Formation of the Regiment in 1702, and of its subsequent Services to 1844. London: Parker, Furnivall, & Parker, 1844. viii, viii, 100 pp., plates. (Cannon's Historical Records Series). $8\frac{1}{2}''$
    3 coloured plates of uniform including 1 with colours.

——— Re-issue. 3 colour plates of uniform, 2 of colours.

A Historical Account of the Services of the 34th and 55th Regiments, the linked Battalions in the 2nd or Cumberland and Westmorland Sub-District Brigade, from the periods of their Formation until the present time.   Compiled from the most authentic sources by George Noakes, Quarter-Master Serjeant.   Carlisle: C. Thurnam & Sons, 1875.   xi, 159 pp., plate.   7¼″

The Border Regiment in the Great War.   By Col. H. C. Wylly.   Aldershot: printed and published for the Regimental Committee by Gale & Polden Ltd. [1924].   ix, 272 pp., plates, maps.   9¾″
 For Private Circulation only.

The Story of the Border Regiment, 1939-1945.   By [Major-Gen.] Philip J. Shears.   With a Foreword by Brig.-Gen. G. Hyde Harrison, Colonel, The Border Regiment.   London: Nisbet & Co. Ltd. [1948].   xv, 184 pp., maps.   8½″

Talks about the Border Regiment (formerly 34th and 55th Regiments) intended for the Instruction of Recruits.   By Major L. H. Caird.   London: T. Fisher Unwin, 1903.   32 pp.   8¼″

A Short History of The Border Regiment.   Aldershot: Gale & Polden Ltd. [1922].   23 pp., plates.   7¼″
 1 coloured plate of uniform and 1 of colours; badge in colour on paper covers.

——— 5th edition.   [1938].   25 pp., plates.   7¼″

The Border Regiment.   [A brief summary of 250 years' service], 1702-1952. [Hastings: printed by F. J. Parsons, Ltd., 1952].   28 pp., illustrations.   9¼″
 6 coloured illustrations of uniform and colours.

The Border Regiment.   Centenary of the Battle of Arroyo-dos-Molinos, 28th October, 1811.   [Aldershot: Gale & Polden Ltd., 1911].   35 pp., portraits, illustrations.   6½″×8″
 Coloured illustrations of uniform, colours, drums etc.

Reminiscences of the Crimean Campaign with the 55th Regiment.   By John R. Hume, Major-General.   London: printed for the author by Unwin Brothers, 1894.   xi, 190 pp., portraits, plates, plans.   6¾″

The Border Regiment in South Africa, 1899-1902.   From photographs by Officers of the Regiment.   [No text].   London: Eyre & Spottiswoode.   [c. 1902]. 64 ff.   Portraits, illustrations.   8¾″

Records of the XIth (Service) Battalion Border Regt. (Lonsdale), from September, 1914, to July 1st, 1916.   Commanding Officer: Lieut.-Colonel P. W. Machell. Compiled by V.M. from Notes by the C.O. and Officers of the Battalion. Appleby: J. Whitehead & Son, printer [c. 1916].   46 pp., portraits, map.   9½″

THE ROYAL SUSSEX REGIMENT [35 and 107]

An Historical Memoir of the 35th Royal Sussex Regiment of Foot. Compiled by Richard Trimen, late Captain. Southampton: The Southampton Times Newspaper and Printing and Publishing Co. Ltd., 1873. viii, 343 pp., plates. 8½″
    6 coloured plates of uniform.

A History of the Royal Sussex Regiment; a history of the old Belfast Regiment and the Regiment of Sussex, 1701-1953. By G. D. Martineau. Chichester: Moore & Tillyer Ltd. [1955]. 324 pp., sketch maps. 8½″

A Short History of the Royal Sussex Regiment from 1701 to 1905. London: Waterlow & Sons Ltd., 1905. 54 pp., plates. 5¼″
    1st edition issued in 1889. 2 plates of colours.

A Short History of the Royal Sussex Regiment, 1701-1915. No imprint. 38 pp. 7″

A Short History of the Royal Sussex Regiment (35th Foot—107th Foot), 1701-1926. With brief particulars of the part taken in the Great War by the various Battalions of the Regiment. Aldershot: Gale & Polden Ltd., 1941. x, 111 pp., portraits, plates, illustrations. 7″
    4 coloured plates, including 1 of uniform and 1 of colours; originally published in 1927.

An Outline History of the Royal Sussex Regiment, 1701-1949. [Brighton: The Dolphin Press Ltd., 1949]. 23 pp. 7½″

The Royal Sussex Regimental Handbook, 1701-1955. Plymouth: printed by Clarke, Doble & Brendon Ltd., 1956. 36 pp., illustrations. 8½″

Two Years on Trek; being Some Account of the Royal Sussex Regiment in South Africa. By the late Lt.-Col. Du Moulin, with a Preface by Col. J. G. Panton. Edited by H. F. Bidder, Captain. London: Murray & Co., The Middlesex Printing Works, 1907. v, 323, xi pp., plans, map. 8½″

Tour of Duty of 1st Battalion The Royal Sussex Regiment in London, 1932. Aldershot: Gale & Polden Ltd., 1932. 24 pp., portraits, plates.   7¼″×9¾″
    Souvenir album, containing Roll and reproductions of photographs.

A Short History of the Second Battalion The Royal Sussex Regiment. Compiled from various Sources by Lieut. J. H. Dumbrell. Singapore: C. A. Ribeiro & Co. Ltd. [1925]. [8], 78 pp., map, plate of badges. 9¼″

The History of the Seventh (Service) Battalion The Royal Sussex Regiment, 1914-1919. Compiled by a Committee of Officers of the Battalion. Edited by Owen Rutter, with an Introduction by Gen. Sir Hubert Gough. Preface by Brig.-Gen. W. L. Osborn (Colonel of The Royal Sussex Regiment). London: The Times Publishing Co. Ltd. xix, 347 pp., portraits, plates, maps. 9¾″

THE ROYAL HAMPSHIRE REGIMENT   [37 and 67]

Annals of the Thirty-Seventh North Hampshire Regiment.   [By Capt. J. E. Whitting].   Winchester: Warren & Son [1878; 83].   55, 8 pp.   7¼″

Historical Record of The Sixty-Seventh, or The South Hampshire Regiment; containing an Account of the Formation of the Regiment in 1758, and of its subsequent Services to 1849.   Compiled by Richard Cannon, Esq., Adjutant-General's Office, Horse Guards.   London: Parker, Furnivall, & Parker, 1849. xxxii, 52 pp., plates.   8½″
   1 coloured plate of uniform and 1 of colours.

The Battle Story of the Hampshire Regiment 1702-1919.   By F. E. Stevens. With Foreword by the Right Hon. The Earl of Selborne.   Southampton: Hampshire Advertiser Company Ltd. [1919].   65 pp., portraits, plates, maps. 9¾″

Regimental History The Royal Hampshire Regiment.   Vols. 1, 2.   By C. T. Atkinson.   Glasgow: printed for the Regiment by Robert Maclehose & Co. Ltd., 1950-52.   9¼″
   Vol. 1.   To 1914.   xx, 497 pp., portraits, maps, illustrations.

   Vol. 2.   1914-1918.   xx, 515 pp., portraits, plate, plans, sketch maps.

   Vol. 3.   1918-1954.   By David Scott Daniell, with a Foreword by Lieut.-Gen. Sir Frederick A. M. Browning.   Aldershot: Gale & Polden Ltd., 1955.   xiii, 294 pp., portraits, maps, plans, end-paper maps.   9¼″

The History of the Hampshire Regiment (37th and 67th Foot).   By G.E.B., revised by H.W.M.M.   Aldershot: Gale & Polden Ltd., 1928.   48 pp., plates, illustrations, maps.   5½″
   2 coloured plates of uniform and 1 of colours.

—— [Another edition].   1933.   52 pp., plates, maps, illustrations.   5½″
   2 coloured plates of uniform and 2 of colours.

—— Reprinted, August, 1940.   52 pp., plates, illustrations.   5½″
   3 coloured plates of uniform and 2 of colours.

Presentation of Colours to the 37th Regiment, at Dover, April, 1865 and Historic Memoir of the Corps, with Account of Memorial Window in All Saints' Church, Aldershot.   [Aldershot: W. Sheldrake, army printer, 1865].   40 pp.   6¼″

———————————

Some Account of the 10th and 12th Battalions The Hampshire Regiment, 1914-1918.   [Edited by Major W. S. Cowland].   Winchester: Warren and Son Ltd. [1930].   78 pp.   8½″

THE SOUTH STAFFORDSHIRE REGIMENT   [38 and 80]

A History of the South Staffordshire Regiment (1705-1923).   By James P. Jones. Wolverhampton: Whitehead Brothers (Wolverhampton) Ltd. [1923].   xx, 483 pp., portraits, plates, maps.   8¾″
  1 coloured plate of uniform.

A Short History of The South Staffordshire Regiment.   No imprint [1922?]. 20 pp., map.   7¼″

A Short History of The South Staffordshire Regiment.   [By Col. W. L. Vale]. [Wolverhampton: Whitehead Brothers Ltd., 1949].   27 pp., illustrations.   8¾″

Your Men in Battle.   The Story of The South Staffordshire Regiment, 1939-45. [Edited by L. B. Duckworth].   Wolverhampton: "Express & Star" [c. 1945]. 47 pp., portraits, illustrations, maps.   9¾″

Extracts from the Records of the Services of the First Battalion South Staffordshire Regiment, late 38th Regiment.   Gibraltar: Beanland, Malin & Co., 1887. 24 pp.   8vo.

The Thirty-Eighth Regiment of Foot, now the First Battalion of the South Staffordshire Regiment.   By Major William J. Freer.   London: Harrison & Sons, 1915.   28 pp., portrait, plates.   (Reprinted from *The British Numismatic Journal*, vol. 11).   9¼″

With the 38th in France and Italy; being a Record of the Doings of the 1st Battalion South Staffordshire Regiment from 26th September, 1916, to 26th May, 1918.   By Lieut.-Col. A. B. Beauman.   Lichfield: A. C. Lomax's Successors, 1919.   48 pp.   7″

1st Battalion The South Staffordshire Regiment.   [Aldershot: Gale & Polden Ltd., 1936].   32 pp., portraits, plates.   7¼″×9¾″
  Souvenir album, cont. reproductions of photographs.

The Unbreakable Coil.   [By Major A. L. K. Anderson].   [Wolverhampton: Whitehead Brothers (Wolverhampton) Ltd., 1923].   viii, 86 pp.   6¼″
  2nd Battalion, Oct.-Dec. 1914.

The History of the Seventh South Staffordshire Regiment.   Edited by Major A. H. Ashcroft.   London: printed by Boyle, Son & Watchurst Ltd. [1919]. 204 pp.   7½″

THE DORSET REGIMENT   [39 and 54]

Historical Record of The Thirty-Ninth, or The Dorsetshire Regiment of Foot; containing an Account of the Formation of the Regiment in 1702, and of its subsequent Services to 1853.   Compiled by Richard Cannon, Esq., Adjutant-General's Office, Horse Guards.   London: Parker, Furnivall, & Parker, 1853. Printed by George E. Eyre and William Spottiswoode for H.M. Stationery Office, xix, xii, 104 pp., plates. $8\frac{1}{2}''$
  1 coloured plate of uniform and 1 of colours.

Records of the 1st Battalion, The Dorset Regiment, late 39th Regiment.   From 1853 to 1893.   [Compiled by Capt. P. R. Phipps].   Cairo.   No imprint. 45 pp. $7\frac{3}{4}''$

Record of the 54th Regiment.   Roorkee: printed at the Thomason Civil Engineering College Press, 1881.   87, xxiv pp., plates. $8\frac{1}{2}''$

The Dorsetshire Regiment.   The Thirty-Ninth and Fifty-Fourth Foot and the Dorset Militia and Volunteers.   By C. T. Atkinson.   Oxford: Privately printed at the University Press, 1947.   2 vols., maps and plans. $9\frac{1}{4}''$
  Vol. 1.   Part I.   The Thirty-Ninth.   xviii, 355 pp.

  Vol. 2.   Part II.   The Fifty-Fourth.   Part III.   The Dorsetshire Regiment. [9], 223, 284 pp.

History of The Dorsetshire Regiment, 1914-1919.   Compiled for the Regimental History Committee.   Dorchester: Henry Ling Ltd. [1933].   x, 306, 152, 205, 64 pp., maps. $9\frac{1}{2}''$
  Part I.   The Regular Battalions.

  Part II.   The Territorial Units.   By Major H. C. Lock and the 1st Volunteer Battalion The Dorsetshire Regiment.   By O. C. Vidler.

  Part III. The Service Battalions.
    Each part, with general prefatory pages and Appendix was also issued separately.

A Short History of the Dorsetshire Regiment.   Aldershot: Gale & Polden Ltd. [1922].   24 pp. $7\frac{1}{4}''$
  Coloured plate of uniform; colours and badge in colour on paper covers.

———— [Another edition].   1937.   24 pp. $7\frac{1}{4}''$

———— Reprint, without plate.   1941.   24 pp. $7\frac{1}{4}''$

A Short History of the Dorsetshire Regiment, 1702-1948.   Dorchester: Henry Ling Ltd., 1948.   28 pp. $8\frac{1}{2}''$

The 39th Regiment of Foot and the East India Company, 1754-1757.   By John Roach.   Reprinted from the " *Bulletin of the John Rylands Library*," vol. 41, No. 1, September, 1958.   Manchester: John Rylands Library, 1958.   39 pp. $9\frac{5}{8}''$

"The Fine Fighting of the Dorsets"; three battles of 1st Battn. The Dorsetshire Regiment in 1914 and 1915. By Major-Gen. A. L. Ransome. Dorchester: The Regtl. Museum. [1959]. 35 pp., illustrations, maps. $9\frac{3}{4}''$

Three Assault Landings. The Story of the 1st Battn. The Dorsetshire Regiment in Sicily, Italy and N.W. Europe. By Lt.-Col. A. E. C. Bredin, with a foreword by Lt.-Gen. Sir Brian Horrocks. Aldershot: Gale & Polden Ltd., 1946. xvi, 172 pp., portraits, plates, maps. $7\frac{1}{4}''$

The First Battalion The Dorset Regiment (39th and 54th) in the Far East. [Pictorial Souvenir]. Hong Kong: printed by South China Morning Post Ltd., 1954, 32 pp., portraits, illustrations. $8\frac{3}{4}'' \times 11\frac{1}{4}''$

Straight on for Tokyo. The War History of the 2nd Battalion The Dorsetshire Regiment (54th Foot), 1939-1948. By Lieut.-Col. O. G. W. White. Aldershot: Gale & Polden Ltd., 1948. xix, 426 pp., portraits, illustrations, maps, end-paper, maps. $8\frac{1}{2}''$

A Medallic Record of the War Services of The Dorsetshire Regiment (39th and 54th). By Lieut.-Col. P. R. Phipps. [Dorchester: Henry Ling Ltd.], 1932. 10 pp., plates (reprinted from the Dorsetshire Regimental Quarterly, Vol. 6, 1931, and revised). $9\frac{3}{4}''$

THE SOUTH LANCASHIRE REGIMENT (THE PRINCE OF WALES'S VOLUNTEERS) [40 and 82]

A Short Record of the 1st Battalion The Prince of Wales's Volunteers (South Lancashire Regiment), formerly the 40th (2nd Somersetshire) Regiment. By Capt. R. H. Raymond Smythies, on the occasion of the Presentation of new Colours to the Battalion, 16th July, 1891. Jersey: "Jersey Times," 1891. 120 pp., portraits, plates. $8''$

Historical Records of the 40th (2nd Somersetshire) Regiment, now 1st Battalion The Prince of Wales's Volunteers (South Lancashire Regiment). From its Formation, in 1717, to 1893, By Capt. R. H. Raymond Smythies. Devonport: printed for the subscribers by A. H. Swiss, 1894. xvi, 620 pp., portraits, plates, illustrations. $8\frac{1}{2}''$
  9 coloured plates of uniform. 250 copies only.

Historical Record of the Eighty-Second Regiment of Prince of Wales's Volunteers. Dedicated to his brother Officers by Brevet-Major Jarvis, 82nd Regt. London: W. O. Mitchell, 1866. xv, 123 pp. Coloured plate of colours. $8\frac{1}{4}''$

" Ich Dien." The Prince of Wales's Volunteers (South Lancashire), 1914-1934. By Capt. H. Whalley-Kelly. Aldershot: Gale & Polden Ltd., 1935. xvi, 336 pp., portraits, plates, maps, maps in end-pocket. $9\frac{1}{2}''$

The South Lancashire Regiment, The Prince of Wales's Volunteers. By Col. B. R. Mullaly. Bristol: The White Swan Press [1955]. 520 pp., portraits, plates, maps. 8½"

A Short History of The Prince of Wales's Volunteers (South Lancashire). Compiled by Lieut.-Col. F. E. Whitton. Aldershot; Gale & Polden Ltd., 1928. [viii], 54 pp., portraits, plates. 9¾"
    10 coloured plates, including 4 of uniform and 1 of colours.

A Short History of The South Lancashire Regiment (The Prince of Wales's Volunteers). [Aldershot: Gale & Polden Ltd., 1946]. 16 pp., illustrations. 6"
    2 coloured illustrations of uniform and 1 of colours.

———— [Another edition]. [By Lt.-Col. F. Jebens]. Aldershot, 1951. 16 pp., illustrations. 6"

Formation and Events in the Services of the Fortieth or 2nd Somersetshire Regt., 1717 to 1799. Calcutta: printed by Thomas S. Smith, City Press, 1879. 54 pp., illustrations. 8¼"

1st Battalion The Prince of Wales's Volunteers (South Lancashire). London, Chelsea Barracks, August 15th to September 19th, 1928. [Aldershot; Gale & Polden Ltd., 1928]. 32 pp., portraits, plates. 7¼"×9¾"
    Souvenir album, containing Roll and reproductions of photographs.

The Prince of Wales's Volunteers. The Royal Tournament, 1932. [Aldershot: Gale & Polden Ltd., 1932]. 32 pp., plates. 7¼"×9¾"
    Souvenir album containing reproductions of photographs.

THE WELCH REGIMENT   [41 and 69]

A History of the Services of the 41st (the Welch) Regiment (now 1st Battalion The Welch Regiment), from its Formation, in 1719 to 1895. By Lieut. and Adjt. D. A. N. Lomax. Devonport: printed by Hiorns & Miller, 1899. xiv, 407 pp., portraits, plates, illustrations, maps. 8½"
    9 coloured plates, including 7 of uniform and 2 of colours.

A Narrative of the Historical Events connected with the Sixty-Ninth Regiment. By W. F. Butler, 69th Regt. London: W. Mitchell & Co., 1870. v, 130 pp., plate. 8½"

The History of The Welch Regiment. Cardiff: Western Mail and Echo Ltd., 1932. xii, 273, vii, 275-592 pp., portraits, plates, maps, map in end-pocket. 9½"
    Part I.   1719-1914; by Major A. C. Whitehorne.
    Part II. 1914-1918; by Major-Gen. Sir Thomas O. Marden, Colonel, The Welch Regiment.

The History of The Welch Regiment, 1919-1951. Based on the original work of Capt. J. de Courcy and amplified and enlarged by Major-Gen. C. E. N. Lomax, Colonel, The Welch Regiment. Cardiff: Western Mail & Echo Ltd. [1952]. 337 pp., portrait, maps. 9¾"

A Short History of The Welch Regiment. Aldershot: printed by Gale & Polden Ltd., 1929. 22 pp. 8½"

――――― [Another edition] Cardiff: Western Mail & Echo Ltd., 1938. 35 pp. 8½"

THE BLACK WATCH (ROYAL HIGHLAND REGIMENT)
[42 and 73]

A Short History of the Highland Regiment. London: printed for Jacob Robinson, 1743. 51 pp., plate. 8½"

――――― Another edition . . .; interspersed with Some Occasional Observations as to the Present State of the Country, Inhabitants and the Government of Scotland. With a Foreword by Col. Paul P. Hutchinson. Cornwallville, N.Y.: Hope Farm Press, 1963. x, 51 pp., plate. 8⅞"

Historical Record of The Forty-Second, or, The Royal Highland Regiment of Foot; containing an Account of the Formation of Six Companies of Highlanders in 1729, which were termed " The Black Watch " and were regimented in 1739: and of the subsequent Services of the Regiment to 1844. London: Parker, Furnivall, & Parker, 1845. viii, xxiv, 198 pp., plates. (Cannon's Historical Records Series). 8½"
    4 coloured plates of uniform (1 includes colours).

Historical Record of The Seventy-Third Regiment; containing an Account of the Formation of the Regiment from the period of its being raised as the Second Battalion of the Forty-Second Royal Highlanders, in 1780 and of its subsequent Services to 1851. Compiled by Richard Cannon, Esq., Adjutant-General's Office, Horse Guards. London: Parker, Furnivall, & Parker, 1851. xxxii, 76 pp., plates. 8½"
    3 coloured plates of uniform and 1 of colours.

History of the 42nd Royal Highlanders—" The Black Watch," now The First Battalion " The Black Watch " (Royal Highlanders), 1729-1893. By Lieut.-Col. Percy Groves. Illustrated by Harry Payne. Edinburgh: W. & A. K. Johnston, 1893. 30 pp., plates. (Illustrated Histories of the Scottish Regiments, Book No. 1). 12¼"
    5 coloured plates of uniform.

The " Black Watch." The Record of an Historic Regiment. By Archibald Forbes. London: Cassell & Company Ltd., 1896. vii, 316 pp., plate. 7¾"

The "Black Watch." New edition. London: Cassell & Co. Ltd., 1903. vii, 326 pp., plates. 8⅛″

────── New edition, containing the further Record of the Regiment from 1885 to the present day by a former Commanding Officer. London: Cassell & Company Ltd., 1910. vii, 335 pp., plates. 7½″

A History of The Black Watch [Royal Highlanders] in the Great War, 1914-1918. Edited by Major-Gen. A. G. Wauchope. London: The Medici Society Ltd., 1925-26. 3 vols., portraits, plates, maps, plans. 10″

The Black Watch and the King's Enemies. By Bernard Fergusson. With a Foreword by Field Marshal Earl Wavell. London: Collins, 1950. 348 pp., maps. 8½″

The Great Deeds of the Black Watch. By L. Cope Cornford and F. W. Walker. London: J. M. Dent & Sons Ltd. [1915]. 181 pp., coloured plate of uniform. (The Story of the Regiments). 7″

A Short History of The Black Watch (Royal Highlanders), 1725-1907; to which is added An Account of the Second Battalion in the South African War, 1899-1902. [By Capt. A. G. Wauchope]. Edinburgh: William Blackwood & Sons, 1908. xv, 241 pp., maps. 8½″

A Brief History of The Royal Highland Regiment, The Black Watch. By John Stewart, a Captain in the Regiment. Edinburgh: printed for the Regiment by T. & A. Constable, 1912. 74 pp., plates. 5½″

────── 2nd edition. 1914. 74 pp., plates. 5½″

────── New edition, containing A Record of The Great War by the Author. Edinburgh: T. & A. Constable, 1924. 105 pp., plates. 5½″

The Black Watch. By Lauchlan Maclean Watt. Edinburgh: W. P. Nimmo, Hay & Mitchell [1916]. 63 pp., plates. 6¼″
    3 coloured plates.

The Black Watch. A Short History. By Bernard Fergusson, sometime Lieut.-Col. in the Regiment. Glasgow: printed for the Regiment by Collins, 1955. 128 pp., plates. 5½″

Chronology and Book of Days of the 42nd Royal Highlanders, The Black Watch, from 1729 to 1874. By J.W. Edinburgh: William Elgin & Son, 1874. 63 pp. 6½″

────── 4th edition with the title Chronology of the 42nd Royal Highlanders The Black Watch, from 1729 to 1905. Berwick-on-Tweed: Martin's Printing Works, 1906. 70 [ii] pp. For private circulation only. 6⅜″
    Earlier editions: Malta, 1843; India, 1859.

The Chronicle of The Royal Highland Regiment, The Black Watch, 1913. Edinburgh: printed by T. & A. Constable [1913]. Portrait, plates. 8½″
    The first and only issue of what was intended to be an annual publication.

The Official Records of the Mutiny in The Black Watch. A London Incident of the year 1743. Compiled and edited by H. D. MacWilliam, with an Introduction, notes and illustrations. London: Forster, Groom & Co. Ltd., 1910. cxxviii, 240 pp., portraits, plates. 11"

A Black Watch Episode of the year 1731. Compiled from contemporary records, with Introduction and notes by H. D. MacWilliam. Edinburgh: W. & A. K. Johnston, 1908. ix, 50 pp. 8½"

The Black Watch at Ticonderoga. By Frederick B. Richards. New York [1911]. 98 pp., portraits, plate, map. (Excerpt from Vol. X of the *Proceedings of the New York State Historical Association*). 8½"

The Black Watch in South Africa. [In *The Military History of Perthshire*, 1899-1902; edited by the Marchioness of Tullibardine, 1908, pp. 1-29]. Portraits, plate. 9¾"

2nd Battalion The Black Watch (Royal Highlanders) illustrated. With brief Historical account of the services of the Regiment. Peshawar, India, 1907. Photographs and publication by F. Bremner, Photographer, Lahore. [ii], 44 pp., illustrations. 9½" × 12¼"

With a Highland Regiment in Mesopotamia, 1916-1917. By one of its Officers. [Capt. H. J. Blampied, 2nd Battalion]. Bombay: The Times Press, 1918. xi, 165 pp., portraits, plates. 7¼"

Officers of The Black Watch, 1725 to 1937. [By Lt.-Col. Neil McMicking]. Perth: Thomas Hunter & Sons Ltd., 1937. 81 pp. 11"

———— Revised edition . . . 1725 to 1952. Perth: Thomas Hunter & Sons Ltd., 1953. 95 pp. 11"

———— Vol. 2; being a Roll of all Militia, Volunteer, Reserve, Territorial, Special Reserve, Temporary, Supplementary Reserve, Emergency Commissioned, Short Service and National Service Officers who have served in the Black Watch. Compiled by Major-Gen. Neil McMicking. Perth: Thomas Hunter & Sons Ltd. [1955]. 134 pp. 11"

The Black Watch Tartan. By H. D. MacWilliam. Inverness: " The Northern Chronicle " Office, 1932. 40 pp., portrait. 8½"

The Royal Highland Regiment, The Black Watch, formerly 42nd and 73rd Foot. Medal Roll, 1801-1911. (Compiled by J.S., i.e. Capt. John Stewart). Edinburgh: printed by T. & A. Constable [published by William Brown], 1913. ix, 350 pp., plates. 10"

The Black Watch Museum. Balhousie Castle, Perth. Catalogue of Principal Exhibits. Perth: Printed by D. Leslie [1964]. 36 pp., 6 coloured illustrations. 9¼"

THE OXFORDSHIRE AND
BUCKINGHAMSHIRE LIGHT INFANTRY [43 and 52]

Historical Records of the Forty-Third Regiment, Monmouthshire Light Infantry, with a Roll of the Officers and their Services from the period of embodiment to the close of 1867.   By Sir Richard George Augustus Levinge, Bart.   London: W. Clowes & Sons, 1868.   352 pp.   1 coloured plates of uniform.   10½"

Historical Record of the Fifty-Second Regiment (Oxfordshire Light Infantry) from the year 1755 to the year 1858.   Compiled under Direction of the Committee and edited by W. S. Moorsom, late Captain.   London: Richard Bentley, 1860.   xvii, 437 pp., portraits, plates, plans.   10"
    3 coloured plates of uniform.

The History of Lord Seaton's Regiment (The 52nd Light Infantry) at the Battle of Waterloo; together with various Incidents connected with that Regiment, not only at Waterloo, but also at Paris, in the North of France, and for several years afterwards: to which are added many of the Author's Reminiscences of his Military and Clerical Careers, during a period of more than fifty years.   By the Rev. William Leeke . . who carried the 52nd Regimental Colour at Waterloo. London: Hatchard and Co., 1866.   2 vols., portrait, plans.   8½"

———— Supplement.   1871.   68 pp., plans (also contains 2 pamphlets (8, 10 pp.) of Letters reprinted from the *Army and Navy Gazette*, both printed by Fletcher and Sons, Norwich).

The Story of the Oxfordshire and Buckinghamshire Light Infantry (The old 43rd and 52nd Regiments).   By Sir Henry Newbolt.   London: " Country Life."   1915.   x, 224 pp., portraits, plates, plans, map.   (" Country Life " Series of Military Histories).   9"
    2 coloured plates of uniform.

History of the 43rd and 52nd (Oxfordshire and Buckinghamshire) Light Infantry in the Great War, 1914-1919.   Aldershot: Gale & Polden Ltd., 1938.   Portraits, plates, illustrations, maps.   9¼"
Vol. 1.   The 43rd Light Infantry in Mesopotamia and North Russia.   By Capt. J. E. H. Neville.   No more published.

A Short History of The Oxfordshire and Buckinghamshire Light Infantry, 1741-1922, for the Young Soldiers of the Regiment.   By Lieut.-Col. R. B. Crosse.   Aldershot: printed by Gale & Polden Ltd., 1925, v, 47 pp.   8½"

———— 3rd edition.   1944.   viii, 48 pp.

The Oxfordshire Light Infantry in South Africa.   A Narrative of the Boer War. From the Letters and Journals of Officers of the Regiment, and from other Sources.   Edited by Lieut.-Col. A. F. Mockler-Ferryman.   London: Eyre and Spottiswoode, 1901.   314 pp., portraits, illustrations, maps.   8½"

A Record of H.M. 52nd Light Infantry in 1914.   By Lt.-Col. R. B. Crosse. Warwick: Spennell Press Ltd., 1956.   [6], viii, 139 pp., portraits, plates.   8½"
    Privately published by the author.   200 copies only.

1923. A Record of the Year's Work. By Lt.-Col. R. B. Crosse. Prepared for publication in 1925 and printed with several small additions in 1953. Warwick: Spennell Press Ltd., 1953. 124 pp., portraits, plates. 8½"

A Short History of the Oxfordshire Light Infantry. [Compiled by John Hanbury-Williams]. Wycombe: South Bucks Standard Printing Co. [1892]. 19 pp. 8vo.

An Alphabetical List of the Officers of the Forty-Third, or Monmouthshire Light Infantry from 1800 to 1850. By Henry Stooks Smith. London: Simpkin, Marshall & Co., 1851. ii, 40 pp. 8½"

Medals and Campaigns of the 43rd Foot, now 1st Battalion of the Oxfordshire and Buckinghamshire Light Infantry. By Major William J. Freer. (Reprinted from *The British Numismatic Journal*, vol. 8). London: Harrison & Sons, 1912. 27 pp., plates. 9¼"

Memorial Record of the Seventh (Service) Battalion The Oxfordshire and Buckinghamshire Light Infantry. Compiled and edited by Lieut.-Col. C. Wheeler. With a Foreword by Major-Gen. J. Duncan. Oxford: Basil Black-well. 1921. xxxii, 224 pp., portraits, plates, maps. 8½"

Regimental War Tales, 1741-1914. Told for the Soldiers of the Oxfordshire and Buckinghamshire Light Infantry (The Old 43rd and 52nd). By Lieut.-Col. A. F. Mockler-Ferryman. Oxford: Alden & Co., Ltd., 1915. vi, 253 pp., portraits, plates (1 coloured), maps, illustrations. 6¼"

The 43rd & 52nd Light Infantry Chronicle, 1892; 1893; 1894.
      [continuing as]
The Oxfordshire Light Infantry Chronicle, 1895 (to 1908). An Annual Record of the First and Second Battalions, formerly the 43rd and 52nd Light Infantry.
      [continuing as]
The Oxfordshire and Buckinghamshire Light Infantry Chronicle, An Annual Record, etc., 1909 (to 1957).
      [continuing as]
Chronicle of 1st Green Jackets, 43rd and 52nd and the Oxfordshire and Bucking-hamshire Light Infantry, 1958 (to 1963) [*in progress*]. Various editors and publishers London: Oxford: Aldershot: Exeter. Portraits, plates, illustrations, maps. 8½"

The volumes for 1914-15; 1915-16; 1916-17; 1917-18 and 1918-19 have title . . . together with the War Records of the other Battalions and are lettered on cover *The Great War*, 1-5.
The volumes for 1939-1945 have title . . . The Record of the 43rd, 52nd, 4th, 5th, [6th, 7th, 70th] and 1st Buckinghamshire Battalion in the Second German War. Edited by Lieut.-Col. Sir J. E. H. Neville, Bt.

  Vol. 1. September, 1939-June, 1940.
  Vol. 2. June, 1940-June, 1942.
  Vol. 3. July, 1942-May, 1944.
  Vol. 4. June, 1944-December, 1945.

THE ESSEX REGIMENT   [44 and 56]

Historical Record of The Forty-Fourth, or The East Essex Regiment of Foot. Compiled by Thomas Carter, Adjutant-General's Office. London: W. O. Mitchell, 1864. xxiii, 222 pp., portrait, plates, plan. 8¼″
 1 coloured plate of uniform and 1 of colours.

—— Second edition. Chatham: Gale & Polden, 1887. xxiii, 197 pp. 7″
 1 coloured plate of uniform.

Historical Record of The Fifty-Sixth, or The West Essex Regiment of Foot; containing an Account of the Formation of the Regiment in 1755, and of its subsequent Services to 1844. London: Parker, Furnivall, & Parker, 1844. viii, viii, 62 pp., plates. (Cannon's Historical Records Series). 8¾″
 2 coloured plates of uniform and 1 of colours.

The Essex Regiment. By John Wm. Burrows. Published by arrangement with the Essex Territorial Army Association. Southend-on-Sea: John H. Burrows & Sons, Ltd. Portraits, plates, maps, plans. 8½″

 1st Battalion (44th), 1741-1919. [1923]. xiv, 158 pp., 1 coloured plate. (Essex Units in the War, 1914-1919, Vol. 1)

 —— [2nd edition. 1931]. xxxi, 293 pp., 6 coloured plates, including 3 of colours.

 2nd Battalion (56th) (Pompadours). [1927]. xxvi, 203 pp. (Essex Units in the War, 1914-1919, Vol. 2)
  1 coloured plate of uniform and 1 of colours.

 —— [2nd edition. 1937]. xxviii, 232 pp.

The Essex Regiment, 1929-1950. By Col. T. A. Martin. Brentwood: The Essex Regiment Association. 1952. xx, 668 pp., portraits, plates, maps, end-paper maps. 8½″
 1 coloured plate of formation badges.

A Short History of the 1st and 2nd Battalions The Essex Regiment. With the Names of all those who laid down their lives for their Country, 1914-1918. [Aldershot: printed by Gale & Polden Ltd., 1921]. 50 pp. 7¼″

The Essex Regiment; short history and chronology. By John Wm. Burrows. Southend-on-Sea: John H. Burrows & Son Ltd. [1938]. 40 pp., plates, map. 8½″
 1 coloured plate of colours.

The 1st Battalion Essex Regiment in South Africa, 1899 to 1902. Thayetmo, Burma: Regimental Press, 1908. 38, viii. 8vo.

2nd Battalion The Essex Regiment "The Pompadours," 'D' Day to 'VE' Day in North West Europe. [By Lieut. A. A. Vince]. No imprint [1945]. 54 pp., illustrations, maps. 8″
 Coloured plate of formation badges.

The Essex Regiment. 9th, 10th, 11th, 13th and 15th Battalions. By John Wm. Burrows. Southend-on-Sea: John H. Burrows & Sons Ltd. [1935], xx, 457 pp., portraits, plates, maps. (Essex Units in the War, 1914-1919, Vol. 6). $8\frac{1}{2}$"
   1 coloured plate.

With the 10th Essex in France. By Lt.-Col. T. D. Banks and Capt. R. A. Chell. London: printed and published for the 10th Essex Old Comrades Association by Burt & Sons, 1921. vi, 290 pp., portraits, plates, illustrations. $7\frac{1}{2}$"

——— Second edition. London: Gay & Hancock, 1924. 334 pp.

THE SHERWOOD FORESTERS
(NOTTINGHAMSHIRE & DERBYSHIRE REGIMENT)
[45 and 95]

History of The 1st & 2nd Battalions The Sherwood Foresters, Nottinghamshire and Derbyshire Regiment, 1740-1914. 45th Foot—95th Foot. Compiled by Col. H. C. Wylly. [Frome: printed by Butler & Tanner Ltd.], 1929. 2 vols., portraits, plates, plans, maps. $9\frac{3}{4}$"

The 1st and 2nd Battalions The Sherwood Foresters (Nottinghamshire and Derbyshire Regiment) in the Great War. Compiled by Col. H. C. Wylly. Aldershot: published for the Regimental Committee by Gale & Polden Ltd. [1924]. xv, 224, portrait, plates, plans, maps in end-pocket. $9\frac{3}{4}$"

The History of The Sherwood Foresters (Nottinghamshire and Derbyshire Regiment), 1919-1957. By Brig. C. N. Barclay. Produced under the direction of the Regimental Affairs Committee, The Sherwood Foresters. London: William Clowes & Sons Ltd., 1959. xvi, 182 pp., portrait (coloured), plates, maps. $9\frac{1}{2}$"

A Short History of The Sherwood Foresters (Nottinghamshire and Derbyshire Regiment). Aldershot: Gale & Polden Ltd. [1925]. 23 pp. $7\frac{1}{4}$"
   1 coloured plate of uniform and colours and badge in colour on paper covers.

——— [Another edition]. 1940. 32 pp. No plates. $7\frac{1}{4}$"

——— [Another edition]. 1945. 32 pp. No plates. $7\frac{1}{4}$"

The Sherwood Foresters. A tribute to their own Regiment of which the people of Nottinghamshire and Derbyshire are justly proud. London: Practical Press, 1955. 84 pp. [33 pp. of advertisements], portraits, illustrations. 8"

History of the 45th Nottinghamshire Regiment (Sherwood Foresters). By Col. P. H. Dalbiac. London: Swan, Sonnenschein & Co. Ltd., 1902. viii, 255 pp., plates, plans, maps. $8\frac{1}{2}$"
   1 coloured plate of colours. Also a special edition containing 4 coloured plates of uniform.

History of the 1st Battalion Sherwood Foresters (Notts. and Derby Regt.) in the Boer War, 1899-1902. By Capt. Charles J. L. Gilson. With an Introduction by Lieut.-Gen. Sir H. L. Smith-Dorrien. London: Swan, Sonnenschein & Co. Ltd., 1908. xxiii, 236 pp., portraits, plate, plans, maps in end-pocket. 8½"

South African War Record of the 1st Battalion Sherwood Foresters, Derbyshire Regiment, 1899-1902. Hongkong: printed by Noronha & Co., 1904. 195 pp. 9"

The Derbyshire Campaign Series.

No. 1. The 95th (The Derbyshire) Regiment in the Crimea. By Major H. C. Wylly. With an Introduction by Major-Gen. J. F. Maurice. London: Swan, Sonnenschein & Co. Ltd., 1899. xv, 151 pp., portrait, plans, map. 7½"

No. 2. The 95th (The Derbyshire) Regiment in Central India. By Gen. Sir Julius Raines. With an Introduction by Col. H. D. Hutchinson. London: Swan, Sonnenschein & Co. Ltd., 1900. xv, 90 pp., portrait, plans. 7½"

No. 3. The 2nd Battalion Derbyshire Regiment in Egypt, 1882. By Officers of the Regiment. London: George Allen & Company Ltd., 1914. vii, 68 pp., portraits, maps. 7½"

No. 4. The 2nd Battalion Derbyshire Regiment in the Sikkim Expedition of 1888. By Capt. H. A. Iggulden, with an Introduction by Sir Steuart Bayley. London: Swan, Sonnenschein & Co. Ltd., 1900. xii, 116 pp., maps. 7½"

No. 5. The 2nd Battalion Derbyshire Regiment in Tirah. By Capt. A. K. Slessor. With an Introduction by Brig.-Gen. Sir R. C. Hart. London: Swan, Sonnenschein & Co. Ltd., 1900. xxiii, 187 pp., portrait, plates, maps. 7½"

The Story of the 2nd Battalion The Sherwood Foresters, 1939-1945. By Capt. John W. A. Masters. With a Foreword by Lieut.-Gen. Sir Henry Willcox. Aldershot: Gale & Polden Ltd., 1946. ix, 109 pp., portrait, plates, maps. 8½"

Record of Services of the Officers of the 1st and 2nd Battalions The Sherwood Foresters, Nottinghamshire and Derbyshire Regiment, 45th and 95th, 1741-1931. Compiled by Col. H. C. Wylly. [Duplicated]. [1931]. iv, 210 pp., portraits. 9¾"

Regimental Annual. The Sherwood Foresters, Nottinghamshire and Derbyshire Regiment. 1909-1914; 1920-1938. [Edited by Col. H. C. Wylly & others]. [Various printers]. 1909-38. Portraits, plates. 8½"

The Men from the Greenwood; being the War History of the 11th (Service) Battalion Sherwood Foresters. By Percy Fryer. Nottingham: Cresswell & Oaksford [1920]. 169 pp., portraits, plans, maps. 6¾"

A Short History of The 16th Battalion The Sherwood Foresters (Chatsworth Rifles). By Lieut.-Col. R. F. Truscott. With a Foreword by The Duke of Devonshire. [London: Truscotts]. 288 pp., portraits, plates, maps. 8½"

THE LOYAL REGIMENT (NORTH LANCASHIRE)
[47 and 81]

An Historical Sketch of the 47th (Lancashire) Regiment and of the Campaigns through which they passed. By Major H. G. Purdon. Preston: The Guardian Printing Works, 1907. 227 pp. 9½"

Historical Record of The Eighty-First Regiment, or Loyal Lincoln Volunteers; containing an Account of the Formation of the Regiment in 1793 and of its subsequent Services to 1872. [By S. Rogers]. Gibraltar: printed by the Twenty-Eighth Regimental Press, 1872. [vi], 256 pp., plates. 8½"
  1 coloured plate of uniform and 1 of colours.

The Loyal North Lancashire Regiment. By Col. H. C. Wylly. London: The Royal United Services Institution, 1933. 2 vols., portraits, plates, maps, plans. 9¾"

The Loyal Regiment (North Lancashire), 1919-1953. By Capt. C. G. T. Dean. Preston: Regimental Headquarters, 1955. 329 pp., portraits, plates, maps, end-paper maps. 9"

The Loyals in Malaya; the First Battalion The Loyal Regiment (N.L.) Malaya, Dec. 1958. [By Frank Allen]. Bolton: Tillotsons Newspapers Ltd., 1959. 24 pp., portraits, illustrations. (Reprinted from *The Bolton Journal & Guardian*). 9¾"

A Short History of The Loyal Regiment (North Lancashire). Preston: T. Snape & Co. Ltd., 1946. v, 37 pp., plates, illustrations, sketch maps. 8½"

The Loyal Regiment (North Lancashire) Roll of Honour, 1939-1945. Preston: [printed by T. Snape & Co. Ltd.], 1948. 20 pp. 8½"

The Record of the 11th Battalion of the King's (Liverpool) Regiment subsequently the 15th Battalion of the Loyal North Lancs. Regiment, Pioneers, 14th Light Division. August, 1914-March, 1919. London: R. E. Thomas & Co., printers, 1920. 46 pp., maps. 7"

THE NORTHAMPTONSHIRE REGIMENT [48 and 58]

History of the Northamptonshire Regiment, 1742-1934. By Lieut.-Col. Russell Gurney. Aldershot: Gale & Polden Ltd., 1935, xix, 464 pp., portraits, plates, illustrations, plans, maps. 9¾"
  10 coloured plates, including 3 of uniform and 1 of colours.

The Northamptonshire Regiment, 1914-1918. Compiled under the direction of the Regimental History Committee. Aldershot: Gale & Polden Ltd. [1932]. [vii], 366 pp., map in end-pocket. 8½″

The History of the Northamptonshire Regiment, 1934-1948. Written by Brig. W. J. Jervois on behalf of the Regimental Council. [Northampton]: The Regimental History Committee, 1953. xxiii, 448 pp., portraits, plates, illustrations, maps. 9½″
    4 coloured plates, including 2 of uniform.

The History of the Northamptonshire Regiment, 1948-1960. Compiled under the Direction of the Regimental Council by Lt.-Col. C. J. M. Watts. Northampton: Regimental History Committee, 1963. xiv, 89 pp., portraits, plates, maps. 9½″
    1 coloured plate of uniform and 1 of colours.

A Short History of the Northamptonshire Regiment [compiled by J. D. Wyatt]. London: Gale & Polden Ltd. [1920]. 20 pp. 7″
    1 coloured plate of uniform and coloured reproduction of colours and badge on paper covers.

────── Revised edition. Aldershot, 1933. 48 pp. 7¼″

A Short History of the Northamptonshire Regiment (48th/58th), 1741-1951. [Northampton: J. Stevenson Holt Ltd., printers]. 1951. 11 pp. 6½″

The First Three Months. The Impressions of an Amateur Infantry Subaltern. By E. J. Needham, late Capt. 3rd Battn. Aldershot: Gale & Polden Ltd. [1936]. [xii], 113 pp., plates, maps. 9¾″

Regimental Records of the 58th (Rutlandshire) Regiment, now the 2nd Battalion Northamptonshire Regiment. Compiled by Capt. & Qr.-Mr. Robert Wallace principally from the Official Documents in the Depot. Northampton: printed by Jos. Tebbutt, 1893. 21 pp. 8½″

A Short History of the "58th" Regiment, 1755. The Rutlandshire Regt. 1782. 2nd Battalion The Northamptonshire Regiment, 1881. Lahore: printed by the "Fifty-eighth Press" 1922 [xii], 60, [4] pp. 7″

A History of the 58th, 1939-1945. 2nd Battalion The Northamptonshire Regiment. [By Major R. S. Wallis]. Aldershot: Gale & Polden Ltd. [1947]. xi, 152 pp., plates, maps. 8½″
    1 coloured plate of colours.

────────────

7th (S.) Battalion Northamptonshire Regiment, 1914-1919. By H. B. King, late Captain. Aldershot: Gale & Polden Ltd., 1919. Portraits, plates, maps. 7¼″

History of the Raising of the 7th (Service) Battalion Northamptonshire Regiment (48th and 58th Foot); And its Records from the Formation until it proceeded on Active Service, 14th Sept., 1914-31st August 1915. By Capt. Guy Paget. Aldershot: printed by Gale & Polden Ltd. [1915], 47 pp., illustrations. 7″

THE ROYAL BERKSHIRE REGIMENT
(PRINCESS CHARLOTTE OF WALES'S) [49 and 66]

The Royal Berkshire Regiment (Princess Charlotte of Wales's) 49th-66th Foot. By F. Loraine Petre. Reading: The Barracks, 1925.   2 vols., portraits, plates, plans, maps.   9½″
   Vol. 1 contains 2 coloured plates of uniform.

The History of The Royal Berkshire Regiment (Princess Charlotte of Wales's), 1920-1947. By Brig. Gordon Blight, with a Foreword by Gen. Sir Miles Dempsey. London: Staples Press [1953]. xx, 499 pp., portraits, plates, maps, end-paper maps.   8½″

Notes for Instructors on the History of the 49th and 66th 1st and 2nd Battalions The Royal Berkshire Regiment (Princess Charlotte of Wales's). By Capt. H. Pawle and Capt. V. G. Stokes. [Reading: Bradley & Sons, printers, 1925].   77 pp.   8½″

A Short Regimental History of The Royal Berkshire Regiment (Princess Charlotte of Wales's). From Notes compiled by W. O. J. E. Perry [Reading: Bradley & Son Ltd., 1939].   39 pp.   8½″

The 66th Berkshire Regiment. A Brief History of its Services at Home and Abroad, from 1758 to 1881. Compiled from the Regimental Records, and other MSS., by J. Percy Groves. Reading: Joseph J. Beecroft, 1887.   viii, 159 pp., plate.   7¼″

The Fighting Tenth. A Short History of the 10th Battalion, The Royal Berkshire Regiment, 1940 to 1944. By David R. C. West. With a Foreword by Lieut.-Col. G. H. Sawyer, 10th Royal Berks Reunion Committee. [Marlborough: printed by J. W. Gale, 1950].   63 pp., portrait, plate, sketch maps.   8½″

THE QUEEN'S OWN ROYAL WEST KENT REGIMENT
[50 and 97]

The History of the 50th or (The Queen's Own) Regiment from the earliest date to the year 1881. By Col. [A.] Fyler. London: Chapman and Hall Ltd., 1895. xviii, 380 pp., plates, illustrations, plans, maps.   9″
   2 coloured plates of uniform and 2 of colours.

The Queen's Own Royal West Kent Regiment, 1881-1914. By Lt.-Col. H. D. Chaplin. Maidstone: Regimental History Committee, 1959.   xvii, 174 pp., maps, plate.   8⅞″

The Queen's Own Royal West Kent Regiment, 1914-1919. By C. T. Atkinson, late Captain, Oxford University O.T.C. London: Simpkin, Marshall, Hamilton, Kent & Co. Ltd., 1924.   xxviii, 629 pp., portraits, plate, maps.   8½″

The Queen's Own Royal West Kent Regiment, 1920-1950. [By] Lieut.-Col. H. D. Chaplin. London: Michael Joseph. [1954]. 510 pp., portraits, plates, maps, end-paper maps. 9″

The Queen's Own Royal West Kent Regiment, 1951-1961. [By] Lieut.-Col. H. D. Chaplin. The Regimental Museum Committee. [Maidstone: printed by *The Kent Messenger*, 1964]. xvii, 168 pp., portraits, plates, maps. 9½″

A Short History of The Queen's Own (Royal West Kent Regiment). London: Gale & Polden Ltd. [1920]. 23 pp. 7¼″
    1 coloured plate of uniform & colours and badge in colour on paper covers.

A Short History of The Queen's Own Royal West Kent Regiment. Maidstone: "Kent Messenger," 1930. [iv], 64 pp. 8½″

The Queen's Own Royal West Kent Regiment. A Short Account of its Origins, Service & Campaigns, 1756-1956. By Lieut.-Col. H. D. Chaplin. Maidstone: Kent Messenger, 1956. 47 pp., sketch maps. 8½″

A Short History of the Queen's Own Royal West Kent Regiment. By Brig. N. I. Whitty. No imprint, 1949. 12 pp., illustrations. 5¼″

" Invicta." With the First Battalion The Queen's Own Royal West Kent Regiment in the Great War. By Major C. V. Molony. London: Nisbit & Co. Ltd. [1923]. xi, 326 pp., portraits, plates, maps. 8½″

2nd Battalion The Queen's Own Royal West Kent Regiment. Ballykinlar, Ireland. [Aldershot: Gale & Polden Ltd., 1924]. 20 pp., portraits, plates. 7¼″×9¾″
    Souvenir album containing reproductions of photographs.

A Short Record of the Colours of The Queen's Own Royal West Kent Regiment. By Capt. H. N. Edwards. No imprint, 1933. 38 pp., illustrations. (Reprinted, from the *Queen's Own Gazette*). 8½″

The Queen's Own Royal West Kent Regiment. 50th (The Queen's Own)—97th (The Earl of Ulster's) Medal Roll. Part One, 1793-1881. [Compiled by Lieut. H. N. Edwards]. Published by The Queen's Own Relics Fund as a Supplement to the " *Queen's Own Gazette*." No imprint [1928]. 66 pp., plate. 11″

The History of the Eighth Battalion The Queen's Own Royal West Kent Regiment, 1914-1919. [By Lieut.-Col. H. J. Wenyon & Major H. S. Brown]. London: Hazell, Watson & Viney Ltd., privately printed, 1921. xiii, 286 pp., portraits, plates, maps. 8½″

The History of the 11th (Lewisham) Battalion The Queen's Own Royal West Kent Regiment. Written and compiled by Capt. R. O. Russell, with Foreword by Lieut.-Gen. Sir Sidney T. B. Lawford and Messages from Brig.-Gen. F. W. Towsey and Lieut.-Col. A. C. Corfe. London: Lewisham Newspaper Co. Ltd., 1934. xvi, 259 pp., portrait, plates, illustrations, maps. 9¾″

THE KING'S OWN YORKSHIRE LIGHT INFANTRY
[51 and 105]

A Record of the Services of the Fifty-First (Second West York), The " King's Own Light Infantry " Regiment. With a List of Officers from 1755 to 1870. By W. Wheater. London: Longmans, Green and Co., 1870. iv, 277 pp. 9″

Historical Records of the One Hundred and Fifth Regiment of Light Infantry. Meerut: Printing Press 105th L.I., October 1871. 49 pp. 7¾″

History of The King's Own Yorkshire Light Infantry. By Col. H. C. Wylly. London: Percy Lund, Humphries & Co. Ltd. [1926]. 2 vols., portraits, plates, plans, maps. 8½″
  Vol. 1 contains 3, and vol. 2, 1 coloured portraits.

———— Vol. 3. With title: History . . . Infantry in the Great War, 1914-1918. By Lt.-Col. Reginald C. Bond. [1930]. xviii, [351] pp. 8½″

———— Vol. 4. A Register of Officers who have served on a Regular Commission in the Regiment since its formation on the 19th December, 1755, until the end of the War on the 15th August, 1945. By Gen. Sir Charles P. Deedes. [1946]. 247 pp., portraits. 8½″

———— Vol. 5. With title: Never Give Up. The History . . . Infantry, 1919-1942. By Lieut.-Col. Walter Hingston, 1950. xvi, 243 pp., portraits, plates, illustrations, sketch maps. 8½″

———— Vol. 6. 1939-1948. By Brig. G. F. Ellenberger. Aldershot: Gale & Polden Ltd., 1961. xvi, 184 pp., maps. 8½″

Short History and Traditions of The King's Own Yorkshire Light Infantry. London: Gale & Polden Ltd. [1920]. 32 pp. 7¼″
  Coloured plate of uniform and colours and badge in colour on paper covers.

A Short History of The King's Own Yorskhire Light Infantry, 1755-1928. Pontefract: printed by W. McGowan, 1929. 30 pp., portrait, plate. 7¼″

———— Another edition . . . 1755-1947. Pontefract: The McGowan Press Ltd. [1947]. [4], 36 pp., portrait, plate. 7¼″

The King's Own Yorkshire Light Infantry. London: Hutchinson & Co. (Publishers) Ltd. [1941]. 94 pp. (The Roll of the Drum Histories of the Regiments of the British Army; edited by Wolmer Whyte). 7½″

————————

A Brief History of the 12th Bn. King's Own Yorkshire Light Infantry (Pioneers) " The Miners' Battalion." By Capt. R. Ede England. [Wakefield: printed by John Lindley Ltd.], n.d. 143 pp., portraits, plates, maps. 8½″
  2 coloured plates of badges.

THE KING'S SHROPSHIRE LIGHT INFANTRY   [53 and 85]

Historical Record of The Fifty-Third, or The Shropshire Regiment of Foot; containing an Account of the Formation of the Regiment in 1755, and of its subsequent Services to 1848.   Compiled by Richard Cannon, Esq., Adjutant-General's Office, Horse Guards.   London: Parker, Furnivall, & Parker, 1849. xxxv, 69 pp., plates.   8½"
   1 coloured plate of uniform and 1 of colours.

Historical Records of the 53rd (Shropshire) Regiment, now the 1st Battalion The King's (Shropshire L.I.), from the Formation of the Regiment in 1755 down to 1889.   Compiled and edited by Col. W. Rogerson, from the Orderly Room Records.   London: Simpkin, Marshall, Hamilton, Kent & Co. [1890].   xxii, 248 pp., portraits, plates.   8½"
   4 coloured plates, including 3 of uniform and 1 of colours.

The Eighty-Fifth King's Light Infantry (now 2nd Battn. The King's Shropshire Light Infantry).   By " One of Them."   Edited by C. R. B. Barrett.   London: Spottiswoode & Co. Ltd., 1913.   xx, 551 pp., portraits, plates, illustrations, maps. 9¾"
   11 coloured plates of uniform.

The History of The King's Shropshire Light Infantry in the Great War, 1914-1918.   Edited by Major W. de B. Wood.   London: The Medici Society Ltd., 1925.   xvi, 471 pp., maps.   8½"

A Short History of The King's Shropshire Light Infantry (53rd and 85th Foot). Aldershot: Gale & Polden Ltd. [1920].   28 pp.   7¼"

——— [Another edition] . . . 1755-1955.   32 pp.   7¼"

The King's Shropshire Light Infantry, 1755-1955.   No imprint.   24 pp., portrait, plates.   10"
   1 coloured plate of colours.

History of the 2nd Battalion The King's Shropshire Light Infantry (85th Foot) in N.W. Europe, 1944-1945.   By Major G. L. Y. Radcliffe assisted by Capt. R. Sale.   Oxford: Basil Blackwell, 1947.   [6], 96 pp., maps.   8¾"

An Alphabetical List of the Officers of the Eighty-Fifth Bucks Volunteers, The King's Light Infantry Regiment, from 1800 to 1850.   By Henry Stooks Smith. London: Simpkin, Weaver & Co., 1851.   xii, 56 pp.   8½"

Regimental Colours, their Origin and History; together with Notes on the Colours of the 1st and 2nd Bns. The King's Shropshire Light Infantry.   By Col. L. H. Torin.   [Shrewsbury: Livesey Ltd., 1946].   31 pp.   7¼"

The King's Shropshire Light Infantry.   Special Supplement [to the Regimental Journal] to commemorate the Presentation of Colours to the First Battalion by Field Marshal Sir John Harding, at Göttingen, Germany, 15th October 1954. No imprint [Shrewsbury], 1955.   20 pp., portraits, illustrations.   9¾"
   2 coloured plates of colours.

THE MIDDLESEX REGIMENT
(DUKE OF CAMBRIDGE'S OWN) [57 and 77]

Historical Records of the Fifty-Seventh, or, West Middlesex Regiment of Foot, compiled from Official and Private Sources, from the Date of its Formation in 1755, to the Present Time, 1878.   With Preface and Epitome, together with the Services of the Honorary Colonels and Lieutenant-Colonels Commanding, and Appendix by the Editor.   Edited by Lieut.-Gen. H. J. Warre.   London: W. Mitchell & Co., 1878.   xl, 304 pp., plates. $8\frac{1}{2}''$
   2 coloured plates, 1 of colours.

History of the Fifty-Seventh (West Middlesex) Regiment of Foot, 1755-1881. Compiled from Official and other Sources.   By H. H. Woollright, Capt.   London Richard Bentley and Son, 1893.   xxiii, 406 pp., portraits, plates, maps. $8\frac{3}{4}''$
   4 coloured plates of uniform.

Records of the Seventy-Seventh (East Middlesex), The Duke of Cambridge's Own Regiment of Foot, now the Second Battalion The Duke of Cambridge's Own (Middlesex Regiment).   Compiled from Official and other Sources.   By Major H. H. Woollright.   London: Gale & Polden Ltd. [1907].   xviii, 191 pp., portraits, plates. $8\frac{1}{2}''$

The Story of The Duke of Cambridge's Own (Middlesex Regiment).   By Charles Lethbridge Kingsford.   London: " Country Life" [1916].   xiv, 244 pp., portraits, plates, illustrations, maps.   (" Country Life " Series of Military Histories). $9''$
   1 coloured plate of uniform.

The Die-Hards in the Great War.   A History of the Duke of Cambridge's Own (Middlesex Regiment), 1914-1919.   Compiled from the Records of the Line, Special Reserve, Service and Territorial Battalions.   By Everard Wyrall.   London: Harrison & Sons Ltd. [1926-30].   2 vols., plans, maps. $8\frac{1}{2}''$

The Middlesex Regiment (Duke of Cambridge's Own), 1919-1952.   Compiled under the direction of a Regimental Committee.   Written and edited by Lieut.-Commdr. P. K. Kemp.   With a Foreword by Lieut.-Gen. Sir Brian G. Horrocks. Aldershot: Gale & Polden Ltd., 1956.   xvi, 462 pp., portraits, illustrations, maps. $8\frac{1}{2}''$

A Short History of the Middlesex Regiment (Duke of Cambridge's Own). Aldershot: Gale & Polden Ltd. [1921].   30 pp. $7\frac{1}{4}''$
   1 coloured plate of uniform and colours and badge in colour on paper covers.

———— Reprint, without plate etc.   n.d.   31 pp.

The Die-Hards; the Story of the Middlesex Regiment.   London: Hutchinson & Co. (Publishers) Ltd. [1941].   86 pp.   (The Roll of the Drum; Histories of the Regiments of the British Army; edited by Wolmer Whyte). $7\frac{1}{2}''$

Our County Regiment. The Duke of Cambridge's Own Middlesex Regiment, " The Die-Hards "; its history—1755-1915; being the Battle Story of the 57th and 77th Regiments of the Line and their Militias, Special Reserve, Volunteer and Territorial Battalions. Compiled by Col. Sir Reginald Hennell. London: Cadet Publications Ltd., 1915. 40 pp., portraits.   8½"

Some Reminiscences of the " Die-Hards " (57th West Middlesex Regiment). By Sergeant-Major E. Bezar. Dunedin, N.Z.: Mills Dick & Co., 1891. 105 pp.   7"

Jottings in the Jungle, being Notes taken on the line of march of the 2nd Battalion Duke of Cambridge's Own Middlesex Regiment from Kamptee to Mhow. January 24th to March 6th, 1890. [Simla: printed at the A.T.A. Press, 1890]. 101 pp., plates.   8½"

Second Battalion, The Middlesex Regiment (D.C.O.). Campaign in N.W. Europe, June 6th, 1944-May 7th, 1945. By Major R. B. Moberley. Cairo: R. Schindler, 1946. Portraits, plate, sketch maps.   7½"

The 16th (Public Schools) Service Battalion (The Duke of Cambridge's Own) Middlesex Regiment and the Great War, 1914-18. A Short History of the Battalion from its Formation to Disbandment, compiled from Official Records, contemporary newspapers, extracts from " The Die-Hards in the Great War " by Everard Wyrall, " How I filmed the War " by Lieut. Geoffrey Malins . . . and from numerous diaries, maps, photographs, letters and other documents . . . By H. W. Wallis Grain, formerly Orderly Room Sergeant. [London: printed by F. P. Lewingdon, 26 & 27 Evershott St., N.W.1, 1935]. 105 pp., plates, maps.   8½"

THE KING'S ROYAL RIFLE CORPS   [60]

The Annals of The King's Royal Rifle Corps. London: Smith, Elder & Co. (Smith, Elder & Co., vols. 1, 2 and Appendix; John Murray, vols. 3-5), 1913; 23; 26; 29; 32. Portraits, plates, maps, plans.   9½"

   Vol. 1. "The Royal Americans"; by Lewis Butler, formerly Capt.   (Including 1 coloured plate of flag).
   Vol. 2. " The Green Jacket "; by Lieut.-Col. Lewis Butler.
   Vol. 3. The K.R.R.C.; by Lieut.-Col. Lewis Butler.
   Vol. 4. The K.R.R.C.; by Major-Gen. Sir Steuart Hare.
   Vol. 5. The Great War; by Major-Gen. Sir Steuart Hare (1 coloured portrait).

Appendix dealing with Uniform, Armament and Equipment. By S. M. Milne and Major-Gen. Astley Terry. (incl. 25 coloured plates of uniform, 1 of colours and 11 plates of badges).

Swift and Bold. The Story of The King's Royal Rifle Corps in the Second World War, 1939-1945. Editors: Major-Gen. Sir Hereward Wake, Bt., Major W. P. Deedes. Aldershot: Gale & Polden Ltd., 1949. xvi, 416 pp., portraits, plates, maps.   8½"

A Brief History of The King's Royal Rifle Corps, 1755 to 1915. Compiled and edited by Lieut.-Gen. Sir Edward Hutton. 2nd edition. [Winchester: Warren and Son Ltd.], 1917. 84 pp., maps. $8\frac{3}{4}''$
    The 1st edition was issued in 1912 being Reprinted by permission from *The King's Royal Rifle Corps Chronicle* of 1911. (Winchester, 52 pp.)

—— Third edition . . . 1755 to 1948. Compiled and edited by the Historical Committee of the Celer et Audax Club. Aldershot: Gale & Polden Ltd., 1948. x, 115 pp., portrait, plates, maps. $8\frac{1}{2}''$
    5 coloured plates of uniform.

The Old Sixtieth. The Story of The King's Royal Rifle Corps. London: Hutchinson & Co. (Publishers) Ltd. 1941. 96 pp. (The Roll of the Drum Histories of the Regiments of the British Army; edited by Wolmer Whyte). $7''$

The Battle Honours of The King's Royal Rifle Corps, 1755-1918. Compiled and edited by Capt. T. N. F. Wilson. Winchester: Warren and Son Ltd.,1927. 72 pp., map. $9\frac{3}{4}'' \times 7\frac{1}{2}''$

The Royal Americans. By Richard Walden Hale, Jr. Ann Arbor; The William L. Clements Library, 1944. 28 pp., plate. $8''$

A Regimental Chronicle and List of Officers of The 60th, or The King's Royal Rifle Corps, formerly The 62nd, or The Royal American Regiment of Foot. By Nesbit Willoughby Wallace, Capt. London: Harrison, 1879. viii, 312 pp., errata leaf, portraits, plates. $9\frac{3}{4}''$
    Including 8 coloured plates of uniform, etc., and 1 of colours.

Celer et Audax; its Origin as the Motto of the King's Royal Rifle Corps. By Major-Gen. Gibbes Rigaud. Oxford: E. Pickard Hall, M.A., and J. H. Stacy, printers to the University, 1882. 20 pp. $7\frac{1}{4}''$

Schweizer Offiziere als Indianerkrieger und Instruktoren der englischen leichten Infanterie. Von Prof. Dr. A. Lätt. Zürich; Kommissionsverlag Beer & Co., 1933. 46 pp., portraits, illustrations, plans, map [125. Neujahrsblatt der Feuerwerker Gesellschaft (Artillerie-Kollegium) in Zürich]. $10\frac{1}{4}''$

Celer et Audax. A Sketch of the Services of the Fifth Battalion Sixtieth Regiment (Rifles) during the twenty years of their existence. By Major-Gen. Gibbes Rigaud. Oxford: E. Pickard Hall, M.A., and J. H. Stacy, printers to the University. 1879. xv, 291 pp., portraits, map. $7\frac{1}{4}''$

The King's Royal Rifle Corps Chronicle, 1901-64, [*in progress*]. Winchester: Warren & Son, The Wykeham Press [volumes for 1903-1958]; London: Jordan-Gaskell Ltd. [and others 1959 onwards]. Portraits, plates, maps. 1904-65. $8\frac{1}{2}''$

A Short History of the 20th Battalion King's Royal Rifle Corps (B.E.L. Pioneers), 1915-1919. By Capt. A. S. Turberville. Hull: Goddard, Walker & Brown Ltd., 1923, viii, 143 pp. $8\frac{1}{2}''$

THE WILTSHIRE REGIMENT (DUKE OF EDINBURGH'S)
[62 and 99]

The Story of The Wiltshire Regiment (Duke of Edinburgh's); the 62nd and 99th Foot (1756-1959), the Militia and the Territorials, the Service Battalions and all those others who have served or been affiliated with The Moonrakers.   By Col. N. C. E. Kenrick, with a Foreword by The Colonel-in-Chief, H.R.H. The Duke of Edinburgh.   Aldershot: Gale & Polden Ltd., 1963.   xi, 324 pp., portrait, plates, maps, end-paper maps.   8½″
   3 coloured plates of uniform.

A Short History of the Wiltshire Regiment (Duke of Edinburgh's) (62nd and 99th Foot) from 1756 to 1918.   By Lieut.-Col. R. M. T. Gillson.   London: Gale & Polden Ltd. [1921].   43 pp., portraits, plates.   7¼″
   3 coloured plates of uniform, colours and badge in colours on paper cover.

   ———— from 1756 to 1936.   Aldershot [1936].   [4],   46 pp., portraits, plates (as before).   7¼″

"The Wiltshire Regiment for Wiltshire."   By W. W. Ravenhill, Honorary Secretary of the Wiltshire Society.   (Read before the Society at Salisbury, August, 1876).   [Devizes: H. F. & E. Bull, 1876].   43 pp.   A Short History of the 62nd Regt.   8½″

Historical Retrospect of the Wiltshire Regt., etc. [signed H.M.C., i.e., Harry M. Carter].   Aldershot: Gale & Polden Ltd. [1899].   12 pp.   7¼″

The Springers.   By H. M. C. [i.e., H. M. Carter].   Dublin: William Carson [1891].   [78] pp.   8″
   A Collection of articles: The Springers—Carrickfergus—The 62nd in Sicily and Italy—The 62nd in the West Indies—The Six and Twos.

2nd Battn. The Wiltshire Regiment (Duke of Edinburgh's).   Centenary, Bangalore, India, 1924.   [Aldershot: Gale & Polden Ltd., 1924].   32 pp., portraits, plates.   7¼″×9¾″
   Souvenir album, containing Short History, with reproductions of photographs.

The 2nd Battalion Wiltshire Regiment (99th).   A Record of their Fighting in the Great War, 1914-18.   By Major W. S. Shepherd.   Aldershot: Gale & Polden Ltd., 1927.   [8], 182 pp., maps.   8½″

THE MANCHESTER REGIMENT [63 and 96]

The History of the late 63rd (West Suffolk) Regiment. By Major James Slack. London: The Army and Navy Co-operative Society Ltd., printers, 1886. xvi, 263 pp. 8½"

History of The Manchester Regiment (late the 63rd and 96th Foot). Compiled by Col. H. C. Wylly, with illustrations by Gerald C. Hudson. London: Forster Groom & Co. Ltd., 1923-25. Portraits, plates, maps and maps in end-pocket. 9¾"

Vol. 1 contains 7 coloured plates, including 5 of uniform and 2 of colours.

Vol. 2 contains 4 coloured plates of uniform.

The Manchesters. A History of the Regular, Militia, Special Reserve, Territorial, and New Army Battalions since their formation; with a Record of the Officers now serving and the Honours and Casualties of the War of 1914-16. Compiled by Capt. G. L. Campbell. London: Picture Advertising Co., Ltd., 1916. 179 pp. 7"

History of the Manchester Regiment. First and Second Battalions 1922-1948. By Lieut.-Commdr. A. C. Bell. Altrincham: John Sherratt and Son, 1954. xx, 554 pp., portraits, plates, maps. 8½"

A Short History of the Manchester Regiment (Regular Battalions). By Col. H. C. Wylly. 3rd edition. Aldershot: Gale & Polden Ltd. [1933]. 32 pp. 7¼" Colours and badge in colour on paper cover.

———— 4th revised edition. Aldershot, 1950. 43 pp. 7¼"

The Manchester Regiment. London: Hutchinson & Co. (Publishers) Ltd. [1941]. 95 pp. (The Roll of the Drum Histories of the Regiments of the British Army; edited by Wolmer Whyte). 7¼"

Diary of Siege of Ladysmith. 1st Battalion, Manchester Regiment. 31st October 1899-28th February, 1900. No imprint. 12 pp. 7"

Rough Diary of the Doings of the 1st Battn. Manchester Regt. during the South African War, 1899 to 1902. Compiled by Major A. W. Marden and Capt. and Adjt. W. P. E. Newbigging. Manchester: John Haywood [1902]. 151 pp., plans. 7¼"

Records of the 2nd Battalion The Manchester Regiment, formerly 96th Foot. Compiled for use of Non-Commissioned Officers and Men of the Battalion. No imprint [1899]. 40 pp. 4¾"

Sixteenth; Seventeenth; Eighteenth; Nineteenth Battalions The Manchester Regiment (First City Brigade). A Record 1914-1918. Manchester: Sherratt & Hughes, 1923. xvi, 357 pp., portraits, maps. 8½″

Manchester City Battalions of the 90th & 91st Infantry Brigades. Book of Honour. Edited by Brig.-Gen. F. Kempster and Brig.-Gen. H. C. E. Westropp. London: Sherratt & Hughes, 1917. xxxviii, 922, 56 pp., portraits, plates. 9¾″
  16th-23rd Battalions The Manchester Regiment.

The 21st Battalion of the Manchester Regiment; a History. By a Committee of Old Members of the Regiment. Manchester: Sherratt & Hughes, 1934. v, 141 pp., plates. 8¾″

The Oldham Battalion of Comrades (24th Battalion Manchester Regiment) Book of Honour. Edited by Alderman Herbert Wilde. London: Sherratt & Hughes, 1920. 106, 48 pp., portraits. 10″

THE NORTH STAFFORDSHIRE REGIMENT
(THE PRINCE OF WALES'S)   [64 and 98]

Memoirs of the Services of the 64th Regiment (Second Staffordshire), 1758 to 1881. By H. G. Purdon. London: W. H. Allen & Co. [1883]. 112 pp., plates. 8½″
  3 coloured plates of uniform.

An Historical Sketch of the 64th (Second Staffordshire) Regiment, and of the Campaigns through which they passed. By Major H. G. Purdon. [Preston: The Guardian Works, 1915]. 242, [4] pp. 8½″
  To 1881 only, re-written.

A Short History of the Prince of Wales's (North Staffordshire Regt.). London: Gale & Polden Ltd., 1920. 20 pp. 7¼″
  Coloured plate of uniform, colours and badge in colour on paper cover.

History of The 1st & 2nd Battalions The North Staffordshire Regiment (The Prince of Wales's), 1914-1923. Longton, Staffs.: Hughes & Harber Ltd. [1933]. [7], 120 pp., portraits, plans, maps. 10″

Second Battalion The Prince of Wales' North Staffordshire Regiment (late 98th Foot). Illustrated. With brief historical Account of the Services of the Battalion. Mooltan, India, 1908. Lahore: F. Bremner [1908]. 42 pp., portraits, illustrations. 14½″×9½″

The North Staffordshire Regiment (The Prince of Wales's); a short history, 1756-1945. Hednesford; 1948. iv, 20 pp., portrait, illustrations, map. 8vo.

The History of the 7th (Ser.) Bn. Prince of Wales's (North Staffordshire Regiment), 1914-1919. By L. R. Missen (late Capt. and Adjt.). Cambridge: W. Heffer & Sons Ltd., 1920. ix, 140 pp., portraits, maps. 7½″

History of the 8th North Staffords. Longton, Staffs.: Hughes & Harber Ltd., 1921. 111 pp., portraits, plates, maps. 10″

THE YORK AND LANCASTER REGIMENT [65 and 84]

Memoirs of The 65th Regiment, 1st Battn. The York and Lancaster Regt., 1756 to 1913. Edited by Lieut.-Col. E. C. Broughton. London: William Clowes & Sons Ltd., 1914. xi, 174 pp., portraits, illustrations. 10″

The York and Lancaster Regiment, 1758-1919. 65th Foot—84th Foot. By Col. H. C. Wylly. [Frome & London: printed by Butler & Tanner Ltd.], 1930. 2 vols., portraits, plates, plans, maps. 9¾″

———— Vol. 3. . . . 1919-1953. By Major O. F. Sheffield. Aldershot: Gale & Polden Ltd., 1956. xv, 297 pp., portraits, plates, maps. 9¾″

A Concise History of The York and Lancaster Regiment. By A. Payne. Bristol: J. W. Arrowsmith, Ltd., 1922. viii, 51 pp., plates, illustrations. 8½″
    2 coloured plates of colours.

A Short History of the York and Lancaster Regiment, 1758 to 1946. Pontefract: The McGowan Press, 1946. 16 pp. 8½″

———— 1758 to 1960. No imprint, 1960. 20 pp. 8½″

War Record of the York and Lancaster Regiment, 1900-1902. From Regimental and Private Sources. By A. H. C. Kearsey. With a Preface by Col. Kirkpatrick. Illustrated with photographs and sketches by H. R. Headlam and E. Cooke. London: George Bell & Sons, 1903. x, 277 pp., portraits, plates, illustrations, maps. 8¼″

Roll of the Officers of The York and Lancaster Regiment, containing a Complete Record of their Services, including dates of commission, &c. By Major G. A. Raikes. The First Battalion, formerly 65th (2nd Yorkshire, North Riding) Regiment, from 1756 to 1884. London: Richard Bentley & Son, 1885. xvi, 135 pp. 8½″

———— The Second Battalion, formerly The Royal Highland Emigrants (1775-1783) late 84th (York and Lancaster) Regiment, from 1758 to 1884. London: Richard Bentley & Son, 1885. xvi, 160 pp. 8½″

Roll of the Officers of The (84th) York and Lancaster Regiment, containing A Record of their Services, including dates of commission; to which is added the Officers' Medal Roll for the Peninsular War, and a Short Account of the Colours used by the Battalion from 1759-1910. This Roll was Compiled by Major G. A. Raikes in 1885, and revised, enlarged, and brought up to June, 1910, by Capt. R. E. Key. London: William Clowes & Sons Ltd., 1910. xx, 233 pp., portraits, plate. 8½″

————————————

History of the 7th Service Battalion The York and Lancaster Regiment (Pioneers), 1914-1919. [By Capt. M. T. Gilvary]. London: The Talbot Press Ltd., 1921. viii, 131 pp., portraits, maps. 8½″

A History of the 9th (Service) Battalion The York and Lancaster Regiment, 1914-19. [By J. B. Montagu]. Duplicated [1934]. [4], 110 pp. 10½″

History of the 12th Service Battalion York and Lancaster Regiment. By Richard A. Sparling. [Sheffield: printed by J. W. Northend Ltd., 1920]. xv, 143 [6] pp., portraits, plates. 8¾″

THE DURHAM LIGHT INFANTRY   [68 and 106]

The Durham Light Infantry. By the Hon. W. L. Vane, Lieut.-Col. London: Gale & Polden Ltd., 1914. xii, 334 pp., portrait, plates. 9¾″

The D.L.I. at War. The History of the Durham Light Infantry, 1939-1945. By Major David Rissik. Brancepeth Castle: The Depot of the D.L.I. [1953]. xvi, 352 pp., portraits, plates, maps. 8½″

Faithful; the Story of the Durham Light Infantry. By S. G. P. Ward. London: Thomas Nelson & Sons Ltd. [1963]. xx, 574 pp., portrait (coloured), maps. 9¾″

A Short Record of the Durham Light Infantry, from 1758 to 1894. By Lieut.-Col. W. Gordon, Commanding 1st Battalion. Devonport: A. H. Swiss, 1894. 47 pp. 8½″

A Short History of The Durham Light Infantry (1st and 2nd Battalions). Aldershot: Gale & Polden Ltd., 1938. 3rd edition (revised). 33 pp. 7¼″

The Story of the Durham Light Infantry. By Capt. E. W. Short. Newcastle-upon-Tyne: J. & P. Bealls Ltd. [1946]. 32 pp., plates. 7¼″
  1 coloured plate of colours.

Durham Light Infantry, 2nd Battalion. A record of the services of the Battalion, to which is added a reproduction of photographs including every man in the Corps, and other views, specially taken at Poona, India, February, 1897. Lt.-Col. F. H. Whitby, Commanding. Made by The Historical Publishing Co., Philadelphia, Pa., U.S.A., published by C. B. Burrows, care of Wm. Watson & Co., Bombay and London [1897]. 105, 11 pp., portraits, plates. 11″ × 13½″

The Durham Forces in the Field, 1914-1918. By Capt. Wilfrid Miles. Vol. 2. The Service Battalions of the Durham Light Infantry. London: Cassell and Co. Ltd., 1920. xii, 380 pp., portraits, plates, maps. 8½″
  No more published.

War History of the 18th (S.) Battalion Durham Light Infantry. By Lieut.-Col. W. D. Lowe. With a Foreword by Lieut.-Col. H. Bowes. London: Humphry Milford, Oxford Univ. Press, 1920. xix, 205 pp., plates, map in end-pocket. 8½″

The History of the locally raised 20th (Service) Battalion Durham Light Infantry. Sunderland: R. Youll, printer [1920].   65 pp., portraits, map.   9¾"

The History of the 16th Battalion the Durham Light Infantry, 1940-1946.   By Major Laurence E. Stringer.   [Graz, Austria: printed at the "Styria," 1946]. 79, [8] pp., maps.   9"

THE HIGHLAND LIGHT INFANTRY
(CITY OF GLASGOW REGIMENT)   [71 and 74]

Regimental Records of the Highland Light Infantry (old 71st and 74th).   [Glasgow: printed by John Horn, Ltd., 1914].   158 pp.   4¾"

Proud Heritage. The Story of the Highland Light Infantry.   By Lt.-Col. L. B. Oatts.   4 vols., vols. 1, 2 London: Thomas Nelson & Sons Ltd., vols. 3, 4. Glasgow: House of Grant Ltd., 1953-63.   9"

Vol. 1.   The 71st H.L.I., 1777-1881.   1953.   4 coloured plates of uniform.

Vol. 2.   The 74th Highlanders, 1787-1882.   1959.   5 coloured plates including 2 of uniform.

Vol. 3.   The Regular, Militia, Volunteer, T.A. and Service Battalions H.L.I., 1882-1918.   1961.   4 coloured plates, including 3 of uniform.

Vol 4.   The Regular, Territorial, and Service Battalions H.L.I. and the H.L.I. of Canada, 1919-1959.   1963.

Historical Record of The Seventy-First Regiment, Highland Light Infantry; containing an Account of the Formation of the Regiment in 1777, and of its subsequent Services to 1852.   Compiled by Richard Cannon, Esq., Adjutant-General's Office, Horse Guards.   London: printed by George E. Eyre and William Spottiswoode for H.M. Stationery Office: published by Parker, Furnivall & Parker, 1852.   xix, xvi, 196 pp., plates.   8¾"
1 coloured plate of uniform and 1 of colours.

Historical Record of the 71st Regiment, Highland Light Infantry, 1777-1876. By Lieut. Henry J. T. Hildyard.   London: Harrison & Son, 1876.

Historical Record of The Seventy-Fourth Regiment (Highlanders); containing an Account of the Formation of the Regiment in 1787, and of its subsequent Services to 1850.   Compiled by Richard Cannon, Esq., Adjutant-General's Office, Horse Guards.   London: Parker, Furnivall & Parker, 1850.   xl., 146 pp., plates.   8¾"
2 coloured plates of uniform and 1 of colours.

Historical Records of The 74th Highlanders (now 2nd Battalion Highland Light Infantry), from 1787 to 1887. (From Official and other Authentic Sources). Illustrated with engraved portraits of past and present Officers, Colours, etc. London and Dumfries: James MacVeigh, 1887. (The Centenary Memorial). pp. 603-651, [3], of *A History of the Scottish Highlands, Highland Clans and Highland Regiments;* edited by J. S. Keltie, with a new title-page.   10$\frac{3}{4}$″
  Coloured plate of colours.

The 2nd Battalion Highland Light Infantry in the Great War. Compiled by Major A. D. Telfer-Smollett, Major C. J. Wallace, Capt. H. Ross Skinner. Glasgow: John Horn Ltd. [1929].   154, xxviii pp., portraits, plates, plans, maps.   7$\frac{1}{4}$″

Early Days of the 74th Highland Regiment (later 2nd Battalion, The Highland Light Infantry), 1787-1805.   Compiled by Col. John Grahame, of Lingo Largo-ward, Fife.   Printed [i.e. duplicated] regimentally, 1951.   235 pp., portraits, plates, map.   12$\frac{3}{4}$″

Notes on the Dress of The Seventy-First Regiment, formerly The 73rd (Lord Macleod's) Regiment of Highland Foot & presently The 1st Battalion The Highland Light Infantry.   Collected by Arthur Neil Edmonstone Browne.   [Glasgow: John Horn, Ltd.], 1934. xiv, 89 pp., plates, illustrations.   50 copies only.   9$\frac{1}{4}$″ × 11$\frac{1}{2}$″

Notes on the History of The Highland Light Infantry (City of Glasgow Regiment). [Glasgow: published by the "H.L.I." Chronicle, 1949].   23 pp.   7$\frac{1}{4}$″

The Highland Light Infantry.   By Lauchlan Maclean Watt.   Edinburgh: W. P. Nimmo, Hay & Mitchell [1916].   63 pp., plates.   6$\frac{1}{4}$″
  3 coloured plates.

An Epic of Glasgow.   History of the 15th Battalion The Highland Light Infantry (City of Glasgow Regiment).   Compiled by Thomas Chalmers.   Illustrations by A. M. Burnie.   Glasgow: John McCallum & Co., 1934.   xvi, 226 pp., portraits, plates, illustrations, sketch maps.   8$\frac{1}{2}$″

A Saga of Scotland.   History of the 16th Battalion The Highland Light Infantry (City of Glasgow Regiment).   Edited by Thomas Chalmers.   With a Foreword by Principal R. S. Rait, University of Glasgow.   Glasgow: John McCallum & Co. [1930].   xv, 174 pp., portraits, plates, illustrations, maps.   8$\frac{1}{2}$″

The Seventeenth Highland Light Infantry (Glasgow Chamber of Commerce Battalion).   Record of War Service, 1914-1918.   Glasgow: David J. Clark, 1920.   136 pp., portraits, plates, map.   8$\frac{1}{2}$″
  Coloured plate of colours.

SEAFORTH HIGHLANDERS
(ROSS-SHIRE BUFFS, THE DUKE OF ALBANY'S)
[72 and 78]

Historical Record of the Seventy-Second Regiment, or The Duke of Albany's Own Highlanders; containing an Account of the Formation of the Regiment in 1778, and of its subsequent Services to 1848. Compiled by Richard Cannon, Esq., Adjutant-General's Office, Horse Guards. London: Parker, Furnivall, & Parker, 1848. xxxvi, 72 pp., plates. 8¾"
   1 coloured plate of uniform and 1 of colours.

Historical Records of the 72nd Highlanders, now 1st Battalion Seaforth Highlanders, 1777-1886. Edinburgh: William Blackwood & Sons, printed for private circulation, 1886. 197 pp. 8"

The Jubilee Memorial. The Historical Records of The 78th Highlanders, or Ross-shire Buffs (now 2nd Battalion Seaforth Highlanders), from 1793 to 1887, from Official and Authentic Sources. By James MacVeigh. Dumfries: J. Maxwell & Son, printers, 1887. [4], 328 pp., portraits. 8"
   Coloured plate of colours.

History and Services of the 78th Highlanders (Ross-shire Buffs). Compiled from the Manuscripts of the late Major Colin Mackenzie and other Sources. By Major H. Davidson, 1793-1881. With illustrations by R. Simkin. Edinburgh: W. & A. K. Johnston, 1901. 2 vols., portraits, plates, plans, maps. 11¼"
   Vol. 1 contains 5 coloured plates of uniform; vol. 2 contains 3 of uniform and 1 of colours. There was a remainder issue, the 2 volumes bound in 1 without the coloured plates.

The Great Deeds of the Seaforth Highlanders. By F. W. Walker. London: J. M. Dent & Sons Ltd. [1916]. 174 pp. (The Story of the Regiments). 7"
   Coloured plate of uniform.

The Seaforth Highlanders; South Africa, 1899-1902. [Edited by Major H. Davidson]. Edinburgh: printed by W. & A. K. Johnston, 1904. vi, 86 pp., plates, map. 10"

Seaforth Highlanders. Edited by Col. John M. Sym. Aldershot: Gale & Polden Ltd., 1962. xvi, 416 pp., plates. 8½"
   3 coloured plates of uniform and 1 of colours.

With the 72nd Highlanders in the Sudan Campaign. By Granville Egerton. London: Eden Fisher & Co. Ltd., 1909. 52 pp., illustrations. (Reprinted from " The Green Howards Gazette "). 7¼"

Photographs and Short Record of Services of some of the senior Officers of The Seaforth Highlanders (Ross-shire Buffs, The Duke of Albany's), 1793-1925. [Edinburgh: published for The Seaforth Highlanders' Regimental Association by J. Burn & Sons, 1926]. [5], 79 ff., portraits. 10"

Pipers and Pipe Music in a Highland Regiment. A Record of Piping in the 1st Seaforth Highlanders, originally the Earl of Seaforth's or 78th (Highland) Regiment, afterwards the 72nd Highlanders, and latterly the 72nd or Duke of Albany's Own Highlanders. By Major I. H. Mackay Scobie. Dingwall: The Ross-shire Printing and Publishing Co. Ltd. [1924]. [8], 63 pp., portraits, plates. (Reprinted with additions and revisions from " Cabar Feidh," the Regimental Magazine of The Seaforth Highlanders). 9¾"

Rules and Records of the Officers' Mess, 72nd Regiment, Duke of Albany's Own Highlanders, 1808-1896. Edinburgh: William Blackwood & Sons, 1897. For private circulation. [10], 240 pp. 8¼"
  100 copies only printed.

The Seaforth Highlanders. By Lauchlan Maclean Watt. Edinburgh: W. P. Nimmo, Hay & Mitchell [1916]. 63 pp., plates, portrait. 6¼"
  3 coloured plates, including 1 of uniform.

10th Battalion The Seaforth Highlanders in the Great War. (With Record of War Services of Officers of The Seaforth Highlanders who had been at Edinburgh University). By Lieut.-Col. Chilton L. Addison Smith. Edinburgh: J. Bain & Sons, printed for private circulation, 1927. 87 pp., portraits, plates. 11½"
  100 copies printed.

THE GORDON HIGHLANDERS   [75 and 92]

The Life of a Regiment; The History of the Gordon Highlanders from its Formation in 1794 to 1816. By Lt.-Col. C. Greenhill Gardyne. Edinburgh: David Douglas, 1901. xxi, 525 pp., plates, illustrations, plans, maps. 8¾"
  6 coloured plates of uniform.

———— Vol. 2. From 1816 to 1898, including An Account of the 75th Regiment from 1787 to 1881. 1903. xxvii, 415 pp., plates, illustrations, plans, maps. 8¾"
  2 coloured plates of uniform.

———— [2nd edition]. London: The Medici Society Ltd., 1929. 2 vols. 9¾"

———— [Vol. 3]. From 1898 to 1914. By Lt.-Col. A. D. Greenhill Gardyne. London: The Medici Society Ltd., 1939. xix, 521 pp., portraits, plates, illustrations, plans, maps. 9¾"

———— Vol. 4. The Gordon Highlanders in the First World War, 1914-1919. [By] Cyril Falls. Aberdeen: The University Press, 1958. xv, 276 pp., sketch maps. 9¾"

———— Vol. 5. The Gordon Highlanders, 1919-1945. [By] Wilfrid Miles. Aberdeen: The University Press, 1961. xv, 422 pp., portraits, plates, maps. 9¾"

Historical Record of the Ninety-Second Regiment, originally termed "The Gordon Highlanders" and numbered the Hundredth Regiment; containing an Account of the Formation of the Regiment in 1794 and of its subsequent Services to 1850. Compiled by Richard Cannon, Esq., Adjutant-General's Office, Horse Guards. London: Parker, Furnivall, & Parker, 1851. xliii, 150 pp., plates, plan. 8¾"
    2 coloured plates of uniform and 1 of colours.

The Valour Story of a Century: Battle History of the Gordon Highlanders. By James Cromb. Edinburgh: John Menzies & Co., 1894. 68 pp. 8vo.

The Gordon Highlanders; being the Story of these Bonnie Fighters. Told by James Milne. London: John MacQueen, 1898. 110 pp., portraits, plates. 7¼"
    Coloured reproduction of uniform on paper cover.

The Gordon Highlanders. By Lauchlan Maclean Watt. Edinburgh: W. P. Nimmo, Hay & Mitchell, 1915. 61 pp., portraits, plates. 6¼"
    2 coloured plates of uniform and 1 of colours.

The Gordon Highlanders; being a Short Record of the Services of the Regiment. By Rev. P. D. Thomson. Devonport: Swiss & Co. [4th impression], 1921. [8], 172, [11] pp. 5¾"
    8 coloured plates, including 5 of uniform and 1 of colours.
    1st impression, 1916.

————— New 2nd edition. Aberdeen. 1933. x, 210, 10 pp.

A Short History of the Gordon Highlanders. [Aberdeen: 1948]. No imprint. 16 pp., portrait. 5½"

With the Gordons at Ypres. [1st Battn.]. By Rev. A. M. Maclean. Paisley: Alexander Gardner, 1916. 70 pp. 7½"

The Gay Gordons. The Story of the 2nd Battalion, Gordon Highlanders. By Wolmer Whyte. London: John Dicks [1905]. 46 pp. 8½"
    First and last of a series "Famous Regiments," price 1d.

Historical Diary of The Gordon Highlanders. By Lieut.-Col. F. H. Neish. Dundee: John Leng & Co. Ltd., 1914 [actually issued January 1918]. First edition. 55 pp. 9¾"

The Gordon Highlanders. The History of their Origin, together with a Transcript of the First Official Muster. [By] John Malcolm Bulloch. Banff: Banffshire Field Club, 1913. vii, 67 pp. 9"
    Coloured plate of uniform. 500 copies printed.

The Gordon Highlanders Casualties in the Peninsular Campaign. By J. M. Bulloch. Banff: Banffshire Field Club, 1915. 20 pp. 10"
    350 copies printed.

The Gordon Highlanders Second Battalion (as quartered in Banff, 1811-12). By J. M. Bulloch. [Buckie: W. F. Johnston & Sons, 1915], 4 pp.   10″
  50 copies printed.

Gordon Highlanders Roll of Honour at Quatre Bras and at Waterloo. [By] J. M. Bulloch. [Aberdeen: Rosemount Press], 1915. Privately printed. 8 pp. 10″
  50 copies printed.

Gordon Highlanders wounded at Waterloo. [By] J. M. Bulloch. [Aberdeen: Aberdeen Daily Journal Office], 1916. Privately printed. 8 pp. 10″
  60 copies printed.

Gordon Highlanders Muster Roll at the period of Waterloo. [By] J. M. Bulloch. [Aberdeen: Aberdeen Press and Journal Office]. Privately printed, 1927. 13 pp. 10″
  80 copies printed.

Battlefield Discipline as it was enforced on the Gordon Highlanders One Hundred years ago. [By] J. M. Bulloch. [Buckie: W. F. Johnston & Sons], 1915. Privately printed. 8 pp. 10″
  50 copies printed.

The Making of the West Indies: The Gordon Highlanders as colonists. By J. M. Bulloch. Buckie: W. F. Johnston & Sons, 1915. 46 pp.   10″

The Truth about Gordon Tartan. By J. M. Bulloch. Glasgow: Maclehose, Jackson & Co., 1924. (Reprinted from *Scottish Historical Review*, April, 1924). 8 pp.   10″

Bibliography of the Gordon Highlanders. By J. M. Bulloch. (In his *Territorial Soldiering in the North-East of Scotland*, 1759-1814). Aberdeen: The New Spalding Club, 1914. 10″

The 11th Battalion Gordon Highlanders [1914-1916]. Glasgow: Published for the 11th Battalion Gordon Highlanders by Maclure, Macdonald & Co. Ltd., 1916. 115 pp., portraits, plate. 8¼″

THE QUEEN'S OWN CAMERON HIGHLANDERS [79]

Historical Record of The Seventy-Ninth Regiment of Foot, or Cameron Highlanders. By Capt. Robert Jameson. Edinburgh: William Blackwood & Sons, 1863. xii, 143 pp. 7½″

Historical Records of the 79th Queen's Own Cameron Highlanders. Compiled and edited by Capt. T. A. Mackenzie, Lieut. and Adjut. J. S. Ewart, and Lieut. C. Findlay, from the Orderly Room Records. London: Hamilton, Adams & Co.—Devonport: A. H. Swiss, 1887. viii, 309 pp., portraits, plates. 8½″
  1 coloured plate of colours.

The Historical Records of the 79th Highlanders (The Queen's Own Cameron Highlanders), from 1793 to 1888. From Official and authentic sources. By James MacVeigh. [Dumfries: printed by J. Maxwell & Son], 1888. [2], 148 pp., portraits. 8½"
  1 coloured plate of colours.

History of the 79th Queen's Own Cameron Highlanders, now the First Battalion Queen's Own Cameron Highlanders, 1794-1893. By Lieut.-Col. Percy Groves. Illustrated by Harry Payne. Edinburgh: W. & A. K. Johnston, 1893. 30 pp., plates. (Illustrated Histories of Scottish Regiments, Book No. 3). 12¼"
  5 coloured plates of uniform.

Historical Records of the Queen's Own Cameron Highlanders. Edinburgh: William Blackwood & Sons, 1909; 31; 52. 6 vols., portraits, plates, plans, maps. 10"
  Vol. 1 contains 8 and Vol. 2, 1 coloured plates of uniform.

———— Vol. 7. 1949-1961. Contains Biographical Notes on all Officers from the formation. Edinburgh: William Blackwood & Sons, 1961. xxiv, 616 pp., portraits, plates. 10"

Queen's Own Cameron Highlanders. A Short Regimental History for the Use of Recruits. By Lt.-Gen. Sir Spencer Ewart. Inverness: printed by The Northern Counties Newspaper and Printing and Publishing Co. Ltd., 1927. 43 pp., plates. 6¾"
  2 coloured plates of uniform.

———— Another edition. Re-edited by Lt.-Col. R. D. M. C. Miers. Inverness: Northern Counties Newspaper etc. Co. Ltd., 1948. 56 pp., plates. 7"
  2 coloured plates of uniform.

Some Account of the Part taken by the 79th Regiment or Cameron Highlanders in the Indian Mutiny in 1858. By Capt. Douglas Wimberley. Inverness: printed at the " Northern Chronicle " Office, 1891. Plan in end-pocket. (Reprinted from ' The Highland Monthly ' Magazine, 1891). 8½"

———— Appendix. 1892. 14 pp.

Narrative of the Part taken by the 79th Queen's Own Cameron Highlanders in the Egyptian Campaign, 1882. By Capt. and Adjut. K. S. Baynes. [London: printed by Henry Hansard & Son], 1883. Printed for private circulation. 34 pp., portrait. 8½"

South African War Record of the 1st Battalion Queen's Own Cameron Highlanders, 1900-1-2. Inverness: The Northern Counties Printing and Publishing Co. Ltd., 1903. [8], 258 pp., plans, maps. 9¾"

An Alphabetical List of the Officers of the Seventy-Ninth Regiment or Cameron Highlanders, from 1800 to 1851. By Henry Stooks Smith. London: Simpkin, Marshall & Co., 1852. 44 pp. 8½"

Cameron Highlanders. Officers present at the various Campaigns, Battles, &c. in which the Regiment has taken part. Lists, with indices and appendices. Compiled by Seymour Clarke, Major; with a Preface by Lieut.-Gen. Sir J. S. Ewart. Edinburgh: William Blackwood & Sons, 1913. xvi, 147 pp. 10″

The Cameron Highlanders. By Lauchlan Maclean Watt. Edinburgh: W. P. Nimmo, Hay & Mitchell [1916]. 63 pp., plates, portrait. 6¼″
  4 coloured plates including 1 of uniform.

The 79th Calendar, 1793-1911. Bazaar in Waverley Market, Edinburgh, December 1911, in aid of the Scottish Naval and Military Veterans' Residence at Whitefoord House. No imprint. 12 pp. 9¾″
  4 coloured plates of uniform.

2nd Battalion The Queen's Own Cameron Highlanders. London, Chelsea Barracks, 14th August to 14th September 1934. [Aldershot: Gale & Polden Ltd., 1934]. 16 pp., plates. 7¼″×9¾″
  Souvenir album containing Roll and reproductions of photographs.

Biographical List of Officers (other than Regular, Militia and Territorial) The Queen's Own Cameron Highlanders. (Published, in Ten Supplements, in . . . the " 79th News " from September 1957 to September 1960). Compiled by Col. Maurice J. H. Wilson. No imprint [Inverness]. 195 pp. 9½″

The Fifth Camerons. By Capt. J. H. F. McEwen. Edinburgh: David Macdonald Ltd. [1938]. 108 pp. 7¼″

Souvenir Booklet of the Sixth Cameron Highlanders. [Edited by W.D.R.]. London: Spottiswoode & Co. Ltd., 1916. 61 pp., portraits, plates. 8″

The History of the 7th Battalion Queen's Own Cameron Highlanders. By Col. J. W. Sandilands and Lt.-Col. Norman MacLeod. Stirling: Eneas Mackay, 1922. 208 pp., portraits, plates. 7¼″

THE ROYAL ULSTER RIFLES   [83 and 86]

Memoirs and Services of the Eighty-Third Regiment (County of Dublin), from 1795 to 1863; including the Campaigns of the Regiment in the West Indies, Africa, the Peninsula, Ceylon, Canada, and India. Edited by Brevet-Major E. W. Bray. London: Smith, Elder & Co., 1863. vii, 71 pp. 8¾″

——— from 1793 to 1907. London: Hugh Rees Ltd., 1908. 99 pp. 8¾″

Historical Record of the Eighty-Sixth, or The Royal County Down Regiment of Foot; containing an Account of the Formation of the Regiment in 1793, and of its subsequent Services to 1842. London: John W. Parker, 1842. viii, vii, 72 pp., plates. (Cannon's Historical Records Series). 8¾″
  1 coloured plate of uniform and 1 of colours.

Royal Irish Rifles, 2nd Battalion, being The Record of the Service of the Battalion; together with a Series of Reproductions of Photographs taken by F. B. Stewart at Poona, India, February, 1897. Lt.-Col. H. A. Eagar, Commanding. Made by The Historical Publishing Co., Philadelphia, U.S.A., published by C. B. Burrows, care Wm. Watson & Co., Bombay and London. [1897]. 97 ff. portraits, plates. $11'' \times 13\frac{1}{2}''$

History of the Royal Irish Rifles. By Lieut.-Col. George Brenton Laurie. London: Gale & Polden Ltd., 1914. xxiv, 540 pp., portraits, plates, illustrations, maps, plans. $11''$
   9 coloured plates of uniform and 1 of colours.

——— Vol. 2. The History of the First Seven Battalions The Royal Irish Rifles (now The Royal Ulster Rifles) in the Great War. By Cyril Falls, formerly Captain. Aldershot: printed for the Regimental Committeee by Gale & Polden Ltd., 1925. xv, 189 pp., portrait, plates, maps, plans. $11''$

——— Vol. 3. The Royal Ulster Rifles. Covering the period 1919-1948 and including a short account of the Battalions which served with the 36th Ulster Division 1914-1918. By Charles Graves. Published by the Royal Ulster Rifles Regimental Committee. [Mexborough: printed by The Times Printing Co. Ltd., 1950]. [viii], 345 pp., maps, end-paper maps. $8\frac{1}{2}''$

The Royal Ulster Rifles, 1793-1957. [History prepared by Lt.-Col. M. J. P. M. Corbally]. [Glasgow: The Paramount Press], 1959. Pp. 33-180 [remainder adverts.], portraits, illustrations. $8\frac{1}{2}''$

——— [Another edition] . . . . 1793-1960. Pp. 33-188. 1960. $8\frac{1}{2}''$

A Short History of the Royal Irish Rifles, the 83rd and 86th Regiments of Foot. Aldershot: Gale & Polden Ltd., 1920. 23 pp. $7\frac{1}{4}''$

A Short History of The Royal Ulster Rifles. Aldershot: Gale & Polden Ltd. [1925]. [viii], 40 pp. $7\frac{1}{4}''$
   1 coloured plate of uniform, and Colours and badge in colour on paper covers.

The Story of the Eighty-Third and Eighty-Sixth Regiments of Foot, The Royal Ulster Rifles. By John Body. Belfast: British Broadcasting Corporation, Northern Ireland, 1953. 41 pp. Duplicated. $13''$

The Royal Ulster Rifles in Korea. Belfast: Wm. Mullan & Son (Publishers) Ltd., 1953. 104 pp., illustrations, maps, end-paper maps. $8\frac{1}{2}''$

With the Ulster Division in France. A Story of the 11th Battalion Royal Irish Rifles (South Antrim Volunteers), from Bordon to Thiepval. In Four Parts, including Photographs and Maps by A.P.I. S[amuels] and D.G.S. Belfast: Wm. Mullan & Son [1918]. 97 pp., portraits, plates, maps. $7\frac{1}{4}''$

THE ROYAL IRISH FUSILIERS
(PRINCESS VICTORIA'S)   [87 and 89]

The Records of His Majesty's 87th Regiment; or the Royal Irish Fusiliers. London: Matthew Iley, 1830.   75, [2] pp.   8½″

Historical Record of The Eighty-Seventh Regiment, or The Royal Irish Fusiliers; containing an Account of the Formation of the Regiment in 1793, and of its subsequent Services to 1853.   Compiled by Richard Cannon, Esq.   Adjutant-General's Office, Horse Guards.   London: printed by George E. Eyre and William Spottiswoode for H.M.'s Stationery Office, published by Parker, Furnivall & Parker, 1853.   xix, xii, 100 pp., plates.   8¾″
   4 coloured plates, including 2 of uniform, 1 of colours and 1 of Eagle.

The First Battalion The Faugh-a-Ballaghs in the Great War.   By Brig.-Gen. A. R. Burrowes.   Aldershot: printed and published for the Regimental Committee by Gale & Polden Ltd. [1925].   [10], 182 pp., portrait, plates, maps.   9¾″

Historical Record of the Eighty-Ninth Princess Victoria's Regiment.   Compiled by Rowland Brinckman, Capt. and Adjutant.   Chatham: Gale & Polden, 1888.   xxvi, 235 pp., portrait, plates.   7¼″
   3 coloured plates of uniform and 2 of colours.

The Royal Irish Fusiliers, 1793-1950.   [By] Marcus Cunliffe.   London: Oxford University Press, 1952.   xvi, 517 pp., portraits, plates, maps.   9¾″

Outline History of The Royal Irish Fusiliers (Princess Victoria's).   Aldershot: Gale & Polden Ltd. [1938].   23 pp.   7¼″
   1 coloured plate of uniform and badge and uniform in colour on paper covers.

———— [Another edition].   Aldershot: Gale & Polden Ltd., 1948.   30 pp., coloured plate.   7¼″

———— [Another edition].   Aldershot.   1955.   31 pp., coloured plate.   7¼″

The Royal Irish Fusiliers: the story of the 87th and 89th Regiments of Foot, known jointly today as The Royal Irish Fusiliers (Princess Victoria's).   By John Body.   Belfast: British Broadcasting Corporation, Northern Ireland, 1953. 49 pp.   Duplicated.   13″

With the Irish Fusiliers from Alexandria to Natal, 1899-1900.   Diary of Bt.-Major D. W. Churcher.   [Reading: J. Read, printer], n.d. 92 pp., illustrations. 8″
   Title on cover: "From Alexandria to Ladysmith with the 87th".

Fifty Years of Sport in the Royal Irish Fusiliers, Compiled by Col. G. V. W. Hill.   35 pp.   Duplicated.   13″

————————————————

A Short Record of the Service and Experiences of the 5th Battalion Royal Irish Fusiliers in the Great War.   [By Lt.-Col. F. W. E. Johnson].   [Dublin: Hely's Ltd., printers, 1919].   45 pp., portrait, map.   7¼″

THE CONNAUGHT RANGERS   [88 and 94]

The Connaught Rangers.   By Lieut.-Col. H. F. N. Jourdain and Edward Fraser. London: The Royal United Service Institution. 1924, 26, 28. 3 vols., portraits, plates, plans, maps.   9¾"
   Vol. 1.   1st Battalion, formerly 88th Foot.   3 coloured plates of uniform.

   Vol. 2.   2nd Battalion, formerly 94th Foot; The Militia: 3rd and 4th Battalions.
    3 coloured plates, including 1 of uniform.

   Vol. 3.   The 5th and 6th (Service) Battalions.   1 coloured plate of uniform.

Historical Record of the Eighty-Eighth Regiment of Foot, or, Connaught Rangers; containing an Account of the Formation of the Regiment in 1793, and of its subsequent Services to 1837.   London: printed by William Clowes & Sons, 1838. [10], viii, 103 pp. (Cannon's Historical Records Series).   8¾"
   1 coloured plate of uniform and colours.

The Crimean Campaign with "The Connaught Rangers," 1854-55-56.   By Lieut.-Col. Nathaniel Steevens.   London: Griffith and Farran, 1878.   xvi, 359 pp., map.   8¾"

The Connaught Rangers.   Regimental Records, 1899-1902.   Cape Town: W. & A. Richards & Sons, 1902.   137 pp., maps.   7¾"

An Alphabetical List of the Officers of the 88th Regiment, or Connaught Rangers, from 1800 to 1852.   By Henry Stooks Smith.   London: Simpkin, Marshall & Co., 1852.   8¾"
   No. 1, pp. 5-12; no more publ.

An Alphabetical List of the Officers of the Ninety-Fourth Regiment, "Scotch Brigade," from 1800 to 1869.   By Henry Stooks Smith.   London: Longmans, Green, Reader, and Dyer, 1869.   x, 58 pp.   8½"

Medals and Decorations.   The Connaught Rangers, late 88th and 94th Regiments, 1793-1922.   Catalogue of Orders, Honorary Distinctions and Medals . . . in the Collection of Lieut.-Col. H. F. N. Jourdain.   [Frome & London: printed by Butler & Tanner Ltd., 1922].   52 pp.   9¾"

A History of the Mess Plate of the 88th The Connaught Rangers.   By Captain H. F. N. Jourdain.   Edinburgh: The Ballantyne Press, privately printed, 1904. xii, 148 pp., plates.   9¾"

———————————

Record of the 5th (Service) Battalion The Connaught Rangers from 19th August, 1914 to 17th January, 1916.   Oxford: University Press, printed for private circulation [1916].   231 pp., plans, map.   8½"

THE ARGYLL AND SUTHERLAND HIGHLANDERS (PRINCESS LOUISE'S)   [91 and 93]

Short Summary of the Record of the XCI. Argyllshire Highlanders.   [London: T. Pettitt & Co., printers, 1875].   8 pp. $8\frac{1}{4}''$

History of the 1st Battalion Princess Louise's Argyll and Sutherland Highlanders. Compiled from the Regimental Records and other authorities by Lieut.-Col. H. G. Robley and P. J. Aubin.   Cape Town: Murray & St. Leger, printers, 1883 [-84].   62, 4 pp. $9\frac{1}{4}''$

Historical Records of the 91st Argyllshire Highlanders, now the 1st Battalion Princess Louise's Argyll and Sutherland Highlanders; containing an Account of the Formation of the Regiment in 1794 and of its subsequent Services to 1881. Arranged by G. L. Goff.   London: Richard Bentley and Son, 1891.   xvi, 361 pp., portraits, plates, illustrations, maps. $8\frac{3}{4}''$
    1 coloured plate of uniform and 1 of colours.

History of the 91st Princess Louise's Argyllshire Highlanders, now the 1st Battalion Princess Louise's Argyll and Sutherland Highlanders, 1794-1894.   By Lieut.-Col. Percy Groves.   Illustrated by Harry Payne.   Edinburgh: W. & A. K. Johnston, 1894.   43 pp., plates. $9\frac{3}{4}''$
    9 coloured plates of uniform, colours and tartan.   Limited to 530 copies.

The History of the 91st Argyllshire Highlanders, now the 1st Battalion Princess Louis's (Argyll and Sutherland Highlanders).   By R. A. Dunn-Pattison, late Lieutenant.   Edinburgh: William Blackwood & Sons, 1910.   xvi, 413 pp., portraits, plates, plans, maps. $11\frac{3}{4}''$

History of the Argyll and Sutherland Highlanders.   1st Battalion, 1909-1939. By Brig. R. C. B. Anderson.   With a Foreword by Gen. Sir Gordon MacMillan of MacMillan and Knap.   Edinburgh: privately printed by T. & A. Constable Ltd., 1954.   xvii, 192 pp., portraits, plates, maps. $9\frac{3}{4}''$

History of the Argyll and Sutherland Highlanders.   1st Battalion, 1939-1954. By Brig. R. C. B. Anderson.   With a Foreword by Gen. Sir Gordon MacMillan of MacMillan and Knap.   Edinburgh: T. & A. Constable Ltd., 1956.   xvi, 304 pp., portraits, illustrations, maps. $9\frac{5}{8}''$

History of the Argyll and Sutherland Highlanders.   1st Battalion (Princess Louise's), 1939-1945.   [By] Lt.-Col. F. C. C. Graham.   With a Foreword by Major-Gen. G. H. A. MacMillan.   London: Thomas Nelson & Sons Ltd. [1948].   x, 262 pp., portraits, plates, maps. $9''$

Historical Records of the 93rd Sutherland Highlanders; now the 2nd Battalion Princess Louise's Argyll and Sutherland Highlanders.   Compiled and edited by Roderick Hamilton Burgoyne.   London: Richard Bentley & Son, 1883.   xvi, 430 pp., portraits, plates, plans. $8\frac{3}{4}''$
    2 coloured plates of uniform and 1 of colours.

History of the 93rd Sutherland Highlanders, now the 2nd Battalion Argyll and Sutherland Highlanders, 1800-1895. By Lieut.-Col. Percy Groves. Illustrated by Harry Payne. Edinburgh: W. & A. K. Johnston, 1895. 49 pp., plates. 9¾"
  9 coloured plates of uniform, colours and tartan.

Am Reisimeid Chataich. The 93rd Sutherland Highlanders, now 2nd Bn. The Argyll & Sutherland Highlanders (Princess Louise's), 1799-1927. By Brig.-Gen. A. E. J. Cavendish. [Frome & London: Butler & Tanner Ltd.]. Published privately, 1928. xxvi, 446 pp., portraits, plates, illustrations, plans, maps. 10¾"
  1 coloured plate of uniform.

History of the Argyll & Sutherland Highlanders. 2nd Battalion (The Thin Red Line). Malayan Campaign, 1941-42. [By] Brig. I. MacA. Stewart. With a Foreword by Field Marshal Earl Wavell. London: Thomas Nelson & Sons Ltd. [1927]. xviii, 171 pp., plates, maps. 9"

——— 2nd Battalion (Reconstituted). European Campaign, 1944-45. [By] Major W. L. McElwee. With a Foreword by Major-Gen. G. H. A. MacMillan. London: Thomas Nelson & Sons Ltd. [1949]. xi, 212 pp., portraits, plates, maps. 9"

The Thin Red Line Almanac, 1908. Edinburgh: W. & A. K. Johnston Ltd., 1908. 102 pp., maps. 9¾"

The Story of the Argyll and Sutherland Highlanders, 91st and 93rd Foot. By J. H. Stevenson. Glasgow: James Maclehose & Sons, 1915. viii, 72 pp. 7"

The Argyll and Sutherland Highlanders. By Lauchlan Maclean Watt. Edinburgh: W. P. Nimmo, Hay & Mitchell [1916]. 63 pp., plates, portrait. 6¼"
  3 coloured plates, including 1 of uniform.

The History of the Argyll and Sutherland Highlanders (Princess Louise's), 1794-1930. [By Capt. G. I. Malcolm. Edinburgh: M'Lagan & Cumming, printers, 1930]. 60 pp. 6¾"

——— 1794-1949. By Lt.-Col. G. I. Malcolm of Poltalloch. Edinburgh: McLagan & Cumming Ltd., 1955. 96 pp. 6¾"
  Coloured plate of uniform.

The Argylls in Korea. [By] Lieut.-Col. G. I. Malcolm of Poltalloch. London: Thos. Nelson & Sons Ltd. [1952]. xii, 97 pp., portraits, plates, map. 8"

————————

The 10th Battalion Argyll and Sutherland Highlanders, 1914-1919. By Lieut.-Col. Herbert G. Sotheby. With a Preface by Major-Gen. John Kennedy. London: John Murray, printed for private circulation, 1931. xxii, 163 pp., portraits, plates, maps. 7½"

THE PRINCE OF WALES'S LEINSTER REGIMENT (ROYAL CANADIANS)   [100 and 109]

The History of the Prince of Wales's Leinster Regiment (Royal Canadians), late The 100th Prince of Wales's Royal Canadian Regiment descended from The 100th Prince Regent's County of Dublin Regiment of Foot disbanded in Canada in 1818: and The 109th Foot formerly The Honourable East India Company's 3rd Bombay European Regiment: to which were added in 1881 as 3rd, 4th and 5th Battalions respectively The King's County Militia; The Queen's County Militia and The Royal Meath Militia; and the 6th and 7th Service Battalions raised in 1914 on the Outbreak of the Great War.   Compiled and edited by Lieut.-Col. Frederick Ernest Whitton.   Aldershot: Gale & Polden Ltd. [1924]. 2 vols., portraits, plates, maps. $8\frac{1}{2}$

The Annals of The Prince of Wales's Leinster Regiment (Royal Canadians), late the 100th Prince of Wales's Royal Canadian Regiment and the 109th Foot (formerly H.E.I.C. 3rd Bombay European Regiment); amalgamated under the above title 1881, ordered to be disbanded 1922.   Edited by Lieut.-Col. F. E. Whitton.   Aldershot: Gale & Polden Ltd. [1922].   104 pp., portraits, plates, illustrations. $9\frac{3}{4}''$

THE ROYAL MUNSTER FUSILIERS   [101 and 104]

The History of the Bengal European Regiment, now the Royal Munster Fusiliers and how it helped to win India.   By Lieut.-Col. P. R. Innes.   London: Simpkin, Marshall & Co., 1885.   xii, 572 pp. $8\frac{1}{2}''$
Coloured plate of colours.

History of the Royal Munster Fusiliers.   By Capt. S. McCance.   Aldershot: printed by Gale & Polden Ltd., 1927.   2 vols., portraits, plates, plans, maps. $9\frac{3}{4}''$
Vol. 1 contains 5 coloured plates including 2 of uniform and 1 of colours.
Vol. 2 contains 3 coloured plates including 1 of uniform.

The 2nd Munsters in France.   By Lieut.-Col. H. S. Jervis.   With a Foreword by Lieut.-Gen. Sir Herbert S. G. Miles.   Aldershot: printed by Gale & Polden Ltd., 1922.   xii, 71 pp., plates, plans, maps. $9\frac{3}{4}''$

The Story of the Munsters at Etreux, Festubert and Rue du Beis.   By Mrs. Victor Rickard.   [Dublin: printed by the Wood Printing Works for The New Ireland Publishing Co. Ltd., 1915].   55 pp., portraits, plans. $8\frac{1}{2}''$
Coloured reproduction of colours on paper cover.

The Story of the Munsters at Etreux, Festubert, Rue du Bois and Hulluch. By Mrs. Victor Rickard. With an Introduction by Lord Dunraven, Honorary Colonel, 5th Royal Munster Fusiliers. London: Hodder and Stoughton, 1918. xvi, 116 pp., portraits, plates, plans. 7¼″

The Roll of Officers of the 101st and 104th Fusiliers and The Royal Munster Fusiliers. Compiled by Lieut.-Col. S. T. Banning. London: [Spottiswoode & Co., printers], 1912. [8], 47 pp. 8½″

Royal Munster Fusiliers, 1652 to present day. [A Calendar compiled by Col. H. S. Jervis]. No imprint, 1949. 27 pp., map. 10½″

The late Royal Munster Fusiliers and Colonel David George Johnstone, an Old Glenalmond, the Father of the Regiment. A Reminiscence. [By Henry, Lord Johnston]. [Edinburgh: printed at The Darien Press, 1926]. ii, 17 pp. 7½″

THE ROYAL DUBLIN FUSILIERS [102 and 103]

A Sketch of the Services of the Madras European Regiment during the Burmese War. By an Officer of the Corps, Lieut. Butler. London: Smith, Elder & Co., 1839. vii, 104 pp. 9″

Historical Record of The Honourable East India Company's First Madras European Regiment; containing An Account of the Establishment of Independent Companies in 1645; their Formation into a Regiment in 1748; and its subsequent Services to 1842. By a Staff Officer. [Brig.-Gen. J. G. S. Neill]. London: Smith, Elder & Co., 1842. xxx, 575 pp., portrait, plates, plans. 8¾″

Services of the 102nd Regiment of Foot (Royal Madras Fusiliers), from 1842 to the Present Time. Being a Sequel to the "Services of the Madras European Regiment; by a Staff Officer." By Col. Thomas Raikes. London: Smith, Elder & Co., 1867. 68 pp. 8½″

The Regimental Records of The First Battalion The Royal Dublin Fusiliers, formerly The Madras Europeans, The Madras European Regiment, The First Madras Fusiliers, The 102nd Royal Madras Fusiliers, 1642-1842. By One whose whole service was passed in the Corps and who had the honour of commanding it. [Col. G. J. Harcourt]. London: Hugh Rees Ltd., 1910. xv, 152 pp., portraits, plates, map. 8½″

The Regimental Records of 1st Batt. Royal Dublin Fusiliers, formerly 102nd Royal Madras Fusiliers, 1st Madras Fusiliers, The Madras European Regiment, 1842-1904. By One who has served over 30 years in it [Lieut.-Col. S. G. Bird]. [Guildford: Biddle & Shippam, 1905]. viii, 164, [8] pp., portraits, plates, maps. 8½″

Neill's "Blue Caps"; being the Record of the Antecedents and Early History of the Regiment variously known as the East India Company's European Regiment, The Madras European Regiment, the 1st Madras European Regiment, the 1st Madras European Fuziliers, the 1st Madras Fuziliers, the 102nd Royal Madras Fuziliers, and the 1st Battalion Royal Dublin Fusiliers. Compiled from the works of Brigadier Neill, Colonels Harcourt and Bird, and from the Notes and Manuscript of Major Dale by Col. H. C. Wylly. Aldershot: Gale & Polden Ltd., for private circulation only [1924]. 3 vols., portraits, plates, plans, maps. 9½"
    9 coloured plates including 1 of uniform in vol. 2; 2 of uniform and 1 of colours and 1 of badges in vol. 3.

Records of H.M.'s 1st Regiment of Bombay European Infantry " Fusiliers"; containing A Brief Account of the Formation in 1662, and Services to 1861. Poona: Observer Press, for private circulation only. 1861. 40 pp. 8½"

———— Another version, with title Records of the 1st Regiment, etc. [Newport, I.W.: printed by T. Kentfield] for private circulation only. 1861. 40 pp. 8½"

Historical Records of the 103rd Royal Bombay Fusiliers. Devonport: A. H. Swiss [1874]. 81, [9] pp. 8¾"

The Second Battalion Royal Dublin Fusiliers in the South African War, with a Description of the Operations in the Aden Hinterland. By Majors C. F. Romer and A. E. Mainwaring. London: Arthur L. Humphreys, 1908. xiv, 271 pp. portraits, plates, illustrations, plans. 8½"

Crown and Company. The Historical Records of the 2nd Batt. Royal Dublin Fusiliers, formerly the 1st Bombay European Regiment, 1666-1911. By Major Arthur Mainwaring. London: Arthur L. Humphreys, 1911. xxii, 437 pp., portrait, plates, plans, maps. 10"
    11 coloured plates including 5 of uniform.

———— Vol. 2, 1911-1922. By Col. H. C. Wylly. Aldershot: Gale & Polden Ltd., for private circulation only [1923]. xii, 234 pp., portraits, plates, maps. 9½"
    1 coloured plate of uniform and 1 of colours.

A Pocket History of the Royal Dublin Fusiliers. By Sergt.-Major Charles V. Brumby. Aldershot: Gale & Polden Ltd. [1912]. 2nd edition. vii, 54 pp. 4¾"
    1st edition has title The Recruit's History of the Royal Dublin Fusiliers.

————————————————

The Pals at Suvla Bay; being the Record of "D" Company of the 7th Royal Dublin Fusiliers. By Henry Hanna. With a Foreword by Lieut.-Gen. Sir Bryan T. Mahon. Dublin: E. Ponsonby Ltd. [1917]. 244 pp., portraits, plates, illustrations, maps. 9½"

THE PARACHUTE REGIMENT

The Red Beret.   The Story of the Parachute Regiment at War, 1940-1945.   By Hilary St. George Saunders.   With a Foreword by Field Marshal The Viscount Montgomery of Alamein.   London: Michael Joseph [1950].   336 pp., plates, maps. $7\frac{7}{8}''$

History of the 2nd Battalion The Parachute Regiment from its Formation to the Battle of Arnhem.   Aldershot: Gale & Polden Ltd., 1946.   43 pp., sketch maps. $8\frac{1}{2}''$

The Parachute Regiment.   Presentation of Colours to the First, Second and Third Battalions by His Majesty The King, Queen's Parade, Aldershot, 19th July, 1950.   [Aldershot: Gale & Polden Ltd.], 1950.   15 pp. $8\frac{1}{2}''$
  Coloured illustrations of colours.   Title on paper cover: A Brief History of the Regiment.

THE RIFLE BRIGADE (PRINCE CONSORT'S OWN)

Sketch of the Field Service of the Rifle Brigade from its Formation to the Battle of Waterloo.   By Lieut.-Col. Leach.   London: T. & W. Boone, 1838.   32 pp. $8''$

The History of The Rifle Brigade (The Prince Consort's Own), formerly the 95th. By Sir William H. Cope, Bart., late Lieutenant.   London: Chatto & Windus, 1877.   xxvi, 537 pp., plates, plans. $8\frac{1}{2}''$
  5 coloured plates of uniform.

The Rifle Brigade.   By Walter Wood.   London: Grant Richards, 1901.   xx, 215 pp., portraits, plate.   (British Regiments in War and Peace). $7\frac{1}{2}''$

History and Campaigns of The Rifle Brigade.   By Col. Willoughby Verner. London: John Bale, Sons & Danielsson Ltd., 1912; 19.   2 vols., portrait, plates, maps, plans. $11''$
  Part I.   1800-1809.
  Part II.   1809-1813.
  3 coloured plates of uniform in Part II.

The History of The Rifle Brigade in the War of 1914-1919. With a Foreword by Field Marshal H.R.H. The Duke of Connaught, Colonel-in-Chief. London: The Rifle Brigade Club Ltd., 1927; 36. Portraits, plates, maps, plans. 9¾"

Vol. 1. August 1914-December 1916. By Reginald Berkeley (Capt.).

Vol. 2. January 1917-June 1919. By William W. Seymour (Brig.-Gen.).

Appendix. List of Officers and Other Ranks of The Rifle Brigade awarded Decorations, or Mentioned in Despatches for Services during the Great War. Compiled by Lieut.-Col. T. R. Eastwood and Major H. G. Parkyn.

The Rifle Brigade, 1939-1945. Compiled and edited by Committee of The Rifle Brigade " Chronicle." London: The Rifle Brigade Club and Association, 1946. 8¼"

Vol. 1. [4], 133 pp.

Vol. 2. [4], 174 pp., portraits, plates.

The Rifle Brigade in the Second World War, 1939-1945. By Major R. H. W. S. Hastings. Foreword by H.R.H. The Duke of Connaught. Aldershot: Gale & Polden Ltd., 1950. xx, 475 pp., portraits, plates, maps. 8½"

A Short Account of The Rifle Brigade. By Col. Willoughby Verner. N.p., 1922. 45 pp., plates, map. 5½"

2 coloured plates of uniform.

———— Revised by Major H. G. Parkyn. [Aldershot: Gale & Polden Ltd.], 1951. 40 pp., plates. 5½"

2 coloured plates of uniform.

———— 3rd (Revised) edition by Col. W. P. S. Curtis, with title: A Short Account of 3rd Green Jackets, The Rifle Brigade. 44 pp., plates. 5½"

1 coloured plate of uniform.

A Short History of The Rifle Brigade. By Major H. G. Parkyn. With an Introduction by Col. Willoughby Verner. 2nd edition. London: John Bale, Sons & Danielsson Ltd., 1922. x, 73 pp., portrait. 8½"

1st edition was issued in 1912.

The First British Rifle Corps. By Capt. Willoughby Verner. London: W. H. Allen & Co., 1890. 149 pp. 7¼"

Coloured plate of uniform.

An Alphabetical List of the Officers of The Rifle Brigade, from 1800 to 1850. By Henry Stooks Smith. London: Simpkin, Marshall & Co., 1851. viii, 68 pp. 8¾"

The Rifle Brigade Century. An Alphabetical List of the Officers of The Rifle Brigade (The Prince Consort's Own) (Regular Battalions) from 1800 to 1905. Compiled by Col. Gerald Edmund Boyle. London: William Clowes and Sons Ltd., 1905. xvi, 205 pp. 8½"

The Rifle Brigade Chronicle for 1890 to 1964 [*In progress*]. [Various editors].
London: R. H. Porter; John Bale, Sons & Danielsson Ltd., etc., 1891-1965.
Portraits, plates, maps. 8½″

For the Duration. The Story of the Thirteenth Battalion The Rifle Brigade.
By D. H. Rowlands. With a Foreword by Capt. W. B. Maxwell. London:
Simpkin, Marshall, Ltd. (for the 13th Battn. The R.B. Old Comrades' Asso-
ciation [1932]. 158 pp., portraits, plates. 7½″

The History of 61 Infantry Brigade, May 1944-June 1945. [Klagenfurt, Austria:
printed by Ferd. v. Kleinmayr, 1945]. 146 pp., maps. 8¼″
   2nd, 7th and 10th Battalions The Rifle Brigade for most of the period.

From the Beaches to the Baltic. The Story of ' G ' Company 8th Battalion.
The Rifle Brigade during the campaign in North-West Europe. [By Noel Bell].
Aldershot: Gale & Polden Ltd., 1947. [10], 123 pp., maps. 8¼″

The War Diary of H Company 8th Bn. The Rifle Brigade. No imprint.
Schleswig, 1945. 82 pp., end-paper maps. 8″

SPECIAL AIR SERVICE REGIMENT

Born of the Desert. By Malcolm James. London: Collins, 1945. Portraits,
plates, 320 pp. 7½″

These Men are Dangerous. The Special Air Service at War. London: Cassell
& Co. Ltd., 1957. xiii, 240 pp., portraits, plates. 7⅞″

DEPARTMENTS: CORPS

ROYAL ARMY CHAPLAINS' DEPARTMENT

My Predecessors in Office. By The Very Rev. A. C. E. Jarvis. (In the *Journal of the Royal Army Chaplains' Department*, Vol. 3, pp. 289-302, 361-382, 444-520; Vol. 4, pp. 14-77, 320-358; Vol. 5, pp. 9-29, 95-114, 420-445, 1930-37). Brighton: Garratt, Mepham & Fisher Ltd.   9¼"
   These biographies of Chaplains-General to the Forces form a history of the Royal Army Chaplains' Department.

Ministers to the Soldiers of Scotland; a history of the military chaplains of Scotland prior to the War in the Crimea. [By] Alexander Crawley Dow. Edinburgh: Oliver & Boyd, 1962.   viii, 288 pp.   8½"

Some Chaplains in Khaki. An Account of the Work of Chaplains of the United Navy and Army Board. By Frederic C. Spurr. London: H. R. Allenson Ltd. [1916].   2nd edition.   157 pp., portraits.   7¼"

Ministering to the Forces; the story of the Baptist and Congregational Chaplains and the Work of the United Navy, Army and Air Force Board, 1914-1964. By the Rev. Ronald W. Thomson. London: Baptist Union of Gt. Britain & Ireland & The Congregational Union of England & Wales [1964].   64 pp.   8½"

ROYAL ARMY SERVICE CORPS

The Predecessors of the Royal Army Service Corps. By Lieut.-Col. C. H. Massé. Illustrated by C. C. P. Lawson. Aldershot: Gale & Polden Ltd., 1948.   xvi, 116 pp., plates.   9½"
   Contents: The Royal Waggoners, 1794/5. The Royal Waggon Corps and Train, 1799-1833. The Land Transport Corps, 1855-57. The Military Train and Commissariat Staff Corps, 1856-69. The Army Service Corps, 1869-81. The Commissariat and Transport Staff and Commissariat and Transport Corps, 1880-88.
   2 coloured plates and many sketches of uniforms.

The Royal Army Service Corps. A History of Transport and Supply in the British Army. Cambridge: University Press, 1930, 31.   8½"

   Vol. 1. By John Fortescue. Portraits, maps.

   Vol. 2. By Col. R. H. Beadon. With an Introduction by John Fortescue. Diagrams, maps.

The Story of the Royal Army Service Corps, 1939-1945. London: published under the direction of the Institution of the R.A.S.C. by G. Bell and Sons Ltd., 1955.   xxii, 720 pp., portraits, plates, maps, end-paper map.   9¾"

Short History of the Royal Army Service Corps.   Aldershot: Gale & Polden Ltd. [1959].   [vii], 72 pp., portrait, plates. $7\frac{1}{4}''$
   3 coloured plates of uniform.

——— [Another edition] Aldershot: Gale & Polden Ltd. [1946].   20 pp. $7\frac{1}{4}''$

With the Army Service Corps in South Africa.   By Sir Wodehouse Richardson, Colonel, Deputy Adjutant-General for Supplies and Transport in South Africa, 1899-1900.   London: Richardson & Co., 1903.   161 pp. $8\frac{1}{2}''$

Memories of the 71st and 83rd Companies, R.A.S.C., M.T., 1914-1918.   By Stanley J. Levy.   [London: The Abbey Press Ltd., printed for private circulation].   176 pp., portraits, illustrations. $9''$

The Peregrinations of the 34th Divisional (M.T.) Coy. (179 Coy. R.A.S.C.) during the Great War of 1914-1919.   Written by Mechanist Sergt.-Major G. Lipscombe.   Aldershot: Gale & Polden Ltd., 1920.   [12], 76 pp., portraits, plates. $7\frac{1}{4}''$

Historical Record of 180 Coy. Royal Army Service Corps, Mechanical Transport.   (At the time of writing its War designation being) The 18th Ammunition Sub-Park.   Written by Mechanist Sergt.-Major G. Lispcombe.   Aldershot: Gale & Polden Ltd., 1919.   [12], 116 pp., portraits, plates. $7\frac{1}{4}''$

The History of 376 H.A.M.T. Company, R.A.S.C. (Commanded by Capt. J. W. Rooke) attached to 43rd Siege Battery, R.G.A.   1915-1919, Egypt, Gallipoli, Macedonia, Serbia, Bulgaria.   Compiled from Notes taken on the field by Harry A. Epstein.   London: [Letchworth Garden City Press], 1919.   32 pp. $7\frac{1}{4}''$

From the Gulf to the Caspian, being the Souvenir Booklet of the 33rd Motor Ambulance Convoy which served in Mesopotamia and North Persia, 1916 to 1919.   Written by various Members of the Unit who remain anonymous. No imprint, *n.d.*   43 pp., plates, map. $8'' \times 10\frac{1}{2}''$

D Day to VE Day with the R.A.S.C.   [502 Coy., R.A.S.C. Independent Armoured Brigade.   By Capt. T. S. Morris and others].   [Aldershot: Gale & Polden Ltd., 1946].   x, 95 pp., plates. $8\frac{1}{2}''$

ROYAL ARMY MEDICAL CORPS

The Story of our Services under the Crown.   A Historical Sketch of the Army Medical Staff.   By Surgeon-Major Albert A. Gore.   London: Baillicre, Tindall and Cox, 1879.   [8], 194.   (Reprinted from Colburn's United Service Magazine). $8\frac{3}{4}''$

A Short History of the Royal Army Medical Corps.   By Col. Fred Smith. Aldershot: Gale & Polden Ltd. [1929].   [12], 111 pp., plates. $7\frac{1}{4}''$

——— 2nd edition.   1931.   xii, 111 pp. $7\frac{1}{4}''$

Not least in the Crusade: a Short History of the Royal Army Medical Corps. By Peter Lovegrove.   Aldershot: Gale & Polden Ltd., 1951, xii, 90 pp., plates. 7¼″
   1 coloured plate of uniform.

The Jubilee Scrapbook of the Royal Army Medical Corps. A Souvenir Scrap-book of fifty years' Corps History published in aid of the R.A.M.C. War Memorial Fund.   Produced under the auspices of the Royal Army Medical Corps Associa-tion.   Aldershot: Gale & Polden Ltd., 1948.   41 pp., portraits, illustrations. 9¼″

The Wings of Healing; the Story of the Airborne Medical Services, 1940-1960. By Lt.-Col. Howard N. Cole; with a Foreword by Lt.-Gen. Sir Frederick Browning.   London: Wm. Blackwood & Sons Ltd., 1963.   xviii, 227 pp., plate, maps.   8½″

A List of the Commissioned Medical Officers of the Army, Charles II to Accession of George II, 1660 to 1727.   Compiled by Col. Alfred Peterkin.   Aberdeen: The University Press, 1925.   viii, 38 pp.   9¾″

Roll of Commissioned Officers in the Medical Service of the British Army who served on full-pay within the period between the Accession of George II and the Formation of the Royal Army Medical Corps, 20 June 1727 to 23 June 1898, with an Introduction showing the Historical Evolution of the Corps.   By the late Col. William Johnston.   Edited by Lieut.-Col. Harry A. L. Howell. Aberdeen: The University Press, 1917.   lxxii, 638 pp., portrait.   10¼″

Fifth Division, 13th, 14th and 15th Field Ambulances.   Diary of their Move-ments in France, Italy and Belgium, 1914-1919.   With a Foreword by Major-Gen. J. Ponsonby.   London: War Narratives Publishing Co., 1919.   For private circulation.   32 pp.   9¾″

With the Forty-Fourths, being a Record of the Doings of the 44th Field Ambu-lance (14th Division).   London: Spottiswoode, Ballantyne & Co. Ltd., 1922. 83 pp., portraits, illustrations, maps.   8½″

Via Ypres.   Story of the 39th Divisional Field Ambulances.   By Allan Jobson. With a Foreword by Gen. Sir Hubert de la Poer Gough.   London: The West-minster City Publishing Co. Ltd., 1934.   [14], 237 pp., portrait, plates.   8½″

The Story of the 18th General Hospital, 1939-45.   By T. D. Pratt and G. A. Bramley.   [Leeds: printed by J. Rostron & Son Ltd.], n.d.   34 pp., portraits, plates.   8″

The Third British Field Dressing Station, R.A.M.C.   [Souvenir booklet; by Major R. W. L. Hall and others].   No imprint, 1945.   112 pp., illustrations.   8¼″

[Brief Sketch of the part played by No. 1 Field Dressing Station with the British Liberation Army during the campaign in North-West Europe, 1944-1945].   By A. F. Harmer.   [Rendsburg, Germany: printed by Heinrich Möller Söhne, 1945]. 48 pp., portraits, plates.   8½″

The Names of the Officers, Warrant Officers, Non-Commissioned Officers, and Men of the Royal Army Medical Corps who gave their Lives in The Great War, 1914-1919. London: The Chiswick Press for the R.A.M.C. War Memorial Fund, 1924. 168 pp., plates. 8½″

The Book of Remembrance. A Roll of Honour of all Ranks of the Royal Army Medical Corps who fell in the Second World War, 1939-1945. [Aldershot: Gale & Polden Ltd., 1949]. 79 pp., illustrations. 8¼″

The Story of the R.A.M.C. [Booklet for recruits]. [London: Sapphire Press Ltd., 1964]. 13 pp. 8¼″

ROYAL ARMY ORDNANCE CORPS

A History of the Army Ordnance Services. By Major-Gen. A. Forbes. London: The Medici Society Ltd., 1929. 3 vols., portraits, plates, illustrations, maps. 8½″

Vol. 1. Ancient History.

Vol. 2. Modern History.

Vol. 3. The Great War.

A Summary of the History of the Royal Army Ordnance Corps. [London: printed by Walter Bargery, 1921]. 40 pp. 5½″

The First Five Hundred Years; an Outline History of the Predecessors of the Royal Army Ordnance Corps from the beginnings to 1914. By Henry E. Harris. Aldershot: Gale & Polden Ltd., 1962. [viii], 120 pp., illustrations. 7¼″

Royal Army Ordnance Corps. Record of Services; Tilbury Fort Detachment and Northfleet Magazine Detachment, 1914-1919. [Aldershot: Gale & Polden Ltd.], 1919. 23 pp. 7¼″

21 Army Group Ordnance. The Story of the Campaign in North West Europe. By Major J. Lee-Richardson. Illustrations by Sjt. W. Savage. [Printed and published in Germany, 1946]. 94 pp., illustrations, maps. 9¾″

A Brief History of 30 Armoured Brigade Ordnance Field Park, R.A.O.C. By Major R. F. Davidson. Aldershot: Gale & Polden Ltd. [1946]. [4], 28 pp. 7¼″

ROYAL ELECTRICAL AND MECHANICAL ENGINEERS

10 Corps Troops Workshops, R.E.M.E., 1942-1945. [By Lt.-Col. P. D. Powell]. [C.M.F., 1946]. 40 pp., maps on paper covers. 7¼″×9¾″

CORPS OF ROYAL MILITARY POLICE

The History of the Office of the Provost Marshal and the Corps of Military Police. [By Capt. A. V. Lovell-Knight]. [Aldershot: printed by Gale & Polden Ltd., 1943]. [10], 174 pp. 7¼"

The History of the Corps of Royal Military Police. By Major S. F. Crozier. Aldershot: Gale & Polden Ltd., 1951. xvi, 224 pp., portraits, plates, maps. 8½"
1 coloured plate.

ROYAL ARMY PAY CORPS

The Royal Army Pay Corps. [Abridged History edited by Col. L. H. Mackenzie. Stockport: The Chester Press Ltd., 1951]. 24 pp. 4¼"×6½"

ROYAL ARMY VETERINARY CORPS

A History of the Royal Army Veterinary Corps, 1796-1919. By Major-Gen. Sir Frederick Smith, formerly Director-General Army Veterinary Service. London: Bailliere, Tindall & Cox, 1927. xii, 268 pp., portraits, plates. 9¾"
10 coloured plates of uniform.

The History of the Royal Army Veterinary Corps, 1919-1961. By Brig. J. Clabby, with a Foreword by Gen. Sir Cecil S. Sugden. London: J. A. Allen & Co., 1963. 244 pp., portrait, plates, illustrations, maps. 9¾"

SMALL ARMS SCHOOL CORPS

A Brief History of the Small Arms School Corps and the Small Arms Wing, School of Infantry, Hythe, 1853-1953. By Capt. A. J. Parsons. [Maidstone: British Legion Press, 1953]. 38 pp., portrait, illustrations. 8½"

MILITARY PROVOST STAFF CORPS

A History of the Provost Marshal and the Provost Services. By Capt. H. Bullock. Aberdeen: Milne & Hutchison, 1929. [vi], 71 pp. 7¼"

ROYAL ARMY EDUCATIONAL CORPS

The Story of Army Education, 1643-1963. By Col. A. C. T. White. With a Foreword by Gen. Sir Hugh Stockwell. London: George G. Harrap & Co. Ltd., 1963. 286 pp., portrait, plates. $8\frac{1}{2}''$

ROYAL ARMY DENTAL CORPS

The History of the Army Dental Service. Issued by The War Office (AMD.6), 1959. 24 pp. *Duplicated.* $8''$

ROYAL PIONEER CORPS

The Pioneer. British Army of the Rhine, 1943-1946. Souvenir. [Major E. Mottram, editor]. [Germany: B.A.O.R., 1946]. 60 pp., portraits, illustrations. $10\frac{1}{4}''$

The Story of the Royal Pioneer Corps. [Weymouth: printed by Sherren & Son Ltd., 1953]. 12 pp., illustrations. $6\frac{7}{8}''$

A War History of the Royal Pioneer Corps, 1939-1945. By Major E. H. Rhodes-Wood. Aldershot: Gale & Polden Ltd., 1960. xvi, 368 pp., portraits, plates, maps. $8\frac{1}{2}''$

ARMY PHYSICAL TRAINING CORPS

History of the Army Physical Training Corps. Part 1. The Army Gymnastic Staff, 1860-August 1914. [By Lt.-Col. E. A. L. Oldfield]. [Aldershot: Gale & Polden Ltd., 1949]. 19 pp., portraits, illustrations. $8\frac{1}{2}''$
   No more published in this form.

History of the Army Physical Training Corps. By Lieut.-Col. E. A. L. Oldfield. Aldershot: Gale & Polden Ltd., 1955. xii, 169 pp., portraits, plates. $8\frac{1}{2}''$

Army Physical Training Corps, incorporating the Army Gymnastic Staff and the Army Physical Training Staff; centenary, 1860-1960. [By Major T. L. Fletcher and Major L. Lambert]. Aldershot: printed by Gale & Polden Ltd., 1960. 44 pp., portraits, illustrations. $8\frac{1}{2}''$

QUEEN ALEXANDRA'S ROYAL ARMY NURSING CORPS

One Hundred years of Army Nursing. The Story of the British Army Nursing Services from the Time of Florence Nightingale to the present day. By Ian Hay [Major-Gen. J. H. Beith]. London: Cassell & Co. Ltd. [1953]. 387 pp., plates, maps. 8½"

Reminiscent Sketches, 1914 to 1919. By Members of Her Majesty Queen Alexandra's Imperial Military Nursing Service. London: John Bale, Sons & Danielsson Ltd., 1922, vii, 80 pp., plates. 7¼"

SECTION IV
AUXILIARY FORCES

FENCIBLES

ENGLAND AND WALES

DENBIGHSHIRE

Historical Records of the Denbighshire Hussars Imperial Yeomanry . . . With Note on the . . . Ancient British Fencible Cavalry, by Engr. Lieut. B. F. M. Freeman, R.N.   Wrexham: Woodall, Minshall, Thomas & Co., 1909.   8½″

DURHAM

The Durham Fencibles.   By Lt.-Col. the Hon. W. L. Vane.   No imprint. 46 pp., 1912.   5″

ISLE OF MAN

The Royal Manx Fencibles.   By B. E. Sargeaunt.   Aldershot: Gale & Polden Ltd., 1947.   101 pp., portraits, plates, map.   8½″

A Military History of the Isle of Man.   [By] B. E. Sargeaunt.   [Incl. Fencibles, etc.].   Arbroath: T. Buncle & Co. Ltd.   [1949].   8½″

NEW ROMNEY

The New Romney Fencible Cavalry (Duke of York's Own), 1794 to 1800.   By Col. E. A. C. Fazan.   Ashford: Headley Brothers.   Reprinted from *Archaeologia Cantiana*, vol. LXII, 1950, pp. 11-20, plates.   8½″

NORFOLK

Records of the Norfolk Yeomanry Cavalry, to which is added The Fencible and Provincial Cavalry of the same county from 1780 to 1908.   Compiled by Lieut.-Col. J. R. Harvey.   London: Jarrold & Sons, 1908.   Portrait.   11″

WARWICKSHIRE

The Warwickshire Fencible Cavalry [in *History of the Warwickshire Yeomanry Cavalry;* by the Hon. H. A. Adderley, pp. 1-9].   Warwick: W. H. Smith & Son. 1912.   8″

SCOTLAND

Sketches of the Character, Manners, and Present State of the Highlanders of Scotland; with details of the Military Service of the Highland Regiments. By Col. David Stewart. 2nd edition. Edinburgh: Archibald Constable & Co., 1822. 2 vols. 8½″
  Vol. 2 contains short accounts of the following Fencible regiments:—

Argyle, 1759	Rothsay and Caithness, 1794
Sutherland, 1759	Dumbarton, 1794
Argyle, or Western, 1778	Reay, 1794
Gordon, 1778	Inverness, 1794
Sutherland, 1779	Fraser, 1794
Grant or Strathspey, 1793	Lochaber, 1799
Breadalbane, 1793-4	Clan Alpine, 1799
Sutherland, 1793	Regiment of the Isles, 1799
Gordon, 1793	Argyle, Glengarry, etc., 1794

A History of the Highlands and of the Highland Clans; with an extensive selection from the hitherto inedited Stuart Papers. By James Browne. Edinburgh: A. Fullarton & Co., 1852-53. 4 vols. New edition. 9½″
  Contains Fencible regiments, as in Stewart above.

Territorial Soldiering in the North-East of Scotland during 1759-1814. By John Malcolm Bulloch. Aberdeen: The New Spalding Club. 1914. lxviii, 517 pp. 10″
  Contains accounts of the following regiments:
  The Northern Fencibles, 1778-83, pp. 73-128.
  The Northern Fencibles, 1793-99, pp. 141-172.
  The Strathspey Fencibles, 1793-99., pp. 173-184.
  The Aberdeenshire or Princess of Wales's Fencibles, 1794-1803, pp. 263-269.
  The Banffshire or Duke of York's Own Fencibles, 1798-1802, pp. 270-275.

CAITHNESS
The Caithness Fencibles, and a Recruiting Card of 1799. By Major I. H. Mackay Scobie. [In *Society for Army Historical Research, Journal*, vol. 6, 1927, pp. 96-106]. Coloured portrait and coloured plate of uniform. 9¼″

GLENGARRY
Sketches illustrating the Early Settlement and History of Glengarry in Canada . . . and the Services of the . . . Glengarry Fencible or British Highland Regiment, etc. By J. A. Macdonell (of Greenfield). Montreal: Wm. Foster, Brown & Co., 1893. 9¾″

GRANT, OR STRATHSPEY
The Grant, Strathspey or First Highland Fencible Regiment, 1793-1799. By H. B. Mackintosh. Elgin: James D. Yeadon, 1934. 128 pp., portraits, plates. 10″
  2 coloured portraits in uniform.
See also Territorial Soldiering in the North-East of Scotland; by J. M. Bulloch, *above.*

NORTHERN OR GORDON.   1778-83 and 1793-9
The Duke of Gordon's Second Regiment. Muster Roll of the Northern Fencibles, 1778-82.   By J. M. Bulloch.   [Keith: privately printed], 1909.   8 pp.   10"

The 4th Duke of Gordon's Third Regiment. Muster Roll of the Northern Fencibles, 1793-9.   By J. M. B. [Keith: privately printed], 1909.   8 pp.   10"

The Northern or Gordon Fencibles, 1778-1783.   By H. B. Mackintosh. [Edinburgh: Turnbull & Spears], privately printed, 1929.   106 pp., plates.   10"
   2 coloured plates of uniform.   250 copies printed.
   See also Territorial Soldiering in the North-East of Scotland; by J. M. Bulloch, *above.*

PERTHSHIRE.
A Military History of Perthshire, 1660-1902.   Edited by the Marchioness of Tullibardine.   Perth: R. A. & J. Hay, 1908.   9¾"
   Contains accounts of the following regiments:
   The 4th (or Breadalbane) Regiment of Fencible Men, 1793-1802.
   The Perthshire Fencible Cavalry, 1794-1800.
   The Perthshire Regiment of Fencibles, 1794-99.
   The Drummond of Perth Fencibles.
   The Royal Clan Alpine Fencible Infantry, 1799-1802.

REAY
The Reay Fencibles or Lord Reay's Highlanders.   Compiled from Documents supplied by the War Office, "Musgrave's History of the Irish Rebellion of 1798"; "History of the House and Clan of Mackay" and other Documents.   By John Mackay.   Glasgow: for the Clan Mackay Society by Charles Mackay, 1890.   59 pp.   7¼"

An Old Highland Fencible Corps.   The History of the Reay Fencible Highland Regiment of Foot, or Mackay's Highlanders, 1794-1802.   With an Account of its Services in Ireland during the Rebellion of 1798.   By Capt. I. H. Mackay Scobie.   Edinburgh: William Blackwood & Sons, 1914.   xlii, 413 pp., portraits, plates, illustrations, maps.   10"
   3 coloured plates of uniform.

Reay Fencibles [in *Old Scottish Regimental Colours;* by Andrew Ross, 1885, pp. 124-5].   Coloured plate.   Edinburgh: William Blackwood & Sons.   15"

SUTHERLAND
The Fencible Regiments of Sutherland [in *Am Reisimeid Chataich.   The 93rd Sutherland Highlanders . . . 1797-1927.   By Brig.-Gen. A. E. J. Cavendish].   1928   10¾"

MILITIA: SPECIAL RESERVE

ENGLAND AND WALES

The Royal Militia and Yeomanry Cavalry Army List; containing . . . A History of the Services, Organization, and Equipment of the Regiments of Militia etc. Arranged and compiled from official Documents by Arthur Sleigh, late Lieut. London: British Army Despatch Press, 1850. Published half-yearly. No. 1, April, 1850. *No more published.* xxxviii, 190 pp. 8½"

An Epitomized History of The Militia (The " Constitutional Force "), together with the Origin, Periods of Embodied Service, and Special Services (including South Africa, 1899-1902), of Militia Units existing October 31, 1905. Compiled by Col. George Jackson Hay. London: " United Service Gazette " Offices. [1906]. [iv], 444 pp. 9½"

ANGLESEY
Memoirs of the Anglesea Militia, including the Principles of the Militia Laws, illustrated by several Cases and Decisions, with Observations on the Evidence against William Peacocke late Lieutenant Colonel, sentenced to be cashiered by a Court Martial held at Portsmouth, August the 6th, 1782, etc. [London]: J. Mathews [1783]. iv, 44 pp. 9½"

BEDFORDSHIRE
Regimental Records of the Bedfordshire Militia from 1759 to 1884. By Lieut.-Col. Sir John M. Burgoyne, Bart. London: W. H. Allen & Co., 1884. iv, 124 pp. 7½"

BERKSHIRE
History of the Royal Berkshire Militia: now 3rd Battalion, Royal Berks Regiment). [By Miss E. E. Thoyts]. Reading: printed by Joseph Hawkes, 1897. xx, 352 pp., portraits (1 coloured), plates. 8¼"

BRECON, *see under* MONMOUTHSHIRE

CAMBRIDGESHIRE
A Short Historical Record of the 4th Batt. Suffolk Regiment (late Cambridgeshire Militia). By Col. H. Frost. Cambridge: printed and published by A. T. Naylor, " Chronicle " Office [1896]. iv, 82 pp., portraits. 7¼"

CORNWALL
" The Royal Miners." A History of the Stannaries Regiment of Miners, late Cornwall and Devon Miners Royal Garrison Artillery Militia, commonly called " The Royal Miners." By G. Cavenagh-Mainwaring (late Captain in the Regiment), including a Short Account of contemporary Military events affecting Cornwall and Devon and the Militia generally. London: Harrison and Sons Ltd., 1913. 129 pp., portraits, plates. 9¾"

DEVON
Annals of the Militia; being The Records of the South Devon Regiment; prefaced by An Historical Account of Militia Organization.　Plymouth: William Brendon and Son [1874].　116 pp.　8¼″

Historical Records of the 1st Devon Militia (4th Battalion, The Devonshire Regiment); with a Notice of the 2nd and North Devon Militia Regiments.　By Col. H. Walrond.　London: Longmans, Green & Co., Ltd., 1897.　xvi, 444 pp., portraits, plates.　8¾″

DORSET
The Dorsetshire Regiment.　The Thirty-Ninth and Fifty-Fourth Foot and the Dorset Militia etc.　By C. T. Atkinson.　Oxford: privately printed at the University Press, 1947.　Part II.　9¼″

History of the Dorsetshire Regiment, 1914-1919.　Part I [pp. 273-9, History of the 3rd Battn.; by Major H. C. C. Batten].　Dorchester: Henry Ling Ltd., 1933.　9½″

DURHAM
The Durham Light Infantry.　By the Hon. W. L. Vane, Lieut.-Col.　[Chapter on Militia Battn.].　London: Gale & Polden Ltd., 1914.　9¾″

Faithful; the Story of the Durham Light Infantry.　By S. G. P. Ward.　[Including the Militia].　London: Thomas Nelson & Sons Ltd. [1963].　9¾″

ESSEX
The Essex Regiment.　The Essex Militia.　By J. W. Burrows.　Southend-on-Sea: John H. Burrows & Sons Ltd. [1929].　xxiv, 238 pp., portraits, plates, illustrations.　(Essex Units in the War, 1914-1919, vol. 4).　[Covers history since formation].　8½″
　2 coloured plates of uniform.

GLOUCESTERSHIRE
The Royal North Gloucester: being notes from the Regimental Orders and Correspondence of the Royal North Gloucestershire Militia, with introductory chapters.　(Founded upon an account of the regiment commenced by the late Sir J. Maxwell Steele-Graves, Bart.).　Compiled by Wilfrid Joseph Cripps, Capt.　London: printed for the compiler by Nicholls and Sons, 1875.　x, 188 pp.　8½″

——— [Another edition with title].　The Royal North Gloucester Militia; with Notes by Capt. the Hon. M. H. Hicks-Beach and Major B. N. Spraggett, on the modern history of the Corps from its constitution as the 4th Batt. of the Glo'stershire Regiment to its disbandment in 1908.　Cirencester: Wilts and Gloucestershire Standard Printing Works [1915].　x, 224 pp., plates.　8½″

A Short History of the 3rd Battalion The Prince of Wales's Volunteers (South Lancashire Regiment) formerly 4th Royal Lancashire (The Duke of Lancaster's Own) Light Infantry Militia, being principally extracts from the Regimental Records.   Manchester: Taylor, Garnett, Evans & Co. Ltd., 1909.   112 pp.   9⅞″

LEICESTERSHIRE
The Leicestershire Militia in South Africa.   [By Major G. H. P. Burne].   [Leicester: Clarke & Satchell, printers, 1902].   116 pp., plates.   6″×9¾″

LINCOLNSHIRE
Annals of the 3rd Battalion Lincolnshire Regiment, formerly the Royal North Lincoln Militia, 1759-1901.   By Capt. W. V. R. Fane.   Lincoln: James Williamson, printer, 1901.   48 pp.   7½″

LONDON
The 7th Battalion The Rifle Brigade (The Prince Consort's Own) late King's Own Royal Tower Hamlets Light Infantry Militia.   [By Sergt.-Major Grant Hodder].   Enfield Press, printed by J. A. Meyers, 1884.   68 pp.   8½″

The Trained Bands of London.   By Major G. Goold Walker.   [In *Journal of the Honourable Artillery Company*, vols. 15-17, 1938-40].   9¼″

MERIONETH
The Merioneth Militia.   [In *Echoes of Old Merioneth;* by Hugh J. Owen, pp. 24-40].   Dolgelley: Hughes Bros., 1949.   8½″

MONMOUTHSHIRE
Some Records of the Royal Monmouthshire Militia (at one time the Monmouth and Brecon Militia).   By Capt. W. F. N. Noel, Royal Engineers, Adjutant.   Monmouth: printed by Bailey and Son, 1886.   111 pp.   9″

The Royal Monmouth Militia; being a Detailed Description of the Regiment from the year 1660 to the time of its Transfer to the Special Reserve.   By B. E. Sargeaunt.   London: The Royal United Service Institution, 1910.   xii, 302 pp., portraits, plates.   9¾″

MONTGOMERYSHIRE
Records of the Royal Montgomery Regiment of Militia, 4th Batt. The South Wales Borderers.   Arranged by R. J. Harrison.   Reprinted from the " *Montgomeryshire Collections*."   London: Whiting & Co., 1884.   56 pp.   8vo.

A Memento of the Royal Montgomeryshire Militia—4th Batt.   The South Wales Borderers.   A Resume of the Battalions History by R. Owen.   Reprinted from the " *Montgomery County Times* " with a Report of the Laying up of the Colours reprinted from the " *Montgomeryshire Express*."   Welshpool: R. & M. Owen [1908].   30 pp.   8vo.

NORFOLK
Diary of the Norfolk Artillery, 1853-1894.   By J. Sancroft Holmes, Major and
Hon. Lieut.-Col.   Norwich: Jarrold & Sons, printers [1894].   110 pp.   10″

—— Another Edition . . . 1853-1909.   Norwich: Jarrold & Sons [1909].
169 pp., plates (1 coloured).   10½″

The History of the 4th Battalion Norfolk Regiment (late East Norfolk Militia).
Compiled by Col. Sir Charles Harvey, Bart.   London: Jarrold & Sons, 1899.   iv,
290 pp., portraits, plates.   11″

The History of the Norfolk Regiment, 1685-1918.   By F. Loraine Petre.   Vol. 1
(Deals with the Militia).   Norwich: Jarrold & Sons Ltd., 1924.   9½″

NORTHAMPTONSHIRE AND RUTLAND
Records of the Services of the Northamptonshire and Rutland Militia from
1756 to 1889.   Northampton: Cordeux & Sons [1890].   42, [10] pp.   9″

Memoirs and Records of the Northamptonshire & Rutland Militia, together
with a brief outline of the origin and history of the Militia Force of Great Britain
to the present time.   By the Captain of No. 1 Company [R. J. D'Arcy].   London:
Edward Stanford, 1875.   viii, 288 pp.   For subscribers only.   8½″

The History of the Northamptonshire & Rutland Militia: now the 3rd Battalion
(Militia) of the Northamptonshire Regiment, from 1756 to 1919.   By Major
C. A. Markham.   London: Reeves and Turner, 1924.   xii, 224 pp., portraits,
plates.   9″
    1 coloured plate of colours.

NORTHUMBERLAND
Notices of the Services of the 27th Northumberland Light Infantry Militia, with
a brief account of several Local Corps of Volunteers which were enrolled in the
county of Northumberland, and in the town and county of Newcastle-upon-Tyne,
during the war with France, towards the close of the last and the commencement
of the present century.   Compiled and edited, with Notes by William Adamson,
Senior Capt. and Hon. Major.   Newcastle-upon-Tyne: Robert Robinson, 1877.
95 pp.   8½″

—— [Another edition with title]: The Services of the 27th Northumberland
Light Infantry Militia, now 3rd Battalion Northumberland Fusiliers . . . and
continued up to the present time by Major and Hon. Lieut.-Col. Robert Scott.
Newcastle-upon-Tyne: Andrew Reid & Co. Ltd., 1914.   152 pp.   9¾″

NOTTINGHAMSHIRE
Historical Record of the Royal Sherwood Foresters: or Nottinghamshire Regiment of Militia.   By Capt. A. E. Lawson Lowe.   London: W. Mitchell & Co.,
1872.   viii, 84 pp.   9½″

OXFORDSHIRE

Oxfordshire Militia. Sketch of the History of the Regiment. John Winston, Duke of Marlborough, K.G., Lord Lieutenant. John William Fane, Lieut.-Col. Commandant. [By John M. Davenport, Clerk of the Lieutenancy. Oxford: E. W. Morris, jun., printer], 1869. 37 pp. 8″

History of the Oxfordshire Regiment of Militia (Fourth Battalion Oxfordshire Light Infantry), 1778-1900; including the Diary of the late Lieut.-Col. Thomas Mosley Crowder, 1853-1885. By Lieut.-Col. Frank Willan. Oxford: Horace Hart, printer to the University, 1900. [xii], 188 pp., portraits, plates. 8¾″

PEMBROKESHIRE

An Abstract of the History and Services of The Royal Pembrokeshire Militia. By Col. C. W. Willis, Commanding the Pembroke R.F.R.A. No imprint. [Preface dated Bournemouth, 1st June, 1909]. 16 pp. 5″×4″

RADNORSHIRE

Notes on the Militia, with special reference to The Royal Radnor Regular Militia (The 50th Regiment of Regular Militia). By Lieut.-Col. Gilbert Drage. Llandrindod Wells: published by the Radnorshire Society and Printed by Sayce Brothers, 1937. 56 pp., plate. 9¾″

RUTLAND, *see under* NORTHAMPTONSHIRE

SOMERSET

Records of the 1st Somerset Militia (3rd Battalion Somerset Light Infantry). By W. J. W. Kerr, late Capt. and Hon. Major. Aldershot: Gale & Polden Ltd. [1930]. xii, 110 pp., plates. 9¾″

STAFFORDSHIRE

Historical Record of the 1st King's Own Stafford Militia, now 3rd and 4th Battalions, South Staffordshire Regiment. Compiled by Capt. C. H. Wylly, Adjutant. Lichfield: A. C. Lomax, 1893. 70 pp. 7″

———— [Another edition] . . . to 1892, and by Col. Charrington and Capt. Bulwer, to 1902. Lichfield: A. C. Lomax's Successors, 1902. 87 pp. 7″

Historical Records of the 3rd King's Own Staffordshire Militia, now the 4th Battalion, The Prince of Wales's North Staffordshire Regiment. By Capt. C. C. W. Troughton. Lichfield: A. C. Lomax, 1894. iv, 86 pp. 7″

———— [2nd edition with title] Historical Records of the King's Own Stafford Rifles (3rd K.O. Stafford Militia), now the 4th Battalion, The Prince of Wales's North Staffordshire Regiment. Lichfield: A. C. Lomax's Successors, 1903. 149 pp. 7″

SUFFOLK
History of the 12th (The Suffolk) Regiment, 1685-1913.   By Lieut.-Col. E. A. H. Webb; including a Brief History of the East and West Suffolk Militia, the latter being now the 3rd Battalion Suffolk Regiment.   London: Spottiswoode & Co. Ltd., 1914.   (Pp. 442-449), plates. $9\frac{3}{4}''$

The History of the Suffolk Regiment, 1914-1927.   By Lieut.-Col. C. C. R. Murphy.   (Chapter on the 3rd (Special Reserve) Battalion, pp. 322-331). London: Hutchinson & Co. (Publishers) Ltd. [1928]. $9''$

SURREY
Historical Records of the Second Royal Surrey, or Eleventh Regiment of Militia, with Introductory Chapters.   Compiled by John Davis, Capt.   London: Marcus Ward & Co., 1877.   xxvi, 468 pp., portraits, plates. $8\frac{1}{2}''$
    1 coloured plate of colours.

Historical Record of the 3rd Royal Surrey Regiment of Militia, No. 118.   Raised in 1798—Revived in 1853.   Head Quarters: Kingston-on-Thames.   With which is incorporated A short sketch of the History of the Militia.   By Capt. Lamorock Flower.   London: W. Mitchell & Co., 1869.   60 pp., portrait. $9''$

WARWICKSHIRE
History of the 53rd, or 2nd Warwickshire Regiment of Militia, now the 6th Battalion Royal Warwickshire Regiment.   Warwick: printed by Evans & Co., "Advertiser" Office, 1903.   72 pp., plates. $8\frac{1}{2}''$
    2 coloured plates of uniform and 1 of colours.

WILTSHIRE
The Story of the Wiltshire Regiment (Duke of Edinburgh's); the 62nd and 99th Foot (1756-1959), the Militia, etc.   By Col. N. C. E. Kenrick.   Aldershot: Gale & Polden Ltd. $8\frac{1}{2}''$

WORCESTERSHIRE
Historical Record of the Third and Fourth Battalions of the Worcestershire Regiment.   By Capt. Robert Holden.   London: Kegan Paul, Trench & Co., 1887.   xvi, 326 pp., portraits. $10''$

YORKSHIRE
The Records of the Third Battalion Prince of Wales's Own West Yorkshire Regiment, late Second West York Light Infantry Militia.   Compiled for the Regiment by Lieut.-Col. G. I. Hay.   [London: printed by The Army and Navy Co-operative Society, Ltd.]   January, 1882.   xi, 61 pp. $8\frac{1}{2}''$

———— Revised edition . . . and revised 1897 by Col. G. J. Hay.   No imprint [1897].   xiii, 92 pp. $8\frac{1}{2}''$

The Record of the 4th Battalion West Yorkshire Regiment (Prince of Wales's Own) during the Boer War, 1899-1902.   By Capt. A. B. Ritchie.   York: John Sampson, 1903.   [iv], 63 pp. $7\frac{1}{4}''$

The West Yorkshire Regiment in the War, 1914-1918. A History of the 14th, The Prince of Wales's Own (West Yorkshire Regt.) and of its Special Reserve . . . Battns. By Everard Wyrall. London: John Lane, The Bodley Head. 2 vols. 1924-27. 9½"

Origin and Services of the Third West Yorkshire (Light Infantry) Regiment of Militia; with notices of the formation of West Riding Militia. By William Sheardown. Communicated to the Doncaster Gazette, May 6, 13, 20 and 28, 1870. Doncaster: printed at the Gazette Office. 54 pp. 7½"

Historical Records of the First Regiment of Militia; or, Third West York Light Infantry. By Capt. G. A. Raikes. London: Richard Bentley & Son, 1876. xvi, 335 pp., portraits, plates. 8½"
  1 coloured plate of colours.

. . . A Continuation of The Historical Records of the First Regiment of Militia or Third West York Light Infantry, now the Third Battalion, York and Lancaster Regiment, from 1875 to 1905. By Major E. C. Broughton. London: William Clowes & Sons, Ltd. 1906. x, 106 pp., portraits, plates. 8½"

The York and Lancaster Regiment, 1758-1919. By Col. H. C. Wylly. Vol. 2 [Chapter on 3rd (Sp. Res.) Bn. (3rd West York) Militia, 1758-1919]. [Frome & London: printed by Butler & Tanner Ltd.] 1930. 9¾"

Records of the 3rd Battalion The Duke of Wellington's (West Riding) Regiment, formerly 6th West York Militia, The Halifax Militia (including Companies of Volunteer Militia, formed under Act 34, George III), 1760-1910. Compiled by Capt. N. H. Moore. London: Gale & Polden Ltd. [1910]. viii, 166 pp., plates. 8½"

The History of the North York Militia, now known as the Fourth Battalion, Alexandra, Princess of Wales's Own (Yorkshire Regiment). By Robert Bell Turton, Major. Leeds: J. Whitehead & Son, 1907. viii, 212 pp. 9"

SCOTLAND

ABERDEENSHIRE
The Raising of the Aberdeen Militia, MDCCXCVII. [By] J. M. Bulloch. [Aberdeen: The Rosemount Press]. Privately printed, 1915. 7 pp. 10"
  50 copies printed.

The Aberdeenshire Militia and the Royal Aberdeenshire Highlanders, now the Third Battalion, the Gordon Highlanders, 1798 to 1882. By Col. Thomas Innes. [Aberdeen: printed at the Aberdeen Journal Office], 1884. 38 pp. 4to.

Territorial Soldiering in the North-East of Scotland during 1759-1814. By John Malcolm Bulloch. [Account of the Militia, pp. 276-286 and Local Militia, pp. 370-384]. Aberdeen: The New Spalding Club, 1914. 10"

ARGYLLSHIRE
The Argyll or Campbell Militia, 1745-6.   By Major I. H. Mackay Scobie.   [In
Society for Army Historical Research, Journal.   Vol. 24, 1946, pp. 12-29].
Illustrations, map.   9¼″

AYRSHIRE
Records of the Ayr Militia from 1802 to 1883.   [Introductory note signed
H.R.D., i.e., Hon. Sir Hew R. Dalrymple].   Edinburgh: privately printed,
1884.   31 pp.   8vo.

BANFFSHIRE
Territorial Soldiering in the North-East of Scotland during 1759-1814.   By
John Malcolm Bulloch.   [Account of the Militia, pp. 287-291 and Local Militia,
pp. 384-6].   Aberdeen: The New Spalding Club, 1914.   10″

BORDER COUNTIES
A History of the Scottish Borderers Militia.   Compiled from Authentic Sources
by the Rev. R. W. Weir.   Dumfries: printed at The Herald Office, 1877.   vi,
77 pp.   8½″

The History of the 3rd Batt. King's Own Scottish Borderers, 1798-1907.
By Rev. R. W. Weir.   Dumfries: "Courier and Herald" Office [1908].   viii,
238 pp., portraits, plates.   9½″

EDINBURGH AND LOTHIANS
History of the Edinburgh, or Queen's Regiment of Light Infantry Militia (now)
Third Battalion The Royal Scots; with Account of the origin and progress of the
Militia, and a Brief sketch of the old Royal Scots.   By Major R. C. Dudgeon,
Adjutant.   Edinburgh: William Blackwood & Sons, 1882.   xviii, 184 pp.,
portraits, plates.   8½″
  3 coloured plates of uniform and 1 of colours.

The Regimental Records of The Royal Scots.   Compiled by J. C. Leask and
H. M. McCance, Capt.   [3rd Battalion The Royal Scots (Spec. Res.) late The
Queen's Regt. of Light Infantry Militia; by Col. Lord Henry Scott, pp. 577-588].
Dublin: Alexander Thom & Co. Ltd., 1915.   10″
  Coloured plate of uniform.

The Society of Trained Bands of Edinburgh.   Edited from the original manuscript,
with Preface and Introductory Remarks by William Skinner.   Edinburgh:
H. & J. Pillans & Wilson, 1889.   158 pp., plates, large folding plan.   8½″
  Coloured plate of colour.

GLASGOW
Proud Heritage.   The Story of the Highland Light Infantry.   By Lt.-Col. L. B.
Oatts.   Vol. 3: The Regular, Militia, etc., Battalions, 1882-1918.   Glasgow:
House of Grant Ltd., 1961.   9″

INVERNESS-SHIRE
Historical Records of the Queen's Own Cameron Highlanders.   Vol 2 [pp. 45-65, History of the 3rd Battalion prior to 1881].   Edinburgh: William Blackwood & Sons, 1909.   10"

LANARKSHIRE
With the 4th Battalion The Cameronians (Scottish Rifles) in South Africa, 1900-1901.   By Col. A. H. Courteney.   Edinburgh: printed for the Author by William Brown, 1905.   [viii], 95 pp.   7¼"

PERTHSHIRE
THE PERTHSHIRE MILITIA.   [In *A Military History of Perthshire;* edited by the Marchioness of Tullibardine, 1908, pp. 103-145], plates.   Perth: R. A. & J. Hay.   9¾"

STIRLINGSHIRE
Records of the Stirlingshire, Dumbarton, Clackmannan, and Kinross Militia, Highland Borderers Light Infantry, now 3rd Battalion Argyll and Sutherland Highlanders (Princess Louise's).   Compiled by A. H. Middleton, Col. Stirling: Eneas Mackay, 1904.   xiv, 255 pp., portraits, plates.   9⅞"

IRELAND

ANTRIM
An Irish Militia Surgeon.   David McAnally, 1765-1818.   By [Sir] Henry McAnally.   Dundalk: W. Tempest, 1947.   24 pp.   7½"
   Coloured portrait in uniform.

History of the 4th Battalion Royal Irish Rifles (late Queen's Royal Irish [sic *i.e.* Antrim] Rifles).   By Fred. J. Tobin, Capt. and Adjut.   Belfast: printed by Marcus Ward & Co. Ltd., 1885.   16 pp.   7¼"

CARLOW
The Carlow Militia.   By Victor Haddon.   [In *Carloviana*, Journal of the Old Carlow Society, 1960, pp. 20-24].   Illustrations.   11"

CORK
Regimental Records of the 3rd Battalion, Royal Munster Fusiliers, formerly South Cork Light Infantry Militia.   [By Lieut.-Col. G. S. Ormerod].   Cork: Purcell & Co., 1906.   viii, 134 pp.   7"

Some Account of the North Cork Regiment of Militia (now the 9th Battalion King's Royal Rifle Corps).   Especially with reference to its Services in the year 1798.   By Rev. Canon Courtenay Moore.   [In *Journal of the Cork Historical and Archaeological Society*, Vol. 4, pp. 222-241; vol. 5, pp. 45-52, 147-152, 1898-99].   Cork: Gay & Co. Ltd.   10"

A Short Sketch of the North Cork Regiment of Militia, 9th Bn. K.R.R.; raised 1793, disbanded March 31st, 1908.   By Robert Day.   [In *Journal of the Cork Historical and Archaeological Society*, 2nd Ser., vol. 14, 1908].   Cork: Gay & Co. Ltd.   9 pp., illustrations.   10"

The Irish Militia, 1793-1816.   Raising the Force in Cork City and County.   By Sir Henry McAnally.   [Reprinted from *Journal of the Cork Historical and Archaeological Society*].   Cork: Gay & Co. Ltd., 1940.   10 pp.   10"

DOWN

Royal Downshire Militia; extracts from Order Books etc.   By Col. Robert Hugh Wallace.   [In *Ulster Journal of Archaeology*, vol. 12, 1906, pp. 145-155; vol. 13, 1907, pp. 24-28]. $9\frac{3}{4}"$
   5th Bn., Royal Irish Rifles.

GALWAY

The Connaught Rangers; by Lt.-Col. H. F. N. Jourdain and E. Fraser, vol. 2, 1926, pp. 469-492 [The 3rd Battalion, 1661-1922].   London: The Royal United Service Institution.   Portrait. $9\frac{3}{4}"$

KILKENNY

Documents connected with the City of Kilkenny Militia in the Seventeenth and Eighteenth Centuries.   By John G. A. Prim.   [In *Proceedings and Transactions of the Kilkenny and South-East of Ireland Arch. Society*, vol. 3, Part II, 1855, pp. 231-274].   [4th Bn. Royal Irish Regiment]. $9\frac{3}{4}"$

KING'S COUNTY

Record of Services of the 3rd Battn. The Prince of Wales's Leinster Regiment (Royal Canadians) in the South African War, 1900, 1901, 1902.   By Col. F. Luttman-Johnson.   London: Army and Navy Co-operative Society Ltd., 1913. 148 pp. [pp. 135-148, The Old King's County Militia], portraits, plates, maps. $8\frac{1}{2}"$

The History of the Prince of Wales's Leinster Regiment (Royal Canadians) . . . to which were added in 1881 as 3rd . . . Batt. respectively The King's County Militia &c.   Compiled and edited by Lt.-Col. F. E. Whitton.   2 vols.   Aldershot: Gale & Polden Ltd. [1924]. $8\frac{1}{2}"$

LONGFORD

A Short History of the Royal Longford Militia, 1793-1893.   Edited and compiled by Henry Alexander Richey.   Dublin: Hodges, Figgis & Co. Ltd., 1894.   viii, 126 pp. $8\frac{1}{2}"$
   Large folded sheet List of Officers at end.
   6th Bn. Rifle Brigade, disbanded 1908.

LOUTH

Notes on the Militia of County Louth, 1793-1806.   By Sir Henry McAnally. Offprint from Tempest's Annual, 1940.   4 pp. $8\frac{1}{2}"$
   6th Bn., Royal Irish Rifles.

MAYO

The Connaught Rangers; by Lt.-Col. H. F. N. Jourdain and E. Fraser.   Vol. 2, 1926, pp. 523-4 [The 3rd Battalion, 1661-1922].   London: The Royal United Service Institution. $9\frac{3}{4}"$

MEATH

Record of the Formation, Services, Marches etc. of the Fifth Battalion the Prince of Wales's Leinster Regiment (Royal Canadians). Dublin, 1882. 33 pp.

The History of the Prince of Wales's Leinster Regiment (Royal Canadians) . . . to which were added in 1881 as . . . 5th Batt. respectively . . . The Royal Meath Militia. Compiled and edited by Lt.-Col. F. E. Whitton. 2 vols. Aldershot: Gale & Polden Ltd. [1924]. 8½"

MONAGHAN

Records of the Monaghan Militia. Written by Quarter Master William Watson in 1871. [Extract from ' The Northern Standard,' Monaghan, March-April, 1928]. c. 14,000 words.
    5th Bn., Royal Irish Fusiliers, disbanded 1908.

QUEEN'S COUNTY

The History of the Prince of Wales's Leinster Regiment (Royal Canadians) . . . to which were added in 1881 as . . . 4th Batt. respectively . . . The Queen's County Militia. Compiled and edited by Lt.-Col. F. E. Whitton. 2 vols. Aldershot: Gale & Polden Ltd. [1924]. 8½"

ROSCOMMON

The Connaught Rangers; by Lt.-Col. H. F. N. Jourdain and E. Fraser. Vol. 2, 1926, pp. 493-500. [The 4th Battalion, 1793-1922]. London: The Royal United Service Institution. Portraits. 9¾"

TIPPERARY

Records of The Tipperary Artillery, with a list of Officers who have served in the regiment from 1793 to 1889. By Major C. A. Ryan. Clonmel: The Chronicle Steam Printing Works, 1890. ii, 140 pp. 8vo.

The Mutiny of the Nth Tipperary Militia on the 7th July 1856. A Full Account of the Famous Outbreak. By E. H. Sheehan. No imprint. 17 pp. 9½"
    3rd Bn., Royal Irish Regiment.

TYRONE

Historical Record of the 2nd (now 80th), or Royal Tyrone Fusilier Regiment of Militia, from the Embodiment in 1793 to the Present Time. By Quartermaster John Core. Omagh: printed by Alexander Scarlett, 1872. viii, 102 pp. 8½"
    3rd Bn. Royal Irish Fusiliers.

WATERFORD

Records of the Waterford Militia, 1584 to 1885 continued to 1891. Waterford Artillery Militia, now 6th Brigade South Irish Division, Royal Artillery, Head Quarters—Waterford. Compiled by Major Otway Wheeler Cuffe, Adjutant. No imprint, 1885(-91). [xxv], 148, [xliv] pp. 8"

WICKLOW
An Outline of the History of the County Wicklow Regiment of Militia: together with a Succession List of the Officers of the Regiment from its Formation in 1793 to the Present Time.   Compiled by Major E. B. Evans, Adjutant.   Published by The Officers of the County Wicklow Militia, 1885.   No imprint.   x, 58 pp., 2 photographs, plates.   8½"

CHANNEL ISLANDS

The Royal Guernsey Militia: a brief sketch of its services &c., from 800 to 1895. By Lieut.-Col. J. Percy Groves.   Guernsey: printed by Frederick Claᵣke, 1895. 97 pp.   9½"

Norman Ten Hundred.   By A. Stanley Blicq.   A Record of the 1st (Service) Bn. Royal Guernsey Light Infantry.   Guernsey: The Guernsey Press Co. Ltd., 1920. [vi], 104 pp., plans.   7"

YEOMANRY

The Royal Militia and Yeomanry Cavalry Army List; containing . . . A History of the Services, Organization, and Equipment of the Regiments of Militia, etc. Arranged and compiled from official Documents by Arthur Sleigh, late Lieut. London: British Army Despatch Press, 1850.   Published half-yearly.   No. 1, April, 1850.   *No more published.*   xxxviii, 190 pp.   8½"

His Majesty's Territorial Army.   A Descriptive Account of The Yeomanry, Artillery, Engineers, and Infantry, etc.   By Walter Richards.   With illustrations by R. Caton Woodville.   London: Virtue & Co., 1910-11.   4 vols., 184 pp. each volume.   12¾"
   32 coloured plates (8 in each volume).
   Outline histories of regiments.

ENGLAND AND WALES

BEDFORDSHIRE
Some Notes on the Bedfordshire Yeomanry Lancers.   By Commander Benson Freeman.   Published serially in the *Bedfordshire Times and Independent*, 1925.   Gives history to 1827.   About 5,000 words.

The Bedfordshire Yeomanry in the Great War.   By L. J. C. Southern.   With a Foreword by Lieut.-Col. J. B. Walker and an Introductory chapter by Lieut.-Col. C. M. Headlam.   Bedford: Rush & Warwick Ltd., 1935.   xix, 146 pp.   8½"

O. C. Beds. Yeomanry. By Col. Sidney Peel. London: Oxford University Press, 1935. 102 pp. 8½"

BERKSHIRE
Journal of the Royal Berks Yeomanry Cavalry, 1895-6. Reading: published for the Regiment by Herbert Beecroft, 1897. 35 pp. 9¾"
    Contains a Short History of the Regiment, with 2 coloured plates of uniform and 1 of standard; compiled by Capt. F. F. Colvin, Adjutant & R.S.M. S. Bradley.

The Yeomanry in Berkshire. By Major G. Tylden. [In *Society for Army Historical Research, Journal*, Vol. 28, 1950, pp. 96-101]. Plates. 9¼"

BUCKINGHAMSHIRE
The Royal Buckinghamshire Hussars Imperial Yeomanry. By Benson Freeman. Published in the *Volunteer Service Gazette*, October, 1904. 3,000 words.

History of the Buckinghamshire Yeomanry. By Engineer-Commdr. Benson Freeman, R.N. Published serially in the *South Bucks Free Press*, 1919-1920. This is a much expanded version of the item above. About 38,000 words.

The Royal Bucks Hussars. In *The Citizen Soldiers of Buckinghamshire*, 1795-1926; compiled by Major-Gen. J. C. Swann, pp. 16-30, 58-77. London: published for the Buckinghamshire Territorial Army Association by Hazell, Watson & Viney Ltd., 1930. 9½"

CARDIGANSHIRE, *see under* PEMBROKESHIRE

CARMARTHENSHIRE, *see under* PEMBROKESHIRE

CARNARVONSHIRE, *see under* DENBIGHSHIRE

CHESHIRE
The Earl of Chester's Regiment of Yeomanry Cavalry; its Formation and Services, 1797 to 1897. [By Frederick Leary]. Edinburgh: privately printed at the Ballantyne Press, 1898. viii, 312 pp., portraits, plates. 9¾"

5000 Miles with the Cheshire Yeomanry in South Africa. A Series of Articles compiled from Letters and Diaries, written by Officers, Non-Commissioned Officers and Men of the 21st and 22nd (Cheshire) Companies of Imperial Yeomanry, relating their experiences during the South African War in the years 1900-01, etc. Compiled by John H. Cooke. Warrington: Mackie & Co. Ltd., 1913-14, xxxiii, 434 pp. Portraits, plates, illustrations. 9½"
    500 copies printed.

CUMBERLAND, *see under* WESTMORLAND

SECTION IV AUXILIARY FORCES

DENBIGHSHIRE

Historical Records of the Denbighshire Hussars Imperial Yeomanry from their Formation in 1795 till 1906.   With Note on the Flintshire, Royal Maylor, and Carnarvonshire Yeomanry Corps, and the Ancient British Fencible Cavalry, by Engr.-Lieut. B. F. M. Freeman, R.N.   Compiled by Col. Ll. E. S. Parry and Eng.-Lieut. B. F. M. Freeman, R.N.   Wrexham: Woodall, Minshall, Thomas & Co., 1909.   xii, 246 pp., portraits, plates.   8½″
    7 coloured plates of uniform and 1 of standards.

DERBYSHIRE

A Record of the Volunteer Cavalry of Derbyshire, from the first formation of that force in the year 1794, till the amalgamation of the Independent Troops into a Corps, on the 1st of April, 1864.   By Charles R. Colville, Lieut.-Col.-Commandant; with an Appendix.   London: Bemrose & Sons, 1868.   47 pp. [*Preceded by*] The Standing Regulations of the Derbyshire Corps of Yeomanry Cavalry, 1868, [*and*] The Standing Regulations regarding the Dress and Appointments of the Officers of the Derbyshire Corps of Yeomanry Cavalry, 1868. xxi pp.   9¼″
    500 copies only printed.

The Derbyshire Yeomanry War History, 1914-1919.   Edited by Lieut.-Col. G. A. Strutt.   Derby: Bemrose & Sons Ltd. [1929].   xvi, 212 pp., portraits, plates.   7½″

1st Derbyshire Yeomanry.   Scrapbook, 1939-1947.   [By Lt.-Col. Sir Ian Walker, Bart, and others].   [Derby: printed by Bemrose & Sons Ltd., 1948]. xii, 184 pp., portraits, illustrations, maps.   10¾″

The Second Derbyshire Yeomanry.   An Account of the Regiment during the World War, 1939-45.   By Capt. A. J. Jones.   Bristol: The White Swan Press Ltd., 1949.   134 pp., illustrations, maps.   8¼″

DEVON

The Yeomanry of Devon, 1794-1927.   By Eng.-Commdr. Benson Freeman, R.N.   Edited by Earl Fortescue.   London: The St. Catherine Press, 1927. xx, 302 pp., portraits, plates, maps.   10″
    6 coloured plates, including 3 of uniform and 2 of guidons.

Diary of Lt.-Col. Viscount Hambledon, September 26, 1915-January 4, 1916, and a Memorandum of the Work of the 1/Royal First Devon Yeomanry at Suvla Bay.   [London: W. H. Smith & Son, 1919].   56, 20 pp.   7½″

Royal Devon Yeomanry.   The Story of 142 Field Regiment R.A., 1939-1945. Eastbourne: The Baskerville Press, 1947.   [xiv], 142 pp., plates, maps.   8½″

DORSET

Records of the Dorset Yeomanry (" Queen's Own ").   Compiled by C. W. Thompson, Capt.   Dorchester: " Dorset County Chronicle " Printing Works, 1894.   ii, 192, xxvi, 6 pp., portraits, plates.   8¾″

Records of the Dorset Yeomanry [Vol. 2]. Records of the Dorset Imperial Yeomanry, 1894-1905. Edited by Capt. M. F. Gage. Sherborne: F. Bennett, 1906. iv, 266 pp., portraits, plates, map. 8¾"
    13 coloured plates of uniform.

——— Another edition without coloured plates. 1906.

Records of the Dorset Yeomanry (Queen's Own), 1914-1919. By Major-Gen. C. W. Thompson. Sherborne: F. Bennett & Co. Ltd., 1921. xii, 156 pp., portraits, plate, maps. 8¾"

A Short Account of the Queen's Own Dorset Yeomanry, 1794-1939. By Major R. H. Glyn, with an Introduction by Brig.-Gen. the Earl of Shaftesbury. [Dorchester: printed by Henry Ling Ltd., 1948]. Published by The Queen's Own Dorset Yeomanry Old Comrades' Association. viii, 65 pp., portraits, illustrations, maps. 8½"
    Coloured plate of uniform.

DURHAM, *see under* NORTHUMBERLAND

ESSEX
The Essex Yeomanry; containing also a Short Account of Military Activity in the County during the Napoleonic War. By John Wm. Burrows. Published by arrangement with the Territorial Army Association. Southend-on-Sea: John H. Burrows & Sons Ltd. [1925]. x, 208 pp., portraits, plates, maps. 8½"
    Vol. 3 of the series " Essex Units in the War, 1914-1919."
    Coloured plate of guidon.

The 10th (P.W.O.) Royal Hussars and The Essex Yeomanry during the European War, 1914-1918. By Lt.-Col. F. H. D. C. Whitmore. Colchester: Benham & Co. Ltd., 1920. viii, 326 pp., plates, maps. 11"

A History of the Essex Yeomanry, 1919-1949. [Edited by P. W. Gee]. Colchester: Benham & Co. Ltd., 1950. xxvii, 309 pp., portraits, plates, maps, chart. 8½"

[147th (Essex Yeomanry) Fld. Regt., R.A.] Europe 1944-1945. [Kiel, Germany: Essex Press, 1946]. 53 pp., plates, maps. 7¼"

A Brief Summary of the Services of the West Essex Yeomanry Cavalry, 1830-77. By Gerald O. Rickword. Colchester: Benham & Co. Ltd., 1948. (Reprinted from *The Essex Review*, vol. 57). 16 pp., illustrations. 8½"
    Coloured plate of uniform.

Essex Volunteer Cavalry in the Napoleonic Wars. By the Rev. Llewellyn Bullock. (In *The Essex Review*, vol. 28, 1919, pp. 41-48). 8½"
    Plate of Freshwater Vol. Cavalry colours.

FLINTSHIRE, *see also under* DENBIGHSHIRE
Memoir of the Flintshire Yeomanry Cavalry; commanded by Major The Earl Grosvenor. Chester: printed by T. Griffith, 1838. viii, 98 pp. 8½"

GLOUCESTERSHIRE

The Yeomanry Cavalry of Gloucestershire and Monmouth. By W. H. Wyndham Quin, late Major. Cheltenham: Westley's Library, 1898. viii, 266 pp., portraits. 8¾″

A Brief History of the Bristol Volunteers . . .; to which is added an Account of the . . . Royal Gloucestershire Hussars. By Edwin T. Morgan, Qr.-Mr.-Sergt. Bristol: " Bristol Times and Mirror " Ltd. [1908]. 48 pp. 8½″

The History of the Royal Gloucestershire Hussars Yeomanry, 1898-1922. The Great Cavalry Campaign in Palestine. By Frank Fox. London: Philip Allan & Co. [1923]. xvi, 336 pp., portraits, plates, maps. 8¾″

Second Royal Gloucestershire Hussars. Libya-Egypt, 1941-1942. By Major Stuart Pitman, with a Foreword by the Duke of Beaufort, Hon. Col. London: The Saint Catherine Press Ltd., 1950. xix, 96 pp., portraits, plates, maps. 8½″

Early Years of the Royal Gloucestershire Yeomanry Cavalry. By Roland Austin. (In *Transactions of the Bristol and Gloucestershire Archaeological Society*, Vol. 43, 1921, pp. 253-266). Kendal: printed for the Society by Titus Wilson & Son.
   Minute Book of the City of Gloucester Troop.

HAMPSHIRE

Historical Records of the Hampshire Yeomanry Regiments. By Lieut.-Commdr. Benson Freeman, R.N. Published serially in the *Hampshire Chronicle*, beginning July 1923. About 98,000 words.

A Look Back. East Hants (Portsdown) Yeomanry Light Dragoons: the Story of its history. By Benson Freeman. Published serially in the *Hampshire Telegraph and Post*, 1925.
   Part of the history published in the *Hampshire Chronicle*, with much added matter. About 13,250 words.

The Loyal Vectis Yeomanry Light Dragoons. By Benson Freeman.
   A further part of the *Hampshire Chronicle* series republished, with considerable additions in an Isle of Wight newspaper in 1925.

New Forest Yeomanry; early days of Home Defence. By Lieut.-Commdr. Benson Freeman. Published serially in the *Hampshire Advertiser and Independent* in 1925.
   A further part of the *Hampshire Chronicle* series republished with much added matter. About 29,000 words.

Records of Service 1/1st Hampshire Carabineers Yeomanry, August 1914-19. Winchester: printed by Warren & Son Ltd. [1924]. 31 pp. 7″

HERTFORDSHIRE

A Brief Record of the Herts. Yeomanry and the Herts. Artillery. By Major A. L. P. Griffith. Hertford: Geo. Creasy & Sons, printers [1927]. 56 pp. Chart. 9¼″

A Short Account of the Formation and Record of 79 (Herts Yeomanry) H.A.A. Regiment R.A. from 1938 to 1945.   No Imprint   [1945].   16 pp.   8"

Diary of the 135th (Herts. Yeomanry) Field Regiment R.A.(T.A.) during the Campaign in Malaya and Singapore, January-February 1942. *Duplicated.* 30 pp.   13"

479 H.A.A. Regiment R.A. (Herts. Yeomanry) T.A. [London: Goddard-Lawrence & Co., 1949].   30 pp., illustrations.   5½"×8"
    Recruiting brochure containing short history.

KENT

A Century of Yeoman Service.   Records of the East Kent Yeomanry (The Royal East Kent Mounted Rifles).   By Col. The Lord Harris.   Ashford: "The Kentish Express" Ltd., 1899.   vii, 72 pp., plates.   8½"
    7 coloured plates of uniform.

Some Historical Records of the West Kent (Q.O.) Yeomanry, 1794-1909.   By Lt.-Col. J. F. Edmeades.   London: Andrew Melrose, 1909.   viii, 150 pp., plates, maps.   8½"
    6 coloured plates of uniform.

West Kent (Q. O.) Yeomanry and 10th (Yeomanry) Battalion The Buffs, 1914-1919.   By Charles Ponsonby, Lieut.-Col. London: Andrew Melrose Ltd., 1920. xviii, 206 pp., plates, maps.   8½"
    The 10th (Yeomanry) Battalion The Buffs consisted of the combined East & West Kent Yeomanries.

Yeoman Service.   A Short History of the Kent Yeomanry, 1939-1945.   By Lt.-Col. Franklin Lushington.   London: The Medici Society Ltd., 1947. x, 227 pp., illustrations, maps.   8½"
    1 coloured plate of uniform.

LANCASHIRE

List of Officers who have served in The Lancashire Hussars Yeomanry Cavalry; with some short Notes and Annals of the Regiment since its formation in 1848 to the present time.   By T. Algernon Earle.   [Liverpool: T. Brakell], 1889. vi, 60 pp., 4to.
    3 coloured plates of uniform.

The Duke of Lancaster's Own Yeomanry Cavalry, 23rd Co., I.Y.; a record of incidents connected with the services of the first contingent of the D.L.O.Y.C. in the South African Campaign of 1899-1900-1901-1902, of interest also to the Westmorland and Cumberland, 24th Co., I.Y. who were our partners and comrades-in-arms, etc. [By L. H. Johnson.   Bolton: the Author, 1902]. 158 pp., portraits, plates, maps.   8½"

Shabash—149; the War Story of the 149th Regiment R.A., 1939-1945.   By E. W. Capleton.   [Liverpool: printing by C. Tinling & Co. Ltd., 1963].   xix, 268 pp., maps, end-paper maps.   8½"

Brief History of The Duke of Lancaster's Own Yeomanry. [1951]. *Duplicated.*
5 pp.   8″

Old Time Yeomanry.   The Manchester Corps.   By Col. Percy Hargreaves and
Eng.-Lieut. Benson Freeman, R.N.   Published serially in the *Chester Courant*
in 1910.   c. 12,000 words.

A Furness Military Chronicle.   By Alfred Fell (Chapter on The Furness Troop
of Yeomanry Cavalry).   Ulverston: Kitchin & Co., 1937.   10″

LEICESTERSHIRE
An Outline of the History of The Leicestershire (Prince Albert's Own) Yeomanry.
By Col. G. R. Codrington.   London: printed for private circulation only by
W. H. Smith & Son, 1928.   48 pp.   7½″

──── Another Edition.   London: Eyre & Spottiswoode, 1955.   61 pp.   7½″

153rd Leicestershire Yeomanry Field Regiment R.A.T.A., 1939-1945.   [By
Lt.-Col. the Hon. B. T. Brassey & Major P. D. Winslow].   Hinckley: W.
Pickering & Sons Ltd., 1947.   xvi, 101 pp., plates, sketch maps.   8½″

" There is an Honour likewise . . ."   The Story of 154 (Leicestershire Yeomanry)
Field Regiment, R.A.   By Lt.-Col. G. E. Bouskell-Wade.   Leicester: Edgar
Backus.   [1948].   xi, 143 pp., portrait, plates, illustrations, sketch maps.   9¾″

Rhodesia—and after; being the Story of the 17th and 18th Battalions of Imperial
Yeomanry in South Africa.   By S. H. Gilbert.   London: Simpkin & Co. Ltd.,
1901.   Illustrations, maps.   8½″
    17th Battalion included Companies from Leicestershire, etc.

LONDON
Records of the Rough Riders (XXth Battalion, Imperial Yeomanry) Boer War,
1899-1902.   By Capt. H. G. Mackenzie Rew.   Bedford: Brown & Wilson,
1907.   289 pp., portraits, illustrations, maps.   8½″

The City of London Yeomanry (Roughriders).   By A. S. Hamilton.   With a
Foreword by Gen. Sir George de S. Barrow.   London: The Hamilton Press
Ltd., 1936.   xii, 244 pp., plates, maps.   8½″
    Coloured plate of uniform.

2nd County of London (Westminster Dragoons) Yeomanry.   The First Twenty
Years; a summary.   Compiled by Major Edward Rowe.   London: printed by
Wm. Clowes & Sons Ltd., 1962.   xiii, 154 pp., portrait, plates, maps, end-paper
maps.   8½″

The Story of the Westminster Dragoons in North West Europe from June 6th
1944 to May 8th, 1945.   [Lüneburg, Germany: Lüneburger Landeszeitung,
1945].   52 pp., illustrations.   11¾″

Historical Record of the 3rd County of London (Sharpshooters) Imperial Yeomanry, 1900-1905.   By Lieut.-Commdr. Benson Freeman.   [London: W. P. Griffith & Sons Ltd., 1905].   72 pp.   5¼"×4"
  Privately printed for the Regiment from articles in the *Volunteer Service Gazette*, August, September, 1905.

The Call to Arms, 1900-1901, or A Review of the Imperial Yeomanry Movement and some subjects connected therewith.   By Henry Seton-Karr.   London: Longmans, Green & Co., 1902.   xviii, 330 pp., frontispiece.   7½"
  Deals largely with the Sharpshooters.

Rhodesia—and after; being the Story of the 17th and 18th Battalions of Imperial Yeomanry in South Africa.   By S. H. Gilbert.   London: Simpkin & Co., Ltd., 1901.   350 pp., portraits, plates, maps.   8½"
  18th Battalion were Sharpshooters.

Through Rhodesia with the Sharpshooters.   By R. Stevenson.   London: Macqueen, 1901.   200 pp.   7½"

Men and Sand.   [4th County of London Yeomanry (The Sharpshooters) later 3rd/4th in 2nd World War].   By the Earl of Onslow; with a Foreword by Gen. Sir R. L. McCreery.   London: The Saint Catherine Press Ltd., 1962.   xi, 140 pp., portraits, plates, maps.   8½"

Sharpshooters at War; the 3rd, the 4th and the 3rd/4th County of London Yeomanry 1939 to 1945.   By [Col.] Andrew Graham.   London: Sharpshooters Regimental Association, 1964.   xviii, 252 pp., portraits, plates, maps, end-paper maps.   8¾"

Standing Orders of the 3rd/4th County of London Yeomanry, " Sharpshooters." No imprint [printed in Germany, 1945].   75 pp., contains Brief History, 14 pp. 8½"

ISLE OF MAN
A Military History of the Isle of Man.   [By] B. E. Sargeaunt.   [Including Yeomanry etc.].   Arbroath: T. Buncle & Co. Ltd. [1949].   8½"

MIDDLESEX
The Story of the 34th Company (Middlesex) Imperial Yeomanry, from the point of view of private No. 6243.   By William Corner.   London: T. Fisher Unwin, 1902.   xx, 540 pp., portraits, plates, map.   8¾"

Reminiscences of the 34th Battalion Imperial Yeomanry.   By Thomas C. Wetton, Ex-Trooper.   London: Sidey & Bartlett [1908].   260 pp., portraits, illustrations.   7"

Historical Records of the Middlesex Yeomanry, 1797-1927.   By Charles Stonham and Benson Freeman, Eng.-Commdr., R.N.   Edited by J. S. Judd. Published for the Regimental Committee, Duke of York's Headquarters, Chelsea, 1930.   x, 242 pp., portraits, plates, maps.   8½"
  4 coloured plates of uniform.

The Yarn of a Yeoman.   By S. F. Hatton.   Foreword by Field-Marshal Viscount Allenby.   London: Hutchinson & Co. Ltd. [1930].   286 pp., illustrations, maps.   8½″

MONMOUTHSHIRE, *see under* GLOUCESTERSHIRE

MONTGOMERYSHIRE
The Historical Records of the Yeomanry and Volunteers of Montgomeryshire, 1803-1908.   Compiled by Lieut.-Col. R. W. Williams Wynn; Benson Freeman. Oswestry: Woodall, Minshall, Thomas & Co., 1909.   xii, 138 pp., plates.   8½″

―――― Vol. 2.   The Historical Records of the Montgomeryshire Yeomanry, with a Short Account of the service in Palestine and France of the 25th Montgomeryshire and Welsh Horse Yeomanry Battalion R.W.F., 1909-1919.   Compiled by Col. R. W. Williams Wynn and Major W. N. Stable.   Oswestry: Woodall, Minshall, Thomas & Co. Ltd., 1926.   x, 186 pp., portraits, plates, maps.   8½″

NORFOLK
Records of the Norfolk Yeomanry Cavalry, to which is added The Fencible and Provisional Cavalry of the same County from 1780 to 1908; together with the Account of the 43rd and 44th Squadrons of Imperial Yeomanry, who volunteered for the South African War, 1900.   Compiled by Lieut.-Col. J. R. Harvey. London: Jarrold & Sons, 1908.   416 pp., portraits, plates.   11″
   5 coloured plates of uniform and 1 of standard.

The History of the Norfolk Regiment.   By F. Loraine Petre.   Vol. 2, pp. 301-332 [The 12th (Yeomanry) Battalion in Gallipoli, Egypt, Palestine and France]. Norwich: Jarrold & Sons Ltd., 1924.   9¾″

NORTHERN IRELAND
The North Irish Horse.   Battle Report: North Africa and Italy.   Belfast: W. & G. Bird, Ltd., 1946.   108 pp., maps.   8½″

NORTHAMPTONSHIRE
The 1st and 2nd Northamptonshire Yeomanry, 1939-1946.   Drawings by Major D. G. Bevan.   Brunswick, Germany: Printing Office Joh. Heinr. Meyer, 1946. 141 pp., portraits, plates, illustrations, maps.   9½″

The First Northamptonshire Yeomanry in Northwest Europe.   By Capt. R. F. Neville, with drawings by Major D. G. Bevan.   Brunswick, Germany: Printing Office Joh. Heinr. Meyer, 1946.   104 pp., plates, illustrations, maps.   9½″

NORTHUMBERLAND
The History of the Northumberland (Hussars) Yeomanry, 1819-1919, with Supplement to 1923.   Edited by Howard Pease.   With a Foreword by Field-Marshal the Earl of Ypres.   London: Constable & Co. Ltd., 1924.   xx, 296 pp., portraits, plates, maps.   8¾″
   3 coloured plates of uniform.

History of the Northumberland Hussars Yeomanry, 1924-1949. By Joan Bright. With the Foreword of Col. The Right Hon. D. Clifton Brown, M.P. Newcastle-upon-Tyne: Mawson Swan & Morgan Ltd., 1949. xvi, 406 pp., portraits, plates, maps. 8¾"

On Active Service with the Northumberland and Durham Yeomanry, under Lord Methuen (South Africa, 1900-1901). By Karl B. Spurgin. With an Introduction by Major Savile Clayton. London: The Walter Scott Publishing Co. Ltd. [1902]. xx, 324 pp., portraits, plates. 7"

NOTTINGHAMSHIRE
History of the South Notts Yeomanry Cavalry, 1794 to 1894. By George Fellows, Capt. and Hon. Major. Nottingham: Thomas Forman & Sons, 1895. 166 pp., portraits, plates. 8½"

Historical Record of the South Nottinghamshire Hussars Yeomanry, 1794 to 1924. By the late George Fellows, Major and the late Benson Freeman, Eng.-Commdr., R.N. With a Foreword by Col. Sir Lancelot Rolleston. Aldershot: Gale & Polden Ltd., 1928. xxii, 352 pp., portraits, plates, maps. 9½"
    5 coloured plates of uniform and 1 of standard.

History of the South Nottinghamshire Hussars, 1924-1948. By Eric B. Dobson. With a Foreword by Major-Gen. M. E. Dennis. York: printed by Herald Printing Works, 1948. xix, 402 pp., portraits, plates, maps in end-pocket 9¾"

307 (South Notts. Hussars Yeo.) Field Regt., R.A., T.A. A Brief History of the Regiment, 1794-1950. By " Hussar." [Nottingham: printed by Nottingham Paper Bag Co. Ltd., 1950]. 16 pp. 7¼"

History of the 3rd Regiment Imperial Yeomanry, 28-1-00 to 6-8-02. By Lieut.-Col. R. L. Birkin. Nottingham: J. & J. Vice, printer, 1905. viii, 143, [76] pp., illustrations, map. 13"×8"
    Nottingham Contingent from the Sherwood Rangers and the South Notts. Hussars.

The Sherwood Rangers Yeomanry in the Great War, 1914-1918. By Major H. Tallents. London: Philip Allan & Co. Ltd. [1926]. xii, 186, plates, maps. 8½"

Sherwood Rangers. (The Story of the Nottinghamshire Sherwood Rangers Yeomanry in the Second World War). By T. M. Lindsay. London: Burrup, Mathieson & Co. Ltd., 1952. [xii], 182 pp., portraits, plates, plans. 9½"

Through Palestine with the Twentieth Machine-Gun Squadron Sherwood Rangers Yeo.—South Notts Hussars. [By Lieut. A. O. W. Kindell]. [London: J. M. Baxter & Co. for private circulation, 1920]. [7], 180 pp., plates, maps. 8½"

A Short History of the Sherwood Rangers Yeomanry, 1794-1953. [By Lt.-Col. D. C. Barbour]. [Worksop: Sissons & Son, Ltd., 1953]. 48 pp., portrait, maps. 8½"

OXFORDSHIRE

Trooper 8008 I.Y.   By the Hon. Sidney Peel.   London: Edward Arnold, 1902.
xii, 68 pp., plates, map.   8¾″
   40th (Oxfordshire) Company, 10th Battalion, Imperial Yeomanry in South
   Africa.

The Oxfordshire Hussars in the Great War (1914-1918).   By Adrian Keith-
Falconer.   London: John Murray, 1927.   xiv, 392, pp., portraits, plates, maps.
8½″

PEMBROKESHIRE

Notes on the Historical Records of the Pembrokeshire (Castlemartin) Imperial
Yeomanry, 1794 to 1905; with Appendices on the:
   Haverfordwest (Dungleddy) Yeomanry Light Cavalry, 1794-1827.
   Independent Pembrokeshire Yeomanry Cavalry, 1798-1813.
   Carmarthenshire Yeomanry Cavalry, 1794-1828.
   Published serially in *The Welshman*, Carmarthen, beginning September 15th,
   1905.   c. 12,500 words.

146 Field Regt., R.A.—146 Medium Regt. R.A. (Pembroke & Cardiganshire
Yeomanry, T.A.) The Regimental Itinerary, 1939-1945.   [By Denys Evans].
No imprint   [Aberystwyth, 1946].   64 pp.   8¼″

The Pembroke Yeomanry, 1794-1947.   [In *The Last Invasion of Britain;* by
Commdr. E. H. Stuart Jones, pp. 282-294].   Cardiff: University of Wales Press,
1950.   8½″
   Illustrations of guidons.

History of the Pembroke Yeomanry.   With a foreword by Major-Gen. L. H. O.
Pugh.   Haverfordwest: T.A. Centre, 1959.   107, 3 pp., portraits, illustrations,
map.   8½″

A History of the Pembrokeshire Imperial Yeomanry.   By Col. F. C. Meyrick
and Eng.-Lieut. B. F. M. Freeman.   London: Elliot Stock.   Illustrated.
   This work was announced "for publication shortly" in the *Army and Navy
   Gazette*, 8th June, 1907, but never appeared.   The MS. was in possession
   of Sir T. F. Meyrick, Bart.

SHROPSHIRE

Historical Record of the Shropshire Yeomanry Cavalry, from its Formation in
1795 up to the year 1887.   Compiled by Col. Wingfield.   Shrewsbury: Admitt
& Naunton, 1888.   220, [24] pp., plates.   9½″
   7 coloured plates of uniform.

The Shropshire Yeomanry, MDCCXCV-MCMXLV.   The Story of a Volunteer
Cavalry Regiment.   By E. W. Gladstone.   With a Foreword by Lieut.-Gen.
Sir Oliver Leese, Bt. [Manchester]: The Whitehorn Press, 1953.   xix, 496 pp.,
portraits, plates, maps.   8¾″
   4 coloured plates of uniform.

SOMERSET

The North Somerset Regiment of Yeomanry Cavalry.   Bath: printed by H. E. Carrington, 1850.   72 pp., plates. $9\frac{1}{2}''$
  3 plates of uniform.

A Brief History of the Bristol Volunteers . . .; to which is added an Account of the North Somerset Yeomanry Cavalry, etc.   By Edwin T. Morgan, Qr.-Mr.-Sergt. , Bristol: "Bristol Times and Mirror" Ltd., 1908.   48 pp. $8\frac{1}{2}''$

A Short Report on the North Somerset Yeomanry during the European War, 1914-1918.   Privately printed by the Regiment.   Bath: Flower [1919].   11 pp. $7\frac{1}{2}''$

A Record of the West Somerset Yeomanry, 1914-1919.   By Capt. R. C. Boyle, with a Foreword by Brig.-Gen. R. Hoare.   London: St. Catherine Press, 1922. xvi, 188 pp., portraits, plates, maps. $8\frac{3}{4}''$

The Adventures of the West Somerset Yeomanry from 'D Day' to 'VE Day.'   By Major J. R. S. Peploe.   40 pp.   Produced in the field.   *n.d.* $7\frac{7}{8}''$

STAFFORDSHIRE

The Records of the Queen's Own Royal Regiment of Staffordshire Yeomanry. Compiled by P. C. G. Webster, Adjutant.   Lichfield: Thomas George Lomax. London: Longmans, Green & Co., 1870.   viii, 192, xlvi pp., plates. $8\frac{1}{4}''$
  2 coloured plates of uniform.

The Staffordshire Yeomanry (Q.O.R.R.) in the First and Second World Wars, 1914-1918 and 1939-1945.   Compiled under the direction of a Regimental Committee.   Written and edited by Lieut.-Commdr. P. K. Kemp, R.N., Aldershot: Gale & Polden Ltd., 1950 xii, 168 pp., portrait, plates, sketch map. $8\frac{1}{2}''$

The Story of The Staffordshire Yeomanry (Queen's Own Royal Regiment). [Burton-on-Trent: The Regiment, 1952].   6 pp. $5\frac{3}{4}''$

Letters on the subject of the Arm'd Yeomanry, addressed to the . . . Earl Gower Sutherland, Colonel of the Staffordshire Volunteer Cavalry.   By Francis Percival Eliot, Major of the above Corps.   Stafford: printed by Arthur Morgan. 1794.   29 pp. $8\frac{1}{2}''$

——— [Another edition].   Six Letters . . . London: printed for the Author, and sold by T. Egerton, 1797.   xv, 230 pp., plates. $8\frac{1}{2}''$
  An enlarged edition containing Field Instructions, Manoeuvres, etc., with plate of uniform.

SUFFOLK

Records of the Norfolk Yeomanry Cavalry : . . 1780 to 1908.   Compiled by Lieut.-Col. J. R. Harvey.   London: Jarrold & Sons, 1908. $11''$
  Chapters IX and X contain the History of the Suffolk Yeomanry, 1793-1901

The Suffolk Yeomanry and 15th (Yeomanry) Battalion Suffolk Regiment.   In *The History of the Suffolk Regiment*, 1914-1927.   By Lt.-Col. C. C. R. Murphy, 1928. $9''$

SURREY
The History and War Records of the Surrey Yeomanry (Queen Mary's Regt.), 1797-1928.   Written and compiled by E. D. Harrison-Ainsworth.   London: printed for the Regimental Committee by C. & F. Layton, 1928.   xvi, 336 pp., portraits, plates, maps.   9¼"
   1 coloured plate of uniform.

SUSSEX
The Sussex Yeomanry and 16th (Sussex Yeomanry) Battalion Royal Sussex Regiment, 1914-1919.   By Lieut.-Col. H. I. Powell-Edwards.   London: Andrew Melrose Ltd. [1921].   398 pp., plates, maps.   8½"

WALES
Welsh Horse.   For the 25th Montgomeryshire and Welsh Horse Yeomanry Battalion Royal Welch Fusiliers, 1914-1919, *see under* MONTGOMERYSHIRE.

WARWICKSHIRE
History of the Warwickshire Yeomanry Cavalry.   Compiled by the Hon. H. A. Adderley (Lieut.).   Warwick: printed by Henry T. Cooke & Sons [1896].   [9], 200, xviii pp., portraits, plates.   8½"
   3 coloured plates of uniform.

———— [Another edition].   Warwick: W. H. Smith & Son, 1912.   [14], 248, xvi pp., plates [as above].   8"

With the Warwickshire Yeomanry in South Africa.   By M. Hunt.   Birmingham: Cornish Bros., 1902.   174 pp., portraits, illustrations.   9"

The Warwickshire Yeomanry in the Great War.   Compiled by the Hon. H. A. Adderley (Capt.).   Warwick: printed by W. H. Smith & Son [1922].   x, 222, xvi pp., portraits, plates, maps.   8"

The Charge of the Warwickshire and Q.O. Worcestershire Yeomanry at Huj, 8th November, 1917.   [By Major E. G. Pemberton].   Petersfield: Childs, printers, *n.d.*   11 pp.   5⅜"×8¾"

WESTMORLAND
The Westmorland and Cumberland Yeomanry.   Historical Sketch of the Regiment.   Penrith: R. Scott, " Observer " Office, 1912.   47 pp.   8¼"
   Reprinted from series of articles in the *Penrith Observer* in April and May 1912 as a contribution towards a complete history; signed Daniel Scott.

The Duke of Lancaster's Own Yeomanry Cavalry, 23rd Co., I.Y.; a record of incidents . . . in the South African Campaign, 1899-1902, of interest also to the Westmorland and Cumberland Yeomanry, 24th Co., I.Y. who were our partners. [By L. H. Johnson.   Bolton: The Author, 1902].   158 pp., portraits, plates, map.   8½"

WILTSHIRE
A List of the Wiltshire Regiment of Yeomanry Cavalry. Commanded by the Right Hon. Lord Bruce. By William Pettit, Lieut. and Adjut. Corrected to the First of January, 1799. Salisbury; printed by B. C. Collins, 1799. 40 pp. 5¾″

The Annals of the Yeomanry Cavalry of Wiltshire; being a Complete History of the Prince of Wales's Own Royal Regiment; from the time of its formation in 1794 to October, 1884. With Six Appendices. By Henry Graham. Liverpool: D. Marples & Co. Ltd., 1886. x, 268 pp., portraits. 8½″

——— Vol. 2: being a Complete History of the Prince of Wales's Own Royal Regiment from 1893 to 1908. By Henry Graham. Devizes: Geo. Simpson, " Gazette " Printing Works, 1908. vii, 192 pp., portraits, plates, maps. 8½″

Royal Wilts. The History of the Royal Wiltshire Yeomanry, 1920-1945. By Lieut.-Col. P. W. Pitts. London: Burrup, Mathieson & Co. Ltd., 1946. 234 pp., plate, maps, diagrams, end-paper maps. 9⅝″

Yeomanry Light Cavalry Uniforms in Wiltshire. By F. Stevens. [In the *Wiltshire Archaeological and Natural History Magazine*, vol. xlix, pp. 339-345, 1940]. 8½″
   6 plates of uniform.

WORCESTERSHIRE
Memoranda relative to the Worcestershire Yeomanry Cavalry, now the Queen's Own, raised by Other Archer, 6th Earl of Plymouth, in 1831 now under the command of Lieut.-Col. The Hon. Robert Henry Cave, M.P. London: printed by S. & J. Bentley, Wilson & Fley, 1843. viii, 124 pp. 8¾″

——— Continuation of Memoranda . . . 1st April, 1843 to 31st March, 1854. London: printed by Woodfall and Kinder, 1854. 120 pp. 8½″

The Yeomanry Cavalry of Worcestershire, 1794-1913. By Q. L. Privately printed. [Devizes: Geo. Simpson], 1914. xii, 240 pp., portraits, plates, maps. 9¾″
   4 coloured plates of uniform.

The Yeomanry Cavalry of Worcestershire, 1914-1922. By C. [i.e. Lord Cobham]. Stourbridge: Mark & Moody Ltd., 1926. xii, 252 pp., plates, maps. 9¾″

The Queen's Own Worcestershire Hussars, 1922-1956. By D. R. Guttery. Stourbridge: Mark & Moody Ltd., 1958. ix, 159 pp., portraits, plates, sketch maps. 8½″

The Charge of the Warwickshire and Q.O. Worcestershire Yeomanry at Huj, 8th November, 1917. [By Major E. G. Pemberton]. Petersfield: Childs, printers, *n.d.* 11 pp. 5⅜″×8¾″

YORKSHIRE
The First West York Regiment of Yeomanry Cavalry: its Formations and Services; with Brief Notices of other Regiments of West Riding Volunteer Yeomanry Cavalry.   By W. Sheardown, Esq.   (Communicated to the Doncaster Gazette, 29th December, 1871-1st March, 1872).   Doncaster: " Gazette " Office [1872]. 96 pp., plate. $7\frac{1}{4}''$

History of the old Second West York Yeomanry Cavalry (1843-1894), supplemented by the Records of the Huddersfield Cavalry Association (1798-1802), of the Huddersfield Corps of Yeomanry Cavalry (Major John Lister Kaye's Regiment (1803-1808), and of the Huddersfield Yeomanry (1817-1828); with introduction by Robert Potter Berry and Benson F. M. Freeman, Engr.-Lieut., R.N. Huddersfield: " Daily Chronicle " Printing Works, 1905.   160 pp. $8\frac{1}{2}''$

The Northern Regiment of West Riding Volunteer Yeomanry Cavalry, 1794-1804.   By Wilfred Robertshaw.   Offprint from *The Bradford Antiquary;* the Journal of the Bradford Historical and Antiquarian Society, N.S., Part 23, pp. 99-120; Part 24, pp. 1-22.   Bradford: printed by Outhwaite Bros., 1929-31. Portraits. $9\frac{3}{8}''$

Europe Revisited.   The East Riding Yeomanry in the Liberation of Europe and the Defeat of Germany.   By V. C. Ellison.   [Hull: A. Brown & Sons Ltd., 1946]. ix, 101 pp., plates, maps. $8\frac{1}{2}''$

A History of the Yorkshire Hussars.   [In *The Yorkshire Hussars Magazine*, July 1927 to July 1939].   Portraits, plates. $9''$
    Coloured illustration of uniform on covers.

An Alphabetical List of the Officers of The Yorkshire Hussars, from the Formation of the Regiment to the Present Time.   By Henry Stooks Smith.   London: Simpkin, Marshall & Co., 1853.   xxvi, 28 pp., plates. $8\frac{1}{2}''$
    Pp. i-xxvi contain a History of the Regiment.
    1 coloured plate of uniform.

A Short Record of the Queen's Own Yorkshire Dragoons, 1794-1930.   [Edited by Col. C. J. Hirst and Major R. Warde-Aldam].   [Doncaster], no imprint, 1931. 30 pp. $5''$

———— [Another edition] . . . 1794-1954.   [Aldershot: Gale & Polden Ltd., 1954]. 31 pp., portrait. $7\frac{1}{4}''$

SCOTLAND

ANGUS, *see* FIFE and FORFAR

AYRSHIRE, *see also under* GLASGOW.
A History of the Ayrshire Yeomanry Cavalry.   By W. S. Cooper, Captain. Edinburgh: David Douglas.   viii, 108 pp.   1881.   8vo.

The Proud Trooper. The History of the Ayrshire (Earl of Carrick's Own) Yeomanry from its raising in the Eighteenth Century till 1964. By Major W. Steel Brownlie. London: Collins, 1964. 639 pp., portraits, plates, maps. 9"
    5 coloured plates of uniform.

A Short History of the Ayrshire Yeomanry (Earl of Carrick's Own) 151st Field Regiment, R.A., 1939-1946. Compiled and edited by Major I. A. Graham Young and Capt. R. I. Gray. Ayr: Observer Office, 1947. 80 pp., portraits, plates, maps. 8½"

BORDER COUNTIES, *see also* LOTHIANS.
Historical Records of the Border Yeomanry Regiments. By Eng. Lieut. Benson F. M. Freeman, R.N. Reprinted from the *Kelso Mail*. [1906]. 42 pp. 9¾"
    Berwickshire Yeomanry Cavalry; Peebleshire Yeomanry Cavalry; Roxburgh-shire Light Dragoons Yeomanry Cavalry and the Selkirkshire Light Dragoons Yeomanry Cavalry from 1797 to 1828.

FIFE and FORFAR
A History of the Fife Light Horse. By Col. Anstruther Thomson. Edinburgh: William Blackwood & Sons, 1892. x, 284 pp., portraits. 9¼"

The Fifes in South Africa; being a history of the Fife and Forfar Yeomanry in the South African War, 1900-1901. By 9176 I.Y. [Trooper J. P. Sturrock]. Cupar Fife: A. Westwood & Son, 1903. xii, 197 pp., portraits, plates, maps. 8½"

The Fife & Forfar Imperial Yeomanry and its Predecessors. Compiled by Capt. Gerald Burgoyne from Regimental and Troop Order Books, etc., and from an MS. History of the Regiment by Lieut. Benson Freeman, R.N. Cupar-Fife: J. & G. Innes, "Fife Herald and Journal," 1904. 103 pp., plates. 7½"

The Fife and Forfar Yeomanry and 14th (F. & F. Yeo.) Batt. R.H., 1914-1919. By Major D. D. Ogilvie. With a Preface by Major-Gen. E. S. Girdwood. London: John Murray, 1921. xii, 212 pp., plates, maps. 7¼"
    Chapter VIII deals with "The Predecessors of the Fife and Forfar Yeomanry."

The Fife and Forfar Yeomanry, 1919-1956. By R. J. B. Sellar. With a Fore-word by Lt.-Gen. Sir Brian Horrocks. Edinburgh: Wm. Blackwood & Sons Ltd., 1960. xii, 288 pp., portraits, plates, maps. 8½"

GLASGOW
Scottish Yeomanry in South Africa, 1900-1901. A Record of the Work and Experiences of the Glasgow and Ayrshire Companies. By Trooper A. S. Orr. Glasgow: James Hadderwick & Sons, 1901. 160 pp., plates. 8½"

The Queen's Own Royal Glasgow Yeomanry, 1848-1948. Glasgow: printed for the Regiment by Robert Maclehose & Co. Ltd. [1949]. 126 pp., portraits, illustrations. 9½"

INVERNESS-SHIRE

532 Light Anti-Aircraft Regiment R.A. (Lovats Scouts) T.A.; short history. Inverness.   No imprint, 1950.   16 pp., $4\frac{3}{4}'' \times 7\frac{1}{2}''$

The Sword of the North: Highland Memories of the Great War.   By Dugald MacEchern.   (Chapter on Lovats Scouts).   Inverness: Robert Carruthers & Sons, "Courier" Office, 1923.   10″

LANARKSHIRE

Records of the Lanarkshire Yeomanry, with some account of the Officers of the Corps, 1819-1910.   By Surg. Lt.-Col. Russell E. Wood.   No imprint, Edinburgh, 1910.   viii, 140 pp., portraits, plates, illustrations. $10\frac{1}{4}''$
   1 coloured plate of uniform.   100 copies printed for private circulation.

593.   The Story of a Field Battery, 1940-1945.   156th (Lanarkshire Yeomanry) Field Regiment, R.A.   Commenced at Anzio 1944—completed in Germany, 1945.   Edited by Gnr. Hodgson, H. B., printed at Pinneberg, Germany, 1945, by A. Beig, xxiv, 328 pp., portraits, plates, illustrations, maps.   8″
   600 copies.

A Short History of The Lanarkshire Yeomanry, R.A.C. (T.A.) Lanark: The Regiment, 1951.   15 pp., illustrations.   7″

LOTHIANS

War Record of 4th Bn. King's Own Scottish Borderers and Lothians and Border Horse, etc.   Edited by W. Sorley Brown (Lieut.) Galashiels: John McQueen & Son, 1920.   216 pp., portraits, plates, maps. $8\frac{1}{2}''$

Outline of Regimental History of the 19th (Lothians and Border Horse) Armoured Car Co.   By Major James Rissik Marshall.   Edinburgh: Thomas Allen & Sons [1928].   24 pp.   8″

The 19th (Lothians and Border Horse) Armoured Car Company.   Brief Outline of the Regimental History.   No imprint, 1933.   8 pp. $6\frac{1}{4}''$

A Short Account of the 1st Lothians and Border Yeomanry in the Campaigns of 1940 and 1944-45.   [By W. A. Woolward].   Published by The Lothians and Border Regimental Association.   [Edinburgh: printed by T. & A. Constable Ltd., 1946].   108 pp., plate, maps. $8\frac{1}{2}''$

"Driver Advance"; being a short account of the 2nd Lothians and Border Horse, 1939-1946.   [By D. G. Antonio].   Edinburgh: printed by T. & A. Constable Ltd., 1947.   119 pp., frontispiece, maps. $8\frac{1}{2}''$

PEEBLESSHIRE, *see* BORDER COUNTIES

PERTHSHIRE

The Scottish Horse, 1900-1940.   By the Duchess of Atholl.   With a Foreword by Field Marshall [sic] Lord Milne and a Message from Colonel-Commandant The Duke of Atholl.   Glasgow: Jackson Son & Co., 1940.   58 pp., portrait, plates. $5\frac{3}{8}''$

The Scottish Horse, 1939-1945; being the history of the 79th and 80th (Scottish Horse) Medium Regiments, Royal Artillery. [By R. A. S. Barbour. Glasgow: printed by McCorquodale & Co. Ltd., 1951]. xii, 151 pp., portraits, plates, maps. 8½″

The Scottish Horse [in *A Military History of Perthshire*, 1899-1902; edited by the Marchioness of Tullibardine, pp. 30-63]. Perth: R.A. & J. Hay, 1908. 9¾″

The Scottish Horse [in *The Sword of the North:* Highland Memories of the Great War; by Dugald MacEchern]. Inverness: Robert Carruthers & Sons, 1923. 10″

The Perthshire Yeomanry, 1794-1902. [in *A Military History of Perthshire*, 1660-1902; edited by the Marchioness of Tullibardine]. Perth: R. A. & J. Hay, 1908. Plates. 9¾″

ROXBURGHSHIRE, *see* BORDER COUNTIES

SELKIRKSHIRE, *see* BORDER COUNTIES

VOLUNTEERS: TERRITORIAL FORCE (*later* ARMY)

The British Army and Auxiliary Forces. By Col. C. Cooper King, R.M.A. With 90 [132] full-page plates from original photographs. London: Cassell & Co. Ltd., 1893. 2 vols. 12¾″
    Brief histories of regiments and corps.

His Majesty's Territorial Army. A Descriptive Account of the Yeomanry, Artillery, Engineers, and Infantry, with the Army Service and Medical Corps, comprising "The King's Imperial Army of the Second Line." By Walter Richards. With illustrations by R. Caton Woodville. London: Virtue & Co., 1910-11. 4 vols., viii, 184 pp., in each vol. 12¾″
    32 coloured plates (8 in each volume).
    Outline histories of regiments and corps.

The Fighting Territorials. By P. Hurd. London: "Country Life," 1915-16. 2 vols. 7¼″

Records of the Scottish Volunteer Force, 1859-1908. By Major-Gen. J. M. Grierson. Edinburgh & London: William Blackwood & Sons, 1909. xxvi, 372 pp., plates. 10″
    47 coloured plates of uniform.
    Short histories of all corps.

ENGLAND AND WALES

ANGLESEY, *see under* CARNARVONSHIRE

BEDFORDSHIRE

The History of the Fifth Battalion The Bedfordshire and Hertfordshire Regiment (T.A.). By Capt. F. A. M. Webster. Foreword by Field Marshal The Viscount Allenby. London: Frederick Warne & Co. Ltd., 1930. xiv, 306 pp., portraits, plates. 8½″

Experiences in the Dardanelles of the 1st/5th Beds. Regt. T.F. By E. Pebody. Olney, 1916. 19 pp. 8vo.

The Story of the First-Fifth Bedfords. By Edmund Rimmer. Manchester: Co-operative Wholesale Society's Printing Works, 1917. 79 pp., portraits, illustrations. 7¼″

The 16th Foot. A History of The Bedfordshire and Hertfordshire Regiment. By Major-Gen. Sir F. Maurice. [Including the Territorial Battn.]. London: Constable & Co. Ltd., 1931. 8¾″

BERKSHIRE

Berkshire Royal Horse Artillery. Fine Record of War Service. Story of the Campaign in Egypt, Arabia, Palestine and Syria, 1914-1919. By G. F. Breach. Reading: Reprinted from *The Reading Standard*, 1923. 12 pp., illustrations. 9½″×13″

The War Services of the 1/4 Royal Berkshire Regiment (T.F.). By C. R. M. F. Cruttwell, late Capt. Oxford: Basil Blackwell, 1922. [iv], 160 pp., portraits, sketch maps. 8½″

" D " Company, 4th Battalion, The Royal Berkshire Regiment. Records of the Company from August 4th, 1914, to October 31st, 1928. [By Major A. C. Hughes and C.-S.-M. A. Brant]. 62 pp. Duplicated with printed title-page and cover. 13″

4/6th Battalion The Royal Berkshire Regiment (T.A.); a short history of the origins and formation etc., 1859-1959. [London: Goddard-Lawrence & Co., 1959]. 36 pp., portraits, illustrations. 9½″

The Royal Berkshire Regiment (Princess Charlotte of Wales's) 49th—66th Foot. By F. Loraine Petre. Reading: The Barracks. 2 vols. [Chapters on Volunteers and Territorial Battns. in both vols.]. 1925. 9½″

The History of The Royal Berkshire Regiment (Princess Charlotte of Wales's), 1920-1947. By Brig. Gordon Blight. [Including the Territorial Battns.]. London: Staples Press, 1953. 8½″

BRECKNOCKSHIRE

The South Wales Borderers, 24th Foot, 1689-1937. By C. T. Atkinson. [Including The Brecknockshire Battalion etc.]. Cambridge: University Press, 1937. 10″

The History of The South Wales Borderers, 1914-1918. By C. T. Atkinson. [Including The Brecknockshire Battn.]. London: The Medici Society Ltd., 1931. 10″

BUCKINGHAMSHIRE
The Citizen Soldiers of Buckinghamshire, 1795-1926. Compiled with the kind assistance of many of the Officers of the Corps concerned by Major-Gen. J. C. Swann. London: Published for the Buckinghamshire Territorial Army Association by Hazell, Watson & Viney, Ltd., 1930. xii, 172 pp., portraits, plates, maps. 9½″

The First Buckinghamshire Battalion, 1914-1919. By Capt. P. L. Wright. With a Foreword by Major-Gen. Sir Robert Fanshawe. London: Hazell, Watson & Viney Ltd. [1920]. xiv, 216 pp., portraits, plates, maps. 8½″

The 2nd Bucks Battalion Oxfordshire and Buckinghamshire Light Infantry, 1914-1918. Narrative compiled by Major-Gen. J. C. Swann. No imprint [c. 1929]. 50 pp., map. 8½″

A Record of the 2nd Bucks Battalion T.F., 1914-1918. To commemorate the Patriotism, the Bravery and the Sacrifice of this Battalion during the Great European War, 1914-1918, and the Distinctions won on the Battlefields of France and Belgium by its Officers and Men. Also the Names of the Officers. Presented to the Bucks Territorial Force Association by Lord Anslow, Chairman of the Association. Compiled and edited by Capt. Ivor Stewart-Liberty. No imprint, 1918. [26] pp. 9¼″

The Oxfordshire & Buckinghamshire Light Infantry Chronicle; An Annual Record etc. 1914-15—1918-19; together with the War Record of the other Battalions. 5 vols. 1915-20.
    Lettered on covers, The Great War, 1-5.

———— 1939-45; the Record of the . . . 1st & 2nd Bucks. Battn. in the Second German War. 4 vols. 1949-54. Portraits, plates, maps. 8½″

CAMBRIDGESHIRE
The Cambridgeshires, 1914 to 1919. By Brig.-Gen. E. Riddell and Col. M. C. Clayton. With an Introduction by Major G. B. Bowes. Cambridge: Bowes & Bowes, 1934. xviii, 292 pp., plates. 8¼″
    [Introduction includes short account of the Cambridgeshire R.V.C., 1860-1914; note in Appendix on the V.T.C.].

The Suffolk Regiment, 1928-1946. By Col. W. N. Nicholson. [The Cambridgeshire Regt., pp. 232-249]. 1948. Portraits, maps. 9″

The History of the Cambridge University Rifle Volunteers. By H. J. Edwards. [In *The Volunteer Service Gazette*, October, 1895].

CARNARVONSHIRE

The Society of Garrison of Fort Williamsburg.   The Old Glynllivon Volunteers, c. 1761-1773.   By E. Alfred Jones. [In *Y Cymmrodor. The Magazine of the Honourable Society of Cymmrodorion*, vol. xliv, pp. 80-103, 1935].   London: issued by the Society.   Portraits.   8½"

A Short History of the 6th (Carnarvon and Anglesey) Battalion the Royal Welch Fusiliers.   North West Europe, June 1944 to May 1945.   Caernarvon: Gwenlyn Evans & Sons, printers, 1946.   xvi, 176 pp., portraits, plates, maps.   8½"

Regimental Records of the Royal Welch Fusiliers.   Vol. 4: 1915-1918, Turkey, Bulgaria, Austria.   By Major C. H. Dudley Ward.   [Chapter on 6th Carnarvon & Anglesey Battalion, T.A.]   London: Forster, Groom & Co. Ltd., 1929.   9¾"

The Red Dragon; the Story of the Royal Welch Fusiliers, 1919-1945.   By Lt.-Commdr. P. K. Kemp & J. Graves.   [Chapter on 6th Carnarvon & Anglesey Battalion, T. A.]   Aldershot: Gale & Polden Ltd., 1960.   8½"

CHESHIRE

Notes on the Establishment of Volunteers in Macclesfield in 1797, and other particulars of the early Volunteer Movement.   By Herbert Sandford Claye.   Macclesfield: "Courier" Office, 1894.   8vo.

The Old Chester Volunteers and their Colour.   By Frank Simpson.   Chester: printed for the Author by G. R. Griffith, Ltd., 1911.   22 pp., portrait.   8½"

The Cheshire Royal Engineers, formerly 113 Assault Engineer Regiment [now 113 (Cheshire) Army Engineer Regiment].   Compiled by Capt. T. R. Davies.   [Birkenhead].   No imprint, 1950, with additions to 1960.   ii, 15 pp.   8½"

Historical Records of the 5th Administrative Battalion Cheshire Rifle Volunteers.   Compiled by Capt. Astley Terry (60th Rifles), Adjutant.   Sandbach: printed by Colour-Sergt. Eachus, 16th C.R.V.C., 1879.   118 pp., portrait, plates.   10¼"
   An 8 pp. supplement was issued for each year from 1879 to 1896.   3 coloured plates of uniform and 1 of colours.

The First Hundred Years; the story of 4th Battalion The Cheshire Regiment, 1859-1959.   [Chester: printed by W. H. Evans Sons & Co. Ltd., 1959].   64 pp. portraits, plates.   8½"

The War Record of the 1/5th (Earl of Chester's) Battalion The Cheshire Regiment, August, 1914-June 1919.   By Lieut.-Col. W. A. V. Churton.   Chester: Phillipson & Golder, 1920.   viii, 130 pp., portraits, maps.   10"

War History of the 6th Battalion The Cheshire Regiment (T.F.) Compiled from the War Diaries of the Battalion.   By Charles Smith with the assistance of the Members of the 6th Cheshire Old Comrades Association.   [Stockport]: Published by the 6th Cheshire Old Comrades Association, 1932.   xi, 68 pp., portraits, plates.   9½"

Do You Remember? The Adventures of 7th Bn. The 22nd (Cheshire) Regiment during the World War, 1939-45. [Edited by Lt.-Col. C. S. Durtnell]. No imprint. Privately printed [1947]. 7, 71 pp., portraits, illustrations, sketch maps. 11¼″

The History of The Cheshire Regiment in the Great War. By Arthur Crookenden, Col. [including the Territorial Battalions]. [Chester: W. H. Evans, Sons & Co. Ltd., 1938]. 9¾″

The History of The Cheshire Regiment in the Second World War. By Arthur Crookenden, Col. [including the Territorial Battalions. Chester: W. H. Evans, Sons & Co. Ltd., 1949]. 9¾″

V.T.C., 1914-1918.
History of the Volunteer Movement in Cheshire, 1914-1920. Edited and compiled from Official Documents, for and on behalf of the County Committee, by E. J. W. Disbrowe, Capt. and Adjut. Stockport: Swain & Co. Ltd., 1920. iv, 108 pp., portraits, plates, map. 7¼″

The Chester Volunteers, with special reference to "A" Company, 3rd Volunteer Battalion The Cheshire Regiment (1914-1920). By Frank Simpson. Chester: The Courant Press [c. 1920]. 156 pp., portraits, illustrations. 8½″

The History of No. 3, Hale Platoon, "A" Company, 1st Volunteer Battalion The Cheshire Regiment, 1914-1919. By H. Dorning. Manchester, 1920. 52 pp. 7¼″

CORNWALL
Historical Record of the 1st Cornwall (Duke of Cornwall's) Artillery Volunteers. By Capt. B. A. Milne, Adjut. No imprint, 1885. 188 pp. 8″

Cornwall's Royal Engineers. A History of the Regiment from its Formation up to the early part of the Second World War. By Lieut.-Col. C. J. H. Mead; including a Contemporary Account of the County's Royal Artillery from 1860 and Military Events affecting Cornwall and the Regular and Auxiliary Forces generally. Plymouth: Underhill (Plymouth) Ltd. [1947]. xxvii, 267 pp., portraits, plates. 7¼″
    Edition limited to 375 copies.

With the Cornwall Territorials on the Western Front, being The History of the Fifth Battalion Duke of Cornwall's Light Infantry in the Great War. Compiled from official records and other sources. By E. C. Matthews, Lieut. Illustrated by the Hon. J. R. L. French, John Hassall, R.I., and others. An Introduction by Brig.-Gen. Lord St. Leven. Cambridge: W. P. Spalding, 1921. xliii, 191 pp., portraits, plates, maps. 8½″

The History of The Duke of Cornwall's Light Infantry, 1914-1919. By Everard Wyrall. [Including the Territorial Battalions]. London: Methuen & Co. Ltd., 1932. 9″

CUMBERLAND
History of the 1st Cumberland Royal Garrison Artillery Volunteers. [By R. Saunders]. Carlisle: G. & T. Coward, printers, 1902. 3, 56 pp. 9½″

The Border Regiment in the Great War. By Col. H. C. Wylly. [Chapters on Territorial Battalions]. Aldershot: Gale & Polden Ltd., 1924. 9¾"

The Story of The Border Regiment, 1939-1945. By Major-Gen. P. J. Shears. [Chapters on Territorial Battalions]. London: Nisbet & Co. Ltd., 1948. 8½"

DENBIGHSHIRE
The 4th (Denbighshire) Battalion Royal Welsh Fusiliers in the Great War. By Capt. C. Ellis. Wrexham: Woodall, Minshall, Thomas & Co., Ltd., 1926. xvi, 148 pp., portraits, plates. 7¾"

Regimental Records of the Royal Welch Fusiliers. Vol. 3. 1914-1918, France and Flanders. By Major C. H. Dudley Ward. [Including 4th Denbighshire Battalion]. London: Forster, Groom & Co. Ltd., 1928. 9¾"

The Red Dragon; the Story of The Royal Welch Fusiliers, 1919-1945. By Lt.-Commdr. P. K. Kemp & J. Graves. [Chapter on the 4th Denbighshire Battalion]. Aldershot: Gale & Polden Ltd., 1960. 8½"

DERBYSHIRE
Belper Regiment—Grenadiers. By the Rev. J. Charles Cox. [In *Journal of Derbyshire Archaeological and Natural History Society*, vol. XII, pp. 58-107, 1890]. London: Bemrose & Sons. 8½"
    Orderly Book of Belper Local Militia, 1809-1813, with account of its prede-
    cessor, the Belper, Shottle and Holbrook Volunteers, 1803-1808.

The War History of the Fifth Battalion The Sherwood Foresters, Notts and Derby Regiment, 1914-1918. By L. W. de Grave. With an Introduction by Lt.-Gen. Sir W. Thwaites; an Appreciation by Lt.-Col. A. Hacking and a Com-mendation by Lt.-Col. J. D. Kerr. Derby: Bemrose & Sons Ltd., 1930. xxiv, 228 pp., portraits, plates, maps. 8½"

The Green Triangle; being the History of the 2/5th Battalion The Sherwood Foresters (Notts and Derby Regiment) in the European War, 1914-1918. By W. G. Hall. With a Foreword by Brig.-Gen. T. W. Stansfield. Letchworth: Garden City Press, 1920. xiv, 197 pp., portraits, plates, maps. 7¼"

6th Bn. The Sherwood Foresters, 1914-1918. [By Capt. W. D. Jamieson]. iv, 161 pp., portraits, maps. Chesterfield, 1958. 10¾"
    Duplicated. 25 numbered copies only.

The Irish Rebellion: the 2/6th Sherwood Foresters' part in the Defeat of the rebels in 1916; their early training. [By Capt. G. J. Edmunds]. Chesterfield: printed by Wilfred Edmunds Ltd. [1960]. 32 pp., illustrations, map. 9½"

The History of the Sherwood Foresters (Nottinghamshire and Derbyshire Regiment), 1919-1957. By Brig. C. N. Barclay. [Chapters on Territorial Battns.]. London: Wm. Clowes & Sons Ltd., 1959. 9½"

DEVON

A Short History of the 3rd Volunteer Battalion of the Devonshire Regiment, 1859 to 1908; and some fragmentary information concerning the East Devon Volunteers of 1794. By a Retired Officer of the 3rd Devon [*i.e.* Major W. H. Hastings]. Exeter: Willis, Pollard & Co. Ltd., 1908. 52 pp., portraits, plates. 9½"

The Devonshire Volunteers of eighty years ago. A Lecture delivered by A. H. A. Hamilton to the Members of the Exeter Literary Society, November 1881. Exeter: printed at the ' Flying Post ' Office, 1881. 17 pp. 7"

The Devonshire Regiment, 1914-1918. Compiled by C. T. Atkinson. [Chapter on Territorial Battns.]. Exeter: Eland Bros., 1926. 8½"

The Devons. A History of The Devonshire Regiment, 1685-1945. By Jeremy Taylor. [Including the Territorial Battns.]. Bristol: The White Swan Press, 1951. 8½"

The 4th Devons. A History of the 4th (Territorial) Battalion, The Devonshire Regiment, 1852-1952. By Francis Thoday and Tom Anstey. Exeter: Wm. Pollard & Co. Ltd., 1952. [8], 144 pp., plate, illustrations, sketch maps. 7¼"

V.T.C., 1914-1918.
The Sidmouth Volunteers. No. 9 Platoon, C Company, 1st Volunteer Battalion Devon Regiment, 1914-1918. By John Tindall, Sergt.-Signaller. Sidmouth: E. Culverwell & Sons, 1920. 64 pp., portraits. 7¼"

The Story of the 2/1st Wessex Field Ambulance, 1914-1919. [Edited by Sergt. W. Pearce]. [Newton Abbot: printed by Mid-Devon Newspaper Co. Ltd., published by W. Pearce, Kingsteignton, 1920]. 50 pp., portraits, illustrations. 10"

DORSET

Dorset Volunteers during the French Wars, 1793-1814. By Henry Symonds. Dorchester: F. G. Longman. (Dorset Natural History and Antiquarian Field Club). 1920. 12 pp. 8½"

The 94th (Dorset & Hants) Field Regiment, Royal Artillery, 1939-1945. By Peter Whately-Smith. [Dorchester: The Dorset Press, 1948]. xii, 114 pp., portraits, illustrations, maps. 8½"

History of the 44 L.A.A. Regiment, R.A. [Edited by Capt. Norman Martin. Brighton: Walter Gillett Ltd., 1945]. 27 pp., portraits, illustrations, maps on paper covers. 9¾"

The Dorsetshire Regiment. The Thirty-Ninth and Fifty-Fourth Foot and the Dorset . . . Volunteers. By C. T. Atkinson. Vol. 2. Oxford: privately printed at the University Press, 1947. 9¼"

History of the Dorsetshire Regiment, 1914-1919. Part II. The Territorial Units. By Major H. O. Lock, and the 1st Volunteer Battalion The Dorsetshire Regiment. By O. C. Vidler. Dorchester: Henry Ling Ltd., 1933. 152 pp., maps. 9½"

From Normandy to the Weser. The War History of the Fourth Battalion the Dorset Regiment, June, 1944-May, 1945. [By] G. J. B. Watkins. [Dorchester: printed by Henry Ling Ltd.], *n.d.* viii, 95 pp., portraits, plates, maps. 7¼"

The Story of the 5th Battalion The Dorsetshire Regiment in North-West Europe, 23rd June, 1944 to 5th May, 1945. Jointly written by Major G. R. Hartwell, Major G. R. Pack, Major M. A. Edwards. [Dorchester: Henry Ling Ltd., 1946]. viii, 82 pp., portraits, illustrations. 7¼"

DURHAM

The History of the 3rd Durham Volunteer Artillery, now part of the 274th (Northumbrian) Field Regiment, R.A. (T.A.), 1860-1960. Edited and compiled by Brig. O. F. G. Hogg. South Shields; printed by the Northern Press Ltd., 1961. 188 pp., portrait, plate. 8½"

The 142nd (Durham) Heavy Battery, R.G.A. (T.); being a Brief Record of their Work in France and Belgium. Compiled by J. L. M. Major J. L. Marr. Sunderland: Rutter & King, *n.d.* 64 pp., portraits, illustrations. 11"

87th Heavy Anti-Aircraft Regiment, Royal Artillery, 1939-1945. [Edited by Lt.-Col. I. G. G. Wilkinson]. Newcastle-upon-Tyne: I. Crane Mann & Son Ltd. [1950]. 55 pp. 8½"

150 years of Loyal Service. A Short History of the 582 LAA/SL Regiment, R.A. (D.L.I.) T.A. from 1797 to 1947 . . . and Programme of Events during Celebrations Week, 10th-16th November, 1947. No imprint [Sunderland]. iv, 28 pp., portraits, plates. 8½"

A Short History of the 112 L.A.A. Regiment, R.A. (Durham Light Infantry) T.A., 1794-1945. [Haifa: Warhaftig's Press, 1946]. 71 pp. 9¼"

The Fifth Battalion The Durham Light Infantry, 1914-1918. By Major A. L. Raimes. With a Foreword by Major-Gen. Sir Percival Wilkinson. Published by a Committee of Past and Present Officers of the Battalion. 1931. xvi, 228 pp., portraits, plates, maps. 9¾"

A Few Notes on The 6th Battalion Durham Light Infantry. By W. L. Vane. 1st January, 1910. No imprint. 46 pp. 5¼"
    100 copies only printed.

The Story of the 6th Battalion Durham Light Infantry. France, April, 1915-November, 1918. Edited by Capt. R. B. Ainsworth. London: St. Catherine Press, 1919. 60 pp. 8½"

A Short History of the Sixth Battalion the Durham Light Infantry. [By Capt. W. I. Watson]. Barnard Castle: The Teesdale Mercury Press, 1939. 30 pp., map. 7¼"

8th Battalion The Durham Light Infantry, 1793-1926. A History compiled by Major E. Hardinge Veitch, from the War Diary, and from Documents, Maps, etc., lent by past and present Members of the Battalion. Durham: J. H. Veitch & Sons, 1926. xvi, 282 pp., portraits, plates, maps. 9¾"

8th Battalion The Durham Light Infantry, 1939-1945. A History compiled by Major P. J. Lewis assisted by Major I. R. English from official records, and personal accounts contributed by Members of the Battalion. Newcastle-upon-Tyne: J. & P. Bealls Ltd., 1949. viii, 319 pp., portraits, plates, sketch maps and end-paper maps. 8½"

[A Short History of the 9th Bn. The Durham Light Infantry (T.A.). Aldershot: Gale & Polden Ltd., 1949]. 15 pp., illustrations. 9"
  Brochure prepared for The Laying up of the Colours and Dedication of Memorial.

The Durham Light Infantry. By the Hon. W. L. Vane, Lieut.-Col. (Chapter on Volunteer and Territorial Battns.). London: Gale & Polden Ltd., 1914. 9¾"

The D.L.I. at War. The History of the Durham Light Infantry, 1939-1945. By Major David Rissik. [Including Territorial Battns.]. Brancepeth Castle: Depot of the D.L.I. [1953]. 8½"

Faithful; the Story of The Durham Light Infantry. By S. G. P. Ward. [Including Volunteer and Territorial Battns.]. London: Thomas Nelson & Sons Ltd., 1963. 9¾"

The 1st Battalion Tyneside Scottish, The Black Watch, Royal Highland Regiment. [History, World War II]. [Perth: Hunter's, 1947]. [xii], 96 pp., portraits, maps. 8½"

ESSEX
Romford to Beirut via France, Egypt and Jericho. An Outline of the War Record of " B " Battery, 271st Brigade, R.F.A. (1/2nd Essex Battery, R.F.A.), with many digressions. Compiled in narrative form by Edwin Blackwell and Edwin C. Axe from Diaries, etc. Clacton-on-Sea: R. W. Humphris, 1926. xvi, 193 pp., portraits, plates, maps. 9¾"

The History of the 17th Light Anti-Aircraft Regiment Royal Artillery, 1938-1945. By Lieut.-Col. H. S. Eeles. With a Foreword by Col. Sir Francis H. D. C. Whitmore, Hon. Colonel. Tunbridge Wells: Courier Co. Ltd. [1946]. 251 pp., plates, maps. 8½"

The Spirit of " 310," being the history of a splendid band of Saturday Night Soldiers. Compiled and edited by H. B. Light. [West Bromwich: Joseph Wones Ltd., printers, 1947]. 180 pp., portraits, illustrations. 9½"
  310 Searchlight Battery, 310/74th S.L. Regt., R.A.

The Essex Regiment. Essex Territorial Infantry Brigade (4th, 5th, 6th and 7th Battalions). Also 8th (Cyclists) Battalion The Essex Regiment. By John Wm. Burrows. Southend-on-Sea: John H. Burrows & Sons Ltd., 1932. xxvii, 410 pp., portraits, illustrations, maps. 8½″
(Essex Units in the War, 1914-1919, vol. 5).

With the 1/5th Essex in the East. By Lt.-Col. T. Gibbons. Colchester: Benham & Company Ltd., 1921. xii, 198 pp., plates, maps. 8¾″

1/4th Essex. A Battalion of the Eighth Army. By Major Denis Beckett· London: printed by Wilson & Whitworth Ltd. [1945]. viii, 43 pp., illustrations· maps. 8½″

The Essex Regiment, 1929-1950. By Col. T. A. Martin. [Including the Territorial Battns.]. Brentwood: The Essex Regiment Association, 1952. 8½″

FLINTSHIRE
Regimental Records of the Royal Welch Fusiliers. Vol. 4., 1915-1918, Turkey, Bulgaria, Austria. By Major C. H. Dudley Ward. [Chapter on 5th Flintshire Battn., T.A.]. London: Forster, Groom & Co. Ltd., 1929. 9¼″

The Red Dragon; the Story of the Royal Welch Fusiliers, 1919-1945. By Lt.-Commdr. P. K. Kemp & J. Graves. (Chapter on 60th A/T Regt. R.A. (R.W.F.), form. 5th (Flintshire) Battn.). Aldershot: Gale & Polden Ltd. 1960. 8½″

GLAMORGAN
132 (Welsh) Field Regiment, R.A. 1939-1945. War Diary. Swansea: C. E. Watkins, 1946. 15 pp. 8½″

1/5th Battalion The Welch Regiment. D-Day to VE-Day. By Serjt. Machin. Duisburg, Germany: 1945. 68 pp., illustrations. 8¾″

The 6th Welsh (T.F.) in France, 1914-1919. By R. G. V. M. Bland. Cardiff: The Western Mail Ltd., 1919. 157 pp., portraits, plates. 8¼″

The History of the Welch Regiment. Part I, 1719-1914; by Major A. C. Whitehorn; Part II, 1914-1918; by Maj.-Gen. Sir T. O. Marden. Cardiff: Western Mail & Echo Ltd., 1932. 9½″

────── 1919-1951 . . . by Maj.-Gen. C. E. N. Lomax. Cardiff: Western Mail & Echo Ltd., 1952. 9¾″
[Both above include the Territorial Battns.].

GLOUCESTERSHIRE
Rules of the 1st Gloucester Artillery Volunteer Corps. Bristol: printed by Rose & Harris, 1881. xii, 94, 85 pp. 4″
Contains Records, Nominal Rolls etc.

The Rise, Progress & Military Improvement of the Bristol Volunteers; with an Alphabetical List of the Officers and Privates, correctly arranged by James Brown, Serj. of the 10th Comp. Bristol: W. Matthews, 1798. [Reprinted by the " Bristol Times and Mirror " Ltd., 1916]. 80 pp. 6¼″

1st Gloucestershire (Bristol) Rifle Volunteers; Headquarters, Bristol. Col. Taylor, Commanding.   Programme of Parades, Drills, etc. for 1867, with other information respecting the Corps.   Bristol: I. Arrowsmith, 1867.   60 pp.   8″
  Published annually to 1876.

A Brief History of the Bristol Volunteers from their earliest formation to the establishment of the Territorial Army in 1908; to which is added an Account of the North Somerset Yeomanry Cavalry and the Royal Gloucestershire Hussars. By Edwin T. Morgan, Qr.-Mr.-Sergt.   Bristol: " Bristol Times and Mirror " Ltd., 1908.   48 pp.   8½″

Some Account of the Frampton-on-Severn Volunteers, 1798-1802.   Extracted from documents preserved at Frampton Court and edited by George B. Michell. Gloucester: The Crypt House Press Ltd., 1928.   15 pp.   8″

History of the Loyal Westbury Volunteer Corps from A.D. 1803 to A.D. 1814. By H. J. Wilkins.   Bristol: J. W. Arrowsmith Ltd., 1918.   52 pp.   9½″

The Cotswold Volunteers—past and present.   By the Rev. D. Royce, hon. chaplain to the I Company, 2nd Volunteer Battalion, Glos. Regiment.   Re-printed from Clift's Stow on the Wold Almanack for 1888.   Stow on the Wold: printed by F. A. Clift, 1888.   24 pp.   8vo.

Gloucestershire Volunteers, 1795-1815.   By Brig. H. Bullock.   An alphabetical list of Artillery and Infantry Volunteer Corps in Gloucestershire.   [In *Society for Army Historical Research, Journal*, vol. 38, 1960, pp. 76-82].   9¼″

European War.   With the 5th Glo'sters at home and overseas from 3 August 1914 to 21 March 1918.   [By W. J. Wood].   Gloucester: printed by the Crypt House Press Ltd. [1925].   [viii], 116 pp., portrait.   8½″

The Fifth Gloucester Gazette.   A chronicle, serious and humorous, of the battalion while serving with the British Expeditionary Force.   Gloucester: printed by John Jennings [1922].   xi, 280 pp.   Fo.
  Reproductions of original issues, with introduction by Rev. G. F. Helm; short history of the Battalion up to outbreak of War, 1914, and its work at the Front; roll.

The Story of the 2/5th Battalion Gloucestershire Regiment, 1914-1918.   Edited by A. F. Barnes, Capt.   Gloucester: The Crypt House Press Ltd., 1930.   192 pp. portraits, plates, maps.   8½″

The Gloucestershire Regiment in the War, 1914-1918.   The Records of the . . . . 4th, 5th and 6th (First Line T.A.) Battalions.   By Everard Wyrall. London: Methuen & Co. Ltd., 1931.   8¾″

Cap of Honour: the Story of The Gloucestershire Regiment, 1694-1950.   By David Scott Daniell.   [Chapters on Volunteer & Territorial Battalions].   London: George G. Harrap & Co. Ltd., 1951.   8½″

Record of a Reconnaissance Regiment. A History of the 43rd Reconnaissance Regiment (The Gloucestershire Regiment), 1939-1944. [Edited by Jeremy Taylor]. With a Foreword by Gen. Sir Ivor Thomas. Bristol: The White Swan Press [1950]. 252 pp., portraits, plates, maps. 8½"

Cadets
An Account of the Formation and Progress of the "Cadet Corps," attached to the First Gloucester Engineer Volunteers. By George Brett. 1881, 12 pp. 8vo.

HAMPSHIRE
The Old Hampshire Volunteers. The flags in the Town Hall, Romsey. Their forgotten past. By Florence Horatia Suckling. Reprinted from the *"Hampshire Independent"* of March 16th, 1912, and 2 other articles. 8, [3], [5] pp. 8vo.

History of the Hampshire Territorial Force Association and War Record of Units, 1914-1919. Southampton: *Hampshire Advertiser* Co. Ltd., 1921. 214 pp. 9¾"
Contains short records of all units raised in the County.

History of the 1/1st Hants. Royal Horse Artillery during the Great War, 1914-1919. Edited by Capt. P. C. D. Mundy. Southampton: The Hampshire Advertising Co. Ltd., 1922. 82 pp., plates. 9¾"

The 94th (Dorset & Hants.) Field Regiment, Royal Artillery, 1939-1945. By Peter Whately-Smith. [Dorchester: The Dorset Press, 1948]. xii, 114 pp., portraits, illustrations, maps. 8½"

History of the First Volunteer Battalion Hampshire Regiment 1859 to 1889, with Appendix containing Notes and Illustrations in reference to the Corps from 1890 to 1903. By Col. T. Sturmey Cave. London: Simpkin & Co. Winchester: Warren & Sons, 1905. xvi, 434 pp., portraits, plates. 7¼"

———— large paper edition. 10"

Home Service with a Hampshire Battalion, 1914-1918. [4th, aft. 17th Bn.]. By Major A. F. St. C. Stapleton. Basingstoke: Bird Brothers Ltd. *n.d.* 31 pp. 8½"

2/4th Battalion Hampshire Regiment, 1914-1919. No imprint, *c.* 1919. 68 pp., sketch maps. 9½"

The Isle of Wight Rifles. [Newport]: I. W. County Press, 1937. 29 pp. 6½"
Princess Beatrice's (I. of W.R.) Heavy Bde., R.A., T.A.

Regimental History of The Royal Hampshire Regiment. By C. T. Atkinson. Glasgow: Robert Maclehose & Co. Ltd., 1950-52. 9¼"
Vol. 1. To 1914 [including Volunteers & Territorial Battns.]
Vol. 2. 1914-1918 [including Territorial Battns.].
Vol. 3. 1918-1954. By David Scott Daniell [including Territorial Battns.]. Aldershot: Gale & Polden Ltd., 1955. 9¼"

Cadets
The Winchester College Corps. By J. W. Parr and Remains of Parr. Winchester: P. & G. Wells Ltd., 1957. [v], 122 pp. 8½"

HEREFORDSHIRE
Historical Record of the Herefordshire Light Infantry and its Predecessors. Edited by G. Archer Parfitt. Hereford. 226 pp., 1962. Portraits, plates. Duplicated. 13"

HERTFORDSHIRE
Local Military Forces in Hertfordshire, 1793-1814. By Major J. H. Busby. [In *Society for Army Historical Research, Journal*, vol. 31, 1953, pp. 15-24]. 9¼"

Hertfordshire Field Gazette. Italian Campaign, Aug. 1944-Jan. 1945. No imprint. [Italy, 1945]. v, 105 pp. 6¼"
  1st Battalion The Hertfordshire Regiment.

A Short History of the Hertfordshire Regiment. [Aldershot: Gale & Polden Ltd., 1950]. 16 pp. 5½"

The 16th Foot. A History of The Bedfordshire and Hertfordshire Regiment. By Major-Gen. Sir F. Maurice. [Including The Hertfordshire Regt., T.A.]. London: Constable & Co. Ltd., 1931. 8¾"

Regulations for the Dress of the First Herts Light Horse Volunteers. Bishops Stortford: A. Boardman, 1868. 15 pp. 8vo.

HUNTINGDONSHIRE
The Duke of Manchester's Mounted Volunteer Corps. [1860]. 16 pp 8½"
  Contains a report of a Meeting held at Kimbolton Castle on 30th Dec., 1859, a list of Subscriptions and Donations, and a List of Volunteers for enrolment.

ISLE OF MAN
A Military History of the Isle of Man. [By] B. E. Sargeaunt. Arbroath: T. Buncle & Co. Ltd. [1949]. 94 pp. 8½"
  Contains Militia, Fencibles, Yeomanry & Volunteers.

515 (Isle of Man) L.A.A.Regt., R.A. (T.A.) Douglas: B. & S. Ltd. [1948]. 12 pp., illustrations. 7¼"

KENT
The Kent Artillery Volunteers. A brief history of the 2nd Kent Artillery Volunteers whose military history over 90 years' service is successively: The 2nd Kent Artillery Volunteers; The 9th Kent Artillery Volunteers; The 8th London Howitzer Brigade, T.A.; The 65th (8th London) Field Brigade, T.A.; The 65th (8th London) Field Regiment, T.A.; The 265th (8th London) Heavy Anti-Aircraft Regiment, T.A. Compiled and edited by Lieut.-Col. S. M. Roberts. Lee Green: [The Broadway Press Ltd.], 1951. 16 pp., illustrations. 8½"

The Regimental History of the 415 Coast Regiment R.A.   (Thames & Medway) (T.A.) [By Lt.-Col. D. C. Titchener-Barrett].   No imprint [1952].   24 pp.   4½″

History of the East Kent Volunteers.   By Charles Igglesden.   Ashford: "The Kentish Express" (Igglesden & Co.) Ltd., 1899.   188 pp., portraits.   8½″

Historical Records of The Buffs, East Kent Regiment.   Vol. 3, 1914-1919; Vol. 4, 1919-1948.   [Chapters on Territorial Battalions].   London: The Medici Society Ltd., 1922-51.   8¾″

A Diary of The First-Fourth Battalion The Buffs, East Kent Regiment-Territorial Force, 1914-1919.   No imprint [c. 1920].   42 pp.   7¾″

The Queen's Own Royal West Kent Regiment, 1914-1919.   By C. T. Atkinson, [including the Territorial Battalions].   London: Simpkin, Marshall, Hamilton, Kent & Co. Ltd., 1924.   8½″

———— 1920-1950.   By Lieut.-Col. H. D. Chaplin.   [Chapter on Territorial Battalions].   London: Michael Joseph, 1954.   9″

———— 1951-1961.   By Lieut.-Col. H. D. Chaplin.   [Including Territorial Battalions].   Maidstone: printed by *The Kent Messenger*, 1964.   9½″

From Kent to Kohima; being the History of The 4th Battalion The Queen's Own Royal West Kent Regiment (T.A.), 1939-1947.   By Major E. B. Stanley Clarke & Major A. T. Tillett.   Aldershot: Gale & Polden Ltd., 1951.   xii, 259 pp., plates, maps.   8½″

The History of the Maidstone Companies, Royal Army Medical Corps (Volunteers).   With 28 illustrations.   By Frederick J. Wood, Corporal.   Maidstone: *Kent Messenger* Printing Works, 1907.   90 pp., portraits, plates.   7¼″

LANCASHIRE
The Lancashire Fighting Territorials.   By George Bigwood.   London: " Country Life," 1916.   viii, 156 pp.   7¼″

———— 2nd edition, revised and enlarged.   1916.   xii, 164 pp., portraits, illustrations.   7¼″

A Furness Military Chronicle.   By Alfred Fell.   Ulverston: Kitchin & Co. 1937.   [Chapters on The Ulverston Volunteer Light Infantry; The Furness Troop of Yeomanry Cavalry; The Volunteer Movement].   10″

West Lancashire Territorial Force.   Compiled by Lt.-Col. A. D. Lomas, T.A.S.C.   Southport: "Visitor" Office [1911].   98 pp., illustrations.   7″
   Short histories of all units.   1 coloured uniform plate.

War Diary of the 1st West Lancashire Brigade, R.F.A.   Compiled by Capt. W. W. Wadsworth.   Liverpool: "Daily Post" Printers, 1923.   vi, 160 pp., portraits, plates, maps.   8½″

The Territorial Army.   A Short History of the 1st West Lancashire Artillery Brigade.   Compiled by W. H. Stephenson.   Southport: Robert Johnson & Co. Ltd., 1956.   26 pp., plates.   (1 portrait group)   9¾″

288 (2nd West Lancashire) Light Anti-Aircraft Regiment, Royal Artillery, Territorial Army; a history.   By Capt. A. W. Simpson.   [Blackpool: Gazette, printers], 1960.   40 pp., portrait, illustrations.   8½″

A Short History of the 59th (4th West Lancashire) Brigade, R.A., T.A.   By Col. L. M. Synge.   Liverpool: "Daily Post" Printers, 1934.   32 pp., portraits, plates.   8½″

History of the 359 (4th West Lancs.) Medium Regiment R.A. (T.A.), 1859-1959.   [Liverpool: printed by C. Tinling & Co. Ltd.] 1959.   x, 214 pp., portraits, plates, maps, end-paper maps.   8½″

A History of the 57th (West Lancashire) Divisional Ammunition Column, 1916 to 1919.   England, France & Flanders.   By Lieut.-Col. J. C. Stitt. Wrexham: Edwin Jones & Son, printers, 1919.   20 pp.   8″

A History of the East Lancashire Royal Engineers.   Compiled by Members of the Corps.   London: "Country Life" Ltd, 1921.   xxvi, 268 pp., plates.   Printed for private circulation.   9″

Proceedings of the General Court-Martial in the Trial of Alexander Grant Carmichael, Captain and Adjutant of the Liverpool Fusiliers, on a Charge, exhibited against him by William Earle, Esq., Lieut.-Col. Commandant.   Published from the Notes of a Short-Hand Writer.   Liverpool: Printed by W. Jones. 1804.   98 pp.   8½″

The Fourth Battalion The King's Own (Royal Lancaster Regiment) and the Great War.   [By] Lieut.-Col. W. F. A. Wadham & Capt. J. Crossley.   [London: Crowther & Goodman, printers, 1935].   136, xxiv pp.   8½″

The King's Own T.F.; being a Record of the 1/5th Battalion The King's Own (Royal Lancaster Regiment) in the European War 1914-1918.   Compiled by Albert Hodgkinson, Capt. & Qrmr., from Battalion Records and his personal Diary.   Lewes: printed by The Lewes Press Ltd., 1921.   185 pp., portrait, maps.   9½″

The King's Own.   The Story of a Royal Regiment.   Edited by Col. L. I. Cowper.   [Vol. 2. Chap. VI, etc. deals with the Loyal Lancaster Volunteers, Ulverston Volunteer Infantry, 4th and 5th Battalions and predecessors].   Oxford: University Press, 1939.   Illustrations of uniform.   9″

———— Vol. 3, 1914-1950.   [Including the Territorial Battalions].   Aldershot: Gale & Polden Ltd., 1957.   9″

The History of the 107 Regiment Royal Armoured Corps (King's Own), June 1940—February 1946.   [Lengerich, Westphalia: Bischof & Klein, 1946].   93 pp.

Liverpool Volunteers of 1859. By R. B. Rose. [In *Liverpool Libraries, Museums & Arts Committee Bulletin*, 1956, pp. 47-66]. Portraits, illustrations. 9½″

The Story of the King's (Liverpool) Regiment, formerly the Eighth Foot. By T. R. Threlfall. [Chapter on "The Work of the Territorial Battalions"]. London: "Country Life," 1916. 9″

History of the 2/6th (Rifle) Battalion "The King's" (Liverpool Regiment), 1914-1919, by Capt. C. E. Wurtzburg. With a Foreword by Major-Gen. Sir R. W. R. Barnes. Printed for the Regimental Committee by Gale & Polden Ltd., Aldershot, 1920. xvi, 368 pp., plates, (coloured plate of badges), maps. 9¾″

The Story of the "9th King's" in France. By Enos Herbert Glynne Roberts. Liverpool: The Northern Publishing Co. Ltd., 1922. 134 pp. 8¼″

The Liverpool Scottish, 1900-1919. By A. M. MacGilchrist. Liverpool: Henry Young & Sons, 1930. xi, 333 pp., portrait, plate, maps. 8½″
    10th Battn. The King's, became Cameron Highlanders in 1937.

Historical Records of the Queen's Own Cameron Highlanders. Vols. 6, 7. [Chapters on the Liverpool Scottish]. Edinburgh: William Blackwood & Sons. 1952-61. 10″

Nominal Roll of Officers gazetted to The Liverpool Scottish, 1900-1962. By Col. R. D. M. C. Miers. No imprint, 1963. 6 pp. 9¾″

Historical Record of The King's Liverpool Regiment of Foot . . . (including affiliated . . . Volunteer Battalions). 3rd edition. Enniskillen: Wm. Trimble, 1904. 8½″

The History of The King's Regiment (Liverpool), 1914-1919. By Everard Wyrall. [Including the Territorial Battns.]. 3 vols. London: Edward Arnold & Co., 1928-35. 9¾″

The Story of The King's Regiment, 1914-1948. By Lt.-Col. J. J. Burke Gaffney. [Including the Territorial Battns.] Liverpool: Printed by Sharpe & Kellett Ltd., 1954. 8½″

A History and Some Records of the Volunteer Movement in Bury, Heywood, Rossendale, and Ramsbottom. By T. H. Hayhurst. Bury: Thos. Crompton & Co., "Guardian" Office. Manchester: Abel Heywood & Son, 1887. xii, 332 pp. [Afterwards 5th Battn. Lancashire Fusiliers]. 7½″

At Ypres with Best Dunkley. By Thomas Hope Floyd. London: John Lane, 1920. 245 pp. [2/5th Lancashire Fusiliers]. 7½″

The History of the 2/6th Lancashire Fusiliers (which amalgamated successively with the 1/6th and the 12th Battalion of the same Regiment. The Story of a 2nd Line Territorial Battalion, 1914-1919. By Capt. C. H. Potter and Capt. A. S. C. Fothergill. With Appreciations by Gen. Sir H. A. Lawrence, Gen. Sir Hubert Gough, Gen. Sir Alexander J. Godley, Major-Gen. Sir Neill Malcolm. Rochdale: "Observer" General Printing Works, 1927. xvi, 232 pp., maps. 8½″

The History of the Lancashire Fusiliers, 1914-1918.   By Major Gen. J. C. Latter.
[Including the Territorial Battns.].   Aldershot: Gale & Polden Ltd.   2 vols. 9½"

Regiment of the Line.   The Story of XX The Lancashire Fusiliers.   By Cyril
Ray. [Including the Territorial Battns.].   London: B. T. Batsford Ltd., 1963.   8¾"

History of The East Lancashire Regiment in the Great War, 1914-1918.   [Chap-
ters on Territorial Battns.].   Liverpool: Littlebury Bros. Ltd., 1936.   9½"

History of The East Lancashire Regiment in the War, 1939-1945.   [Chapters on
Territorial Battns.].   Manchester: H. Rawson & Co. Ltd., 1955.   9¾"

A Statement of facts relative to the transfer of service of the Warrington Volunteer
Corps into the Local Militia.   By J. A. Borron, Lieut.-Col. Commandant of the
late Regiment.   Warrington: J. Haddock, 1809.   68 pp.   8¼"

Warrington Volunteers, 1798-1898.   By Walter Crompton and George Venn.
Warrington: " Sunrise " Publishing Co., 1898.   xxviii, 112 pp., portraits,
plates.   8½"

9th and 49th Lancashire Volunteer Rifle Corps, afterwards entitled 1st Volunteer
Battalion Prince of Wales's Volunteers (South Lancashire Regiment).   A few
statistics compiled by Lieut.-Col. J. D. Buckton.   Warrington: " Sunrise "
Publishing Co., 1910.   20 pp., portraits.   7" × 12½"
   The 3 preceding titles deal with the predecessors of the 4th Battn. The South
   Lancashire Regiment.

The Volunteer Service Company (1st South Lancashire Regiment in South Africa
during the Boer War, January 1900-July 1901.   Compiled by Capt. Francis M.
Appleton, with the assistance of the Officers and Men of the Company, etc.
Warrington: Mackie & Co., 1901.   xiv, 178 pp., portraits, illustrations, map. 9¾"

" Ich Dien."   The Prince of Wales's Volunteers (South Lancashire), 1914-1934.
By Capt. H. Whalley-Kelly.   [Chapters on Territorial Battns.].   Aldershot:
Gale & Polden Ltd., 1935.   9½"

The South Lancashire Regiment, The Prince of Wales's Volunteers.   By Col.
B. R. Mullaly.   [Including the Territorial Battns.].   Bristol: The White Swan
Press, 1955.   8½"

The Loyal North Lancashire Regiment.   By Col. H. C. Wylly.   Including the
Territorial Battns.   2 vols.   London: Royal United Service Institution, 1933.
9¾"

The Loyal Regiment (North Lancashire), 1919-1953.   By Capt. C. G. T. Dean.
[Including the Territorial Battns.]   Preston: Regimental Headquarters, 1955.   9"

The War History of the 1st/4th Battalion The Loyal North Lancashire Regiment,
now the Loyal Regiment (North Lancashire), 1914-1918.   Preston: Geo.
Toulmin & Sons Ltd., 1921.   193 pp., portraits, plates, maps.   9¾"
   Coloured plate of colours.

Records of the Mounted Infantry Company 2nd V.B. Manchester Regiment, 1887-1908.   By C. W. Cowell.   Manchester: J. H. Baxter, *n.d.*   59 pp., plates. 8¾″

Records of the 4th Volunteer Battalion, Manchester Regiment.   Compiled by Capt. H. C. Evans.   Manchester: 1900.   224 pp.   8¾″

Letters from Helles.   By Col. Sir Henry Darlington.   With a Preface by Gen. Sir Ian Hamilton.   London: Longmans, Green & Co., 1936.   154 pp.   [1/5th Battn. Manchester Regt.].   End-paper maps.   7¼″

With the Manchesters in the East.   By Gerald B. Hurst.   Manchester: University Press, 1918.   viii, 104 pp., portraits, plates, map.   [Story of the 7th Battalion]. 7¼″

The Seventh Manchesters, July 1916 to March 1919.   By Capt. S. J. Wilson, with a Preface by the Hon. Anthony M. Henley, Brig.-Gen. and an Introduction by Gerald B. Hurst, M.P. (Lieut.-Col. Commanding).   Manchester: University Press, 1920.   xvi, 162 pp., portrait, plates, maps.   7¼″

The Manchesters.   A History of the Regular . . . Territorial . . . Battalions since their formation; with a Record of the Officers now serving and the Honours and Casualties of the War of 1914-16.   Compiled by Capt. G. L. Campbell. London: Picture Advertising Co. Ltd., 1916.   7″

The Story of the 63rd Field Ambulance (2/2 West Lancashire Field Ambulance, T.F.), 1914-1919.   By A. W. Westmore, M. Thomson, J. E. Allison.   [Liverpool: Wood & Sloane Ltd., Printers, 1928].   98 pp.   7¼″

History of the 2/3rd East Lancashire Field Ambulance.   The Story of a 2nd Line Territorial Unit, 1914-1919.   By Sergeant Alfred E. F. Francis.   With Appreciations by Gen. the Hon. Sir H. A. Lawrence and Col. J. Mackinnon.   Salford: W. F. Jackson & Sons, 1930.   x, 150 pp., portraits, plates.   8½″

A Citizen Soldier's Service.   The War Diary of Staff-Sergt. H. Ward, 1914-1919. A record of No. 34 (West Lancs.) C.C.S., R.A.M.C. (T.).   No imprint, *n.d.* 52 pp.   8¼″ × 10½″

Cadets
A Short History of the Rossall School Corps.   By Lt.-Col. L. H. Trist.   Published on the Occasion of the Centenary Parade and Inspection of the Corps by Field Marshal Sir Claude Auchinleck, 10th June, 1960.   [Fleetwood: Fleetwood Chronicle], 1960.   27 pp., portraits, illustrations.   8″

LEICESTERSHIRE
Footprints of the 1/4th Leicestershire Regiment, August 1914 to November 1918. By John Milne, Capt.   With a Foreword by Field Marshal Lord Milne. Leicester: Published for Past and Present Members of the 4th Leicestershire Regiment by Edgar Backus, 1935.   xii, 158 pp., portraits, plates, map.   8½″

The Fifth Leicestershire. A record of the 1/5th Battalion The Leicestershire Regiment T.F., during the War, 1914-1919. By Capt. J. D. Hills. With an Introduction by Lt.-Col. C. H. Jones. Loughborough: The Echo Press, 1919. 10, 380 pp., portraits, plates, maps. $7\frac{1}{4}''$

"The 177th Brigade," 1914-1918. By Lt.-Col. J. P. W. Jamie. Leicester: printed by W. Thornley & Sons, 1931. 73 pp., portraits, illustrations, maps.   9"
   [2/4th, 2/5th Leicestershire Regiment].

LINCOLNSHIRE
A History of the Horncastle Detachment, 4th Battalion The Lincolnshire Regiment (Territorial Army), from the raising of the original Volunteer Corps in 1803 to the present time. By H. R. Tweed. Horncastle: W. K. Morton & Sons, 1936. 50 pp., portraits, illustrations. $8\frac{1}{2}''$

————— Supplement for the years 1936 to 1947.   1947.   36 pp., portraits.

A History of the 5th Battalion The Lincolnshire Regiment. By Col. T. E. Sandall. With a Chapter on its Reconstitution by Major G. H. Teall (Adjutant). Oxford: Basil Blackwell, 1922. viii, 222 pp., portraits, plates. $8\frac{1}{2}''$

"The 177th Brigade," 1914-1918. By Lt.-Col. J. P. W. Jamie. Leicester: printed by W. Thornley & Sons, 1931. 73 pp., portraits, illustrations, maps.   9"
   [2/4th, 2/5th Bns. The Lincolnshire Regt.].

The History of The Lincolnshire Regiment, 1914-1918. Edited by Major-Gen. C. R. Simpson. [Including the Territorial Battns.]. London: The Medici Society Ltd., 1931. $9\frac{3}{4}''$

The History of the Tenth Foot, 1919-1950. Compiled . . . by Major L. C. Gates. [Chapter on the Territorial Battns.]. Aldershot: Gale & Polden Ltd., 1953. $9\frac{1}{2}''$

The History of the Sixth Battalion, The Lincolnshire Regiment. [Edited by A.H.W., i.e. A. H. Wenham, Lt.-Col.]. Leoben, Austria: composed and published by Lincoln Unit Printers and printed by Obersteirische Printing Press, 1946. iv, 54 pp., maps. $9\frac{1}{2}''$

The Orderly Book of Captain Daniel Hebb's Company in the Loveden Volunteers (Lincolnshire), 1803-8. With an Introduction by Col. W. K. Fane. [In *Society for Army Historical Research, Journal*, vol. 4, 1925. pp. 149-161]. $9\frac{1}{4}''$

LONDON
Loyal Volunteers of London & Environs, Infantry and Cavalry, in their respective Uniforms. Representing the whole of the Manual, Platoon, and Funeral Exercise, in 87 plates. Designed and Etch'd by T. Rowlandson, and Dedicated by Permission to His Royal Highness The Duke of Glocester [*sic*] 1799. 87 coloured plates and descriptive letterpress. $13\frac{1}{2}'' \times 11''$

Honourable Artillery Company
The History of The Honourable Artillery Company, of the City of London, from its Earliest Annals to the Peace of 1802.   By Anthony Highmore.   London: Printed for the Author by R. Wilks, Chancery Lane etc., 1804.   xvi, 600 pp., portraits, plates.   8½"

The History of the Honourable Artillery Company.   By Capt. G. A. Raikes. With maps and illustrations.   London: Richard Bentley & Son, 1878-79. 2 vols., portraits, plates, maps.   8½"
    Vol. 1 contains 1 coloured plate of uniform and 1 of Colours; Vol. 2, 1 coloured portrait.

Incidents in the History of the Honourable Artillery Company; being an abridged version of Major Raikes' History of the Company from its Incorporation in 1537 to the Present Time (1887), and including also a Brief History of the American Branch of the Regiment, founded in 1638, and known as the Ancient and Honourable Company of Boston, Mass., U.S.A.   By Capt. Woolmer-Williams. With maps and illustrations.   London: Richard Bentley & Son, 1888.   xx, 206 pp., portraits, plates, plan.   8½"

The Royal Charter of Incorporation granted to the Honourable Artillery Company by Henry VIII, 25th August, 1537; also the Royal Warrants issued by successive Sovereigns from 1632 to 1889, and Orders in Council relating to the Government of the Company, from 1591 to 1634.   Edited by Lieut.-Col. G. A. Raikes and printed by Order of the Court of Assistants.   London: C. E. Roberts & Co., 1889.   xvi, 112 pp.   8½"

The Ancient Vellum Book of the Honourable Artillery Company, being the Roll of Members from 1611 to 1682.   With Notes and Illustrations.   Edited by Lieut.-Col. G. A. Raikes.   Printed by Order of the Court of Assistants.   London: Richard Bentley & Son, 1890.   xx, 186 pp., plates.   9"

The Historie Booke.   Done to keep in lasting remembrance the joyous meeting of the Honourable Artillery Company of London and the Ancient and Honourable Artillery Company of the Massachusetts in the Towne of Boston, A.D. 1903.   Edited by Justin H. Smith.   Privately printed at the Norwood Press [Boston, 1903] for the Ancient and Honourable Artillery Company of the Massachusetts.   lvi, 176 pp., plates, illustrations.   12½"
    6 coloured plates, including 1 of Colours.

The H.A.C. in South Africa.   A Record of the Services rendered in the South African War by Members of the Honourable Artillery Company.   Edited by Basil Williams and Erskine Childers.   With a map.   London: Smith, Elder & Co., 1903.   234 pp.   7½"

The Honourable Artillery Company, 1537-1926. By G. Goold Walker (Major), Secretary of the Company. With a Foreword by the Earl of Denbigh and Desmond (Colonel-Commandant H.A.C.). With Four illustrations in colour and Seventy Four in black and white. London: John Lane, The Bodley Head Ltd., 1926. xvi, 298 pp., portraits, plates, illustrations. 8½"
    4 coloured plates, including 2 of uniform.

———— [2nd edition] . . . 1537-1947. With a Foreword by Field Marshal The Viscount Alanbrooke. Aldershot: Gale & Polden Ltd., 1954. xiii, 380 pp., portraits, plates, illustrations, maps. 8½"
    5 coloured plates, including 2 of uniform.

The Honourable Artillery Company in the Great War, 1914-1919. Edited by Major G. Goold Walker. With an Introduction by the Earl of Denbigh and Desmond. London: Seeley, Service & Co. Ltd., 1930. 592 pp., portraits, plates, sketch maps. 8½"

Regimental Fire! The Honourable Artillery Company in World War II, 1939-1945. By Brig. R. F. Johnson. [London: Printed by Williams, Lea & Co. Ltd.], 1958. xx, 440 pp., portraits, plates, maps. 8⅛"

The Story of the Honourable Artillery Company; being a short account of the long history of the ancient Guild of St. George. By John Betts. Finsbury: Armoury House, 1921. 30 pp., portraits, illustrations. 9½"

Honourable Artillery Company, 1537-1937. [London: W. & S. Ltd., 1937]. 36 pp., portraits, illustrations. 11½"
    8 coloured illustrations, including 6 of uniform and 1 of Colours.

London Gunners. The Story of the H.A.C. Siege Battery in Action. By W. R. Kingham (Ex-gunner H.A.C.). With a Foreword by the Earl of Denbigh. London: Methuen & Co. Ltd. [1919]. xx, 280 pp., portraits, plates, maps. 7½"

With the 11th (H.A.C.) Regiment, R.H.A., in World War II. By Major Kenneth Bolton. [London: Williams, Lea & Co. Ltd., 1945]. 84 pp., illustrations. 9¾"

Light Horse Volunteers
An Historical Record of the Light Horse Volunteers of London and Westminster; with the Muster Rolls from the first Formation of the Regiment in MDCCLXXIX, to the Relodgement of the Standards in the Tower, MDCCCXXIX. By James N. Collyer and John Innes Pocock. London: printed by William Nicol, Shakespeare Press. Published by Wright, 60 Pall Mall, 1843. vi, 388 pp., plates 8¾"
    7 coloured plates of uniform.

The Inns of Court Regiment
A Short History of the Military and Naval Services of The Inns of Court and the Members of the Bench and Bar from the time of the Battle of Hastings. By F. C. Norton, barrister-at-law and sergeant, I.C.R.V. London: William Clowes & Sons Ltd., 1886. 16 pp. 8½"

The Inns of Court Officers Training Corps during the Great War.   Edited by
Lt.-Col. F. H. L. Errington.   London: Printing-Craft Ltd. [1922].   375 pp.,
portrait, plates.   10¾"

Needs must . . . The History of the Inns of Court Regiment, 1940-1945.   [By
Capt. A. F. J. Taggart.   London: F. Mildner & Sons, 1949].   103 pp., portraits,
plates, maps in pocket.   8¼"

An Outline of the History of The Inns of Court Regiment.   No imprint, 1951.
11 pp.   4½"

Artillery
Amateur Gunners.   The Adventures of an Amateur Soldier in France, Salonica
and Palestine in the Royal Field Artillery, recording Some of the Exploits of the
2/22nd County of London Howitzer Battery, R.F.A., on Active Service.   By
A. Douglas Thorburn, Capt.   Liverpool: William Potter [1933].   199 pp., plates.
7¼"

The History of the 53rd (London) Medium Brigade, Royal Artillery.   By Major
B. J. Grimwood.   [South Darenth: The Little Boys' Press, 1936].   66 pp.,
plates.   7¼"

(The History of A/18).   'A' Battery, 18th Army Brigade, R.F.A., 1914-1919.
[London: Battley Brothers Ltd., 1939].   84 pp., portraits.   8¼"

A Short Summary of the War Services and Actions fought by the 7th London
Brigade, R.F.A., and its component Batteries, March, 1915-19.   By Capt.
P. H. Pilditch and Capt. R. B. Ullman.   Introduction by Brig.-Gen. J. C.
Wray.   Woolwich: Royal Artillery Institution, *n.d.*   12 pp.   9"

264 (7th London) Field Regiment Royal Artillery (T.A.).   A Short History
[1860-1947].   [Woolwich: printed at the Royal Artillery Institution, 1948].
[32 pp.], portraits, plates.   8¼"

A Short History of the 454 H.A.A. Regiment R.A. (City of London) Territorial
Army [formerly 54th (City of London H.A.A. Regiment R.A. (T.A.)].   By
Lt.-Col. J. W. Perring.   No imprint.   London, 1950.   16 pp., illustrations.   7¼"

History of the 90th (City of London) Field Regiment R.A. in the Second World
War, 1939-1945.   No imprint [1945].   39 pp., portraits, illustrations, maps.   10"

The ' Ninety-Second '; a Short Outline History of the 92nd Field Regiment, R.A.
during the War of 1939-1945.   By Lieut.-Col. George Aris.   London: printed
by Williams, Lea & Co. Ltd. [1946].   108 pp., illustrations.   9¾"

Lewisham Gunners; a centenary History of 291st (4th London) Field Regiment,
R.A. (T.A.) formerly 2nd Kent R.G.A. (Volunteers) [Chatham: printed by W. &
J. Mackay & Co. Ltd.], 1962.   vi, 74 pp., plates.   8½"

Engineers
History of the 520th (Field) Company, R.E. (T.F.), formerly known as the 2/3rd London (Field) Company, R.E. (T.F.), 1914-1918.   London: War Narratives Publishing Co., 1919.   90 pp., portrait. $9\frac{3}{4}''$

Regimental Centenary; 101st (London) Field Engineer Regiment (T.A.), 1960, 1st Middlesex Engineer Volunteers, 1860.   [Aldershot: Gale & Polden Ltd.], 1960.   12 pp., portrait, illustrations. $8\frac{1}{2}''$

Royal Corps of Signals
Regimental Centenary; 47th (London) Signal Regiment, T.A., 1960, 1st Middlesex Engineer Volunteers, 1860.   [Aldershot: Gale & Polden Ltd.], 1960.   8 pp., illustrations. $8\frac{1}{2}''$

City Imperial Volunteers
Reports on the Raising, Organising, Equipping and Despatching The City of London Imperial Volunteers to South Africa.   Published by Order of the Right Hon. the Lord Mayor (Sir Alfred J. Newton, Bart.).   London: Blades, East & Blades, printers.   June, 1900.   80 pp. $10\frac{3}{4}''$

The C.I.V. and The War in South Africa, 1900.   The "City Press" Illustrated Souvenir of the City of London Imperial Volunteers.   London: published at the "City Press" Offices, 1900.   [48] pp. $10\frac{1}{4}''$

"City Press" C.I.V. War Souvenir.   Portraits of the Officers and Men of the City of London Imperial Volunteers, Pictures of the Enrolment and Departure, full List of the Members of the Regiment, Scenes at the Front, In Action, etc. London: Collingridge, 1900.   144 pp. $10''$

The Journal of the C.I.V. in South Africa.   By Major-Gen. W. H. Mackinnon, Commandant of the Corps.   With plans and illustrations.   London: John Murray, 1901.   xii, 252 pp. $8''$
   Deals with the Infantry Battalion.

One Thousand Miles with the C.I.V.   By J. Barclay Lloyd, Lance Corporal, Cyclist Section.   With frontispiece and map.   London: Methuen & Co., 1901, xii, 288 pp. $7\frac{1}{2}''$
   Deals with the Cyclist Section.

In the Ranks of the C.I.V.—a Narrative and Diary of Personal Experiences with the C.I.V. Battery (Honourable Artillery Company) in South Africa.   By Driver Erskine Childers.   London: Smith, Elder & Co., 1901.   vi, 301 pp., frontispiece. $7\frac{1}{2}''$

The Record of the Mounted Infantry of the City Imperial Volunteers.   Edited by Guy H. Guillum Scott, late Farrier-Sergeant and Geoffrey J. McDonell, late Colour-Sergeant.   London: E. & F. N. Spon, 1902.   xvi, 228 pp., map. $7\frac{1}{2}''$

LONDON REGIMENTS

2nd London Regiment, now part of The Royal Regt. of Artillery
The 2nd City of London Regiment (Royal Fusiliers) in the Great War (1914-1919).
By Major W. E. Grey.   Published from the Headquarters of the Regiment,
1929.   xxxiv, 464 pp., portraits, plates, maps.   9¾"
   The Introduction (11 pp.) deals with its predecessors, 46th & 23rd Middlesex
R.V.

The Royal Fusiliers in the Great War.   By H. C. O'Neill.   [Including the 1st-4th
London Regts.]   London: William Heinemann, 1922.   8½"

4th London Regiment, now part of The Royal Regt. of Artillery
Tower Hamlets Rifle Volunteer Brigade (1st Tower Hamlets Rifle Volunteers),
afterwards, from May 1903, The Fourth Volunteer Battalion Royal Fusiliers
(City of London Regiment).   A History compiled from Official Documents and
other sources.   By Col. E. T. Rodney Wilde.   Second edition.   [London:
Coningham Bros., printers].   1903.   111 pp.   8½"

———— Third edition.   Enlarged and revised to close of Volunteer Force,
31st March, 1908.   With Appendix as to the 4th (City of London) Battalion
The London Regiment (Royal Fusiliers).   London: Printed and published by
Coningham Bros., 1910.   172 pp.   8½"

The History of the Old 2/4th (City of London) Battalion The London Regiment,
Royal Fusiliers.   [Edited by Capt. F. W. Walker].   London: The Westminster
Press, 1919.   192 pp., portraits, plates, maps.   8¾"

The War History of the 4th Battalion The London Regiment (Royal Fusiliers),
1914-1919.   By Capt. F. Clive Grimwade.   London: Headquarters of the 4th
London Regiment, 1922.   xii, 532 pp., plates, maps.   8¾"

*5th London Regiment, now The London Rifle Brigade Rangers, part The 3rd Green
Jackets, R.B.*
The History of the London Rifle Brigade, 1859-1919.   With Introduction by
Major-Gen. Sir Frederick Maurice.   London: Constable & Co. Ltd., 1921.
xx, 516 pp., portraits, plates, sketch maps.   Separate case of maps.   8¾"

Short History of the London Rifle Brigade.   Compiled regimentally.   Aldershot: Gale & Polden Ltd., 1916.   48 pp., portraits, plates, map.   7¼"

Four Years on the Western Front.   By Rifleman Aubrey Smith.   Being the
Experiences of a Ranker in the London Rifle Brigade, 4th, 3rd and 56th Divisions.
London: Odhams Press Ltd., 1922.   xvi, 410 pp., sketch maps.   9¾"

The London Rifle Brigade, 1919-1950.   By Major A. T. M. Durand and Major
R. W. H. S. Hastings.   Aldershot: Gale & Polden Ltd., 1952.   xi, 320 pp.,
portraits, plates, maps.   8½"

6th London Regiment, now part of The Royal Regt. of Artillery
The "Cast-Iron" Sixth.   A History of the Sixth Battalion London Regiment
(The City of London Rifles).   By Capt. E. G. Godfrey.   London: F. S. Stapleton, for the Old Comrades Association, 1938.   xvi, 280 pp., portraits, plates,
maps.   9"

7th London Regiment, now part of The Royal Regt. of Artillery
History of the 7th (City of London) Battalion The London Regiment, embracing
the 3rd London and the 32nd Searchlight Regiment, R.A. (7th City of London).
Compiled by C. Digby Planck, with a Foreword by Brig.-Gen. The Right Hon.
Viscount Hampden.   London: published by The Old Comrades' Association.
[1946].   x, 262 pp., portraits, plates, illustrations.   8½"
    1 coloured plate of uniform and 1 of colours.   Lettered on cover and half-title
    The History of the "Shiny Seventh."

8th London Regiment, amalgamated with 7th London
Regimental Record of 24th Middlesex (formerly 49th Middlesex) Post Office
Volunteers from 1868 to 1896.   London: Spottiswoode & Co. [1896].   128 pp.,
portraits, illustrations.   7¼"

History of the Post Office Rifles, 8th Battalion, City of London Regiment, 1914
to 1918.   [By Lt.-Col. A. D. Derviche-Jones].   Aldershot: Gale & Polden Ltd.,
1919.   45 pp.   9¼"

9th London Regiment, now part of The 2nd Green Jackets, K.R.R.C.
The Cumberland Sharpshooters (formerly the Covent Garden Volunteers),
subsequently The Royal Victoria Rifle Club, then The Victoria Rifles, 1st Middlesex R.V., 1798 to 1853.   By Major John Eustace Anderson.   Printed for private
circulation.   [Richmond: R. W. Simpson & Co. Ltd.], 1897.   30 pp.   8"

The History & Records of Queen Victoria's Rifles, 1792-1922.   Compiled by
Major C. A. Cuthbert Keeson.   London: Constable & Co. Ltd., 1923.   xxiv,
670 pp., portraits, plates, maps.   8¾"

Swift and Bold.   The Story of the King's Royal Rifle Corps in the Second World
War.   [Chapters on the 7th and 8th Battns., Queen Victoria's Rifles].   Aldershot: Gale & Polden Ltd., 1949.   8½"

12th London Regiment, amalgamated with The London Rifle Brigade
The Rangers' Historical Records: From 1859 to the Conclusion of the Great
War.   Edited by Capt. A. V. Wheeler-Holohan and Capt. G. M. C. Wyatt.
[London: Harrison & Sons Ltd., 1921].   xii, 272 pp., portraits, plates, maps.   8½"

Chronicles of the 1st Battalion The Rangers (K.R.R.C.), 1939-1945.   By Col·
R. N. B. D. Bruce.   *Duplicated.*   1958.   vi, 75 pp., plates, maps.   12¾"

Swift and Bold.   The Story of the King's Royal Rifle Corps in the Second World
War.   [Chapters on the 9th and 10th Battns., The Rangers].   Aldershot: Gale
& Polden Ltd., 1949.   8½"

13th London Regiment, now part of The Royal Corps of Signals
The Declaration, with the Rules and Regulations of the Kensington Corps of
Volunteer Infantry.   Kensington: Martin, printing in general, 1803.   16 pp.   6¼"
    Including List of officers, Rules regarding uniform etc.

" The Kensingtons," 13th London Regiment.   By Sergt. O. F. Bailey and Sergt.
H. M. Hollier.   Published for the Regimental Old Comrades Association [1936].
xvi, 440 pp., portraits, plates, maps.   8½"

" The Kensingtons " Princess Louise's Kensington Regiment, Second World War.   Published by the Regimental Old Comrades' Association [1952].   xvi, 392 pp., portrait, plates, maps.   8½"

Army Phantom Signal Regiment (Princess Louise's Kensington Regiment) T.A. [A Brief History] 1859-1959.   Aldershot: Gale & Polden Ltd., 1959.   20 pp., portrait, illustrations.   8¼"
    1 coloured portrait and 2 coloured illustrations of colours.

14th London Regiment, now part of The Gordon Highlanders
London Scottish Volunteer Rifles.   Speech of Lord Elcho, M.P. at Freemasons' Tavern, July 4, 1859.   With a woodcut and appendix.   Published at the request of the Committee.   London: J. Ridgway, 1859.   40 pp., plate.   8½"

A Record of Northern Valour.   How the Volunteers in the counties of Aberdeen, Banff and Kincardine, and the London Scottish Regiment rose in a National Crisis.   [By William Will].   Aberdeen: "Aberdeen Journal," 1901.   52 pp., portraits.   7⅞"×9⅞"

The London Scottish in the Great War.   Edited by Lt.-Col. J. H. Lindsay. With a Foreword by Field Marshal Earl Haig.   London: Regimental Headquarters, 1925.   xvi, 426 pp., portraits, plates, maps.   8½"

Kilts Across the Jordan, being Experiences and Impressions with the Second Battalion " London Scottish " in Palestine.   By Bernard Blaser (Battalion Scout and " Mapper ").   With a Preface by Field Marshal Viscount Allenby.   London: H. F. & G. Witherby, 1926.   252 pp., plates, maps.   8½"

The London Scottish in the Second World War, 1939 to 1945.   With a Foreword by Col. R. J. L. Ogilby, Hon. Col. of the Regiment.   Edited by Brig. C. N. Barclay.   Compiled under the direction and supervision of the Regimental History Committee.   London: William Clowes & Sons Ltd., 1952.   xix, 459 pp., portraits, illustrations, maps.   8½"

The London Scottish (The Gordon Highlanders) T.A.   A Centenary Supplement to the Regimental Gazette.   London: The Regiment, 1959.   41 pp., portraits, illustrations.   9¾"

The Uniform of the London Scottish, 1859-1959.   By J. O. Robson.   London: London Scottish Regiment Ogilby Trust, 1960.   64 pp., portraits, plates.   11"
    4 coloured plates of uniform and 1 of colours.

15th London Regiment, amalgamated with The 16th London
A History of the Civil Service Rifle Volunteers.   (Including the Volunteers of the Bank of England).   By Edward Merrick (Lieutenant, C.S.R.V.).   London: Sheppard & St. John, 1891.   iv, 96 pp., portrait.   7¼"

15th (County of London) Battalion The London Regiment.   [An Illustrated Account of the Battalion].   London, 1913.   4to

The History of the Prince of Wales's Own Civil Service Rifles.   London: printed by Wyman & Sons Ltd., for P.W.O. Civil Service Rifles, 1921.   xvi, 490 pp., portraits, plates, map.   8¼″
    1 coloured plate of uniform.

16th London Regiment, now part of The 2nd Green Jackets, K.R.R.C.
The War History of the 1st Battalion Queen's Westminster Rifles, 1914-1918. By Major J. Q. Henriques.   London: The Medici Society Ltd., 1923.   xvi, 348 pp., portraits, plates, maps.   9¾″

Some Unofficial Adventures of the Second Battalion Queen's Westminster Rifles from 1914 to January 1918.   By "Adjutant Mare."   Illustrations by L. C. Pierpoint.   [Taunton: The Wessex Press, printers], *n.d.*   152 pp., portraits.   7¼″

Swift and Bold.   The Story of the King's Royal Rifle Corps in the Second World War.   [Chapters on the 11th and 12th Battns. Queen's Westminsters]. Aldershot: Gale & Polden Ltd., 1949.   8½″

A Brief History of The Queen's Westminsters (K.R.R.C.).   [London: printed by L. J. Doggett, 1948].   16 pp.   6″

18th London Regiment, now part of The Royal Ulster Rifles
The London Irish Rifles, 18th Battalion London Regt., T.F.: its Work at the Front.   1916.   8 pp.   12mo.

The London Irish at War.   A History of the Battalions of the London Irish Rifles in World War II.   With a Foreword by Field Marshal The Rt. Hon. The Viscount Alexander of Tunis.   London: Published on behalf of the London Irish Rifles Old Comrades' Association [1949].   222 pp., portraits, plates, sketch maps.   8½″

London Irish Rifles, 1859-1959; the regimental centenary.   By Lt.-Col. M. J. P.M. Corbally.   Glasgow: The Paramount Press, 1959.   84 pp., portraits, illustrations.   9⅝″

19th London Regiment, now part of The Royal Regt. of Artillery
The Early History of the 17th (North) Middlesex Volunteer Rifles (formerly the 29th), 1859 to 1889.   By Colour-Sergt. Rudd (R.).   London: R. & J. Widdicombe, 1895.   [8], 128 pp., portraits, plates.   9¾″

The Second Nineteenth; being the History of the 2/19th London Regiment.   By Major F. W. Eames.   London: Waterlow & Sons Ltd., 1930.   208 pp., portraits, plates, maps.   8½″
    Coloured plate of colours.

XIX London Regiment (St. Pancras), 1798-1935.   [Aldershot: Gale & Polden Ltd., 1935].   24 pp., portraits, plates, illustrations.   7¼″×9¾″
    Souvenir album containing Regimental History and reproduction of photographs, including 1 coloured plate of uniform and 1 of colours.

20th London Regiment, now part of The Royal Regt. of Artillery
The Second Twentieth, being The History of the 2/20th Bn. London Regiment.
By Capt. W. R. Elliot (Adjutant). Illustrations by S. A. Court. Maps by
Capt. H. C. Lovell. Aldershot: Printed by Gale & Polden Ltd., 1920. xvi,
314 pp., portraits, plates (3 coloured), maps. $7\frac{1}{4}''$

21st London Regiment, now part of The Royal Regt. of Artillery
A War Record of the 21st London Regiment (First Surrey Rifles), 1914-1919.
[London: H. B. Skinner & Co., printers, 1927].   278 pp., portrait. $8\frac{1}{2}''$

22nd London Regiment, now part of The Queen's Royal Surrey Regt.
History of The Queen's Royal Regiment. Vol. 8, 1924-1948. [Chapter on 6th
Battn. (22nd London)].   Aldershot: Gale & Polden Ltd., 1953. $9\frac{3}{4}''$

23rd London Regiment, now part of The Queen's Royal Surrey Regt.
History of the 4th V.B. East Surrey Regiment; including The Newington Surry
Volunteers, Southwark and Lambeth Rifle Corps, 7th Surrey Rifle Volunteer
Corps, 26th Surrey Rifle Volunteer Corps, now the 23rd Battn. The London
Regiment. Compiled from Official Records by Capt. Albert Barking. Intro-
ductory by the Right Hon. Lord Esher. [London: Gale & Polden Ltd., 1912].
64 pp., portraits, illustrations. $9\frac{3}{4}''$

History of the 23rd London Regiment, formerly 4th V.B. East Surrey Regiment,
The 7th and 26th Surrey Volunteer Corps, Southwark and Lambeth Corps,
Successors of the Newington Surry Volunteers. Compiled by Capt. Albert
Larking. [London: Rangecroft & Co., printers], 1915. 16 pp., portraits,
illustrations. $9\frac{3}{4}''$

The 23rd London Regiment, 1798-1919. Compiled from Contributions by
former Officers of the Regiment, with a Foreword by Field Marshal Viscount
Allenby. London: The Times Publishing Co. Ltd., 1936. xvi, 188 pp., maps
and coloured plate of uniform. $9\frac{1}{2}''$

42nd Royal Tank Regiment, 1938-1944. Compiled from contributions made by
former Members of the Regiment. London: 27 St. John's Hill, S.W.11 [1951].
37 pp., maps. $9\frac{3}{8}''$

24th London Regiment, now part of The Royal Regt. of Artillery
History of The Queen's Royal Regiment. Vol. 8. 1924-1948. [Chapter on
the 7th Battn. (24th London)].   Aldershot: Gale & Polden Ltd., 1953. $9\frac{3}{4}''$

History of the 2/7th Battalion The Queen's Royal Regiment, 1939-1946. By
Roy E. Bullen. With a Foreword by Lieut.-Gen. Sir William Stratton. [Exeter:
printed by Besley & Copp Ltd., 1958].   [xi], 161 pp., portraits, plates, maps. $8\frac{1}{2}''$
  Raised 1939 at Elephant & Castle but were never actually styled 24th London.

The Lambeth and Southwark Volunteers. A Century of Voluntary Service in
the Volunteers and Territorial, 1860-1960. Compiled by J. M. A. Tamplin.
Published by the Trustees of the Regimental Historical Fund. [Printed by John
Bellows Ltd., Gloucester]. 1965. xv, 500 pp. Portraits, plates, illustrations,
sketch maps. $10\frac{1}{2}''$
  Coloured plate of colours.   Limited edition of 600 copies.

25th London Regiment, now part of the Royal Corps of Signals
The London Cyclist Battalion. A Chronicle of Events connected with the 26th Middlesex (Cyclist) V.R.C., and the 25th (C. of L.) Cyclist Battalion The London Regiment, and Military Cycling in General. Published for the 25th London (Cyclist) Old Comrades' Association by Forster, Groom & Co. Ltd., 1932. xii, 292 pp., portraits, plates, maps. 8½"

28th London Regiment The Artists Rifles, now Special Air Service Regiment
Once an Artist Always an Artist. By Capt. C. J. Blomfield. London: Page & Co., 1921. 176 pp., portraits, plates. 7½"

The Regimental Roll of Honour and War Record of the Artists Rifles (1/28th, 2/28th and 3/28th Battalions The London Regiment, T.F.) Commissions, Promotions, Appointments and Rewards for Service in the Field obtained by Members of the Corps since 4th August, 1914. Edited by Major S. Stagoll Higham, with a Foreword by Col. H. A. R. May. London: Howlett & Son, 1922. xliv, 596 pp., portraits, plates. 8½"

Memories of the Artists Rifles. By Col. H. A. R. May (Artists Rifles, 1882-1921). London: Howlett & Son, 1929. xx, 364 pp. Many illustrations from photographs, etc., portraits, illustrations. 9¾"

A Short History of "B" Company of the "Artists" R.V. By Col.-Sergt. F. R. Light. No imprint, *n.d.* 15 pp. 6½"

The 28th (County of London) Battalion Artist's Rifles, Abergavenny Camp, 1913, and other Photographs; in which is incorporated conditions of service and notes on the Regiment. No imprint, 1920. xvi, 30 pp., illustrations. 5¾"

Record of Cyclist Section of 20th Middlesex (Artists') R.V., 1890-1907. [London: Howlett & Son], 1914. 38 pp. 7¼"

R.A.M.C.
The 2/1st London Field Ambulance. An outline of the 4½ years' service of a unit of the 56th Division at home and abroad during the Great War. London: Morton, Burt & Sons Ltd., 1924. 104 pp., portrait, plates, maps. 9"

The "Second-Seconds" in France: the Story of the 2/2nd City of London Field Ambulance. London: Spottiswoode, Ballantyne & Co. Ltd., 1920. 110 pp. portrait, plates, illustrations, maps. 8¼"

Tales of a Field Ambulance, 1914-1918. Told by the Personnel [2/4th London Field Ambulance]. Southend-on-Sea: Borough Printing & Publishing Co., 1935. 282 pp., portrait, plates. [Printed for private circulation]. 8½"

A Brief Record of the 6th London Field Ambulance (47th London Division) during the War. [By Major F. Coleman]. London: John Bale, Sons & Danielsson Ltd. [1924]. 40 pp. 8½"

The History of the First London (City of London) Sanitary Company. With a Record of its Activities in the Great War, 1914-1919. With a Foreword by P. S. Lelean, Brevet-Col. Edited by George W. Foster. [Grimsby: Burnetts (Gy.) Ltd., Printers, 1924]. 114 pp., portraits, plates. 8¾"

The Gazette. 3rd London General Hospital (T.F.) Vol. 1: October, 1915. Vol. 4, No. 10: July, 1919. [Last issue]. London: Iliffe & Sons Ltd.]. Illustrations. 8"

V.T.C., 1914-1918
The C.L.V.C. A Short History of The City of London Volunteer Corps, August, 1914—June 1915. By John Quebec. With a Preface by Sir T. Vansittart Bowater, Bart. London: W. Knott, 1917. viii, 50 pp. 8¾"

3rd Battn. (Old Boys) Central London Regiment (Volunteers). List of Members. [By Cecil J. Wray, Hon. Secretary]. [London: Marchant, Singer & Co., printer, 1915. 56 pp. 7½"

St. Marylebone Volunteers: 21st Batt. County of London Volunteer Regiment. Embodied 31st July, 1915. Officer Commanding: Major J. E. K. Studd Adjutant: Lieut. F. Warburton. Headquarters: The Polytechnic, 309 Regent Street, London. W.I. 16 pp. 4½"×6½"
    Pamphlet for intending recruits.

The National Guard in the Great War, 1914-1918. By A. E. Manning Foster. London: Cope & Fenwick, 1920. xvi, 304 pp., portraits, illustrations. 11¼"

A Record of the United Arts Rifles, 1914-1919. Edited by Edward Potton, Lieut. and Asst. Adjut. London: Alexander Moring Ltd., 1920. viii, 92 pp., portraits, illustrations. 11"

County of London Royal Engineer Volunteers, London Army Troops Companies. London: Headquarters, Balderton Street, W.I. [London: The Electrical Press Ltd., 1918]. 12 pp., illustrations. 9"
    Brochure giving origin, work, etc. of the Corps.

The History of Group II, City of London R.A.S.C., M.T. (V.), popularly known as the M.T.V., 1915-1919. Compiled by the Adjutant, Major G. M. Horn and edited for publication by Capt. Percy Linden and Lieut. Haddon Cave. No imprint [1920]. 46 pp., portraits. 8½"

Cadets
A History of the City of London Army Cadet Force. Produced in the Centenary Year of the Army Cadet Force, 1960. [Colchester: printed by Benham & Co. Ltd.], 1960. 20 pp., portrait. 7¼"

1st Cadet Battalion The Royal Fusiliers. War Record, 1914-1918. [London: Hart & Son Ltd., 1920]. 31 pp. 6½"
    Roll of cadets who served in the Great War.

The Stock Exchange Cadets, 1937. Devised and edited by Robert James. London: "The Stockbroker," 1937. 32 pp., portraits, illustrations. 9¾"
   History and work of Stock Exchange Detachment 1st Cadet Battn., R.F.

Milestones and Memories, 1926-1950. A picture cavalcade of an Army Cadet Force Unit, The Stock Exchange Company, 1st Cadet Battalion The Royal Fusiliers (City of London Regiment). [London: Hillside Publishing Co., 1952]. 67 pp., portraits, illustrations. 7¼"×9¼"

———— 1926-1959; a pictorial cavalcade . . . . now 8th City of London Company (R.F.) A.C.F. Stock Exchange Company. 2nd edition. 1959. 76 pp. 7¼"×9¼"

MERIONETH
Merioneth Volunteers and Local Militia during the Napoleonic Wars (1795-1816). By Hugh J. Owen, Clerk of the Peace and of the County Council of the County of Merioneth. With a Foreword by the Right Honourable Lord Atkin. Dolgelley: Hughes Bros., " Dydd " Office, 1934. 112 pp., portraits, plates. 8½"

The Merioneth Volunteers during the Napoleonic Wars & The Merioneth Local Militia, 1808-1816. [In *Echoes of Old Merioneth;* by Hugh J. Owen, pp. 41-57]. Dolgelley: Hughes Bros., 1949. 8½"

Regimental Records of the Royal Welch Fusiliers. Vol. 4, 1915-1918. By Major C. H. Dudley Ward. (Chapter on 7th Merioneth & Montgomery Battn. T.A.) London: Forster, Groom & Co. Ltd., 1929. 9¾"

The Red Dragon: the Story of the Royal Welch Fusiliers, 1919-1945. By Lt.-Commdr. P. K. Kemp and J. Graves. [Chapter on the 7th Merioneth & Montgomeryshire Battn., T.A.]. Aldershot: Gale & Polden Ltd., 1960. 8½"

MIDDLESEX
Centenary, 571 L.A.A. Regiment R.A. (9th Bn. The Middlesex Regt., D.C.O.) T.A., 1859-1959. [London: Harrison & Sons Ltd.], 1959. 24 pp., portraits, illustrations. 9½"
   Coloured reproduction of colours on paper cover.

General Order Book of the Royal Spelthorne Legion, Bedfont: the " Home Guard " of 1803. By C. ffoulkes. [In *Society for Army Historical Research, Journal,* vol. 21, 1942, pp. 37-48]. 9¼"

Records of the Third Middlesex Rifle Volunteers and of the various Corps which formed the Second and Sixth Middlesex Administrative Battalions, to which is prefixed a General Account of the Volunteer Forces of the United Kingdom. Compiled from Official and Private Sources from 1794 to 1884. By E. T. Evans, Lieut. London: Simpkin, Marshall & Co., 1885. xiv, 352 pp. 8½"

The History of the 7th Battalion Middlesex Regiment. By Col. E. J. King, Hon. Colonel. With a Foreword by Gen. Sir Ivor Maxse, Colonel of the Middlesex Regiment. London: Harrison & Sons Ltd., 1927. xvi, 396 pp., portraits, plates, maps. 8½"

The Story of The Duke of Cambridge's Own (Middlesex Regiment).   By C. L. Kingsford.   [Including Volunteer & Territorial Battns.].   London: "Country Life," 1916.   9″

The Die-Hards in the Great War.   A History of the Duke of Cambridge's Own (Middlesex Regiment), 1914-1919.   Compiled from the Records of the . . . Territorial Battns.   By Everard Wyrall.   London: Harrison & Sons Ltd. [1926-30].   2 vols.   8½″

The Middlesex Regiment (Duke of Cambridge's Own), 1919-1952 . . . by Lieut.-Commdr. P. K. Kemp.   [Chapters on Territorial Battns.].   Aldershot: Gale & Polden Ltd., 1956.   8½″

MONMOUTHSHIRE
The Story of the Monmouthshire Volunteer Artillery.   By Capt. John More and Col. W. L. C. Phillips.   Pontypool: Hughes & Son Ltd., 1958.   xiii, 111 pp., portraits, plates, maps.   9¾″

An Account of the Presentation of Colours to the Monmouth Volunteers by Her Grace the Duchess of Beaufort in the year 1799.   Usk: County Observer Offices [1901].   8vo.
    Reprint of the first edition; limited to 100 copies.

A History of the 2nd Bn. Monmouthshire Regiment.   Compiled by Capt. G. A. Brett.   Pontypool: Hughes & Son, 1933.   156 pp., portraits, plates, maps.   8½″

On the Western Front.   1/3rd Batt. Monmouthshire Regt.   Dedicated to the Honoured Memory of Our Comrades who fell in the Great War, 1914-1918.   Abergavenny: Seargeant Bros. Ltd. [1926].   128 pp., plates, maps.   8½″

History of The South Wales Borderers and The Monmouthshire Regiment, 1937-1952.   Pontypool: Hughes & Son Ltd., 1953-54.   Portraits, plates, maps.   8½″
    Part III.   The Second Battalion The Monmouthshire Regiment, 1933-1952.   By Lt.-Col. G. A. Brett.   1953.   126 pp.
    Part IV.   The 3rd Battalion The Monmouthshire Regiment.   By Major J. J. How.   1954.   134 pp.

A Short History of the South Wales Borderers, 24th Foot and The Monmouthshire Regiment.   Compiled by direction of the Regimental Committee.   Cardiff: printed by Western Mail & Echo Ltd., 1940.   83 pp.   8½″

The South Wales Borderers, 24th Foot, 1689-1937.   By C. T. Atkinson.   [Including The Monmouthshire Regiment, T.A.].   Cambridge: University Press, 1937.   10″

MONTGOMERYSHIRE
The Historical Records of the Yeomanry and Volunteers of Montgomeryshire, 1803-1908.   Compiled by Lieut.-Col. R. W. Williams Wynn and Benson Freeman.   Oswestry: Woodall, Minshall, Thomas & Co., 1909.   xii, 138 pp., plates.   8½″

A Brief Record of the Activities of 7th Batt. The Royal Welch Fusiliers, 1908-1946. By Major R. B. S. Davies. Llandiloes; [printed by J. Ellis], 1950. 46 pp., illustrations, maps.   7¼″

Regimental Records of the Royal Welch Fusiliers. Vol. 4, 1915-1918. By Major C. H. Dudley Ward. [Chapter on Merioneth & Montgomery Battn.]. London: Forster, Groom & Co. Ltd., 1929.   9¾″

The Red Dragon; the Story of the Royal Welch Fusiliers, 1919-1945. By Lt.-Commdr. P. K. Kemp and J. Graves. [Chapter on the 7th Merioneth & Montgomeryshire Battn., T.A.].   Aldershot: Gale & Polden Ltd., 1960.   8½″

NORFOLK

The History of the Yarmouth Battery, 1569-1926. By Major M. A. Castle. With a Foreword by Col. the Earl of Stradbroke.   With 60 illustrations and maps.   Norwich: Jarrold & Sons Ltd., 1927.   xvi, 160 pp., plates, maps.   8½″

The Autobiography of a Military Great Coat; being a Story of the 1st Norfolk Volunteer Active Service Company, 1900-1. By Harold Josling. [Harold Josling Bryant].   London: Jarrold & Sons, 1907.   426 pp.   8″

The History of the Norfolk Regiment, 1685-1918. By F. Loraine Petre. Norwich: Jarrold & Sons Ltd. [1924].   9¾″

    Vol. 1 [including The Militia and Volunteer Battns. to 1881].   Portraits, plates, 1 coloured of uniform.

    Vol. 2.   [Including chapters on 4th, 5th and 6th Territorial Battns.].

——— Vol. 3.   1919-1951.   By Lt.-Commdr. P. K. Kemp.   [Chapters on Territorial Battns.].   Norwich, 1953.   9¾″

A History of 7th Battalion The Royal Norfolk Regiment in World War No. 2. July 1940-August 1944. [By Lieut.-Col. I. H. F. Freeland].   No imprint [printed in Germany].   53 pp., maps.   8½″

NORTHAMPTONSHIRE

A Short History of the Northamptonshire Battery (B/270, R.F.A.).   Compiled from material supplied by Major F. E. C. Stanley and other Officers of the Battery. [Peterborough: The Peterborough Press Ltd., 1926].   Plates, maps.   8¼″

History of the Northamptonshire Regiment, 1742-1934. By Lieut.-Col. Russell Gurney.   [Chapter on Volunteers and Territorials].   Aldershot: Gale & Polden Ltd., 1935.   9¾″

With the Northampton Territorials in Egypt and Palestine.   Reprinted from the *Northampton Independent* with Forewords by the Rt. Hon. Earl Spencer, H.M. Lord Lieutenant of Northamptonshire, and Lt.-Col. Stanley Barry.   By Capt. the Rev. F. J. Walkey.   Published for private distribution by W. H. Holloway, Editor *Northampton Independent*.   Northampton: Archer & Goodman, printers, *n.d.*   24 pp., portraits, illustrations.   6¾″

The 5th Battalion the Northamptonshire Regiment in Italy. [Compiled by Capt. Ian McKee]. [Austria: printed by Fritz Nothhaft etc. in the German Cavalry Corps Mobile Printing Press at Tamsing, Treffling and Ober Vellach, 1945]. 95 pp., maps.   13¼"

The Northamptonshire Regiment, 1914-1918. [Chapter on Territorial Battns.]. Aldershot: Gale & Polden Ltd., 1932.   8½"

The History of the Northamptonshire Regiment, 1934-1948. By Brig. W. J. Jervois. [Chapters on Territorial Battns.].   Northampton: 1953.   9½"

———— 1948-1960.   Compiled by Lt.-Col. C. J. M. Watts.   Northampton: 1963. [Including Territorial Battns.].   9½"

NORTHUMBERLAND

The Volunteers of a Hundred Years ago, with a description of Corps formed in Northumberland and Newcastle-on-Tyne. A Lecture delivered by Col. J. G. Hicks before the North of England Volunteer Service Institution, Newcastle-on-Tyne, 26th February, 1904.   Newcastle-on-Tyne: printed for private circulation for The North of England Volunteer Service Institution, 1904.   60 pp.   7¼"

The Percy Artillery.   Records of The Percy Tenantry Volunteer Artillery, 1805-1814, and of the 2nd Northumberland (Percy) Volunteer Artillery, 1859-1899. By Lieut.-Col. J. G. Hicks.   With introductory notices of the Volunteer Movements of 1799 and 1859.   London: printed by Spottiswoode & Co., 1899. x, 84 pp., portraits.   9"

The War History of the 1st Northumbrian Brigade, R.F.A. (T.F.), later known as the 250th (Northumbrian) Brigade, R.F.A. (T.F.), and now (1927) known as the 72nd (Northumbrian) Field Brigade, R.A. (T.A.), August 1914-July 1919. By Lieut.-Col. C. H. Ommanney.   Newcastle-upon-Tyne: printed for the publishers by J. W. Hindson & Sons, 1927.   xvi, 250 pp.   8½"

The History of the Tyne Electrical Engineers, Royal Engineers.   From the formation of the Submarine Mining Company of the 1st Newcastle-upon-Tyne and Durham (Volunteers) Royal Engineers in 1884 to 1933.   [Newcastle-upon-Tyne: R. W. Ward & Sons Ltd., 1935].   xvii, 273 pp., portraits, plates, maps.   9¾"

Notices of the Services of the 27th Northumberland Light Infantry Militia, with a brief account of several Local Corps of Volunteers which were enrolled in the county of Northumberland, and in the town and county of Newcastle-upon-Tyne, during the war with France, towards the close of the last and the commencement of the present century.   Compiled and edited, with Notes by William Adamson, Senior Capt. and Hon. Major.   Newcastle-upon-Tyne: Robert Robinson, 1877. 95 pp.   8¼"

———— [Another edition with title]: The Services of the 27th Northumberland Light Infantry Militia . . . and continued up to the present time by Major and Hon. Lieut.-Col. Robert Scott.   Newcastle-upon-Tyne: Andrew Reid & Co. Ltd., 1914.   152 pp.   9¾"

When the Lantern of Hope Burned Low: the Story of the 1/4th Northumberland Fusiliers (T.F.) during the German Offensives of March, April, May, 1918. By Rev. R. Wilfrid Callin. [Hexham: J. Catherall & Co.], *n.d.* Portraits, maps. 8¾″

A Diary of an Officer with the 4th Northumberland Fusiliers in France and Flanders, from April 20th to May 24th, 1915. [Signed W. J. B., *i.e.* W. J. Bunbury]. Hexham: J. Catherall & Co. [1918]. 68 pp., maps. 8¾″

War History of the Seventh Northumberland Fusiliers. Edited by Capt. F. Buckley. Newcastle-upon-Tyne: T. M. Grierson, printer [1919]. viii, 155 pp., illustrations, map. 9½″

The History of the Royal Northumberland Fusiliers in the Second World War. By Brig. C. N. Barclay. [Chapters on the Territorial Battns.]. London: Wm. Clowes & Son Ltd., 1952. 9¾″

History of 3rd Reconnaissance Regt. (N.F.) in the Invasion and subsequent Campaign in North West Europe, 1944-1945. No imprint, *n.d.*. 64 pp., illustrations. 9¼″

Wheeled Odyssey. The Story of the Fifth Reconnaissance Regt., Royal Armoured Corps. No imprint, *n.d.* 68 pp., portraits, plates, maps. 7¼″

NOTTINGHAMSHIRE
" The Robin Hoods ": 1/7th, 2/7th and 3/7th Battns. Sherwood Foresters, 1914-1918. Written by Officers of the Battalions. With a Foreword by Gen. Sir H. L. Smith-Dorrien. Nottingham: J. & H. Bell Ltd., 1921. 471 pp., portraits, plates, maps. 7½″

The Sherwood Foresters in the Great War, 1914-1919: 1/8th Battalion. By Capt. W. C. Weetman. With an Introduction by Brig.-Gen. C. T. Shipley. Nottingham: Thos. Forman & Sons, 1920. 323 pp., portraits, plates, maps. 7¼″

The Sherwood Foresters in the Great War, 1914-1918: The 2/8th Battalion. By Lieut.-Col. W. C. Oates. Nottingham: J. & H. Bell Ltd., 1920. 230 pp., portraits, plates, maps. 7¼″

The 8th Battalion The Sherwood Foresters, T.A.; Campaign in Norway, April, 1940. By Col. E. G. C. Beckwith. *Duplicated.* 90 pp. 1958. 13″

The History of the Sherwood Foresters (Nottinghamshire and Derbyshire Regiment), 1919-1957. By Brig. C. N. Barclay. [Chapters on Territorial Battns.]. London: Wm. Clowes & Sons Ltd., 1959. 9½″

V.T.C., 1914-1918
A Record of the Early Volunteer Movement and of the Notts Volunteer Regiment (The Sherwood Foresters), 1914-1919: Compiled from Official Documents at Headquarters. By C. Gerring, Sergt.-Major. Nottingham: Sisson & Parker, 1920. [12], 68 pp., portraits, plates. 8½″

Cadets

Nottingham University Officers' Training Corps, 1909-1964. By G. J. Eltringham. Printed by Hawthornes of Nottingham, Ltd. [for private circulation]. 1964. xii, 75 pp. Portraits. 8½″

OXFORDSHIRE

War Record of the 1/4th Battalion Oxfordshire and Buckinghamshire Light Infantry. Compiled by Major P. Pickford. Banbury: "Banbury Guardian" Office, 1919. 127 pp., portrait, maps. 6″

The Story of the 2/4th Oxfordshire and Buckinghamshire Light Infantry. By Capt. G. K. Rose. With a Preface by Brig.-Gen. The Hon. R. White and an Introduction by Col. W. H. Ames. Oxford: B. H. Blackwell, 1920. xvi, 226 pp., portraits, plates, sketch maps. 8½″

The Oxfordshire & Buckinghamshire Light Infantry Chronicle; An Annual Record, etc., 1914-15—1918-19; together with the War Record of the Territorial Battalions. 5 vols., 1915-1920. [Lettered on covers, The Great War, 1-5].

———— 1939-45; the Record of the . . . 4th and 5th Battns. in the Second German War. 4 vols., 1949-54.
    Portraits, plates, maps. 8½″

RADNORSHIRE

Military History of Radnorshire. [By] G. Archer Parfitt. Llandrindod Wells: Radnorshire Society, 1957-59. Offprint from the *Society's Transactions.* 54 pp., portraits, plates. 9⅜″

SHROPSHIRE

Shropshire Volunteers in 1803-5. By Askew Roberts. [In *Shropshire Archaeological Society, Transactions*, vol. 4, 1881, pp. 409-424]. Shrewsbury. 8½″

Diary of the Shropshire R.H.A., 1947-1960. By L. Ball. Duplicated. Shrewsbury. 1965. 8 pp. 13″

Shropshire Gunners in the Trenches; or a personal account of the Ammunition Column of the 1/1 Welsh Border Mounted Brigade in the Great War, 1914-1918. Duplicated. Shrewsbury. 1965. 4 pp. 13″

The History of the King's Light Infantry in the Great War, 1914-1918. Edited by Major W. de B. Wood. [Chapter on the 4th Battn.]. London: The Medici Society Ltd., 1925. Maps. 8½″

The History of the 4th Battalion King's Shropshire Light Infantry (T.A.), 1745-1945. By Lieut.-Commdr. P. K. Kemp. Shrewsbury: Wilding & Son Ltd., 1955. [8], 183 pp., portraits, plates, maps. 8½″

Historical Records, 4th Battalion, The King's Shropshire Light Infantry (Territorial Army). [By G. Archer Parfitt]. *Duplicated, printed paper cover.* 1959. v, 72 pp., plate. 13″

The Colours of the 4th Bn. K.S.L.I. and its Predecessors. By G. Archer Parfitt. *Duplicated.* 1962. 13″

The Shropshire Rifle Volunteers. 4th Battalion, The King's Shropshire Light Infantry (Territorial Army). [Shrewsbury: Livesey Ltd., printers], 1963. 8 pp. 8¼"

Cadets
A Brief History of the Shropshire Army Cadet Force. Centenary Celebration, 24th March, 1960. By G. Archer Parfitt. Shrewsbury: T. & A. F. Association, 1960. [Duplicated, printed paper cover]. ii, 5 pp., plate. 13"

SOMERSET
The History of Somerset Yeomanry, Volunteer and Territorial Units. By W. G. Fisher. Taunton: Goodman & Son, 1924. [8], 288 pp. 8½"
  Coloured plate of uniform.

Narrative of the 502nd (Wessex) Field Company, R.E., 1914-1918. By Major C. L. Fox. London: Hugh Rees Ltd., 1920. 192 pp., plates, maps. 8½"

History of the 4th Bn. The Somerset Light Infantry (Prince Albert's) in the Campaign in North-West Europe, June 1944-May 1945. [Taunton: printed by E. Goodman & Son Ltd., 1946]. 140 pp., maps. For private circulation only. 8⅛"

The Great War, 1914-1919. The Book of Remembrance of the 5th Battalion (Prince Albert's) Somerset Light Infantry. London: Privately printed at the Chiswick Press, 1930. xv, 121 pp., maps. 12½"

The Story of the Seventh Battalion The Somerset Light Infantry (Prince Albert's). Collected and told by Capt. J. L. J. Meredith. Designs and illustrations by L. R. Stokes. No imprint [Hanover? 1945]. 216 pp., illustrations, maps. 10⅞"
  Title on cover "From Normandy to Hanover, June 1944-May 1945."

The History of The Somerset Light Infantry (Prince Albert's). By Everard Wyrall, 1914-1919. [Chapter on Territorial Battns.]. London: Methuen & Co. Ltd., 1927. 9¾"

———— 1919-1945. Compiled by G. Molesworth. [Incl. Territorial Battns.]. Frome: printed by Butler & Tanner Ltd., 1951. 9¾"

STAFFORDSHIRE
The Stafford Battery. 241/61st Field and Super Heavy Regiment Royal Artillery, 1939-1945. [By Major R. J. C. Evans, Capt. G. R. Lewin and Lieut. E. L. Hamilton. Stafford: Allison & Bowen Ltd., 1947]. 102 pp., portraits, plates, map. 8½"
  A private publication, not for general distribution.

The War History of the Sixth Battalion the South Staffordshire Regiment (T.F.). By a Committee of Officers who served with the Battalion. London: William Heinemann Ltd., 1924. x, 248 pp., portraits, plates. 8¾"

The 5th North Staffords and the North Midland Territorials (The 46th and 59th Divisions), 1914-1919. By Lieut. Walter Meakin. Longton, Staffs., Hughes & Barber Ltd., 1920. 176 pp., portraits, plates, maps. 9¾"

SUFFOLK

Volunteers in Suffolk. By Major E. R. Cooper. [Bury St. Edmunds: Free Press Works]. Reprinted from *The East Anglian Daily Times* and *The Suffolk Regimental Gazette*, 1935. 32 pp., portraits, illustrations. 9¾"

67th (Suffolk) Medium Regiment Royal Artillery (T.A.) Campaign in North West Europe, 6th June, 1944 to 5th May, 1945. [By Lt.-Col. J. K. L. Mardon]. No imprint [1945]. 23 pp. 7"

The History of the 1/5th Battalion "The Suffolk Regiment." Compiled by Capt. A. Fair and Capt. E. D. Walton. With a Foreword by Field Marshal Viscount Allenby. London: Eyre & Spottiswoode Ltd. [1923]. xii, 126 pp., portraits, illustrations, maps. 8"

The History of the Suffolk Regiment, 1914-1927. By Lieut.-Col. C. C. R. Murphy. [Chapters on the Territorial Battns. & The Suffolk Volunteers, by Major E. R. Cooper]. London: Hutchinson & Co. Ltd., 1928. 9"

The Suffolk Regiment, 1928-1946. By Col. W. N. Nicholson. [Chapters on the T.A. Battns.]. Ipswich: The East Anglian Magazine Ltd., 1948. Portraits, maps. 9"

SURREY, *see also* LONDON REGIMENTS, 21st-24th.

A Short Account of the Mortlake Company of the Royal Putney, Roehampton and Mortlake Volunteer Corps, 1803-1806. By Major John Eustace Anderson. Richmond, Surrey: R. W. Simpson, " Herald " Office. Printed for private circulation, 1893. 16 pp. 9¾"

Soldiers and Soldiering in Richmond (Surrey). Four Hundred Years; 1515-1915. By Albert A. Barkas. Reprinted from the *Richmond and Twickenham Times*, 1915. 24 pp. 8½"

The Surrey Rifle Volunteers; a century of Volunteers and Territorial Service, 1859-1959. Compiled by J. M. A. Tamplin, Capt. *Duplicated.* 1959. 13 pp., large folded chart in pocket. 13"
   Printed paper cover with title: A Catalogue of the Surrey Rifle Volunteers, 1859-1959.

An Outline History of 57th (East Surrey) Anti-Tank Regiment Royal Artillery, 1939-1945. [By Major Graham S. Abbott]. [Tolentino: Tipografia " Fidelfo," 1945]. 32 pp. 8¼"

The Records of " I " Company: A Brief History of the East Surrey Volunteers' Service in the South African War. By A. G. Garrish. London: Walbrook & Co. Ltd., 1901. Portrait, illustrations, maps. 8½"

" Military Avalanche." The Story of a Surrey Battalion who fought on after Dunkirk. [2/6th East Surrey Regiment]. *Duplicated.* 89 pp., maps. 13"

History of the East Surrey Regiment. Vols. 2, 3. By Col. H. W. Pearse and Brig.-Gen. H. S. Sloman. [Including Territorial Battns.]. London: The Medici Society Ltd., 1933-34. 9½"

History of the East Surrey Regiment. Vol. 4, 1920-1952. By D. Scott
Daniell. [Chapters on Territorial Battns.]. London: Ernest Benn Ltd., 1957. 8½″

4th The Queen's Royal Regiment. An Unofficial War History. With Chapters
on the 2/5th Battalion. By Capt. Ronald Bannerman. Croydon: H. R.
Grubb, Ltd., 1931. [xii], 105 pp., portraits, plates. 8½″

History of The Queen's Royal Regiment. Vols. 7, 8. [Chapters on the Territorial Battns., 1914-1948]. Aldershot: Gale & Polden Ltd., 1925-53. 9½″

History of the 2nd/5th Battalion The Queen's Royal Regiment, 1939-1945. By
Capt. P. N. Tregoning; with a Foreword by Major-Gen. J. Y. Whitfield. Aldershot: Gale & Polden Ltd., 1947. xii, 104 pp., plates, maps. 7¼″

A History of 2/6th Bn. Queen's Royal Regt. in the Italian Campaign. [Italy:
printed by The Dog Press, 2/6th Bn. Queen's Royal Regt., 1945]. 65 pp., map.
7″

Impact. History 169 Queen's Brigade, March-May 1945. Aldershot: Gale &
Polden Ltd. [1947]. [4], 92 pp., maps. 8½″
  2/5th, 2/6th and 2/7th Battns.

Cadets
Notes on the History of the 1st Cadet Battalion The Queen's Royal Regiment
(West Surrey). [Aldershot: Gale & Polden Ltd., 1944]. 12 pp. 5½″

The Army Cadets of Surrey, 1860-1960. By Lt.-Col. H. C. Hughes. [London:
Owen Spyer & Co. Ltd.], 1960. iv, 34 pp., portraits, illustrations. 6½″×8½″

A Short History of the Frimley and Camberley Cadet Corps. Aldershot: Gale
& Polden Ltd., 1948-62. 2 vols., portraits, illustrations. 7¼″
  Vol. 1. 1908-1948; by Col. F. W. Foley. 48 pp.
  Vol. 2. 1948-1962; by Maj. R. E. Pounds. 31 pp.

SUSSEX
The Prince of Wales's Royal Brighton Volunteer Artillery. By Lieut.-Col.
M. E. S. Laws. [In *Journal of the Royal Artillery*, 1957, pp. 257-261]. Woolwich:
Royal Artillery Institution. 9¼″

113th Field Regiment, R.A. 1939-1945. [Compiled by Sjt. Matthews].
Worthing: Laceys Ltd. [1947]. 103 pp. 7¼″
  Afterwards 313 H.A.A. Regt. R.A. (T.A.).

The Offer of Service, Stipulations, Establishment and Regulations of the North
Pevensey Legion. East Grinstead: printed by T. Palmer, 1803. 10 pp., contains
Roll of Officers. 8vo.

The Story of the Rye Volunteers. By Leopold Amon Vidler. Rye: The Stone
House, 1954. [vi], 85 pp., portraits, plates. 8½″

Record of the Second Volunteer Battalion, Royal Sussex Regiment from 1859 to 1903. Revised and corrected by Major B. T. Hodgson. London: J. J. Keliher & Co. Ltd., 1903. 32 pp. 10¾"

—— [Another edition with title]: Record of the Fourth Battalion, Royal Sussex Regiment from 1859 to 1913. London: Printed for private circulation by Hazell, Watson & Viney Ltd., 1914. 68 pp. 10¾"

A Short History of " The Cinque Ports," 5th (Cinque Ports) Battalion The Royal Sussex Regiment, from the time of its formation until the present day. By E. A. C. Fazan. Wadhurst: R. H. Wadeson, The Alpha Press [1913]. 44 pp. 8½"

A History of the Royal Sussex Regiment . . . 1701-1953. By G. D. Martineau. [Including the Territorial Battns.]. Chichester: Moore & Tillyer Ltd., 1955   8¾"

History of the 44th (Home Counties) Divisional Royal Army Service Corps (Territorial Army), 1908-1935. By Capt. D. H. V. Buckle. Aldershot: Gale & Polden Ltd. [1935]. xii, 58 pp., plates. 7¼"

V.T.C., 1914-1918
The Brighton Volunteers in the Great War: The First Volunteer Battalion (1914-1919) The Royal Sussex Regiment. A Brief Account of the Founding, Development and Disbandment of a War-time Organisation. By P. Fisher. Brighton: Garnett, Mepham & Fisher Ltd., 1932. 24 pp. 7¼"

WARWICKSHIRE
The Overseas Service of 269 (Warwick) Field Battery, Royal Artillery, 1942-1945, during the Second World War. [Birmingham: The Birmingham Printers Ltd., 1945]. 55 pp., portraits, plates. 8½"

Royal Corps of Signals. The History of the 48th (South Midland) Divisional Signals, Territorial Army. Vol. 1, 1908 to 1932. Compiled by Capt. E. A. James. [Birmingham: " Journal," Printers, 1932]. 50 pp. 9¾"

—— [Vol.] II. 1933-1939. No imprint, 1939. 30 pp. 9¾"

The 48th and 61st Divisional Signals, T.A., 1939-1945. Compiled by Brig. E. A. James, with a Foreword by Major-Gen. R. F. B. Naylor. Birmingham: The Journal Printing Offices, 1947. vii, 101 pp., portraits, map. 9¾"
   200 numbered copies only.

The 48th Div. Signal Company in the Great War. By F. W. Dopson. Privately printed. [Bristol: J. W. Arrowsmith Ltd., 1938]. 143 pp., portrait, illustrations, maps. 8¾"

The History of the First Warwickshire (Birmingham) Battalion of Rifle Volunteers: being an Account of its raising, progress and exploits. Compiled from Authentic Sources. By T. H. Gem, Major. Birmingham: Josiah Allen, 1876. 48 pp. 8¾"

The History of the 1st Volunteer Battalion The Royal Warwickshire Regiment and its Predecessors; The Birmingham Independent Volunteers, 1782; The Birmingham Loyal Association, 1797; The Loyal Birmingham Volunteers, 1803. By Col. Charles J. Hart.   Birmingham: The Midland Counties Herald Ltd., 1906. [12], 390 pp., portraits, plates, map.   9¾″
    3 coloured plates of uniform and 2 of medals.

The War Record of the 1/5th Battalion, The Royal Warwickshire Regiment. By Lieut. C. E. Carrington.   Birmingham: Cornish Bros. Ltd., 1922.   x, 97 pp., maps.   7½″

History of the 1/6th Battalion The Royal Warwickshire Regiment. Birmingham: Cornish Bros. Ltd., 1922.   91 pp.   6″

History of the 2/6th Battalion The Royal Warwickshire Regiment, 1914-1919. [With Introductory Note by Lieut.-Col. J. J. Shannessy].   Birmingham: Cornish Bros. Ltd., 1929.   118 pp., portraits.   7¼″

Black Square Memories.   An Account of the 2/8th Battalion The Royal Warwickshire Regiment, 1914-1918.   By H. T. Chidgey, an officer of the same Battalion.   Stratford-upon-Avon: Shakespeare Head Press, 1924.   xv, 184 pp., portrait, map in end-pocket.   7½″   200 copies printed for sale.

8th Battalion The Royal Warwickshire Regiment.   A Short Description of the Battle of Beaumont-Hamel, 1st July, 1916.   Compiled from Accounts of the Survivors and of a Visit to the Field of Battle, March 12th, 1918, by Brig.-Gen. W. R. Ludlow.   No imprint, 1st July, 1918.   15 pp., map.   8″
    For private circulation only.

The Birmingham Territorial Units of the Royal Army Medical Corps, 1914-1919. By Lt.-Col. J. E. H. Sawyer.   Birmingham: Allday Ltd., *n.d.*   230 pp.   7½″

History of the Royal Warwickshire Regiment, 1919-1955.   By Marcus Cunliffe. [Deals with the Territorial Battns.].   London: Wm. Clowes & Sons Ltd., 1956.   8½″

Cadets
A History of the First Hundred Years of the Rugby School Corps, 1860-1960. By Lt.-Col. H. J. Harris.   [London: printed by Brown, Knight & Truscott Ltd.], 1962.   ix, 204 pp., plates.   8½″

WESTMORLAND
Diary of 2/4th Battalion The Border Regiment, 1914-1919.   Carlisle: Chas. Thurnham & Sons, 1920.   39 pp.   10″

The Border Regiment in the Great War.   By Col. H. C. Wylly.   [Chapters on Territorial Battns.].   Aldershot: Gale & Polden Ltd.   1924.   9¾″

The Story of The Border Regiment, 1939-1945.   By Major-Gen. P. J. Shears. [Chapters on Territorial Battns.].   London: Nisbet & Co., Ltd.   1948.   8½″

WILTSHIRE
The History of the 1st Batt. Wilts. Volunteers from 1861 to 1885.   By Robert Dwarris Gibney, Major.   London: W. H. Allen & Co., 1888.   xii, 134 pp.   7¼″

The 1/4th Battalion The Wiltshire Regiment, 1914-1919. By Lieut. George Blick. Edited by Major Gerald Stanley. With Forewords by Lord Roundway and Brig.-Gen. H. J. Huddleston. [Frome: Butler & Tanner Ltd.], 1923. 142 pp., sketch maps. 7¼"

The Maroon Square. A History of the 4th Battalion The Wiltshire Regiment (Duke of Edinburgh's) in North West Europe, 1939-46. Compiled by Majors A. D. Parsons, D. I. M. Robbins and D. C. Gilson. London: Franey & Co. Ltd. [1955]. 231 pp., plates, maps. 8½"

The Fifth Battalion The Wiltshire Regiment in North-West Europe, June 1944-May 1945. By Capt. J. S. McMath. Sketch maps drawn by Private C. J. Hart. [London: printed by Whitefriars Press Ltd., 1946]. 128 pp., plates, maps. 8½"

The Story of The Wiltshire Regiment (Duke of Edinburgh's); the 62nd and 99th Foot (1756-1959) . . . and the Territorials, etc. By Col. N. C. E. Kenrick. Aldershot: Gale & Polden Ltd., 1963. 8½"

WORCESTERSHIRE
A Short History of the 2nd Volunteer Battalion Worcestershire Regiment, 1859 to 1888. Compiled and printed by F. Simms, Captain and Qr.-Mr., at his Private Press, Henwyke, Worcester, June 1888. 133 pp. 7"

The Worcestershire Regiment. War Story of the 1/8th (Territorial) Battalion. By Edward C. Corbett, ex-Regimental Quartermaster-Sergeant. Worcester: Herald Office. 1921. 155 pp. 7"

1/8th Battalion The Worcestershire Regiment, 1914-1918. [By Lt.-Col. H. T. Clarke & Col. W. K. Peake]. London: War Narratives Publishing Co., 1919. 34 pp. 9¼"

The Worcestershire Regiment in the Great War. By Capt. H. Fitzm. Stacke. [Chapters on the Territorial Battns.]. Kidderminster: G. T. Cheshire & Sons, Ltd., 1929. 11"

The Worcestershire Regiment, 1922-1950. By Lieut.-Col. Lord Birdwood. [Chapters on the Territorial Battns.]. Aldershot: Gale & Polden Ltd., 1952. 8½"

YORKSHIRE, EAST RIDING
History of the Hull Artillery. Compiled by Major R. Saunders. Hull: Printed by Walker & Brown, 1907. x, 72, [84] pp., portraits, plates. 8½"

The East Yorkshire Regiment in the Great War, 1914-1918. By Everard Wyrall. [Including the Territorial Battns.]. London: Harrison & Sons Ltd., 1928. 9½"

A History of The East Yorkshire Regiment (Duke of York's Own) in the War of 1939-45. By P. R. Nightingale, Lt.-Col. [including the Territorial Battns.]. York: William Sessions Ltd., 1952. 8½"

V.T.C., 1914-1918.
Records of the East Yorkshire Volunteer Force (1914-1919). Compiled by the County Commandant (Col. W. Lambert White) and Edited by Major F. H. Lock. Hull: Printed by the Eastern Morning and Hull News Co. Ltd., 1920. 82 pp., portraits, plates. 9½″

YORKSHIRE, NORTH RIDING
A Brief History of the Territorial Force Association of the County of York (North Riding), 1908-1919. Compiled by Capt. F. H. Reynard. Northallerton: Printed by Jos. Walker, 1919. 34 pp. 9″

The Green Howards in the Great War, 1914-1919. By Col. H. C. Wylly. [Chapters on the Territorial Battns.]. Richmond, Yorks, 1926. 9¾″

The Story of The Green Howards, 1939-1945. By Capt. W. A. T. Synge. [Chapters on the Territorial Battns.]. Richmond, Yorks., 1952 8½″

History of the King's Own Yorkshire Light Infantry, 1755-1914. By Col. H. C. Wylly. London: Percy Lund, Humphries & Co. Ltd., 1926. Vol. 2 [pp. 655-669, History of the 4th Battn.; pp. 670-676, History of the 5th Battn.]. 8½″

———— Vol. 3, with title History . . . in the Great War, 1914-1918. By Lt.-Col. Reginald C. Bond. [Chapters on Territorial Battns.]. 1930. 8½″

———— Vol. 5, with title Never Give Up, 1919-1942. By Lieut.-Col. Walter Hingston. [Including Territorial Battns.]. 1950. 8½″

———— Vol. 6. 1939-1948. By Brig. F. G. Ellenberger. Aldershot: Gale & Polden Ltd., 1961. [Including Territorial Battns.] 8½″

The War History of the 1/4th Battalion The King's Own Yorkshire Light Infantry. Compiled and written by Major G. C. W. Harland. Austria: printed in the "Buchdrucherei Mürzzuschtag," 1946. 32 pp. 9″

The Story of the 2/4th Battalion The King's Own Yorkshire Light Infantry, 1939-1946. Compiled by Lt.-Col. O. P. S. Jones. Dorking: Adlard & Son Ltd., 1948. 90 pp., map. 8½″

The 187th Infantry Brigade in France, 1917-1918. London: War Narratives Publ. Co., 1919. 44 pp. 9½″
    2/4th; 5th; 2/5th K.O.Y.L.I.; 2/4th; 2/5th York and Lancaster Regt.

V.T.C., 1914-1918
The North Riding of Yorkshire Volunteers, 1914-1919. By Col. Sir James D. Legard. York: The Yorkshire Herald Co., 1919. 95, [12] pp. 7¼″

YORKSHIRE, WEST RIDING
A Short History of the 51st Battalion Royal Tank Regiment. C.M.F., Printing and Stationery Services, 1945. 29 pp. 8″

49 (West Riding) Reconnaissance Regiment, Royal Armoured Corps. Summary of Operations, June 1944 to May 1945. Neuenkirchen: [Sauerländische Druckerei Wilh. Kroscky], 1945. 24 pp., maps. 8¼″

War Services of the 62nd West Riding Divisional Artillery. By Col. A. T. Anderson. With a Preface by Lieut.-Gen. Sir W. P. Braithwaite. Cambridge: [W. Heffer & Sons Ltd.], 1920. xii, 142 pp. 7¼″

A Record of D245 Battery, 1914-1919. By Sergeant A. E. Gee and Corporal A. E. Shaw. London: Renwick of Otley, 1931. 162 pp., portraits, plates, illustrations, maps. 8½″
    11th West Riding Howitzer Battery.

A Short History of The 57th Light Anti-Aircraft Regt. Royal Artillery. Aldershot: Gale & Polden Ltd., 1947. [12], 107 pp., portraits, plates. 7¼″

121 Field/Medium Regiment Royal Artillery, 1939-1946. [Guildford: printed by Biddles Ltd., 1946]. ix, 124 pp., plate, maps. 7¼″

The Royal Regiment of Artillery, Territorial Army: the Field Artillery Regiment of the City of Leeds, 1860-1954; short History of the regiment [269 West Riding Field Regiment]. Leeds: printed by Jowett & Sowry Ltd., 1954. 8 pp. 8½″

Leeds Engineer Volunteers. Colonel W. Child, Commanding. A Brief Record of the work of the 2nd West York Engineer Volunteers, from the Formation of the Corps in 1861 to 1887. Compiled by Quarter-Master Fredk. Green. Leeds: Julian Green, 1887. 64 pp., portrait. 8½″

History of the 2nd West Yorkshire Royal Engineers Volunteers, The Northern Telegraph Companies Royal Engineers Army Troops, The 49th (West Riding) Divisional Signals, 1861-1936. By Col. Walter Boyle. Leeds: printed by The Yorkshire Conservative Newspaper Co. Ltd., 1936. 93 pp. 8″

49th (West Riding) Signal Regiment (T.A.). No imprint. 12 pp., chart. 8½″

A History of the Formation and Development of the Volunteer Infantry, from the Earliest Times, illustrated by the Local Records of Huddersfield and its Vicinity, from 1794 to 1874. By Robert Potter Berry (late) Lieut. London: Simpkin, Marshall, Hamilton, Kent & Co. Ltd., 1903. 566 pp., portraits, plates. 9¾″
    8 coloured plates, including 4 of uniform and 2 portraits.

The West Riding Territorials in the Great War. By Laurie Magnus. With a Foreword by Field Marshal Earl Haig. London: Kegan Paul, Trench, Trubner & Co. Ltd., 1920. xv, 124 pp., portraits, plates, illustrations, maps. 9¼″

The West Yorkshire Regiment in the War, 1914-1918. A History . . . and of its Territorial . . . Battns. By Everard Wyrall. London: John Lane, The Bodley Head Ltd. 2 vols. 1924-27. Plates, maps. 9½″

From Pyramid to Pagoda; the Story of the West Yorkshire Regiment (The Prince of Wales's Own) in the War, 1939-45 and afterwards. By Lieut.-Col. E. W. C. Sandes. [Chapters on Territorial Battns.]. [London: printed by F. J. Parsons Ltd., 1952]. 11″

History of the Sixth Battalion West Yorkshire Regiment. Bradford: Percy Lund, Humphries & Co. Ltd., 1921-23. 2 vols., portraits, plates, maps. 9½″

    Vol. 1. 1/6th Battalion. By Capt. E. V. Tempest. xvi, 352 pp.

    Vol. 2. 2/6th Battalion. By Capt. E. C. Gregory. xvi, 206 pp.

A Short History of the 45/51 (Leeds Rifles) Royal Tank Regt. (T.A.) and 466th (Leeds Rifles) L.A.A. Regt. R.A. (T.A.). London: Reid Hamilton Ltd. [1954]. 32 pp., illustrations. 7¼″

The Early Leeds Volunteers. By Miss Emily Hargrave. [In *Thoresby Society Publications*, vol. 28, pp. 255-319, 1926]. Portrait, illustration. Leeds: Thoresby Society. 8½″

The History of the 1/4th Battalion Duke of Wellington's (West Riding) Regiment, 1914-1919. By Capt. P. G. Bales (formerly Adjut. of the Battalion). Halifax: Edward Mortimer Ltd., 1920. [8], 314 pp., portraits, plates, maps. 9¼″

Brief History of the 5th Duke of Wellington's Regiment (West Riding). Compiled by the Commanding Officer [Lieut.-Col. K. Sykes], February, 1933. [Holmfirth: printed at the " Express " Office], 1933. 12 pp. 6¼″

The History of The Duke of Wellington's Regiment, 1919-1952. Edited by Brig. C. N. Barclay. [Chapters on the Territorial Battns.]. London: William Clowes & Sons Ltd., 1953. 9¾″

The 1/4th (Hallamshire) Battalion York and Lancaster Regiment, 1914-1919. By Capt. D. P. Grant. London: Printed for private circulation by The Arden Press [1931]. 166 pp., maps in end-pocket. 9¾″

The Log Book of the Hallamshire Bn. York & Lancaster Regiment. [27 June 1859-3 Sept. 1939]. Compiled by Capt. T. W. Best and Lt.-Col. W. Tozer. Privately printed. *n.d.* 185 pp. 14″×10″
    Limited to 50 copies.

A Diary of Events: 6th Bn. The York and Lancaster Regiment during the Campaigns in North Africa and Italy, 1943-1945. Taken from a diary compiled by Major R. Elmhirst, including Maps and Sketches of the fighting in Italy, and a Roll of Honour. [Rotherham: printed by Hy. Garnett & Co. Ltd., 1946]. [17, 34] pp., map, plans. 7″×9¾″

The York and Lancaster Regiment, 1758-1919. By Col. H. C. Wylly. Vol. 2. [Chapters on the Territorial Battns.]. [Frome & London: printed by Butler & Tanner Ltd.], 1930. 9¾″

——— Vol. 3, 1919-1953. By Major O. F. Sheffield. [Chapters on the Territorial Battns.]. Aldershot: Gale & Polden Ltd., 1956. 9¾″

Twenty Years Ago with the 1st/2nd West Riding Field Ambulance, R.A.M.C. (T.), 49th Division. By Alfred Johnson. Foreword by Col. A. D. Sharp, A.D.M.S., 49th Division. Presented at the Reunion Dinner in Leeds, 4th February, 1939. No imprint, 1939. 48 pp., portraits, illustrations, maps. 9″

2/1st West Riding Field Ambulance, R.A.M.C. (T.), 1914-1919. Old Comrades. No imprint [1929]. 2nd edition. 24 pp., illustrations. 5¼″ × 3½″

SCOTLAND

GENERAL

Records of the Scottish Volunteer Force, 1859-1908. By Major-Gen. J. M. Grierson. Edinburgh and London: William Blackwood & Sons, 1909. xxvi, 372 pp. 10¼″
  47 coloured plates of uniform.
  Separate histories of all Corps.

The Sword of the North: Highland Memories of the Great War. By Dugald MacEchern. Inverness: Robert Carruthers & Sons, "Courier" Office, 1923. xvi, 672 pp., portraits, illustrations. 10″
  Includes chapters on the 51st (Highland) Division; the Aberdeen Territorial Force Association; Lovats Scouts; Scottish Horse; Inverness-shire R.H.A. and Ammunition Column; 6th and 7th Battn. Black Watch; 4th, 5th, 6th & 2nd Vol. Battns. Seaforth Highlanders; 4th Battn. Queen's Own Cameron Highlanders; and the Highland Mounted Brigade Field Ambulance.

ABERDEEN

The History of the Aberdeen Volunteers, embracing also some account of the Early Volunteers of the Counties of Aberdeen, Banff and Kincardine. By Donald Sinclair. Aberdeen: "Daily Journal" Office, 1907. xxiv, 388 pp. 9¾″

Territorial Soldiering in the North-East of Scotland during 1759-1814. By John Malcolm Bulloch. Aberdeen: The New Spalding Club, 1914. lxviii, 517 pp. 10″
  Contains short histories of Volunteer Corps in Aberdeen and Banff.

The Contribution of the Town of Aberdeen to Volunteer Defence, 1794-1808. By J. M. Bulloch. Privately printed. "Aberdeen Daily Journal" Office, 1915. 20 pp. 9½″

A Record of Northern Valour. How the Volunteers in the counties of Aberdeen, Banff and Kincardine, and the London Scottish Regiment rose in a National Crisis. [By William Will]. Aberdeen: "Aberdeen Journal," 1901. 52 pp., portraits. 7⅛″ × 9⅞″

The Huntly Volunteers: A History of the Volunteer Movement in Strathbogie, from 1798 to 1808. By William Will. Compiled from Documents in the Public Record Office, London. With a Foreword by J. M. Bulloch. Reprinted from the *Huntly Express*. 1915, 59 pp. 7¼″

Records of the 3rd (The Buchan) Volunteer Battalion Gordon Highlanders. Compiled by Capt. and Hon. Major James Ferguson. Peterhead: printed by David Scott, 1894. [6], 64, xx pp. $8\frac{3}{4}''$

"The Lads of the Don." Donside Gordon Highlanders, "D" Company, Alford, 24th August, 1904. Edited by the Rev. Peter Adam. Aberdeen: "Aberdeen Daily Journal" Office, 1904. 76 pp., portraits, plates. [4th Vol. Battn.] $8\frac{1}{4}''$

Records of the 5th (Deeside) Highland Volunteer Battalion Gordon Highlanders. Compiled by Major Patrick Leslie Davidson. 2nd edition. Aberdeen: printed for private circulation by Cornwall, 1898. 74 pp. $8''$

The Sixth Gordons in France and Flanders (with the 7th and 51st Divisions). By Capt. D. Mackenzie. With a Foreword by Lieut.-Gen. Sir G. M. Harper. Aberdeen: printed for the War Mermorial Committee at the Rosemount Press, 1921. xiv, 241 pp., portraits, plates, maps. $9\frac{3}{4}''$

Students under Arms; being the War Adventures of the Aberdeen University Company of the Gordon Highlanders. By Alexander Rule. With an Introduction by J. M. Bulloch. Aberdeen: The University Press, 1934. xv, 220 pp., map. $7\frac{1}{4}''$

The Life of a Regiment.
Vol. 4. The Gordon Highlanders in the First World War, 1914-1919. [By] Cyril Falls. Aberdeen: The University Press, 1958-61. $9\frac{1}{4}''$
Vol. 5. The Gordon Highlanders, 1919-1945. [By] Wilfrid Miles.
　[Both volumes include the Territorial Battns.]

Gordon Highlanders in North Africa and Sicily, August 1942 to October 1943. A Short Account of a Battalion [5/7th] during the Two Campaigns. By Felix Barker. Sidcup: The Bydand Press, 1944. 32 pp., map. $8\frac{1}{2}''$

The Sword of the North: Highland Memories of the Great War. By Dugald MacEchern, Lieut. [incl. chapter on the Aberdeen Territorial Force Association]. Inverness: Robert Carruthers & Sons, 1923. $10''$

ARGYLLSHIRE
Argyllshire Highlanders, 1860-1960. By Lt.-Col. G. I. Malcolm of Poltalloch. Glasgow: The Halberd Press, 1960. viii, 167 pp., portraits, plates. $8''$

Argyll Mountain Battery [In The Sword of the North: Highland Memories of the Great War. By Dugald MacEchern, Lieut.]. Inverness: Robert Carruthers & Sons, 1923. $10''$

History of the Argyll & Sutherland Highlanders. 8th Battalion, 1939-47. [By] Lt.-Col. A. D. Malcolm. With a Foreword by Major-Gen. G. H. A. MacMillan. London: Thomas Nelson and Sons Ltd. [1949], xi, 284 pp., portraits, plates, maps, $9''$

AYRSHIRE

The History of 279 (Ayrshire) Field Regiment R.A.(T.A.) (1st Ayrshire and Galloway Artillery Volunteers), 1859-1956. Troon: *Duplicated.* iv, 39 pp, 1956. 8"

Notes on 279 (Ayrshire) Field Regiment Royal Artillery (Territorial Army), 1859-1959. [Troon]: *Duplicated.* 1959. 5 pp. 13"

The 6th Battalion, Royal Scots Fusiliers, 1939-46. Ayr: printed by T. Gemmell & Son Ltd., 1962. 160 pp., portraits, plates, map. 7¼"

The History of The Royal Scots Fusiliers (1678-1918). By John Buchan. [Including the Territorial Battns.]. London: Thomas Nelson & Sons Ltd., 1925. 9"

———— 1919-39. By Col. J. C. Kemp. [Including the Territorial Battns.]. Glasgow: Robert Maclehose & Co. Ltd., 1963. 8½"

Outposts and Convoys with the Ayrshire Volunteers in South Africa. By R. M'Caw. Kilmarnock: Dunlop & Drennan, 1901. 149 pp. 7½"

BANFFSHIRE

Territorial Soldiering in the North-East of Scotland during 1759-1814. By John Malcolm Bulloch. Aberdeen: The New Spalding Club, 1914. lxviii, 517 pp. 10"
    Contains accounts of all Volunteers raised in the county.

The Beginnings of the Banffshire Volunteers, 1794. By J. M. Bulloch. Privately Printed. No imprint, 1915. 12 pp. 9¾"

Banffshire Volunteers as raised in MDCCXCVII. By J. M. Bulloch. Privately Printed. No imprint, 1915. 20 pp. 9¾"

The Independent Volunteers of Banffshire raised in 1798. By J. M. Bulloch. Privately Printed. No imprint, 1915. 6 pp. 9¾"

The Volunteers of Banff from 1798 to 1808. By J. M. Bulloch. Privately Printed. No imprint, 1915. 8 pp. 9¾"
    50 copies only printed of each of the above 4 pamphlets.

6th Gordons, 1939-1945. A History of the 6th (Banffshire) Battalion The Gordon Highlanders. Aberdeen: printed at " The Press and Journal " Office, 1946. 95 pp., plates, sketch maps. 8¼"

BORDER COUNTIES

With the Border Volunteers to Pretoria. By Lieut. William Home, 2nd V.B. King's Own Scottish Borderers (lately Sergt., 1st Vol. Service Coy., K.O.S.B.). Hawick: W. & J. Kennedy, 1901. 204 pp., portrait, illustrations, map. 7½"

War Record of 4th Bn. King's Own Scottish Borderers and Lothians and Border Horse, with History of the T.F. Association of the Counties of Roxburgh, Berwick and Selkirk. Edited by W. Sorley Brown (Lieut., 4th Bn., K.O.S.B.). Galashiels: John McQueen & Son, 1920. 216 pp., portraits, plates, map. 8½"

The Fourth Bn. King's Own Scottish Borderers. War History, 1939-1945. No title-page or imprint [Galashiels, 1946]. 216 pp., portraits, illustrations. $5\frac{3}{4}'' \times 8\frac{1}{4}''$
   Title on dust cover.

The K.O.S.B. in the Great War. By Capt. Stair Gillon. [Chapter on the 4th Battn.]. London: Thomas Nelson & Son Ltd. [1930]. $8\frac{3}{4}''$

The 6th (Border) Battalion The King's Own Scottish Borderers, 1939-1945. By Capt. J. R. P. Baggaley. [Berwick-on-Tweed: Martin's Printing Works Ltd., 1946]. 111 pp., portraits, maps. $8\frac{1}{4}''$

Borderers in Battle. The War Story of The King's Own Scottish Borderers, 1939-1945. By Capt. H. Gunning. [Including the Territorial Battns.]. Berwick-upon-Tweed: Martin's Printing Works Ltd., 1948. $8\frac{1}{2}''$

CAITHNESS

War Diary of the Fifth Seaforth Highlanders, 51st (Highland) Division. With illustrations and a map. By Capt. D. Sutherland. London: John Lane, The Bodley Head, 1920. 180 pp., portraits, map. $7\frac{1}{2}''$

The Sword of the North: Highland Memories of the Great War. By Dugald MacEchern, Lieut. [Chapter on the 5th Battn. Seaforth Highlanders]. Inverness: Robert Carruthers & Sons, 1923. $10''$

Sans Peur. The History of the 5th (Caithness and Sutherland) Battalion The Seaforth Highlanders, 1942-1945. By Alastair Borthwick. Stirling: Eneas Mackay [1946]. xi, 420 pp., portraits, plates, sketch maps and end-paper maps. $7\frac{1}{4}''$

Seaforth Highlanders. Edited by Col. John Sym. [Including the Territorial Battns.]. Aldershot: Gale & Polden Ltd., 1962. $8\frac{1}{2}''$

CLACKMANNAN

The History of the Volunteers of Clackmannan and Kinross (7th V.B. Argyll and Sutherland Highlanders). (South Africa, 1900-1902). By Edmund E. Dyer, Surgeon-Capt. Alva: Printed by Robert Cunningham, 1907. xvi, 254 pp., portraits, plates. $9\frac{1}{4}''$

DUMBARTONSHIRE

Roll of Officers, 1st Dumbartonshire Volunteer Rifle Corps, 1860-1908; 9th Battalion (The Dumbartonshire) Princess Louise's (Argyll & Sutherland Highlanders) (Territorial Force), 1908-1920; 9th Battalion Princess Louise's (Argyll & Sutherland Highlanders) (Territorial Army), 1920; The Dumbartonshire Volunteer Regiment, 1916-1920 (1st & 3rd Volunteer Battalions Argyll & Sutherland Highlanders). With historical notes, tables of distribution and other information. Compiled from the files of the London Gazette, Official Army Lists, Regimental records, and other sources by Lieut.-Col. F. Rorke. Published with the approval of the Territorial Association for the County of Dumbarton. No imprint, 1937. 174 pp., plates. $8\frac{1}{2}''$

History of the Argyll & Sutherland Highlanders, 9th Battalion, 54th Light A.A. Regiment, 1939-45. [By] Lt.-Col. F. R. P. Barker [& others]. London: Thomas Nelson and Sons Ltd. [1950]. ix, 131 pp., portraits, plates, map. 9"

DUMFRIESSHIRE
War History of the 5th Battalion King's Own Scottish Borderers. By G. F. Scott Elliot, formerly Capt. Under the Auspices of the Territorial Force Associations of the County of Dumfries, the Stewartry of Kircudbright and the Shire of Wigtown. Dumfries: Robert Dinwiddie, 1928. xiv, 328 pp., portraits, illustrations, maps. 8½"

The K.O.S.B. in the Great War. By Capt. Stair Gillon. [Chapter on the 5th Battn.]. London: Thomas Nelson & Sons Ltd., 1930. 8¾"

EDINBURGH AND LOTHIANS
War Record of the 2nd City of Edinburgh Battery, First Lowland Brigade, Royal Field Artillery (" C " Battery, 86th Army Brigade), 1914-1918. Glasgow: Robert Maclehose & Co. Ltd., 1923. 116 pp., portraits, plates, map. 10¼"

History of 57 Medium Regt., R.A., T.A., afterwards 51 Heavy Regt., R.A., 1939-1945. [Edinburgh: printed by Morrison & Gill Ltd.], n.d. 8 pp. 8½"

The History of the Rise, Opposition to, and Establishment of the Edinburgh Regiment, 1778. No imprint, 1778. 18, 2 pp. 9½"

A View of the Establishment of the Royal Edinburgh Volunteers: with an Alphabetical List of the Corps, 15th June, 1795. Published by permission of the Right Honourable Sir James Stirling, Baronet, Lord Provost &c. of Edinburgh. Edinburgh: printed for Manners & Miller, 1795. 60 pp. 8"

———— Jan. 2, 1797. Edinburgh: printed for Manners & Miller, 1797. 85 pp. 8"

History of the Queen's City of Edinburgh Rifle Volunteer Brigade, with Accounts of the City of Edinburgh and Mid-Lothian Rifle Association, The Scottish Twenty Club, etc. By William Stephen, late Second Lieut. Edinburgh: William Blackwood & Sons, 1881. x, 414 pp. [4th and 5th R. Scots]. 7½"

Souvenir of The Queen's Brigade Rifle Volunteer, Royal Scots in 1889. By Capt. Moir-Bryce. Edinburgh: Caldwell Bros. Ltd., 1889. 35ff. Portraits, illustrations. 8¾"×11½"

The Regimental Records of The Royal Scots (The First Regiment of Foot). Compiled by J. C. Leask and H. M. McCance, Capt. [pp. 572-595 deal with all Volunteer/Territorial Battns.]. Dublin: Alexander Thom & Co. Ltd., 1915. 10"

The Royal Scots, 1914-1919. By Major John Ewing. With a Foreword by the Right Hon. Lord Salvesen. [Chapters on the Territorial Battns.] Edinburgh: Oliver & Boyd, 1925. 2 vols. 9"

With the Incomparable 29th. By Major A. H. Mure, 5th Battalion The Royal Scots (Queen's Edinburgh Rifles). London & Edinburgh: W. & R. Chambers Ltd., 1919. 206 pp. 7½"

European War, 1914-1918. 1/8th Battalion The Royal Scots. With an Introduction by Lt.-Col. W. Thorburn. Reprinted from *The Haddington Courier*. Haddington: Croal, *n.d.* 36 pp. 7½"

Record of the 9th (Volunteer) Battalion (Highlanders) The Royal Scots, or The Raising of a Volunteer Regiment and its Conversion into a Full-Strength Battalion of the Territorial Force, 1900-1909. By James Ferguson, Col. London & Edinburgh: W. & A. K. Johnston Ltd., 1909. viii, 182 pp., plates. 8½"
  3 coloured plates of uniform and 1 of colours.

9th Royal Scots (T.F.) B. Company on active service. From a private's diary. February-May, 1915. [By W. P. Young]. 2nd edition. Edinburgh: Turnbull & Spears, 1916. 94 pp. 6½"

9th Battalion (Highlanders) The Royal Scots (The Royal Regiment). No imprint, 1925. 12 pp. 7½"

FIFESHIRE
War History of the 7th Bn. The Black Watch (R.H.R.) (Fife Territorial Battalion) August, 1939-May, 1945. With a Foreword by Major-Gen. Douglas Wimberley. Markinch: printed by The Markinch Printing Co. Ltd., 1948. xii, 146 pp., portraits, plates, maps. 9¾"

A History of The Black Watch Royal Highlanders in the Great War, 1914-1918. Edited by Major-Gen. A. G. Wauchope. London: The Medici Society Ltd., 1926. Vol. 2. The Territorial Battns. Portraits, plates, maps. 10"

The Black Watch and the King's Enemies. By Bernard Fergusson. [Chapters on Territorial Battns.]. London: Collins, 1950. 8½"

GALLOWAY, *see under* AYRSHIRE

GLASGOW, *see also* LANARKSHIRE
The Glasgow Territorials. 52nd (Lowland) Division, 1858-1946. No. 602 (City of Glasgow) (Fighter) Squadron. By William Pratt Paul. Glasgow: McKenzie, Vincent & Co. Ltd., 1946. 104 pp., portraits, illustrations. 9¾"

Youth of Yesteryear. Campaigns, Battles, Service and Exploits of the Glasgow Territorials in the last Great War. By Ion S. Munro. With a Foreword by Ian Hay. Edinburgh: William Hodge & Co. Ltd., 1939. 118 pp. 7¼"

Time Spent; or The History of the 52nd (Lowland) Divisional Reconnaissance Regiment, R.A.C. January, 1941-October, 1945. By Major T. D. W. Whitfield. [Hamilton: The Hamilton Advertiser Ltd., 1946]. 84 pp., maps. 8½"

Mike Target. The Story of the 79th (Lowland) Field Regiment, R.A., in France, Belgium, Holland and Germany. From September, 1944 to May, 1945. [Hanley: Wood, Mitchell & Co. Ltd., 1946] 76 pp., illustrations, maps. 8"

80th (Lowland—City of Glasgow) Field Regiment, R.A., T.A.   A History of the Period 1939-1945, compiled by Members of the Regiment still serving with it in 1945.   Privately printed.   [Glasgow: Robert Maclehose & Co. Ltd.]   1948. 206 pp., maps.   8½″
    420 numbered copies.

The History of Headquarters, Royal Artillery, 52nd Lowland Division during the German War, 1939-1945.   Annan: printed by Dumfriesshire Newspapers Ltd. [1946].   126 pp., maps.   8½″

Glasgow Volunteers, Canal Corps [in *Old Scottish Regimental Colours;* by Andrew Ross, 1885, pp. 127].   Edinburgh: William Blackwood & Sons. Coloured plate.   15″

History of the 1st Lanark Rifle Volunteers: with List of Officers, Prize Winners, Men present at Royal Reviews, etc.   By David Howie.   Glasgow: David Robertson & Co.   London: William Mitchell & Co., 1887.   viii, 448 pp., portraits.   7½″
    Later 5th Battn. Cameronians.

History of the Seventh Lanarkshire Rifle Volunteers, late 4th Ad. Battalion and 29th L.R.V.; also Biographical Notices of Officers, Past and Present, with Statistics and other information regarding the Volunteers of Lanarkshire.   By Capt. James Orr, Adjutant.   Glasgow: Robert Anderson, 1884.   xvi, 642 pp. 8½″
    Later 5th Vol. Battn. Cameronians, disbanded 1897.

With the Cameronians (Scottish Rifles) in France.   Leaves from a Chaplain's Diary.   By the Rev. John White.   Glasgow: John Smith & Son Ltd., 1917. xi, 111 pp. [5th Battalion].   7¼″

The Fifth Battalion The Cameronians (Scottish Rifles), 1914-1919.   Glasgow: Jackson Sons & Co., 1936.   xx, 256 pp., portraits, plates, maps.   8½″

7th Battalion The Cameronians (Scottish Rifles) [with the British Liberation Army in Europe, Oct., 1944 to May, 1945].   No imprint.   Printed in Germany. 32 pp., maps, folding plate.   8¼″

With the 8th Scottish Rifles, 1914-1919.   By Col. J. M. Findlay.   London: Blackie & Son Ltd., 1926.   xvi, 240 pp., portraits, plates, maps.   8½″

History of The Cameronians (Scottish Rifles).   Vol. 2.   1910-1933; by Col. H. H. Story.   Vol. 3.   1933-1946; by Brig. C. N. Barclay.   [Includes Territorial Battns.] 1949; 61   8½″

The Fifth Battalion Highland Light Infantry in the War, 1914-1918.   Glasgow: Printed for private circulation by Maclehose, Jackson & Co., 1921.   x, 250 pp., portraits, plates, maps.   9″

Book of the Sixth Highland Light Infantry.   Glasgow: Clark, 1918.   32 pp., portraits, illustrations.   10″
    Title on cover: The Book of a Glasgow Battalion, 6th H.L.I.

Campaign in Europe. The Story of The 10th Battalion The Highland Light Infantry City of Glasgow Regiment), 1944-1945. Recorded by the late Capt. R. T. Johnston, Capt. D. N. Steward and the Rev. A. Ian Dunlop, Chaplain. [Glasgow: McCorquodale, printers, 1946]. 78 pp., portraits, plates, maps in end-pocket. 8½″

A Silver Lining. The Glasgow Highlanders in France. By D. R. M. [Donald R. McLaren]. Glasgow: John Smith & Son Ltd. [1916]. 91 pp. 7″

1st Bn. The Glasgow Highlanders H.L.I. (from October 1944 to May 1945 during the campaign in North West Europe). [Glasgow: published by the Education Department, 1st Battalion The Glasgow Highlanders H.L.I. 1945]. 24 pp., illustrations, map. 8¼″

Concise Official History of the 2nd Battalion The Glasgow Highlanders, The Highland Light Infantry. Lübeck: 1946. 37 pp., illustrations. ["Not for sale"]. 8¼″

Proud Heritage. The Story of The Highland Light Infantry. By Lt.-Col. L. B. Oatts. Vol. 3. The Regular, Volunteer, T.A. etc. Battns., 1882-1918; Vol. 4. The . . . Territorial Battns., 1919-1959. Glasgow: House of Grant Ltd., 1961-63. 9″

The Whippets; the Book of the 2nd Lowland Field Ambulance. [Glasgow: Maclehose, printers, 1919]. 40 pp., illustrations. 9½″

With the 52nd (Lowland) Division in three continents. By James Young, Lieut.-Col. Commdg. 1/3 Lowland Field Ambulance. Edinburgh: W. Green & Son Ltd., 1920. 112 pp., plates. 9″

V.T.C., 1914-1918
The Glasgow Volunteers: Recollections, 1914-1918. By J. B. Kidston. Glasgow: Hugh Hopkins, 1926. viii, 66 pp., portrait. 7½″

INVERNESS-SHIRE
Historical Records of the Queen's Own Cameron Highlanders. Edinburgh: William Blackwood & Sons, 1909; 31; 52; 61. 10″

Vol. 2. Pp. 66-104, 201-8. History of the 4th Battn. Portraits.

Vol. 3. Pp. 419-468. The Territorial Force Battns. (1/4th, Supernumerary Company, 2/4th, 3/4th). Portraits.

Vol. 4. Pp. 389-390. 10th (Lovat's Scouts) Battn.; pp. 397-408, the 1/1st Battn. of the Northern Counties Highland Volunteer Regiment.

Vol. 6. Chapters on 4th and 5th Territorial Battns.

Vol. 7. Chapters on 4/5th Battn.

4th Battalion Queen's Own Cameron Highlanders (T.A.). A short history. Inverness: Chronicle [1947]. 12 pp. 7¼″

4th Battn. Cameron Highlanders—Inverness-shire R.H.A.—Highland Mounted Brigade, T. & S. Column, R.A.S.C.—Highland Mounted Brigade Field Ambulance. [In *The Sword of the North:* Highland Memories of the Great War. By Dugald MacEchern, Lieut.]. Inverness: Robert Carruthers & Sons, 1923. 10″

KINCARDINESHIRE *see also under* ABERDEEN
The Kincardineshire Volunteers: A History of the Volunteer Movement in Kincardineshire, from 1798 to 1816. By William Will. Compiled from Documents in the Public Record Office, London. Reprinted from the *Aberdeen Weekly Journal, n.d.* 132 pp. 7¼″

KINROSS, *see under* CLACKMANNAN

KIRKCUDBRIGHT, *see under* DUMFRIESSHIRE

LANARKSHIRE, *see also under* GLASGOW
With the Scottish Rifle Volunteers at the Front. By Godfrey H. Smith. Glasgow: William Hodge & Company, 1901. xvi, 140 pp., portraits, illustrations. 7¼″
   4th Vol. Battn. afterwards 8th Battn.

6th (Lanarkshire) Battalion The Cameronians (Scottish Rifles). History of the Regiment and the Battalion, 1689-1936. Hamilton: Printed by the " Hamilton Advertiser " Ltd., 1936. 20 pp., map. 5¼″

The History of 6th (Lanarkshire) Battalion The Cameronians (S.R.) World War II. [Glasgow: John Cossar, 1946]. 150 pp., portraits, plates, maps. 7¼″

History of The Cameronians (Scottish Rifles). Vol. 2. 1910-1933; by Col. H. H. Storey. Vol. 3. 1933-1946; by Brig. C. N. Barclay. [Both volumes include the Territorial Battns.]. 1949: 61. 8½″

LOTHIANS, *see under* EDINBURGH

MORAYSHIRE
3rd V.B. Seaforth Highlanders: A Brief History of their Origin and Development. To be sold for the benefit of the Headquarters Fund Bazaar at Elgin, 13th, 14th, and 15th September, 1906. Elgin: printed at the " Northern Scott " Office, 1906. 47 pp., illustrations. 11″×8¾″

The Great War, 1914-1918. 6th Seaforth Highlanders. Campaign Reminiscences by Capt. R. T. Peel and Capt. A. H. Macdonald. Elgin: W. R. Walker & Co., 1923. 61 pp., portraits. 9½″

6th Battn. The Seaforth Highlanders. [In *The Sword of the North:* Highland Memories of the Great War. By Dugald MacEchern, Lieut.]. Inverness: Robert Carruthers & Sons, 1923. 10″

Seaforth Highlanders. Edited by Col. J. Sym. [Including the 6th Battn.]. Aldershot: Gale & Polden Ltd., 1962. 8½″

NAIRN, *see* INVERNESS-SHIRE

ORKNEY AND SHETLAND
The History of the Orkney and Shetland Volunteers and Territorials, 1793-1958. By D. Rollo.   [Lerwick: The Shetland Times Ltd., 1958].   vi, 37 pp., plates.   8½″

PERTHSHIRE
A Military History of Perthshire, 1660-1902.   Edited by the Marchioness of Tullibardine.   Perth: R. A. & J. Hay, 1908.   [Pp. 185-224, The Perthshire Yeomanry, Volunteers and Local Militia, 1794-1902].   Plates.   9¾″

—— 1899-1902.   Edited by the Marchioness of Tullibardine.   With a Roll of the Perthshire Men of the present day who have seen Active Service under the British Flag.   Compiled by the Editor and Jane C. C. Macdonald.   With portraits, illustrations and maps.   Perth: R. A. & J. Hay, 1908.   xx, 316 pp.   9¾″

Historical Sketch of the 4th (Perthshire) Volunteer Battalion The Black Watch (Royal Highlanders) late 1st Perthshire.   By George D. Pullar, Capt.   Edinburgh: John A. McCulloch, Hillside Printing Works, 1907.   iv, 46 pp., plates.   7½″

A History of the 6th Battalion The Black Watch (Royal Highland Regiment), 1939-1945.   By B. J. G. Madden.   Perth: D. Leslie, 1948.   xvi, 143 pp., illustrations, maps.   8¾″

6th Battalion, Black Watch [in *The Sword of the North:* Highland Memories of the Great War.   By Dugald MacEchern, Lieut.].   Inverness: Robert Carruthers & Sons, 1923.   10″

A History of The Black Watch Royal Highlanders in the Great War, 1914-1918. Edited by Major-Gen. A. G. Wauchope.   London: The Medici Society Ltd., 1926.   Vol. 2, The Territorial Battns., portraits, plates, maps.   10″

The Black Watch and the King's Enemies.   By Bernard Fergusson.   [Chapters on the Territorial Battns.].   London: Collins, 1950.   8½″

RENFREWSHIRE
Volunteer Memories.   By Col. William Lamont, late Commanding 1st (Renfrewshire) Volunteer Battalion Princess Louise's Argyll and Sutherland Highlanders.   With illustrations.   Greenock: James McKelvie & Sons Ltd., 1911. xii, 196 pp., portraits, plates.   [5th Battn.].   7½″

History of the Argyll & Sutherland Highlanders.   5th Battalion, 91st Anti-Tank Regiment, 1939-45.   [By] Major Desmond Flower.   London: Thomas Nelson & Sons Ltd., 1950.   xii, 396 pp., portraits, plates, sketch maps.   9″

—— 6th Battalion, 93rd Anti-Tank Regiment R.A. (A. & S.H.).   Edited by William Pratt Paul.   With a Foreword by Lieut.-Gen. Sir Gordon H. A. MacMillan.   London: Thomas Nelson & Sons Ltd. [1949].   x, 134 pp., portraits, plates, maps.   9″

On Active Service with the Argyll & Sutherland Highlanders. A ranker's reminiscence and war notes. 6th Battalion. By John Maclean. Edinburgh: The Scottish Chronicle Press, 1926. 2 vols. Portraits [vol. 1, 94 pp.; vol. 2, 116 pp.] 7″

ROSS AND CROMARTY

A History of the Fourth Battalion The Seaforth Highlanders. With some Account of the Military Annals of Ross, the Fencibles, the Volunteers, and the Home Defence and Reserve Battalions, 1914-1919. Compiled by Lieut.-Col. M. M. Haldane. Illustrations by Capt. Finlay Mackinnon. London: H. F. & G. Witherby, 1928. 372 pp., plates, maps. 10″
   17 coloured plates, including 1 of colours.

4th Battn. The Seaforth Highlanders—Ross and Cromarty Highland Mountain Battery [in *The Sword of the North:* Highland Memories of the Great War. By Dugald MacEchern, Lieut.] Inverness: Robert Carruthers & Sons, 1923. 10″

Seaforth Highlanders. Edited by Col. John M. Sym. [Incl. the 4th Battn.] Aldershot: Gale & Polden Ltd., 1962. 8½″

ROXBURGH, *see* BORDER COUNTIES

SELKIRK, *see* BORDER COUNTIES

STIRLINGSHIRE

7th Battalion Argyll and Sutherland Highlanders. The Great War, 1914-1919. [By A. D. Morrison]. [Alva: Robert Cunningham & Sons Ltd., *c.* 1925]. 103 pp., portraits, illustrations. 7¼″
   No title page, title on cover.

7th Battalion Argyll and Sutherland Highlanders. To the Undying Memory of of the Officers, Non-Commissioned Officers, and Men who fell during the Great War. [Foreword signed A. D. Morrison]. No imprint. [*c.* 1919]. 56 pp., portraits. 10″

History of the Argyll & Sutherland Highlanders, 7th Battalion from El Alamein to Germany. [By] Capt. Ian C. Cameron. With a Foreword by Major-Gen. D. N. Wimberley. London: Thomas Nelson & Sons Ltd. [1947]. xiii, 242 pp., portraits, plates, maps. 9″

The 7th Battalion Argyll and Sutherland Highlanders (T.A.); their peacetime life, 1908-1958. Glasgow: The Paramount Press [1958]. 63 pp., portraits, illustrations. 8½″

SUTHERLAND, *see under* CAITHNESS

WIGTOWN, *see under* DUMFRIESSHIRE

VOLUNTEERS [& YEOMANRY]

IRELAND

The History of the Volunteers of 1782. By Thomas MacNevin. Dublin: James Duffy, 1845.   250 pp.   5¾″

———— Centenary edition.   Dublin: James Duffy, 1882.   xxii, 250 pp.   5¾″

The Ulster Volunteers of '82; their medals, badges, flags, etc.   By Robert Day [& others] [in *Ulster Journal of Archaeology*, vol. 4, pp. 73-85, 152-9, 255-8; vol. 5, pp. 23-4, 92-5, 218-9; vol. 6, pp. 34-38; vol. 7, pp. 97-102, 1898-1901.]   9¾″

The County Armagh Volunteers of 1778-1793. By T. G. F. Paterson.   [In the *Ulster Journal of Archaeology*, 3rd Ser., IV, pp. 101-127; V, pp. 31-61; VI, pp. 69-105; VII, pp. 76-95.]   Belfast.   1941-44.   Portraits, illustrations. 9¾″

An Account of the Yeomanry of Ireland, 1796 to 1834; with a List of the Corps in County Cork, and the Records of the Doneraile Yeomanry Cavalry.   By Major James Grove White.   Cork: Guy & Co. Ltd., 1893.   33 pp.   4to.

Record of the Doneraile Rangers; with a List of the Volunteer Corps of the County of Cork.   By Major J. G. White.   [In *Journal of the Cork Historical and Archaeological Society*, Jan. 1893].   14 pp.   9½″

Volunteers and Yeomanry of the Newry District.   By Francis C. Crossle, 1906. Reprinted from *The Northern Whig and Belfast Post*.   Belfast: The Northern Whig Ltd.   31 pp., 1934.   7″

Some Mementoes of the Irish Volunteers (& Yeomanry).   By Robert Day. [In *Cork Historical & Archaeological Society, Journal*, vol. 4, pp. 321-7; vol. 5, pp. 37-45, 1898-99.]

   Continued with title:

The Medals and Gorgets of the Irish Volunteers and Militia.   [*ibid*, vol. 5, pp. 183-194; vol. 6, pp. 161-8, 1899-1900].   Illustrations.   9½″

On some Medals and Mottoes of the Irish Volunteers.   By Robert Day.   [In *Cork Historical and Archaeological Society, Journal*, vol. 4, pp. 33-48, 1898]. Illustrations.   9½″

The Yeomanry Corps of County Cork, 1823-1834.   By James Buckley.   [In *Cork Historical and Archaeological Society, Journal*, vol. 19, pp. 37-39.   1913]. 9½″

The Cork Historical and Archaeological Society, Journal, from 1895 onwards contains many other brief articles and notes on Yeomanry and Volunteers.

SECTION V

MISCELLANEOUS

WOMEN'S CORPS

Women in Uniform.   Edited by D. Collett Wadge, formerly Sen. Comd. A.T.S.
London: Sampson Low, Marston & Co. Ltd. [1947].   xi, 386 pp., portraits,
illustrations.   9″
   Short accounts of all women's services.

Britain's Other Army.   The Story of the A.T.S.   By Eileen Bigland.   London:
Nicholson & Watson, 1946.   190 pp., plates.   7¼″

Service with the Army.   By Chief Controller Dame Helen Gwynne-Vaughan.
London: Hutchinson & Co. (Publishers), Ltd. [1942].   168 pp., illustrations.   7¼″

As Thoughts Survive.   By Dame Leslie Whateley, Director of the A.T.S.
Preface by H.R.H. The Princess Royal.   London: Hutchinson & Co. (Publishers) Ltd. [1949].   211 pp., portraits, plates.   9½″

Fanny goes to War.   By Pat Beauchamp.   With an Introduction by Major-Gen.
H. N. Thompson.   London: John Murray, 1919.   x, 290 pp.   7½″
   First Aid Nursing Yeomanry.

Fanny went to War.   By Pat Beauchamp.   With a Foreword by H.R.H.
Princess Alice, Countess of Athlone.   London: George Routledge & Sons Ltd.
[1940].   xi, 240 pp., portraits, plates.   7½″

F.A.N.Y. Invicta.   By Irene Ward, D.B.E., M.P.   With a Foreword by H.R.H.
The Princess Alice, Countess of Athlone.   London: Hutchinson & Co. (Publishers) Ltd., 1955.   348 pp., portraits, plates, illustrations.   8½″

Women's Legion, 1916-1920.   By Molly Colclough.   With a Foreword by Ina
N. Clarke (Chief Commandant).   London: Spearman Publishers [1939].   46 pp.,
portraits, plates.   7¼″

DISBANDED REGIMENTS AND CORPS

The following books contain a number of short histories of disbanded Scottish
regiments.   In order to avoid duplication of titles they are referred to below by
letter only.   For detailed lists of their contents see under GENERAL WORKS,
SCOTTISH.

A   Sketches of the Character, Manners, and Present State of the Highlanders
     of Scotland; with details of the Military Service of the Highland Regiments.
     By Col. David Stewart.   2nd edition.   Edinburgh: Archibald Constable &
     Co., 1822.   2 vols.   8½″

B   A History of the Highlands and of the Highland Clans; with an extensive selection from the hitherto inedited Stuart Papers. By James Browne. Edinburgh: A. Fullarton & Co., 1852-53. Portraits, plates, illustrations, maps. New edition. 4 vols. $9\frac{3}{4}''$

C   A History of the Scottish Highlands, Highland Clans and Highland Regiments, etc. Edited by John S. Keltie. Edinburgh: A. Fullarton & Co., 1875. 2 vols. Portraits, illustrations, maps. $10\frac{1}{2}''$

——— New edition, with the Regimental Portion brought down to the present time from official sources by William Melven. Edinburgh: Jack, 1887. 2 vols., portraits, plates, illustrations. $10\frac{1}{2}''$
    32 coloured plates of tartans and 8 of Regimental Colours.

D   Territorial Soldiering in the North-East of Scotland during 1759-1814. By John Malcolm Bulloch. Aberdeen: The New Spalding Club, 1914. lxviii, 518 pp., portrait, plate, illustration. $10''$

E   A Military History of Perthshire, 1660-1902. Edited by the Marchioness of Tullibardine. Perth: R. A. & J. Hay, 1908. xxiii, 634 pp., portraits, plates, maps. $9\frac{3}{4}''$

F   Old Scottish Regimental Colours. By Andrew Ross. With twenty-eight coloured plates and other illustrations. Edinburgh: William Blackwood & Sons, 1885. x, 158 pp. $15''$

G   The Sword of the North: Highland Memories of the Great War. By Dugald MacEchern. Inverness: Robert Carruthers & Sons, " Courier " Office, 1923. xvi, 672 pp., portraits, illustrations. $10''$

SECTION 1—NUMBERED REGIMENTS

18th (*formerly* 19th) *Light Dragoons*, 1759-1821
The Historical Memoirs of the XVIIIth Hussars. By Col. H. Malet. London: Simpkin & Co. Ltd., 1907. Pp. 1-207. $8\frac{1}{2}''$
    6 coloured plates of uniform.

The Nineteenth and their Times; being an Account of the Four Cavalry Regiments in the British Army that have borne the number Nineteen etc. By Col. John Biddulph. London: John Murray, 1899. Pp. 1-9. $8\frac{3}{4}''$

19th *Dragoons*
The Nineteenth and their Times; being an Account of the Four Cavalry Regiments in the British Army that have borne the number Nineteen etc. By Col. John Biddulph. London: John Murray, 1899. $8\frac{3}{4}''$

    19th Light Dragoons, 1759, re-numbered 18th, 1763. *q.v.* pp. 1-9.
    19th Light Dragoons, 1779-1783. Pp. 10-18.
    19th (formerly 23rd) Light Dragoons, 1781-1821. Pp. 19-219.

20th Dragoons
Notes on the History and Services of the Twentieth Dragoons. [In *Colburn's United Service Magazine*, 1876, Pt. 3; 1877, Pt. 1]. London: Hurst and Blackett, 1876-77. 8½″

20th Light Dragoons, 1759-63. 1876, Pt. 3, pp. 198-199.

20th Light Dragoons, 1779-83. 1876, Pt. 3, pp. 199-200.

20th, or Jamaica Light Dragoons, 1791-1818. 1876, Pt. 3, pp. 200-211, 346-359, 442-455; 1877, Pt. 1, 65-78, 212-222.

21st Dragoons
Notes on the History and Services of the Twenty-First Regiment of Dragoons. [In *Colburn's United Service Magazine*, 1876, Pt. 2]. London: Hurst and Blackett, 1876. 8½″

21st, or Royal Windsor Foresters, 1760-63. Pp. 336-340.

21st Light Dragoons, 1779-83. Pp. 340-341.

21st Light Dragoons, 1794-1820. Pp. 341-351, 490-497.

22nd Dragoons
XXII Dragoons, 1760-1945: The Story of a Regiment. By Raymond Birt. Aldershot: Gale & Polden Ltd., 1950. xxxi, 349 pp., portraits, plates, maps. 8½″
22nd Light Dragoons, 1779-83.
22nd Light Dragoons, 1794-1802.
22nd Light Dragoons, 1802-1820 (raised 1794 as 25th, became 22nd 1802).
22nd Dragoons, 1940-48.

23rd Light Dragoons, 1781-86, see *19th*, above

23rd Hussars, 1940-46
The Story of the 23rd Hussars, 1940-1946. Written and compiled by members of the Regiment. [Printed in Germany, 1946]. 277 pp., portraits, illustrations, maps. 8¼″

'A' Squadron, 23rd Hussars War Diary, June 1944-May 1945. No imprint [1945]. 36 pp., illustrations, maps. 10″

24th Light Dragoons (raised as 27th in 1795, re-numbered 24th in 1802) d. 1819
A Cavalry Regiment of the Mahratta Wars. By C. T. Atkinson. [In *Society for Army Historical Research, Journal*, vol. 33, 1955, pp. 80-87]. 9¼″

71st, Fraser's Highlanders, 1775-83, see also A, B, C, D, above
The 71st Highlanders in Massachusetts, 1776-1780. By Colin Campbell. [In *New England Historical and Genealogical Register*, vol. 92, pp. 265-275; vol. 93, pp. 1-14, 84-95, 1958-59]. Boston, Mass. Plates, maps. 8½″

72nd, Royal Manchester Volunteers, 1778-83
The Royal Manchester Volunteers. By T. H. McGuffie. [In *The Manchester Review*, Summer 1955, pp. 209-222]. Manchester: Manchester Libraries Committee. Illustration. 8½″

74th, Argyle Highlanders, 1778-83, see A, B, C, above

76th, Macdonald's Highlanders, 1777-84, see also A, B, C, above
Historical Record of the 76th " Hindoostan " Regiment. By Lt.-Col. F. A. Hayden. Lichfield: A. C. Lomax's Successors, 1908. [Account of the 76th Macdonald's Highlanders, pp. 135-141]. $8\frac{1}{2}''$

77th, Montgomery's Highlanders, 1757-63, see A, B, C, above

77th, Atholl Highlanders, 1777-83, see also A, B, C, D, E, above
The " Mutiny " of the Atholl Highlanders and An Account of the Sheelagreen Gordons. By J. M. Bulloch. Buckie: W. F. Johnston & Sons, 1911. 23 pp. 10''

78th, Fraser's Highlanders, 1757-63, see A, B, C, above

81st, Aberdeenshire Highland, 1778-83, see A, B, C, D, above

82nd Regiment, 1778-83, see also F, above
History of the Hamilton Regiment. [In *Studies in Nova Scotian History;* by George Patterson, pp. 17-33]. Halifax, N.S.: The Imperial Publishing Co. Ltd., 1940. $8\frac{3}{4}''$

84th Regiment, 1758-63
The York and Lancaster Regiment. By Col. H. C. Wylly. [Frome: Butler & Tanner Ltd.], 1930. [Vol. 2, short account of 84th, 1758-63]. $9\frac{3}{4}''$

Roll of Officers of the York and Lancaster Regiment, containing a Complete Record of their Services etc. By Major G. A. Raikes. The Second Battalion . . . from 1758 . . . included 84th, 1758-63. London: Richard Bentley & Son, 1885. $8\frac{1}{2}''$

——— Revised, enlarged etc., by Capt. R. E. Key. London: William Clowes & Sons Ltd., 1910. $8\frac{1}{2}''$

84th, Royal Highland Emigrants, 1775-84, see also A, B. C. E, above
The " Highland Emigrants " and their Comrades; being an Account of the Siege of Quebec, Canada, in 1775-6. Compiled by Capt. R. E. Key. [In *Journal of the Royal United Service Institution*, vol. 56, 1912, pp. 1247-62]. Plates, maps. $9\frac{1}{2}''$

Sketches illustrating the Early Settlement and History of Glengarry in Canada, relating principally to the Revolutionary War of 1775-83 . . . and the Services of the . . . 84th or Royal Highland Emigrant Regiment etc. By J. A. Macdonell. Montreal: Wm. Foster, Brown & Co., 1893. $9\frac{3}{4}''$

The York and Lancaster Regiment. By Col. H. C. Wylly. [Frome: Butler & Tanner Ltd.], 1930. Vol. 2 [short account of 84th, 1775-84]. $9\frac{3}{4}''$

Roll of Officers of The York and Lancaster Regiment, containing a Complete Record of their Services etc. By Major G. A. Raikes. The Second Battalion, formerly The Royal Highland Emigrants . . . London: Richard Bentley & Son, 1885. $8\frac{1}{2}''$

———— Revised, enlarged etc., by Capt. R. E. Key.   London: William Clowes & Sons Ltd., 1910.   8½″

85th, Royal Volunteers, 1759-63
The Eighty-Fifth King's Light Infantry; edited by C. R. B. Barrett.   London: Spottiswoode & Co. Ltd., 1913.   [Account of 85th Royal Volunteers, pp. 1-21; Roll of Officers, pp. 457-461].   9¾″

85th, Westminster Volunteers, 1779-83
The Eighty-Fifth King's Light Infantry; edited by C. R. B. Barrett.   London: Spottiswoode & Co. Ltd., 1913.   [Account of 85th Westminster Volunteers, pp. 22-29; Roll of Officers, pp. 462-467].   9¾″

86th Regiment (Wall's African Corps), 1758-84
For the history of this corps, see A Statement of Events in Senegal and Goree, 1758 to 1784.   By Major J. J. Crooks.   [In *The United Service Magazine*, vol. 52, 1916, pp. 307-19, 411-20, 530-40].   9″

87th, Keith's Highlanders, 1759-63, see also A, B, C, D, above
Three Prints of Keith's and Campbell's Highlanders (87th and 88th Regiments, 1759-1763).   By Major I. H. Mackay Scobie; [&] The Highlanders in Westphalia, 1760-62 and the Development of Light Infantry.   By C. T. Atkinson.   [In *Society for Army Historical Research, Journal*, vol. 20, 1941, pp. 162-9, 208-223].   Plates.   9¼″

88th, Campbell's Highlanders, 1759-63, see also A, B. C, above
Three Prints of Keith's and Campbell's Highlanders (87th and 88th Regiments, 1759-1763).   By Major I. H. Mackay Scobie; [&] The Highlanders in Westphalia, 1760-62 and the Development of Light Infantry.   By C. T. Atkinson.   [In *Society for Army Historical Research, Journal*, vol. 20, 1941, pp. 162-9, 208-223].   Plates.   9¼″

89th, Highland Regiment, 1759-65, see A, B, C, D, above

94th, Scotch Brigade, 1793-1818, see also F, above

The Connaught Rangers.   By Lt.-Col. H. F. N. Jourdain and E. Fraser.   London: The Royal United Service Institution, vol. 2, 1926.   [Account of the 94th Scotch Brigade, pp. 96-304; vol. 3, 1928, includes Records of Officers Services].   Portraits, plates, maps.   9¾″

For the Scots Brigade in Holland, 1572-1782, see under DISBANDED REGIMENTS: NAMED, below

95th Regiment, 1780-83, see E, above

95th Regiment (raised 1802 as 96th, renumbered 95th, 1816, disbanded 1818), see *96th*

96th Regiments
History of the Manchester Regiment.   Compiled by Col. H. C. Wylly.   London:
Forster, Groom & Co. Ltd., 1923.   Vol. 1.   Plates. $9\frac{3}{4}''$
[Contains accounts of " Regiments that have been numbered 96 "].

96th, 1761-63.

96th, British Musqueteers, 1780-83.

96th, Queen's Royal Irish, 1793-96.

96th (formerly 97th Queen's Germans), 1798-1818.

96th (afterwards 95th), 1802-18.

97th, Inverness-shire Regiment, 1794-95, see also A, B, D, above
The Inverness-Shire Highlanders or 97th Regiment of Foot, 1794-1796.   By
H. B. Mackintosh.   Elgin: J. D. Yeadon, 1926.   79 pp.,   portrait, plates.   10"

97th, Queen's Germans (afterwards 96th), 1798-1818, see *96th*

99th, (raised 1804 as 100th, Prince Regent's County of Dublin Regiment, re-
numbered 99th, 1816, disbanded 1818), see *100th*

100th Regiments
The History of the Prince of Wales's Leinster Regiment (Royal Canadians).
Compiled by Lt.-Col. F. E. Whitton.   Aldershot: Gale & Polden Ltd., 1924.
Vol. 1. $8\frac{1}{2}''$

Contains accounts of:

100th Regiment, 1760-63.

100th Regiment, 1780-85.

100th (afterwards 99th) Prince Regent's County of Dublin, 1804-18.

102nd, New South Wales Corps, 1789-1818
Rum Rebellion.   A Study of the Overthrow of Governor Bligh by John Mac-
arthur and the New South Wales Corps.   By the Hon. Mr. Justice H. V. Evatt.
Sydney: Angus & Robertson Ltd., 1938.   xx, 366 pp. $8\frac{1}{2}''$
Coloured plate of uniform.

A Short History of the New South Wales Corps, 1789-1818.   By R. Maurice
Hill.   [In *Society for Army Historical Research, Journal,* vol. 13, 1934, pp. 135-
140]. $9\frac{1}{4}''$

104th, New Brunswick Fencibles
The 104th Regiment of Foot (The New Brunswick Regiment), 1803-1817.   By
Capt. W. Austin Squires.   Fredericton, N.B.: Brunswick Press, 1962.   246 pp.,
portraits, plates. $8\frac{1}{2}''$

The 104th Regiment.   By Lieut.-Col. E. Cruikshank.   [In *Canadian Military
Institute, Selected Papers,* No. 7, 1896, pp. 9-20].   Welland, Ont.: printed by
The Tribune. $8\frac{3}{4}''$

The New Brunswick Fencibles—afterwards the 104th Foot.   By W. Y. Baldry and A. S. White.   [In *Society for Army Historical Research, Journal*, vol. 1, 1922, pp. 90-92].   9¼″

The New Brunswick Fencibles.   By 2nd Lieut. George F. G. Stanley.   [In *Canadian Defence Quarterly*, vol. 16, Oct. 1938, pp. 39-53].   Ottawa: Runge Press Ltd.   9½″

105*th, Queen's Own Royal Regiment of Highlanders*, 1761-64, see E, above

109*th Regiments*
The History of the Prince of Wales's Leinster Regiment (Royal Canadians). Compiled by Lt.-Col. F. E. Whitton.   Aldershot: Gale & Polden Ltd., 1924. Vol. 1.   8½″

   Contains accounts of:

   109th, 1761-63, see also E, above.

   109th, Aberdeenshire, 1794-95, see also D, above.

113*th, Royal Birmingham Volunteers*, 1794-95
The Short Life and Sudden Death of an English Regiment of Foot; an account of the raising, recruiting, mutiny and disbandment of the 113th Regiment of Foot, or " Royal Birmingham Volunteers " (April, 1794 to September, 1795). By T. H. McGuffie.   [In *Society for Army Historical Research, Journal*, vol. 33, 1955, pp. 16-25, 48-56].   Portrait.   9¼″

116*th Regiment*, 1794-95, see E, above

119*th Regiment*, 1762-63
The 119th Regiment of Foot, 1762 to 1763.   By the Rev. P. Sumner.   [In *Society for Army Historical Research, Journal*, vol. 17, 1938, pp. 63-64].   9¼″
   Coloured plate of uniform.

SECTION 2—NAMED REGIMENTS AND CORPS

Argyllshire Highlanders
The First Highland Regiment: The Argyllshire Highlanders.   By Lt.-Col. Robert MacKenzie Holden.   [In *The Scottish Historical Review*, Oct. 1905, pp. 27-40].   9¾″

Atholl's Troop of Horse, 1666-67
The Earl of Atholl's and Major-Gen. Wm. Drummond's Troops of Horse, 1666-67.   [In *A Military History of Perthshire*, 1660-1902; edited by the Marchioness of Tullibardine, 1908, pp. 1-7].   Perth: R. A. & J. Hay.   9¾″

Cardross's Dragoons
Cardross's Dragoons.   [In *Old Scottish Regimental Colours;* by Andrew Ross, 1885, pp. 47-8].   Edinburgh: William Blackwood & Sons.   Plate.   15″

Claverhouse's Horse
Claverhouse's Horse. [In *Old Scottish Regimental Colours;* by Andrew Ross, 1885, pp. 12-13]. Edinburgh: William Blackwood & Sons. 15″

Commissariat and Transport Corps
The Commissariat and Transport Staff and Commissariat Transport Corps, 1880-1888. [In *The Predecessors of the Royal Army Service Corps;* by Lt.-Col. C. H. Massé, 1948, pp. 82-116]. Aldershot: Gale & Polden Ltd. Plates (1 coloured), illustrations. 9½″

Cromwell's Regiments
Cromwell's Regiments. By Sir Charles H. Firth. [In *Society for Army Historical Research, Journal*, vol. 6, 1927, pp. 16-23, 141-146, 222-228]. 9¼″
   Accounts of the 6 regiments commanded by Cromwell.

Cromwellian Army
The Regimental History of Cromwell's Army. By Sir Charles Firth, assisted by Godfrey Davies. Oxford: Clarendon Press, 1940. 2 vols. 8½″
   Contains short histories of all regiments.

Drummond's Troop of Horse, 1666-67, see under *Atholl's*, above

Garrison Battalions and Companies
Garrison, Reserve and Veteran Battalions and Companies. By A. S. White. [In *Society for Army Historical Research, Journal*, vol. 38, 1960, pp. 156-167]. 9¼″

Glider Pilot Regiment
Lion with Blue Wings. The Story of the Glider Pilot Regiment, 1942-1945. By Ronald Seth, with Forewords by Field Marshal Viscount Alanbrooke and Air Chief Marshal Sir Leslie Holleyhurst. London: Victor Gollancz Ltd., 1955. 245 pp., portraits, plates. 8½″

The Wings of Pegasus. By George Chatterton. London: Macdonald, 1962. xi, 282 pp., portraits, plates. 8½″
   The Story of the Glider Pilot Regiment.

Roll of Honour and Record of Battle Casualties and Honours of the Glider Pilot Regiment in the European War, 3rd September, 1939 to 8th May, 1945. *Duplicated.* 1945. 132 pp. 13″

Gooch's Regiment, 1739-42
Gooch's American Regiment of Foot, 1739-42. By W. Y. Baldry and A. S. White. [In *Society for Army Historical Research, Journal*, vol. 16, 1937, pp. 235-239]. 9¼″

King Edward's Horse
The History of King Edward's Horse (The King's Overseas Dominions Regiment). Edited by Lieut.-Col. Lionel James, with a Foreword by Gen. the Hon. Sir Herbert A. Lawrence. London: Sifton, Praed & Co. Ltd., 1921. xv, 401 pp., portraits, plates, maps. 8½″

King's Life Guard of Horse, 1678
The King's Life Guard of Horse, 1678. [In *A Military History of Perthshire*, 1660-1902; edited by the Marchioness of Tullibardine, 1908, pp. 8-18]. Perth: R. A. & J. Hay. 9¾″

Kingston's Light Horse
The Duke of Kingston's Regiment of Light Horse. By A. C. Wood. [In *Thoroton Society, Transactions*, vol. 49, 1945, pp. 73-83]. Nottingham: printed for the Society by Cooke & Vowles (1940) Ltd., 1946. 8½″

Labour Corps
With a Labour Company in France; being the War Diary of the 58th Labour Company. [By] Capt. T. C. Thomas. Birmingham: Hudson & Son, printers, 1919. 76 pp., illustrations. 8¼″

Land Transport Corps
The Land Transport Corps, 1855-1857. [In *The Predecessors of the Royal Army Service Corps;* by Lt.-Col. C. H. Massé, 1948, pp. 23-36]. Aldershot: Gale & Polden Ltd. Illustrations. 9½″

Loudon's Highlanders, see A, B, C, above

Machine Gun Corps
Machine Guns, their History and Tactical Employment (being also a History of the Machine Gun Corps, 1916-1922. By Lieut.-Col. G. S. Hutchison. London: Macmillan & Co. Ltd., 1938. xvi, 349 pp., plates. 8½″

War Diary, 1st Machine Gun Squadron, 1918-1919. [By Capt. C. H. Reid]. [London: Straker Brothers Ltd., 1922]. 67 pp., portraits, sketch maps. *No title-page.* 8½″

Through Palestine with the Twentieth Machine-Gun Squadron Sherwood Rangers Yeo. South Notts Hussars. [By Lieut. A. O. W. Kindell]. [London: J. M. Baxter & Co. for private circulation, 1920]. [7], 180 pp., plates, maps. 8½″

History and Memoir of the 33rd Battalion Machine Gun Corps and of the 19th, 98th, 100th and 248th M.G. Companies. Written and illustrated by Members of the Battalion. London: printed by Waterlow Brothers & Layton Ltd., 1919. [14], 118 pp., portraits, plates, illustrations. 12¾″
    18 coloured plates. 1600 copies printed for private circulation.

With the Machine Gun Corps from Grantham to Cologne. By Arthur Russell. London: Dranes [1923]. 218 pp. 7¼″

Record of the 110th Company (21st Division), Machine Gun Corps, B.E.F., France, 1916-1917. By W. Grantley Jones. [Bristol], 1962. iii, 29 pp., portraits. Photostat of typescript. 11¾″

Military Train
The Military Train and Commissariat Staff Corps, 1856-1869. [In *The Predecessors of the Royal Army Service Corps;* by Lt.-Col. C. H. Massé, 1948, pp. 37-56]. Aldershot: Gale & Polden Ltd. Illustrations. 9½″

Murray's, Lord John, Regiment
John, Lord Murray's (afterwards Earl of Tullibardine's) Regiment of Foot, 1694-97. [In *A Military History of Perthshire*, 1660-1902; edited by the Marchioness of Tullibardine, 1908, pp. 23-27]. Perth: R. A. & J. Hay. 9¾"

Prince of Wales's Horse
The Prince of Wales's Regiment of Horse, 1642-46. By Major Peter Young. [In *Society for Army Historical Research, Journal*, vol. 31, 1953, pp. 9-12]. 9¼"

Reconnaissance Regiment
This Band of Brothers. A History of the Reconnaissance Corps of the British Army. By Jeremy Taylor. Bristol: The White Swan Press Ltd., 1947. 271 pp., portraits, plates, maps. 7"

Wheeled Odyssey. The Story of the Fifth Reconnaissance Regiment, Royal Armoured Corps. [Edited by Lt.-Col. A. R. Prince]. No imprint, 1946. 68 pp., portraits, plates, maps. 7¼"

The Scottish Lion on Patrol; being the Story of the 15th Scottish Reconnaissance Regiment, 1943-1946. By Capt. W. Kemsley and Capt. M. R. Riesco. Bristol: The White Swan Press Ltd., 1950. 232 pp., portraits, plates, end-paper maps. 8½"

Welsh Spearhead; a History of the 53rd Reconnaissance Regiment, 1941-1946. By Major P. M. Cowburn. Solingen Ohligs: pr. by Wilhelm Muller. 1946. 192 pp., plates, maps. 8½"

Reserve Battalions, see under *Garrison*, above

Scots Brigade, see also 94th, *Scotch Brigade*, 1793-1818, above
An Historical Account of the British Regiments employed since the reign of Queen Elizabeth and King James I in the Formation of the Dutch Republic, particularly of the Scots Brigade. London: printed for T. Kay etc., 1795. viii, 102 pp. 8½"

Papers illustrating the History of The Scots Brigade in the Service of the United Netherlands, 1572-1782. Extracted by permission from the Government Archives at The Hague, and edited by James Ferguson. Edinburgh: printed at the University Press by T. & A. Constable, 1899: 1901. 3 vols. (Publications of the Scottish History Society, vols. 32, 35, 38). 8¾"
  Vol. 1. 1572-1697. Vol. 2. 1698-1782.
  Vol. 3. The Rotterdam Papers, 1709-82—The Remembrance; a Metrical Account of the War in Flanders, 1701-12, by John Scot, soldier.
  3 coloured plates of uniform and 1 of colours in vol. 3.

A Scots Brigade Flag for Amsterdam in 1930; being a Narrative of some Happenings old and new, concerning the Clan Mackay. By George Mackay. Stirling: Eneas Mackay [1931]. 32 pp., portrait, plates. 8½"

The Scots Brigade. [In *The Connaught Rangers;* by Lt.-Col. H. F. N. Jourdain and E. Fraser, vol. 2, pp. 5-95]. London: The Royal United Service Institution, 1926. Portrait, plates, maps. 9¾"

South Irish Horse
The 7th (South Irish Horse) Battalion. [In *The Campaigns and History of the Royal Irish Regiment*, vol. 2, From 1910 to 1922; by Brig.-Gen. S. Geoghegan]. Edinburgh: William Blackwood & Sons, 1927. 10″

Staff Corps, Royal
The Royal Staff Corps, 1800-1837. By Lt.-Col. F. S. Garwood. [In *The Royal Engineers Journal*, vol. 57, 1943, pp. 81-96, 247-260]. Chatham. Maps, plate, diagram. 9″

Veteran Battalions, see *Garrison Battalions*, above

Waggoners, Royal—Waggon Train, Royal
The Royal Waggoners, 1794-1795 and The Royal Waggon Corps and Train, 1799-1833. [In *The Predecessors of the Royal Army Service Corps;* by Lt.-Col. C. H. Massé, 1948, pp. 1-22]. Aldershot: Gale & Polden Ltd. Plates, illustrations. 9½″

COLONIAL

SECTION I—REGULAR

African Colonial Corps, Royal, 1822-40
For the history of this corps see *Records relating to the Gold Coast Settlements, from 1750 to 1874;* by J. J. Crooks, Major. Dublin: Browne & Nolan Ltd., 1923. 8¼″

African Corps, Royal
Historical Records of the Royal African Corps. By J. J. Crooks (Major). Dublin: Browne & Nolan Ltd., 1925. viii, 138 pp. 7¼″

Canadian Rifle Regiment, Royal
The Royal Canadian Rifle Regiment, 1840 to 1870. By Major G. Tylden. [In *Society for Army Hist. Res., Journal*, vol. 34, 1956, pp. 59-62]. Illustration. 9¼″

Cape Mounted Riflemen
History of the Cape Mounted Riflemen; with a Brief Account of the Colony of the Cape of Good Hope. London: John W. Parker, 1842. viii, 32 pp. (Cannon's Historical Records Series). 8¾″
   1 coloured plate of uniform and 1 of standards.

Boot and Saddle. A narrative record of the Cape Regiment, the British Cape Mounted Riflemen, etc. By P. J. Young. Cape Town: Maskew Miller Ltd., 1955. xiv, 193 pp., portraits, plate, sketch map. 8½″

Cape Regiments
The Cape Coloured Regular Regiments, 1793 to 1870. By Major G. Tylden. [In *Africana Notes and News*, vol. 7, 1950, pp. 37-59]. Johannesburg: Radford, Adlington Ltd., 1950. 9″   The Cape Mounted Rifles and predecessors.

Ceylon Regiments
The Ceylon Rifle Regiment.   By an Officer [Surg.-Gen. Henry Lionel Cowen].
[In *Colburn's United Service Magazine*, 1860, Pt. 3, pp. 323-337].   London:
Hurst & Blackett, 1860.   8½″

History of the Ceylon Garrison Artillery.   Colombo.   1927.

The Ceylon Regiments, 1796 to 1874.   By Major G. Tylden.   [In *Society for
Army Historical Research, Journal*, vol. 30, 1952, pp. 124-128].   Plates.   9¼″

Chinese Regiment
On Active Service with the Chinese Regiment.   A Record of the Operations of
the First Chinese Regiment in North China, from March to October, 1900.   By
Capt. A. A. S. Barnes.   London: Grant Richards.   1902.   xv, 228 pp., plates,
maps.   7″

Gold Coast Artillery Corps
For the history of this corps see *Records relating to the Gold Coast Settlements
from 1750 to 1874*.   By J. J. Crooks, Major.   Dublin: Browne & Nolan Ltd.,
1923.   8¼″

The Gold Coast Artillery Corps, 1851-63.   By Major J. J. Crooks.   (Reproduced
from *The Journal of the Royal Artillery*, vol. 38, 1912).   7 pp.   Woolwich:
Royal Artillery Institution.   9¼″

Malta Corps
History of the Royal Malta Artillery.   Abridged for use in Regimental Schools.
Valletta: Criterion Press, 1944.   40 pp.   8″

Historical Records of the Maltese Corps of the British Army.   Compiled by
Major A. G. Chesney, Adjutant, Royal Malta Regiment of Militia.   London:
William Clowes & Sons, Ltd., 1897.   xii, 210 pp., plates.   8¾″
   14 coloured plates of uniform and 3 of colours.

West African Regiment
The West African Regiment, 1898 to 1928.   By Major G. Tylden.   [In *Society
for Army Historical Research, Journal*, vol. 41, 1963, pp. 98-100; vol. 42, 1964,
pp. 100-102].   Plates.   9¼″

West India Regiments
The History of the First West India Regiment.   By A. B. Ellis, Major.   London:
Chapman & Hall Ltd., 1885.   xii, 366 pp., plates, maps.   8¾″
   2 coloured plates of uniform.

The 1st West India Regiment.   A Brief Historical Sketch.   By Col. A. R.
Loscombe.   London: The West India Committee [1905].   20 pp., illustrations.
9″×6¾″

One Hundred Years' History of the 2nd Batt. West India Regiment from date
of raising, 1795 to 1898.   Compiled by Col. J. E. Caulfeild.   London: Forster
Groom & Co., 1899.   222 pp., plates.   8½″

The West India Regiments.   [In *Her Majesty's Army: Indian & Colonial Forces;*
by Walter Richards, pp. 6-13].   London: J. S. Virtue & Co. Ltd., 1892.   11″
   Coloured plate of uniform.

The West India Regiments, 1795 to 1927, and from 1958.   By Major G. Tylden. [In *Society for Army Historical Research, Journal*, vol. 40, 1962, pp. 42-49]. Plates (1 coloured).   9¼″

West Indies Regiment, British
A Few Notes on the History of the British West Indies Regiment.   By Lt.-Col. C. Wood-Hill.   No imprint.   *n.d.*   11 pp.   8½″

The British West Indies Regiment in Jamaica's Part in the Great War, 1914-1918. By Frank Cundall, pp. 27-75.   London: Publ. by the West India Committee. 1925.   9¼″

SECTION II—FENCIBLES: PROVINCIALS

Butler's Rangers
The Story of Butler's Rangers and the Settlement of Niagara.   By Ernest Cruikshank.   Welland, Ont.: Tribune Printing Works, 1893.   114 pp.   (Lundy's Lane Historical Society).   8½″

War Out of Niagara: Walter Butler and the Tory Rangers.   [By] Howard Swiggett.   New York: Columbia University Press, 1933.   xxv, 309 pp., plates.   (New York State Historical Association Series, No. 2).   9″

Roger's Rangers
The History of Rogers Rangers.   By Burt Garfield Loescher.   With coloured plates by Helene Loescher.   San Francisco: [The Author].   1946.   Plates, illustrations, maps, end-paper map.   Vol. 1.   The Beginnings, Jan. 1755-April 6, 1758.   439 pp.   7″
   3 coloured plates of uniform.

Rogers' Rangers.   A History.   By Lieut.-Col. H. M. Jackson.   *No imprint.* [Ottawa] 1953.   [vii], 214 pp., portrait, map.   9″
   Contains also short accounts of
   The   Queen's Rangers, 1776-83.   The King's Rangers, 1779-83

Rogers Rangers and the French and Indian Wars.   By Bradford Smith.   New York: Random House, 1956.   vi, 184 pp., illustrations, map.   8¼″

Incidents in the early Military History of Canada, with Extracts from the Journals of the Officer Commanding the Queen's Rangers during the War 1755 to 1763. A Lecture . . . . by Lt.-Col. R. Z. Rogers.   [In *Canadian Military Institute, Selected Papers*, 1890-91, pp. 1-24].   Toronto.   8½″

Queen's Rangers
History of the Queen's Rangers.   By James Hannay.   [Reproduced from *Royal Society of Canada, Transactions*, vol. 2, pp. 123-186].   Ottawa: printed for the Royal Society of Canada, 1909.   9½″

The Queen's Rangers.   [By George H. Locke and Margaret Ray].   This pamphlet is issued in connection with the presentation of the colours of the Queen's Rangers to the Public Library of Toronto, by Mr. Frederick B. Robins of that city.   [Toronto].   [1924].   30 pp.   10″

The Queen's Rangers, 1st American Regiment. By Capt. H. M. Jackson. (Reprinted from *Bridle and Golfer*, October, 1933). *n.p.* 17 pp. 6"

———— [Another edition] [in *Society for Army Historical Research, Journal*, vol. 14, 1935, pp. 143-154]. Plate. 9¼"

The Queen's Rangers in the Revolutionary War. By the late Col. C. J. Ingles. Edited by Lt.-Col. H. M. Jackson. [Montreal: The Industrial Shops for the Deaf]. 1956. xii, 301 pp., plate, maps. 9"

The Queen's Rangers in Upper Canada, 1792 and after. By Lt.-Col. H. M. Jackson. [Montreal: Industrial Shops for the Deaf]. 1955. 117 pp. 6½"

A Brief Historical Sketch of the Queen's York Rangers, 1st American Regiment. Toronto: Fort York Armoury, 1942. 30 pp. 6"

King's Royal Regiment of New York
The King's Royal Regiment of New York. By Brig.-Gen. E. A. Cruikshank. [In *Ontario Historical Society, Papers and Records*, vol. 27, 1929, pp. 193-323]. Toronto. 9¼"

Loyalists in Arms; a short account of the " Provincial Troops," otherwise known as British American regiments or Loyalist Corps, 1775-1783 [&] Roll of Officers of the British American or Loyalist Corps. Compiled from the original Muster Rolls and arranged alphabetically by W. O. Raymond. [In *New Brunswick Historical Society, Collections*, No. 5, pp. 189-272]. St. John, N.B.: The Sun Printing Co. Ltd., 1904. 9"

Sketches illustrating the Early Settlement and History of Glengarry in Canada . . and the Services of the King's Own Royal Regiment of New York, the Royal Canadian Volunteer Regiment of Foot . . . The Glengarry Light Infantry Regiment, etc. By J. A. Macdonell (of Greenfield). Montreal: Wm. Foster, Brown & Co., 1893. 337 pp. 9¾"

The Royal Canadian Volunteers, 1794-1802. By J. L. Hubert Neilson, Surgeon Major. [In *V.R.I. Magazine;* published by the V.R.I. Club, Vol. 1, 1894-95, pp. 69-82, 111-121]. Montreal: printed by John Lovell & Son, 1895. 8"

The Canadian Fencibles. Records of the Services of the Canadian regiments in the War of 1812; by Lt.-Col. E. Cruikshank, Part 7. [In *Canadian Military Institute, Selected Papers*, No. 11, pp. 9-22]. Welland, Ontario: printed for the C.M.I. by The Tribune, 1901. 8¾"

The King's New Brunswick Regiment, 1793-1802. By Jonas Howe. [In *New Brunswick Historical Society, Collections*, vol. 1, 1894, pp. 13-62]. St. John, N.B. 9½"

The Royal Nova Scotia Regiment, 1793-1802. By Major George F. G. Stanley. [In *Society for Army Historical Research, Journal*, vol. 21, 1942, pp. 157-170]. 9¼"

The Glengarry Light Infantry. Records of the Services of the Canadian regiments in the War of 1812; by Capt. E. Cruikshank, Part 2. [In *Canadian Military Institute, Selected Papers*, No. 6, pp. 9-23]. Welland, Ontario: printed for the C.M.I. by The Tribune, 1895. 8¾"

Sketches illustrating the Early Settlement and History of Glengarry in Canada ... and the Services of ... The Glengarry Light Infantry Regiment, etc. By J. A. Macdonell (of Greenfield). Montreal: W. Foster, Brown & Co., 1893. 337 pp. 9¾"

Newfoundland Regiment, Royal
Skinner's Fencibles; The Royal Newfoundland Regiment, 1795-1802. By David A. Webber. St. John's, Newfoundland: Naval & Military Museum, 1964. viii, 82 pp., portraits, plates. 9¼"

The Royal Newfoundland Regiment. Records of the Services of Canadian regiments in the War of 1812; by Capt. E. Cruikshank, Part 1. [In *Canadian Military Institute, Selected Papers*, No. 5, pp. 5-15]. Welland, Ontario: printed for the C.M.I. by The Tribune, 1894. 8¾"

FOREIGN CORPS IN BRITISH PAY

The Huguenot Regiments. By Charles E. Lart. Reprint from the Proceedings of the Huguenot Society of London. Vol. 9, No. 3, 1912. London: Spottiswoode, Ballantyne & Co. Ltd., 1912. 54 pp. 8"

———— Supplementary Notes. By W. H. Manchee. Reprint from the Proceedings. Vol. 13, No. 4, 1927. 8 pp.

Die " legion britannique," 1760-62. Von C. A. Pentz von Schlichtegroll, Volsrade. Leipzig: Zentralstelle für Deutsche Personen- und Familiengeschichte, 1931. (Flugschriften für Familiengeschichte, Heft 20), 24 pp. 9¼"

Le Royal-Louis; Régiment à la solde de l'Angleterre levé au nom du Roi Louis XVII à Toulon, en 1793. Par A. Jacques Pares. Toulon: Imprimerie P. Beau & C. Mouton, 1927. (Société d'Etudes Scientifiques & Archeologiques de Draguignan, Mémoires, XVI). 64 pp., plan. 9½"

L'exil et la guerre. Les émigrés à cocarde noire, en Angleterre, dans les Provinces belges, en Hollande et à Quiberon. Par René Bittard des Portes. Paris: Emile Paul, editeur, 1908. vi, 638 pp. 9"

Les Corps de Troupe de l'Émigration Française (1789-1815). Par Vicomte Grouvel. Illustrations du Baron Louis de Beaufort. Paris: Editions de la Sabretache, 1957. 12½"
  Tome 1. Service de la Grande-Bretagne et des Pays-Bas. 374 pp., plates, illustrations.
  40 plates of uniform, uncoloured. 500 numbered copies.

Les troupes corses au service de l'Angleterre sous la Revolution et le Premier Empire, 1794-1817. Par le Vicomte Grouvel. [In *Cahiers d'Historie et de Documentation Corses*, Decembre 1950, pp. 235-267]. Grenoble: Imprimerie Allier, 1951. 9¼"

Foreign Artillery Corps in the British Service.   By Lieut.-Col. M. E. S. Laws.
[In *The Journal of the Royal Artillery*, vol. 65, pp. 356-367; vol. 73, pp. 250-260;
vol. 75, pp. 57-63].   1938-48. $9\frac{1}{4}''$
   No. 1.   The French Emigrant Artillery
   No. 2.   The Dutch Emigrant Artillery
   No. 3.   The Royal Foreign Artillery

Foreign Regiments in the British Army, 1793-1802.   By C. T. Atkinson.   [In
Society for Army Historical Research, Journal, vol. 21, pp. 175-181; vol. 22,
pp. 2-14, 45-52, 107-115, 132-142, 187-197, 234-250, 265-276, 313-324], 1942-44.
Plates. $9\frac{1}{4}''$
   General history, followed by brief accounts of the separate regiments.

Greek Light Infantry
Sir Richard Church, K.C.H. and the Greek Light Infantry, 1810 to 1816.   By
Major G. Tylden.   [In *Society for Army Historical Research, Journal*, vol. 41,
pp. 159-161; vol. 42, p. 100], 1963-64. $9\frac{1}{4}''$
   Coloured plate of uniform.

Meuron's Regiment
His Majesty's Regiment de Meuron.   By Julian James Cotton.   [In *The
Calcutta Review*.   Vol. 117, 1903, pp. 192-234].   Calcutta: The City Press. $9''$

His Majesty's Regiment de Meuron.   By Lieut.-Col. F. H. N. Davidson.
(Reprinted from the *Army Quarterly*, October 1936).   London: William Clowes &
Sons Ltd.   15 pp. $8\frac{1}{2}''$

Essai historique sur le régiment de Meuron.   Neuchâtel.   1885.

État nominatif des officiers qui ont servi dans le regiment de Meuron de 1781
à 1816.   Neuchâtel, 1886.

Roll's Regiment
Das Schweizerregiment von Roll in englischen Dienste, 1795 bis 1816.   Von
Oberstlieutenant Adolf Bürkli.   (88. Neujahrsblatt der Feuerwerker-Gesellschaft
(Artillerie-Collegium) in Zürich auf das Jahr 1893).   Zürich: Art. Institut Orell
Fussli.   [1893].   39 pp., map. $12''$

Watteville's Regiment
The Regiment de Watteville; its settlement and services in Upper Canada.   By
John D. P. Martin.   [In *Ontario History*, vol. 62, 1960].   Toronto: Ontario
Historical Society.   14 pp. $9\frac{1}{2}''$

Das Schweizerregiment von Wattenwyl in englischen Dienste, 1801 bis 1816.
Von Oberstlieutenant Adolf Bürkli.   (89. Neujahrsblatt der Feuerwerker-
Gesellschaft (Artillerie-Collegium) in Zürich auf das Jahr 1894).   Zürich: Art.
Institut Orell Fussli.   [1894].   36 pp., portrait. $12''$

York Light Infantry Volunteers
The York Light Infantry Volunteers, 1803 to 1917.   By Major G. Tylden [in
Society for Army Historical Research, Journal, vol. 39, 1961, pp. 140-142]. $9\frac{1}{4}''$
   Coloured plate of uniform.

King's German Legion
History of the King's German Legion.   By N. Ludlow Beamish, late Major.
London: Thomas and William Boone, 1832-37.   2 vols., plates, plans.   9″
   9 coloured plates of uniform (18 figures) in vol. 1.

———— Geschichte der königlich deutschen Legion.   Berlin: Verlag von H.
Barsdorf, 1906.   2te Auflage.   2 vols., plates, plans.
   18 coloured plates of uniform in vol. 1.   510 numbered copies.

Geschichte der Königlich Deutschen Legion, 1803-1816.   Von Bernhard Schwertfeger, Königlich Sächsischer Hauptmann, etc.   Hannover: Hahn'sche Buchhandlung, 1907.   2 vols., plates, illustrations, plans, maps.   9″
   19 coloured plates of uniform, similar to those in Beamish.

Des Königs deutsche Legion bis zur Schlacht bei Talavera, 28. Juli 1809.   Von B.
Ballauff.   Hannover: Verlag von Heinr. Feesche. 1909.   viii, 175 pp., portrait,
maps.   7½″

Die Königlich deutsche Legion, 1803-1816.   Volkstümlich dargestellt von Adolf
Pfannkuche.   Hannover: Helwingsche Verlagsbuchhandlung, 1926.   2te
durchgesehene u. erweiterte Auflage.   xv, 303 pp., portraits, illustrations, maps.
   1st edition was issued in 1910.

Des Königs Deutsche Legion 1803 bis 1816.   Darstellung ihrer inneren Ver-
hältnisse durch B. von Poten, Königlich Preuss.Oberst z.D.   Berlin: Ernst
Siegfried Mittler u. Sohn, 1906.   (Beiheft zum *Militär-Wochenblatt*, 1905,
Elftes Heft).   63 pp.   9¼″

Peninsula-Waterloo.   Zum Gedächtnis der Königlich Deutschen Legion.
Vortrag gehalten im Historischen Verein für Niedersachsen zu Hannover am 21.
Februar 1914 von B. Schwertfeger, Major.   Hannover: Hahnsche Buchhandlung,
1914.   36 pp., portraits, illustrations.   8½″

The Raising and Organizing of The King's German Legion [& other articles].
By Lt.-Col. R. E. F. G. North [& *others*] [In *Society for Army Historical Research*,
Journal, vol. 39, 1961, pp. 167-192].   Illustrations.   9¼″
   1 coloured plate of uniform.

British German Legion
The British German Legion, 1855-1856.   By Lieut.-Col. Arthur Egerton.   [In
Journal of the Royal United Service Institution, August, 1921].   London.   8 pp.,
plate.   9½″

Die britisch-deutsche Legion, 1855-57.   Von R. Wichmann.   Braunschweig.
1861.   110 pp.   8vo.

Unter Englands Fahnen zur Zeit des Krim-Krieges.   Von Th. R. von Oswiecinski.
Hannover, 1875.   2 vols., 8vo.   Vol. 2 contains an account of the formation of
German Military Settlers in South Africa.

Ten Years in South Africa. Only complete and authentic history of the British German Legion in South Africa and the East Indies. By Wm. Westphal. Chicago, 1892. 8vo.

For Men must Work. An account of German immigration to the Cape, with special reference to the German Military Settlers of 1857 and the German Immigration of 1858. Cape Town: Maskew Miller Ltd., 1954. 300 pp., plates. 8½"

British Swiss Legion
Histoire du service militaire des regiments suisses à la solde de l'Angleterre, de Naples et de Rome. Par Henri Ganter, ancien sous-officier au service étranger. Geneve: Ch. Eggimann & Cie. [*c*. 1890]. [Pp. 11-26 deal with The British Swiss Legion, 1854-56]. 1 coloured plate of uniform. 9½"

Die englische Schweizerlegion und ihr Aufenthalt in Orient. Von J. J. Romang. Langenau, Bern, 1857. 128 pp., plates. 8vo.

ROYAL MARINES

An Historical Review of the Royal Marine Corps, from its original Institution down to the Present Era, 1803. By Alexander Gillespie, First Lieut. Birmingham: M. Swinney. xvi, 402, 6 pp., plate. 10½"

Historical Record of the Royal Marine Forces. By Paul Harris Nicolas, Lieut. London: Thomas and William Boone, 1845. 2 vols. 9"

Historical Record of the Marine Corps, containing An Account of their Formation and Services from 1664 to 1748; at which period those corps ceased to form part of the Establishment of the Regular Army. From the year 1755 the present Corps of Royal Marines have been under the control of The Lords Commissioners of the Admiralty. Compiled by Richard Cannon, Esq., Adjutant-General's Office, Horse Guards. London: [Parker, Furnivall & Parker], 1850. xxxiv, 56 pp., plates. 8¾"

  1 coloured plate of uniform and 1 of colours.

  Issued as an Appendix to Cannon's 31st Foot and usually bound with it.

The Historical Records of the Royal Marines, including the Duke of York and Albany's Maritime Regiment of Foot, subsequently styled Prince George of Denmark's Maritime Regiment of Foot; the First and Second Regiments of Marines, afterwards known as Col. Thomas Brudenell's Regiment of Marines, Col. William Seymour's Regiment of Marines, Col. Henry Mordaunt's Regiment of Marines, and Col. Henry Dutton Colt's Regiment of Marines. Compiled and edited by Major L. Edye. London: Harrison & Sons Ltd., 1893. Vol. 1. 1664-1701. xxiv, 610, lxxv pp., portraits, plates, maps. 9¾"

  3 coloured plates of uniform and 2 of colours. No more published.

Britain's Sea Soldiers: a History of the Royal Marines and their Predecessors and of their Services in action, ashore and afloat, and upon sundry other occasions of moment. By Col. Cyril Field. With numerous illustrations and plans. Foreword by Admiral of the Fleet Earl Beatty. Liverpool: The Lyceum Press, 1924. 2 vols., portraits, plates, illustrations, plans, maps. 11″

   Vol. 1.   11 coloured plates, including 9 of uniform and 1 of colours.

   Vol. 2.   12 coloured plates of uniform, including 1 with colours.

Britain's Sea Soldiers. A Record of the Royal Marines during the War 1914-1919. Compiled by Gen. Sir H. E. Blumberg. Devonport: Swiss & Co. [1927]. xxiii, 492 pp., portraits, plates, plans, maps, maps in end-pocket. 11″

The Royal Marines. The Admiralty Account of their Achievement, 1939-1943. Prepared for the Admiralty by the Ministry of Information. London: H.M. Stationery Office, 1944. 80 pp., plates, illustrations, sketch maps. 8½″

Short History of the Royal Marines. By Col. G. W. M. Grover. Illustrated by Lieut.-Col. H. A. Bass. Aldershot: Gale & Polden Ltd., 1948. 68 pp., illustrations, map. 7¼″

——— 2nd edition. 1959. 98 pp. 7¼″

The Royal Marines. A Record of the Tour of Duty in London from 17th August to 19th September, 1935. Aldershot: Gale & Polden Ltd. [1935]. 24 pp., portraits, plates. 7¼″×9¾″
   Souvenir Album containing Roll and reproduction of photographs.

The Marines were there: the Story of the Royal Marines in the Second World War. [By] Sir Robert Bruce Lockhart. London: Putnam, 1950. viii, 229 pp., maps. 8½″

The Royal Marines, 1664-1964. By A. Cecil Hampshire. No imprint. 1964. 80 pp., portraits, illustrations (8 coloured) 8½″

The Story of 45 Royal Marine Commando. The history of the unit from its formation in August, 1943, until it returned from Germany in June, 1945. Published privately for members of the unit and their relations. [London: printed by McCorquodale & Co. Ltd., 1946]. 84 pp., plates, maps. 7¼″

The Story of 46 Commando Royal Marines. By Capt. P. K. W. Johnson. With a Foreword by Lieut.-Col. C. R. Hardy. Aldershot: Gale & Polden Ltd. [1946]. [xii], 56 pp., plates, maps. 7¼″

Haste to the Battle: a Marine Commando at War. By [Major-Gen.] J. L. Moulton. With a Preface by Gen. Sir Richard Gale. London: Cassell, 1963. xvi, 210 pp., portraits, plates, maps. 8½″
   The Story of 48 Royal Marine Commando.

Commando Men. The Story of a Royal Marine Commando [45] in North-West Europe. By Bryan Samain. London: Stevens & Sons Ltd., 1948. xv, 188 pp., portraits, plates, maps, end-paper maps. 8½″

A Short History of the Royal Marines in Deal. By A. D. H. Jones. [Deal: Mercury Printing Service], 1963. 23 pp., illustrations. 7¼″

The Royal Marine Artillery, 1804-1923. By Edward Fraser and L. C. Carr-Laughton. London: Royal United Service Institution, 1930. 2 vols., portraits, plates, plans, maps. 9¾″

Marine Gunner. Twenty-two years in the Royal Marine Artillery. By Patrick Mee. With an Introduction by Surg. Rear-Admiral T. T. Jeans. London: Jonathan Cape [1935]. 286 pp. 8″

BODY GUARDS

Gentlemen-at-Arms
Curialia: An Historical Account of some Branches of the Royal Household, etc., By Samuel Pegge. Vol. 1, consisting of Three Parts, viz.:
    II. An Account of the King's Honourable Band of Gentlemen Pensioners from its Establishment to the present Time. viii, 126 pp.
London: printed by J. Nichols, 1791. 10¾″

Regia Insignia; or An Account of the King's Honourable Band of Gentlemen Pensioners or Gentlemen at Arms. By W. M. Thiselton, Gentleman Pensioner in Ordinary to His Majesty. London: printed for Sherwood, Neely and Jones; and C. Chapple, 1819. [8], 284 pp. 8½″

Some Account of the Ancient Corps of Gentlemen-at-Arms. By James Bunce Curling, Clerk of the Cheque. London: Richard Bentley, 1850. vi, 266 pp., portrait. 8¼″

The Nearest Guard: a History of Her Majesty's Body Guard of the Honourable Corps of Gentlemen-at-Arms from their Institution in 1509 to the year 1892. By Major Henry Brackenbury. London: Harrison & Sons, 1892. vi, 242 pp., plates. 11¾″
    2 coloured plates of uniform.

———— [Another edition with title] The History of His Majesty's Body Guard of the Honourable Corps of Gentlemen-at-Arms, "The Nearest Guard" of the Sovereign and the Principal Military Corps of His Household. By Major Henry Brackenbury. London: Harrison & Sons, 1905. iv, 255 pp., plates, illustrations. 8¾″

His Majesty's Bodyguard of the Honourable Corps of Gentlemen-at-Arms. [By] Brig.-Gen. Harvey Kearsley. London: John Murray. [1937]. xiv, 314 pp., portraits, plates. 8¾″
    1 coloured plate of uniform and 1 of standard.

The Spears of Honour and The Gentlemen Pensioners. By John Glas Sandeman. Hayling Island: Robert Higginbottom, printer, 1912. 34 pp. 9¾″

———— Facsimiles of the Ordinances and Statutes of the Spears of Honour, 1509, and the Oath and Articles of the Gentlemen Pensioners, 1600, being a copy of that drawn up in the time of Henry VIII (1540). 22 facsimiles. 1912. folio.

Yeomen of the Guard
Curialia: or An Historical Account of some Branches of the Royal Household, etc.   By Samuel Pegge.   Vol. 1, consisting of Three Parts, viz. . .
III.   Account of the Yeomen of the King's Guard, from the date of its Institution.   135 pp.   London: printed by J. Nichols, 1791.   10¾"

Some Account of the Royal Body Guard entitled the Ancient Corps of the Yeomen of the Guard, instituted 1485.   With a brief notice of the Warders of the Tower.   By Thomas Smith.   London: W. W. Wright, 1852.   [iv], 47 pp.   7¼"

The Yeomen of the Guard; their History from 1485 to 1885.   And a Concise Account of the Tower Warders.   By Thomas Preston.   London: Harrison & Sons.   [1885].   198 pp., plates, illustrations.   7½"
    1 coloured portrait in uniform.

——— 2nd edition.   London: Whitaker & Co. [1887].   198 pp., plates, illustrations.   7½"
    3 coloured plates of uniform.

The History of The King's Body Guard of the Yeomen of the Guard (Velecti Garde Domini Regis), the Oldest Permanent Body Guard of the Sovereigns of England, 1485 to 1904.   By Col. Sir Reginald Hennell, Lieutenant.   Westminster: Archibald Constable & Co., Ltd., 1904.   xvi, 344 pp., portraits, plates, illustrations.   11¼"
    3 coloured plates of uniform.

Military Knights of Windsor
A Short History of the Military Knights of Windsor.   By Capt. J. C. Coley-Bromfield.   Windsor: Messrs. Oxley & Son Ltd., 1916.   61 pp., portrait, plates.   7¼"
    1 coloured plate of uniform.

The Military Knights of Windsor, 1352-1944.   By Edmund H. Fellowes, Minor Canon of Windsor.   Windsor: printed and published for the Dean and Canons of St. George's Chapel in Windsor Castle by Oxley and Son (Windsor) Ltd.   [1944].   lv, 140 pp.   8½"
    A Roll of the Knights, with biographical details and General Introduction.

Royal Company of Archers
The History of the Royal Company of Archers, The Queen's Body-Guard for Scotland.   By James Balfour Paul.   Published under the Authority and by Direction of the Council.   Edinburgh: William Blackwood and Sons, 1875.   x, 393 pp., portraits, plates.   9¾"
    6 coloured portraits in uniform.

The Royal Company of Archers, 1676-1951.   By Ian Hay (Major Gen. John Hay Beith).   Edinburgh: William Blackwood & Sons Ltd., 1951.   x, 299 pp., portraits, plates (4 coloured).   9¾"

APPENDIX

Showing present day titles of Regiments

Present day (1965) *title*	*Former title before amalgamation or redesignation*
1st The Queen's Dragoon Guards	1st King's Dragoon Guards The Queen's Bays (2nd Dragoon Guards)
The Queen's Own Hussars	3rd The King's Own Hussars 7th Queen's Own Hussars
The Queen's Royal Irish Hussars	4th Queen's Own Hussars 8th King's Royal Irish Hussars
9th/12th Royal Lancers (Prince of Wales's)	9th Queen's Royal Lancers 12th Royal Lancers (Prince of Wales's)
The Queen's Royal Surrey Regiment	The Queen's Royal Regiment (West Surrey) The East Surrey Regiment
The Queen's Own Buffs, The Royal Kent Regiment	The Buffs (Royal East Kent Regiment) The Queen's Own Royal West Kent Regiment
The King's Own Royal Border Regiment	The King's Own Royal Regiment (Lancaster) The Border Regiment
The Royal Warwickshire Fusiliers	The Royal Warwickshire Regiment
The King's Regiment (Manchester and Liverpool)	The King's Regiment (Liverpool) The Manchester Regiment

The Royal Anglian Regiment
  1st (Royal Norfolk and Suffolk) Bn.
  2nd (Duchess of Gloucester's Own Royal Lincolnshire and Northamptonshire) Bn.
  3rd (16th/44th Foot) Bn.
 	
  4th (Royal Leicestershire) Bn.
	The Royal Norfolk Regiment
	The Suffolk Regiment
	The Royal Lincolnshire Regiment
	The Northamptonshire Regiment
	
	The Bedfordshire and Hertfordshire Regiment
	The Essex Regiment
	The Royal Leicestershire Regiment

The Devonshire and Dorset Regiment	The Devonshire Regiment The Dorset Regiment
The Somerset and Cornwall Light Infantry	The Somerset Light Infantry (Prince Albert's) The Duke of Cornwall's Light Infantry

The Prince of Wales's Own Regiment of Yorkshire

The West Yorkshire Regiment (The Prince of Wales's Own)
The East Yorkshire Regiment (The Duke of York's Own)

The Royal Highland Fusiliers (Princess Margaret's Own Glasgow and Ayrshire Regiment)

The Royal Scots Fusiliers
The Highland Light Infantry (City of Glasgow Regiment)

The Lancashire Regiment (Prince of Wales's Volunteers)

The East Lancashire Regiment
The South Lancashire Regiment (The Prince of Wales's Volunteers)

The Staffordshire Regiment (The Prince of Wales's)

The South Staffordshire Regiment
The North Staffordshire Regiment (The Prince of Wales's)

The Duke of Edinburgh's Royal Regiment (Berkshire and Wiltshire)

The Royal Berkshire Regiment (Princess Charlotte of Wales's)
The Wiltshire Regiment (Duke of Edinburgh's)

Queen's Own Highlanders (Seaforth and Cameron)

Seaforth Highlanders (Ross-shire Buffs, The Duke of Albany's)
The Queen's Own Cameron Highlanders

1st Green Jackets, 43rd and 52nd

The Oxfordshire and Buckinghamshire Light Infantry

2nd Green Jackets, The King's Royal Rifle Corps

The King's Royal Rifle Corps

3rd Green Jackets, The Rifle Brigade

The Rifle Brigade (Prince Consort's Own)

ADDENDUM

SECTION I

GENERAL

The Standards and Colours of the Army from the Restoration 1661 to the introduction of the Territorial System 1881. By Samuel Milne. xxiii, 267 pp., 29 plates (16 in colour), 57 illustrations. Leeds: for the subscribers by Goodall and Suddick, 1893. 200 numbered copies only.

British Regiments 1914–1918. By E. A. James. London: Samson Books, 1978. 140 pp.

Welsh Regiments. By John W. Fortescue. London: Macmillan & Co., 1915. 12 pp. 8¾in.

The Army of India Medal Roll 1799–1826. By R. W. Gould and Capt. K. J. Douglas-Morris, RN. 123 pp.

Ashanti 1895–95. By Ian McInnes and Mark Fraser. 156 pp. A complete roll of all who received the Ashanti Star.

British Army Collar Badges, 1881 to the present. By Colin Churchill and Ray Westlake. 1986.

British Regiments. 1914–18. By Brigadier E. A. James, OBE, TD. 1978. 140 pp.

Casualties Sustained by the British Army in the Korean War 1950–53. 85 pp. Lists of killed, wounded and missing by regiments.

Casualty Roll for the Crimea 1854–1855. By F. & A. Cook. 1976. 269 pp. 21 plates.

Casualty Roll for the Zulu and Basuto Wars South Africa 1877–79. Compiled by I. T. Tavender. 53 pp.

Collecting Metal Shoulder Titles. By R. A. Westlake. 1980. 187 pp. Details of shoulder titles worn by over 1200 units. More than 1850 illustrations. Lineage of every unit.

The Distinguished Conduct Medal 1914–1920 Citations. In 77 parts.

1	RFC/RAF	6	The Queen's
1X	Royal Artillery	7	The Buffs
2	Foot Guards	8	The King's Own
3	Yeomanry	9	The Northumberland Fusiliers
4	Cavalry	10	The Royal Warwickshire Regiment
5	The Royal Scots	11	The Royal Fusiliers

12 The King's Regiment
13 The Norfolk Regiment
14 The Lincolnshire Regiment
15 The Devonshire Regiment
16 The Suffolk Regiment
17 Prince Albert's (Somerset Light Infantry)
18 The Prince of Wales's Own (West Yorkshire Regiment)
19 The East Yorkshire Regiment
20 The Beds. & Herts. Regiment
21 The Leicestershire Regiment
22 The Royal Irish Regiment
23 Alexandra Princess of Wales's Own (Yorkshire Regiment)
24 The Lancashire Fusiliers
25 The Royal Scots Fusiliers
26 The Cheshire Regiment
27 The Royal Welsh Fusiliers
28 The South Wales Borderers
29 The King's Own Scottish Borderers
30 The Cameronians
31 The Royal Inniskilling Fusiliers
32 The Gloucestershire Regiment
33 The Worcestershire Regiment
34 The East Lancashire Regiment
35 The East Surrey Regiment
36 The Duke of Cornwall's Light Infantry
37 The Duke of Wellington's West Riding Regiment
38 The Border Regiment
39 The Royal Sussex Regiment
40 The Hampshire Regiment
41 The South Staffordshire Regiment
42 The Dorsetshire Regiment
43 The Prince of Wales's Volunteers (South Lancashire Regiment)
44 The Welch Regiment
45 The Black Watch
46 The Oxfordshire and Buckinghamshire Light Infantry

47 The Essex Regiment
48 The Sherwood Foresters (Nottinghamshire And Derbyshire Regiment)
50 The Loyal North Lancashire Regiment
51 The Northamptonshire Regiment
52 Princess Charlotte of Wales's (Royal Berkshire Regiment)
53 The Queen's Own
54 The King's Own Yorkshire Light Infantry
55 The King's Shropshire Light Infantry
56 The Duke of Cambridge's Own (Middlesex Regiment)
57 The King's Royal Rifle Corps
58 The Duke of Edinburgh's (Wiltshire Regiment)
59 The Manchester Regiment
60 The Prince of Wales's (North Staffordshire Regiment)
61 The York and Lancaster Regiment
62 The Durham Light Infantry
63 The Highland Light Infantry
64 The Seaforth Highlanders
65 The Gordon Highlanders
66 The Queen's Own Cameron Highlanders
67 The Royal Irish Rifles
68 Princess Victoria's (Royal Irish Fusiliers)
69 The Connaught Rangers
70 Princess Louise's (Argyll and Sutherland Highlanders)
71 The Prince of Wales's Leinster Regiment
72 The Royal Munster Fusiliers
73 The Royal Dublin Fusiliers
74 The Rifle Brigade
75 Territorial Regiments (includes all London Regiments), 2 *volumes*
76 Royal Engineers

For Bravery in the Field. The roll of the recipients of the Military Medal from 1919–1991. By C. K. Bate and M. G. Smith. Bayonet Publications. 550 pp. Approx. 40 illustrations. 10in.

India General Service Medal 1895 Casualty Roll. By Anthony Farrington.

Korea 1950–1953, Prisoners of War, the British Army. By Peter Gaston. 28 pp.

Lineage Book of British Land Forces 1660–1978. By J. B. M. Frederick. xxxvi, 1058 pp (2 vols).The origins and subsequent biographical outlines of every land unit of the regular and reserve forces that has ever appeared in the lists of the British Army. 11¼in.

The Military General Service Roll, 1793–1814, Edited by A. L. T. Mullen. 728 pp. 11¾in. London Stamp Exchange 1990.

The Old Contemptibles Honours and Awards: Officers and Men of the Naval and Military Forces of Great Britain and the Empire Mentioned in Despatches with Related Honours and Awards 1914–1915. First published 1915 Army and Navy Gazette. Second edition published 1971 as 'Honours and Awards of the Old Contemptibles.' Amended edition J. B. Hayward 1991. 69 pp.

Regimental Medals Handbook 1745–1895, Vol 1: Regular Army. By J. L. Balmer. Loughborough: Langlands Edition, 1987. 96 pp. Card covers. Numbered catalogue of all medals awarded at regimental level and below. 8¼in.

Regimental & Volunteer Medals 1745–1895, Vol 1: Regular Army. By Major J. L. Balmer. Loughborough: Langlands Edition, 1988. 309 pp., illustrated. Catalogue numbered record of all medals awarded at regimental level and below to make up for lack of government recognition before the middle of the 19th century. Copious footnotes. Also a Subscribers' edition individually named and numbered and quarter leather bound. 10in.

Regiments and Corps of the British Army. By I. S. Hallows. Arms & Armour Press. 1991. 320 pp. Single-source reference to the British regiments and their history, including battle honours, marches, dress, anniversaries and other historical background. Line drawings of every cap badge.

The Second Afghan War 1878–1880. Casualty Roll. By Anthony Farrington. 180 pp.

Shoulder-Belt Plates and Buttons. By Major H. C. Parkyn. 349 pp. A record of some of the many changes in the design of the shoulder-belt plates and buttons worn by the British Regular Army. Each regiment has a page of drawings to illustrate changes and details of regimental title changes, badges and Battle Honours authorized from 1802 to 1855.

Soldiers Died in the Great War 1914–1918. HMSO. 1921. 80 Parts in 74 casebound volumes. Facsimile reprint.

1	Household Cavalry and Cavalry of the Line (including Yeomanry and Imperial Camel Corps)	Artillery Company Batteries), Royal Garrison Artillery
2 & 3	Royal Horse and Royal Field Artillery, Regulars and Territorial Force (including Honourable	4 Corps of Royal Engineers
		5 Foot Guards (including Guards Machine Gun Regiment)
		6 The Royal Scots (Lothian Regiment)

7   The Queen's (Royal West Surrey Regiment)
8   The Buffs (East Kent Regiment)
9   The King's Own (Royal Lancaster Regiment)
10   The Northumberland Fusiliers
11   The Royal Warwickshire Regiment
12   The Royal Fusiliers (City of London Regiment)
13   The King's (Liverpool Regiment)
14   The Norfolk Regiment
15   The Lincolnshire Regiment
16   The Devonshire Regiment
17   The Suffolk Regiment
18   Prince Albert's (Somerset Light Infantry)
19   The Prince of Wales's Own (West Yorkshire Regiment)
20   The East Yorkshire Regiment
21   The Bedfordshire Regiment
22   The Leicestershire Regiment
23 & 32   The Royal Irish Regiment, The Royal Inniskilling Fusiliers
24   Alexandra Princess of Wales's Own (Yorkshire Regiment)
25   The Lancashire Fusiliers
26   The Royal Scots Fusiliers
27   The Cheshire Regiment
28   The Royal Welsh Fusiliers
29   The South Wales Borderers
30   The King's Own Scottish Borderers
31   The Cameronians (Scottish Rifles)
32   The Royal Inniskilling Fusiliers— See Part 23
33   The Gloucestershire Regiment
34   The Worcestershire Regiment
35   The East Lancashire Regiment
36   The East Surrey Regiment
37   The Duke of Cornwall's Light Infantry
38   The Duke of Wellington's (West Riding Regiment)
39   The Border Regiment
40   The Royal Sussex Regiment
41   The Hampshire Regiment
42   The South Staffordshire Regiment
43   The Dorsetshire Regiment
44   The Prince of Wales's Volunteers (South Lancashire Regiment)
45   The Welch Regiment

46   The Black Watch (Royal Highlanders)
47   The Oxfordshire and Buckinghamshire Light Infantry
48   The Essex Regiment
49   The Sherwood Foresters (Nottinghamshire and Derbyshire Regiment)
50   The Loyal North Lancashire Regiment
51   The Northamptonshire Regiment
52   Princess Charlotte of Wales's (Royal Berkshire Regt)
53   The Queen's Own (Royal West Kent Regiment)
54   The King's Own (Yorkshire Light Infantry)
55   The King's (Shropshire Light Infantry)
56   The Duke of Cambridge's Own (Middlesex Regiment)
57   The King's Royal Rifle Corps
58   The Duke of Edinburgh's (Wiltshire Regiment)
59   The Manchester Regiment
60   The Prince of Wales's (North Staffordshire Regiment)
61   The York and Lancaster Regiment
62   The Durham Light Infantry
63   The Highland Light Infantry
64   The Seaforth Highlanders (Ross-shire Buffs, The Duke of Albany's)
65   The Gordon Highlanders
66   The Queen's Own (Cameron Highlanders)
67–69   The Royal Irish Rifles, Princess Victoria's (Royal Irish Fusiliers), The Connaught Rangers
70   Princess Louise's (Argyll and Sutherland Highlanders)
71–73   The Prince of Wales's Leinster Regiment (Royal Canadians), The Royal Munster Fusiliers, The Royal Dublin Fusiliers
74   The Rifle Brigade (The Prince Consort's Own)
75   Machine Gun Corps, Tank Corps
76   The London Regiment, Honourable Artillery Company (Infantry), Inns of Court Officers Training Corps
77   The Monmouthshire Regt, The

Cambridgeshire Regt, The Hertford-
shire Regt, The Herefordshire Regt,
Army Cyclists Corps, The Northern
Cyclist Battalion, The Highland
Cyclists Battalion, The Kent Cyclist
Battalion, The Huntingdonshire
Cyclist Battalion, Royal Defence
Corps
78 Royal Army Service Corps
79 Royal Army Medical Corps
80 Labour Corps, Royal Army Ord-

nance Corps, Royal Army Veteri-
nary Corps, Royal Army Pay Corps,
Corps of Army Schoolmasters,
Channel Island Militia, Corps of
Military Mounted Police, Corps of
Military Foot Police, Corps of the
Small Arms School, Military Provost
Staff Corps, Non- Combattant
Corps, Queen Mary's Army Auxil-
iary Corps

Soldiers Killed on the First Day of the Somme. By Ernest W. Bell. 212 pp.

The South Africa 1853 Medal. By G. R. Everson. 160 pp.

The South African War Casualty Roll: Natal Field Force 20 October 1888—26
October 1900. 237 pp.

The South African War Casualty Roll. The South African Field Force 4th October
1899—June 1902. 782 pp.

The Victoria Cross Roll of Honour, compiled by James W. Bancroft. 123 pp.

The Zulu Rebellion of 1906. Roberts Medals Publications Ltd 1990. vi, 141 pp. A
revised edition of Donald R. Forsyth's original 'Medal Roll For The Zulu Rebellion' published in 1976.

GENERAL WORKS: SCOTTISH

A Short History of Scottish Regiments. By A. W. Keith, Private (retired). The
Highland Light Infantry. Cupar, Fife: J. & G. Innes Ltd., 1935. 35 pp. Humorous
sketches. 7¼in.

The Highland Regiments: Tigers in Tartan. By W. P. Paul. Aberdeen: Impulse
Books, 1971. 221 pp., illustrations.

The Lowland Regiments: Lions Rampant. By W. P. Paul. Aberdeen: Impulse
Publications, 1972. 186 pp., illustrations.

SECTION II

REGULAR ARMY

HOUSEHOLD BRIGADE

The Household Brigade: a pictorial record. London: Pitkin Pictorials Ltd., 1966, 24 pp. portraits, illustrations (many coloured). 9in.

The Standards, guidons and colours of the Household Division 1660–1973. By N. P. Dawney. London: Midas Books, 1975. 272 pp., illustrations. 9¾in.

All the Queens Men: The Household Cavalry and the Brigade of Guards. London: Hamish Hamilton, 1977. 288 pp., illustrations. 9½in.

HOUSEHOLD CAVALRY

The King's Guards: (being a Fighting History of the Household Cavalry). By R. Power Berrey. London: J. Nisbet & Co. 1903. v, 244 pp. 7¼in.

The Household Cavalry Brigade in the Waterloo Campaign. By Capt. Sir Morgan Crofton, Bart. Coloured frontispiece of uniform and folding map. London: Sifton Praed. 1912, 52 pp.

Short history of the Corps of Household Cavalry. The Life Guards and the Blues and Royals (Royal Horse Guards and 1st Dragoons). London: Lowe. *n.d.* [*c.* 1970] 13 pp. 9in.

THE LIFE GUARDS

War Diary of the 1st Life Guards, First Year 1914–1915, 88 pp., frontispiece and a map, 4to, 1919.

ROYAL HORSE GUARDS (THE BLUES)

Royal Horse Guards (The Blues). Club Register. Contains History of the Club. Early history of The Blues (1650–1660). Printed by Service Publications Ltd., Shoreham-by-Sea. 1966. 48 pp. 8¾in.

Royal Horse Guards. (The Blues). By R. J. T. Hills. London: Leo Cooper, 1970. 117 pp., illustrations. 8¾in.

ROYAL ARMOURED CORPS

The Royal Armoured Corps. By J. R. W. Murland. London: Methuen, 1943. viii, 106 pp. illustrations.

The Royal Armoured Corps. By Frank Owen. London. HMSO. 1945. 70 pp., illustrations. 9ins.

Welsh Spearhead. 53rd Reconnaissance Regiment 1941–46, Solingen-Ohligs, February 1946.

QUEEN'S DRAGOON GUARDS

The Queen's Dragoon Guards, by E. Belfield. 1978, 114 pp.

3rd CARABINIERS
(PRINCE OF WALES'S DRAGOON GUARDS)

I Serve: Regimental History of the 3rd Carabiniers (Prince of Wales's Dragoon Guards). By Lt. Col. L. B. Oatts. Chester: 3rd Carabiniers 1966, illustrations. 9¾in.

4th/7th ROYAL DRAGOON GUARDS

A History of the 4th/7th Royal Dragoon Guards and their Predecessors 1685–1980. By J. M. Brereton. Catterick: 4/7 Dragoon Gds, 1982. 494 pp., illustrations, maps. 9¾in.

5th ROYAL INNISKILLING DRAGOON GUARDS

First in Last Out. By J. Pilborough, illustrations by G. W. Sawtrell, 1947.

5TH (PRINCESS CHARLOTTE OF WALES'S)
DRAGOON GUARDS

The Green Horse in Ladysmith: First In Last Out. [Also large paper edition limited to 100 numbered copies.] By J. Pilborough. 1947. 100 pp., plates.

6th DRAGOON GUARDS (THE CARABINIERS)

Extracts from Regimental History of 'The Carabiniers', privately published, *c.* 1911, 12 pp., 6¾in. [Bound with Presentation of Standard, 1906].

1st THE ROYAL DRAGOONS

Short History of the Royal Dragoons. Ipoh: Granier, 1960, 28 pp., 6¾in.

The Royal Dragoons. By R. J. T. Hills. London: L. Cooper, 1972. vi, 109 pp., illustrations. 8¼in.

Attack the Colour! The Royal Dragoons in the Peninsula and at Waterloo. By A. E. Clark-Kennedy. London: Research Publishing Co., 1975. 158 pp., maps, illustrations. 9¾in.

THE ROYAL SCOTS GREYS (2nd DRAGOONS)

The Royal Scots Greys. South Africa 1899–1901. By Sgt. J. McElligott, Royal Scots Greys. Edinburgh: Banks and Co., for the Regiment. 32 pp., *n.d.*, *c.*1901.

Romance of the Greys. London: Drapkin, 1910, 32 pp., illustrations. 19in.

The History and Traditions of the Royal Scots Greys. Privately published for the Regiment, *n.d.* [*c.* 1967], 17 pp., illustrations. 8¾in.

The Royal Scots Greys. By Michael Blacklock. London: L. Cooper, 1971. vi, 126 pp., illustrations. 8¼in.

Royal Scots Greys. By Charles Grant. Reading (Berks): Osprey Publishing, 1972. 40 pp., illustrations. 9¾in.

4th QUEEN'S OWN HUSSARS

Historical records of the Fourth, or, The Queen's Own Regiment of Light Dragoons: containing an account of the formation of the regiment in 1685, and of its subsequent services to 1842. By Richard Cannon. London: John W. Parker 1843. xvi, 115 pp., illustrations.

A Short History of the IV Queen's Own Hussars. — another edition. Gives history up to 1925. Meerut: The Pathek Machine Printing Press. 1925. 92 pp. 5½in.

Irish Hussars. By Maj.-Gen. J. M. Strawson, Brig. H. T. Pierson and Brig. R. J. Rhoderick-Jones. London: The Queen's Royal Irish Hussars Association. 1986. 234 pp., illustrations, maps. 8¾in.

4th Hussar. The Story of the 4th Queen's Own Hussars 1685–1958, by D. S. Daniell. 1959, 416 pp.

7th QUEEN'S OWN HUSSARS

A short history of the Seventh Queen's Own Hussars from 1689 to 1932. Aldershot: Gale & Polden, 1932. 58 pp., illustrations.

7th Hussars. The Dress Distinctions of the 7th Queen's Own Hussars as worn at the time of the amalgamation of the regiment in 1758. 1 pp. and 10 pp. of uniform details. Cambridge: Langbridge, 1959, oblong 4to.

The 7th Queen's Own Hussars. By J. M. Brereton. London: Leo Cooper, 1975. 221 pp., illustrations, 8¾in.

8th KING'S ROYAL IRISH HUSSARS

8th Hussars. The Dress Distinctions of the 8th King's Royal Hussars. Details as above. Cambridge: Langbridge, 1959, oblong 4to.

10th ROYAL HUSSARS (PRINCE OF WALES'S OWN)

The 10th Royal Hussars. By M. Brander. London: Leo Cooper, 1970. 137 pp., illustrations. 8¾in.

11th HUSSARS (PRINCE ALBERT'S OWN)

The Eleventh at War, being the Story of the XI Hussars (Prince Albert's Own) through the years 1934–1945. By Dudley Clarke. Index, coloured frontispiece and 33 illustrations London: Joseph, 1952, 504 pp., illustrations. 9in.

11th Hussars Prince Albert's Own 'The Cherrypickers'. London: Page, *n.d.* [*c.* 1963], 104 pp., illustrations. 8¾in.

The 11th Hussars. By R. Brett Smith. London: Leo Cooper 1970. 325 pp., illustrations. 8¾in.

12th ROYAL LANCERS (PRINCE OF WALES'S)

12th Lancers. History of the XII Royal Lancers (Prince of Wales's). Also 2 volume edition. xvi, x, 516 pp., 13 plates (9 in colour).

13th/18th ROYAL HUSSARS (QUEEN MARY'S OWN)

13th/18th Hussars. 13th Hussars from Marseilles to Baghdad June 1916 to March 1917. [Lt. Col. J. J. Richardson?] Privately [c. 1917].

14th/20th KING'S HUSSARS

Emperor's Chambermaids: The Story of the 14th/20th King's Hussars. By Lt. Col. L. B Oatts. London: Ward Lock, 1973. 518 pp., illustrations, maps. 9½in.

15th/19th THE KING'S ROYAL HUSSARS

A Short History of the 15th/19th The King's Royal Hussars. Compiled by Major J. S. F. Murray. Aldershot: The Forces Press, 1964. viii, 81 pp. Plates. 4 coloured plates of uniform and 1 of guidon. 8¼in.

The History of the 15/19 The King's Royal Hussars 1945–1980. By J. Bastin. Chichester: Keats House, 1981. 165 pp., illustrations, maps. 9¾in.

16th/5th THE QUEEN'S LANCERS

History of the 16th, The Queen's Light Dragoons (Lancers) 1912–1925. By Henry Graham. Devizes: privately printed, 1926. xi, 148 pp., illustrations, maps.

A short history of the 16th/5th Lancers. By H. G. Parkyn. Aldershot: Gale & Polden, 1934. ix, 72 pp., illustrations, maps.

16th/5th The Queen's Royal Lancers. By Major General Sir James Lunt. London: L. Cooper, 1973. xviii, 82 pp., illustrations. 8¼in.

5th Royal (Irish Lancers) Lancers in South Africa 1899–1902, a facsimile reprint drawn from 'The Historical Records of the Fifth (Royal Irish) Lancers, from their Foundation As Wynne's Dragoons (in 1689) To The Present Day' by Walter Temple Willcox, 1908. With a biographical sketch of Colonel Scott Chisholme. A list of Officers and men of the 5th Lancers who were killed, died of disease, and were wounded during the defence of Ladysmith, also an extensive list of officers who have served in the regiment. 108 pp., 2 illustrations and folding maps. York, *c*.1977. Edition limited to 400 copies.

17th/21st LANCERS

17th/21st Lancers ('The Death or Glory Boys')—second edition 1903. viii, 384 pp., 8 plates.

The 17th/21st Lancers. By R. L. V. ffrench Blake. London: Hamish Hamilton, 1968, 173 pp., illustrations. 8½in.

A short history the 17th/21st Lancers. Viersen, Germany: 15 Comp. Ord. Dept, 1975. 6 pp., illustrations. 7¾in.

ROYAL TANK REGIMENT: ROYAL TANK CORPS

A Brief History of No. 24 (Tank Corps) Officer Cadet Battalion. Compiled from Unit Records. Winchester: printed by Warrer & Sons, 1919, 67 pp., plates. 8¼in.

42nd Royal Tank Regiment 1938–1944, roneo/cyclostyled, 37 pp., 7 maps, printed paper wrappers, Clapham Junction, 1951.

The 'Fourth' Royal Tank Regiment. Short History. Celle, Germany: printed by Aug. Linnemann, 1959, oblong sheet folded making 6 pp. uncut. 5in.

To the Green Fields Beyond: a short history of the Royal Tank Regiment. By Kenneth Macksey. London: Royal Tank Regt, 1 Elverton St., S.W.1 1965, x, 92, xvipp., portrait, illustrations, maps. 7in.

A History of the 44th Royal Tank Regiment in the War of 1939–45. 6th Battn. Gloucestershire Regt. up to 1939. Brighton: 44th R.T.R. Association, 1966, xi, 214 pp. maps, plate, 8½in.

Seconds Out! A History of the 2nd Royal Tank Regiment. 2 volumes, 136 pp. and 133 pp. Vol I—1st Round, W.W.I. Vol II—2nd Round, W.W.II. Plates, small folio, roneo/cyclostyled, printed paper wrappers, *c*.1967.

The Royal Tank Regiment. By Kenneth Chadwick. London: L. Cooper, 1970, vi, 158 pp., illustrations. 8¼in.

50th Royal Tank Regiment: the story of a regiment. 50 R.T.R. Old Comrades' Association, 1981, 44 pp., maps.

50th Royal Tank Regiment: the story of a regiment. 50 R.T.R. Old Comrade's Association, 1982, 32 pp. maps.

The Tank Corps Honours and Awards 1916–1919. Midland Medals. vi, 401 pp. Originally published in 1919 as 'The Tank Corps Book of Honour' this edition omits data not of interest to medal collectors, but includes a short history of the Tank Corps.

ROYAL REGIMENT OF ARTILLERY

History of the Royal Regiment of Artillery. By Gen. Sir M. Farndale. London: The Royal Artillery Institute, 1986. 421 pp., illustrations, maps. 10¼in.

History of the Royal Regiment of Artillery. The Forgotten Fronts and the Home Base, 1914–1918. By Gen. Sir Martin Farndale. 1988. 505 pp. 53 illustrations, 82 maps.

The Relief of Ladysmith: The Artillery in Natal, Colenso, Spion Kop, Vaal Krantz and Pieter's Hill. By Capt. C. H. Wilson. London: Wm. Clowes & Sons, 1901, 114 pp., maps. 7¼in.

A Short History of 'S' Battery 1826–1926, 31 pp. plus Officers who served in 'S' Battery. 1926.

11th (City of London Yeomanry) Light Anti-Aircraft Regiment R.A., a diary of the regiment during the North African and Italian Campaigns. Oderse, 1945, 45 pp. 12mo.

Amateur Gunners ... 2/22nd County of London Howitzer Battery, R.F.A. on Active Service. By A. D. Thorburn, Liverpool. 1933.

History of 'A' Battery 84th Army Brigade R.F.A. 1914–1919. By D. F. Grant, 95 pp. including index, Marshall Bros, Fleet Street, c.1922.

Life in Gunner Regiments: 3 Articles by Gunner Subalterns on Life in Gunner Regiments. London: MOD (Army), n.d. [c. 1964], 16 pp., illustrations. 8¼in.

History of the Bolton Artillery, 1860–1928. By B. Palin Dobson. Bolton: Blackshaw, Sykes & Morris, 1929. 230 pp. 7in.

The Regimental History of the 32nd Searchlight Regiment, Royal Artillery (7th City of London T.A.). London: Whittington Rees, 1943, 12 pp., illustrations. 7¾in.

Before the Echoes Die Away. The story of a Warwickshire Territorial Gunner Regiment 1892–1969. By N. D. G. James. The 268th Officers Reunion Association, 1980. 194 pp., maps, illustrations. 9½in.

ROYAL HORSE ARTILLERY

Records of 3rd Troop, 2nd Brigade, R.H.A. now No.1 Depot R.F.A. Woolwich: printed by H. Pryce & Son, 1904, 28 pp. 7in.

A sketch of the history of 'F' Battery Royal Horse Artillery ... from notes by F. W. Stubbs and A. S. Tyndale-Briscoe. London: Spottiswoode and Co., 1905. 64 pp., illustrations, 7¾in.

A Short History of 'S' Battery R.H.A., 1826–1926. By 'O. T. F.' Bristol, 1926, 31 pp. 8½in.

The History of Strange's Royal Artillery 1848–1958. Hong Kong: Ye Olde Printerie Ltd., 1950, 69 pp. 8¼in.

ROYAL FIELD ARTILLERY

A Short History of the 72nd Brigade, R.F.A., 1914–1919. By Brig.-Gen. J. W. Stirling and Lt. Col. F. W. Richey. Woolwich: Royal Artillery Institution, 1920, 50 pp. 9½in.

ROYAL GARRISON ARTILLERY

A Short Record of the 59th Siege Battery R.A. By Frank House. (*n.d.*)

332 Siege Battery R.G.A. an account of its adventures in the Great War, compiled by the officers (1923).

ROYAL ARTILLERY 1939–45

Notes on the Maritime Anti-Aircraft Royal Artillery, 6th May 1941 to 30th September 1942—Maritime Royal Artillery 1st November 1942 to 31st July 1946. Compiled by Brig. H. B. Latham. Based on Official Records in the War Office and the Admiralty. Typewritten. 117 pp., maps, diagrams. 13in.

The history of the 3rd Medium Regiment Royal Artillery 1939–1945. By D. F. Hickson *et al.* Liverpool: The Northern Publishing Co., 1946. 381 pp., illustrations, maps.

The History of the 17th Light Anti-Aircraft Regiment, R.A. 1938–45. By Lt.-Col. H. S. Eeles. Tunbridge Wells Courier Co., 1946. 251p., illustrations. 9in.

113rd Field Regiment Royal Artillery 1939–1945. By C. R. Spincer. London: Laceys, 103p. 7½in.

The War History of 337 Field Artillery R.A. England, South Africa, El Tahag … Tripoli, later 337 Mountain Battery R.A. 2 volumes, viii, 58 pp. and viii, 25 pp. (461 F.B.R.A. later 461 M.B.R.A.), illustrations and maps, Glasgow, c.1946.

125th Anti-Tank Regiment R.A. 1939–45, 49 pp., portraits. Sunderland, 1946.

Ack-Ack. By Frederick Pile. London: Harrap, 1949. 410 pp., illustrations. 8¾in.

92nd Field Regiment Royal Artillery, 108 pp. c.1949.

The history of the 7th Medium Regiment Royal Artillery (now 32nd Medium Regiment R.A.) during World War II, 1939–1945. By F. L. Johns et al. 1951. ix, 222 pp., illustrations, maps.

CORPS OF ROYAL ENGINEERS

The Royal Engineer. By the Rt. Honourable Sir F. B. Head. xii, 371 pp. plus appendix, 7 uncoloured lithograph plates, 1869.

History of Submarine Mining in the British Army, xii, 288 pp., 13 illustrations, Chatham, 1910.

All Rank and No File, a History of the Engineer and Railway Staff Corps R.E. 1865–1965. By C. E. C. Townsend, 138 pp., 5 illustrations, The Engineer and Railway Staff Corps RE (TAVR) London, S.W.1.

Deeds of the Royal Engineers compiled in the Royal Engineers Record Office in compliance with Army Council Instruction No. 850 dated April 19th 1916. Chatham: Royal Engineers Institute, 1918, 81 pp. 9¾in.

Journal of the Operations conducted by the Corps of Royal Engineers, Pt. II, from Feb 1855 to fall of Sebastopol, Sept 1855. London: Eyre & Spottiswoode, 1859, 638 pp. 10½in.

Honourable Conquests. An account of the enduring work of the Royal Engineers throughout the Empire. By A. J. Smithers. Pen & Sword. 208 pp. Peacetime achievements of the R.E. and their contribution to the welfare of mankind in all quarters of the globe: India, Canada, Australia and other parts of the Empire.

History of the Royal Monmouthshire Royal Engineers (Militia), Vol II 1908–1967, 1969.

The History of the Tyne Electrical Engineers, Vol. 2 (1934–1984). xiv, 202 pp. plus 16 pp. of photographs and lineage chart. Includes list of officers (35 pp.). Gateshead: 72 Engineer Regiment, 1984. 10in.

1914–1918 FORMATIONS, UNITS

The Work of the Royal Engineers in the European War 1914–1919

— Water Supply (France), Part I. General Development ... Plant and Water. Operations, 88 pp. and index, many plates and folding maps. Chatham, 1921.

— Bridging, 83 pp. and index, many illustrations and maps Chatham, 1921.

— Egypt and Palestine, Water Supply, 72 pp., many illustrations and maps, Chatham, 1921.

— The Signal Service in the European War of 1914 to 1918 (France), frontispiece and folding plates. By R. E. Priestley. Chatham: Mackay, 1921, 359 pp., illustrations. 9½in.

— Military Mining, 154 pp. and index, 85 photographic plates and plans, Chatham, 1922.

A Short History of the 17th and 22nd Field Companies, 3rd Sappers and Miners in Mesopotamia, 1914–18. Kirkee, 1932.

A Record of the 203rd Field Company (Cambs.) Royal Engineers 1915–1919, 125 pp. Cambridge: Wm. Heffer, 1921.

The 497th at Wipers, 4to, 1935.

Narrative of the 502 (Wessex) Field Company Royal Engineers 1915–19. By C. L. Fox.

1939–1945 FORMATIONS, UNITS

Engineers in the Italian Campaign, 1943–1945, 114 pp., 79 illustrations, 7 folding maps, no imprint, *n.d.*, printed paper wrappers, printed by Printing & Stationery Services, C.M.F. *c.*1945. 9in.

Royal Engineers Battlefield Tour. Normandy to the Seine, 172 pp., 30 illustrations, small folio, August, 1946.

A.R.E. The Story of the 1st Assault Brigade, Royal Engineers. 1943–45, 78 pp., coloured folding maps and photographic illustrations, 4to, privately printed for members of the Brigade, c.1947. 8¾in.

ROYAL CORPS OF SIGNALS

Ths History of 3rd Headquarters and Signal Regiment. Aldershot: printed by The Forces Press (N.A.A.F.I.), 1966, 20 pp., portraits. 7¼in.

Signal Venture. By Brig. L. H. Harris, 278 pp. including index, frontispiece, many illustrations and a map. Aldershot: Gale & Polden Ltd., 1951, 278 pp. 8¾in.

The History of the Royal Army Signals in the Second World War. By Maj.-Gen. R. F. H. Nalder, 366 pp. and index, 2 maps, 1953.

The History of British Army Signals in the Second World War. General Survey. London: R.S I., 1953, 377 pp., illustrations. 9½in.

Through to 1970: Royal Signals Golden Jubilee. 1970, 122 pp.

FOOT GUARDS

The Guards Chapel, 1838–1938. By Nevile Wilkinson. London: Chiswick Press, 1938, xi, 246 pp., illustrations. 8½in.

With the Guards Brigade from Bloemfontein to Koomati Poort and back. By E. P. Lowry. London; Horace Marshall, 1952.

The Brigade of Guards on Ceremonial Occasions. By Col. Henry Legge-Bourke. London: Macdonald, 1962, 64 unnumbered pp. of coloured photographs, 7 of explanatory matter. 10½in.

The story of the Guards. By Julian Paget. London: Osprey, 1976. 304 pp., illustrations. 11in.

The Guards. By John De St Jorre. London: Aurum Press, 1981. 255 pp., illustrations.

GRENADIER GUARDS

Incidents of the South African Campaign, being chiefly the Personal Experiences of the Author. By Pte. J. Hart, 151 pp., The Telegraph Press, St. John, New Brunswick, 1901.

Short History of the Grenadier Guards. Published by Authority. Colchester: Benham & Co. Ltd., 1916, 83 pp., maps. 7½in.

An Alphabetical List of Officers of the Grenadier Guards, from 1800 to 1854. By Henry Stooks Smith. London: Parker, Furnivall & Parker, 1954, 66 pp. 3 coloured plates of colours. 8½in.

3rd Battalion Grenadier Guards 1661–1960. Household Brigade Magazine Special Number, 1961, 65 pp., illustrations. 9½in.

The Grenadier Guards (The First or Grenadier Regiment of Foot Guards). By Maj.-Gen. R. H. Whitworth. Famous Regiments Series. London: Leo Cooper 1974, 120 pp., illustrations. 8¼in.

COLDSTREAM GUARDS

The Coldstream Regiment of Foot Guards. Presentation of Colours to the First Battalion by His Majesty King Edward VII on the 29th Day of May MCMVII at Buckingham Palace. By Nevile R. Wilkinson. London: Chiswick Press, 1907, 59 pp., illustrations. 7¾in.

Presentation of the Colour to the First Battalion, by H.R.H. the King at Buckingham Palace, 29 May 1907, 60 pp., 6 illustrations. Chiswick Press, 1907. Edition limited to 250 copies.

Coldstream Guards, The Colours and Customs for the Use of Officers Only. Aldershot: Gale & Polden, 1931, 40 pp. 6¼in.

The Coldstream Guards. By Charles Grant. Reading: Osprey Publishing, 1971. 40 pp., illustrations. 9¾in.

The Coldstream Guards 1946–1970. By Richard Crichton. London: Coldstream Guards, 1972, xvi, 206 pp., illustrations, maps.

SCOTS GUARDS

Scots Guards. Scotland's Own Regiment of Foot Guards. Glasgow: Paramount Press, 1959, 82 pp., illustrations. 8¼in.

2nd Battalion Scots Guards Malaya 1948–1957. 1961, 90 pp., illustrations, map.

A Short History of the Scots Guards, 1642–1962 with some notes on the Colours, Badges and customs of the Regiment. By J. Swinton. Aldershot: Gale & Polden, 1963, 44 pp., illustrations. 7in.

The Scots Guards. By Anthony Goodinge. London: L. Cooper, 1969, vi, 149; illustrations. 8¼in.

IRISH GUARDS

The Micks: the Story of the Irish Guards. By P. Verney. London: Peter Davies. 1970. 218 pp. and index, 8 illustrations and 15 maps. 9¼in.

WELSH GUARDS

Uniforms of the Welsh Guards, 1915–1975, descriptive text by Eric Collings, 12 large coloured plates by Charles Stadden, each showing several figures. Foreword by H.R.H. Prince Charles, Colonel-in-Chief of the Regiment, oblong small folio, Edition limited to 500 numbered copies, c.1976.

The Welsh Guards. By John Retallack. London: Warne, 1981. xii, 177 pp., illustrations.

History of the Welsh Guards. By C. H. Dudley Ward. 1988 Reprint. v, 505 pp. London: The London Stamp Exchange.

Welsh Guards at War. By L. F. Ellis. Originally published 1946, reprinted by London Stamp Exchange. xiii, 380 pp.

INFANTRY OF THE LINE
(in Army List order and including disbanded Irish Regiments)

THE ROYAL SCOTS (THE ROYAL REGIMENT) [1]

Historical Record of The First, or Royal Regiment of Foot; containing an Account of the Origin of the Regiment in ths reign of King James VI of Scotland and of its subsequent Services to 1838 (Cannon's Historical Records Series). London: Longmans, Orme & Co., 1838. 8, 12, xiii, 277 pp., plates, 3 coloured plates, including 1 of uniform and 1 of colours. 8¼in.

An Old Scots Brigade: being the history of Mackay's regiment now incorporated with the Royal Scots. By John Mackay. Edinburgh: Blackwood, 1885, xv, 260 pp.

The Royal Scots. By Col. G. U. Prior. No imprint, *n.d.* [*c.* 1890], 56 pp. 6¾in.

Diary of Services of the First Battalion the Royal Scots during the Boer War. South Africa, 1899–1902, 84 pp., 22 photographic illustrations and folding plate of Memorial. By Col. W. Douglas, printed for private circulation, Bayswater, 1904.

Royal Scots. Three Centuries of History, 1633–1933. 26 pp., illustrations. 8vo. Aldershot, 1933.

The Royal Scots, The Royal Regiment. Edinburgh: Dunedin Press, *n.d.*, *c.* 1939. 80 pp., illustrations. 7in.

The Royal Scots. History and handbook of the Regiment 1633–1954. No imprint [1954], 136 pp. 8¾in.

The Royal Scots (The Royal Regiment). By Michael A. Brander. London: Leo Cooper, 1976. 111 pp., illustrations.

THE QUEEN'S ROYAL REGIMENT (WEST SURREY) [2]

Memorials of the Principal Events in the Campaigns in North Holland and Egypt, London, 1886.

The Queen's Royal Regiment (West Surrey). By J. Haswell, London: Hamish Hamilton, 1967, 152 pp., illustrations. 8¼in.

A Guide to the Queen's Regiment. By G. Blaxland. Canterbury: Elvey & Gibbs *n.d. c.* 1970. 87 pp., frontispiece, illustrations, maps. 8¼in.

The 1st 10 Years (supplement to the above). By G. Blaxland.

The History of The Queen's Royal Surrey Regiment 1959–1970. By Capt. J. R. Riley. London: The Queens, 1970, 144 pp., Illustrations. 9¾in.

THE BUFFS (ROYAL EAST KENT REGIMENT) [3]

With 'The Buffs' in South Africa. By Lt.-Col. J. B. Backhouse, 173 pp., illustrations, printed for private circulation by Gale & Polden, Aldershot, 1903.

Drums and Drummers (Largely, but not wholly concerned with the band of The Buffs). By G. R. Howe, London: Medici Society, 1932, x, 68 pp., illustrations. 7½in.

The Farewell Years. The Final Historical Records of The Buffs, Royal East Kent Regiment (3rd Kent) Formerly designated The Holland Regiment and Prince George of Denmark's Regiment, 1948–1967. By G. Blaxland. Canterbury: The Queen's Own Buffs Office, 1967, xvi, 231 pp., illustrations. 8½in.

The Buffs. By Gregory Blaxland. Reading: Osprey Publishing, 1972. 40 pp., illustrations. 9¾in.

The Queen's Own Buffs, the Royal Kent Regiment (3rd, 50th and 97th of Foot). By Gregory Blaxland. Canterbury: Q. O. Buff's Regimental Association, 1974 vi, 111 pp., illustrations. 8¾in.

The Third Battalion 'The Buffs' in South Africa. By H. D. Hirst. Canterbury: H. J. Goulden, 1908, 59 pp.

THE KING'S OWN ROYAL REGIMENT
(LANCASTER) [4]

The King's Own Regiment. 1st Battalion Lucknow 1910. Paris: Evrard, 1910. 22 pp., illustrations. 8¾ × 10½in.

The Fourth Battalion the King's Own, (Royal Lancaster Regiment) and the Great War. By Lt.-Col. W. F. A. Wadham and Captain J. Crossley, 150 pp., privately printed, London, 1920.

A Short History of The King's Own Royal Regiment (Lancaster). Aldershot: Gale & Polden Ltd., 1925, 23 pp. 4½in.

The Kings Own Royal Regiment (Lancaster). Morecambe Bay Printers, n.d. [c. 1961], 64 pp., illustrations. 8¾in.

The King's Own Royal Border Regiment. Morecambe: Morecambe Bay Printers, 1963, 70 pp., illustrations. 8¾in.

The King's Own Royal Regiment (Lancaster) (The 4th Regiment of Foot). By Howard Green. London: L. Cooper 1972. viii, 143 pp., illustrations. 8¾in.

The King's Own Royal Border Regiment 1680–1980. A Short History. By Col. Ralph May. Border Regiment. 46 pp., illustrations. 9½in.

THE ROYAL NORTHUMBERLAND FUSILIERS [5]

1st Battalion 5th Fusiliers. Rawalpindi 1910. Paris: Evrard, 1910. 22 pp., illustrations. 8¾ × 10½in.

Northumberland Fusiliers. Extracts from the digest of service, Fifth Fusiliers, in continuation of Cannon's Historical Record 1837–1910. Gharial: Fifth Fusiliers Printing Press, 1911. 54 pp.

The Royal Northumberland Fusiliers. By B. Peacock. London: Leo Cooper 1920, 128 pp. illustrations. 8¾in.

The Royal Regiment of Fusiliers. 100 years service on the Rock. By J. Phillips. Worthing: Stamp Publicity, 1971. 35 pp., illustrations. 4 × 6in.

A History of No.1. Indep. M.G. Coy. Royal Northumberland Fusiliers in the campaign in N.W. Europe, 1944–45. By T. I. Mather and H. B. van der Gucht. 74 pp., plate and sketch map, appendices, roll of honour. Privately published, *n.d. n.p.* [N.W. European publication?], *c.*1945. 7½in.

The 17th (Service) Battalion Northumberland Fusiliers (N.E.R.) (Pioneers). An Account of the Battalion's Formation and Training for six months, September, 1914, to February, 1915. North Eastern Railway Magazine, York. London: The Railway Gazette, 1915, 48 pp, illustrations. 9½in.

The Royal Northumberland Fusiliers. Summary of The History and Traditions of 'The Fifth' The Royal Northumberland Fusiliers, 1674–1967. Privately published, 1967, 6 pp. 13in.

THE ROYAL WARWICKSHIRE REGIMENT [6]

1st Battalion Royal Warwickshire Regiment. Quetta, Baluchistan, 1903. Lahore: F. Bremner, 1907. 44 pp., illustrations. 8¾ × 10½in.

2nd Battalion Royal Warwickshire Regiment. Malta 1913. 24 pp., illustrations. 8¾ × 10½in.

2nd Battalion Royal Warwickshire Regiment. Landi Kotal, N. W. Frontier 1922. 24 pp., illustrations. 8¾ × 10½in.

THE ROYAL FUSILIERS
(CITY OF LONDON REGIMENT) [7]

The Royal Fusiliers (The 7th Regiment of Foot). By Michael Foss. London: Hamish Hamilton, 1967, 153 pp., illustrations. 8½in.

A record of the presents of plate, pictures, books, colours etc. presented to the 1st Battalion Royal Fusiliers. London: Hatchards, 1880. 51 pp.

The Paddington Companies of the 3rd City of London Battalion The Royal Fusiliers 1912–1920. By J. P. Kelleher. London: J. P. Kelleher, 1982. 8 pp. 8¼in.

THE KING'S REGIMENT (LIVERPOOL) [8]

Book of Information for Kingsmen. Printed by Sharpe & Kellet, Liverpool, *n.d.* [*c.* 1960], 34 pp. 6¼in.

A Short History of the Regular Battalions of the King's Regiment (Manchester & Liverpool). By R. P. Macdonald. Aldershot: Gale & Polden, 1962, 16 pp., illustrations. 8¾in.

A short history of the Regular Battalions of the King's Regiment (Manchester and Liverpool). Aldershot: Gale and Polden, 1962. 2nd edition 1971. 16 pp., illustrations. 8¾in.

1st Battalion The King's Regiment, Cyprus October 1977 to April 1978. The King's Regiment, 1978. 93 pp., illustrations. 9½in.

Liverpool Pals. 17th, 18th, 19th, 20th Battalions The King's (Liverpool Regiment). By Graham Maddocks. Leo Cooper. 1991. 12½in. 263 pp.Illustrated with contemporary photographs and maps.

THE ROYAL NORFOLK REGIMENT [9]

The Royal Norfolk Regiment (The 9th Regiment of Foot). By T. Carew. London: Hamish Hamilton, 1967, 156 pp., illustrations. 8½in.

Kitchener's Pioneers, the Story of One Battalion formed from Kitchener's first 100,000 August 1914, Brigadier W. J. Jervois, 66 pp., map, Appendices show details of officers and men killed and wounded, Huntington, 1968.

Crater to the Creggan. The History of the Royal Anglian Regiment 1964–74. By Michael Barthorp. London: Leo Cooper, 1976. 160 pp., illustrations, 8¼in.

THE ROYAL LINCOLNSHIRE REGIMENT [10]

The Lincolnshire Regiment 250th Anniversary 1685–1935, *n.d.*, illustrations. 7½ × 9½in.

A record of the visit of the 1st Battalion (X Foot) The Lincolnshire Regiment to London on Public Duties, 14th Aug to 19th Sept, 1929. Aldershot: Gale and Polden, 1929. 28 pp., illustrations. 6in.

The Royal Lincolnshire Regiment. Roll of Honour 1939–45. No imprint. 86 pp.

Grimsby Chums. The Story of the 10th Lincolnshires in the Great War. By Peter Bryant. Humberside Leisure Services & Peter Bryant 1990. 213 pp. More than thirty photographs and 24 maps.

THE SUFFOLK REGIMENT [12]

The Suffolk Regiment. By G. Moir. London: Leo Cooper, 1969. 140 pp., illustrations. 8¼in.

THE SOMERSET LIGHT INFANTRY
(PRINCE ALBERT'S) [13]

The Light Bob Gazette, Royal Silver Jubilee and 250th Anniversary Number. Taunton: Phoenix Press, 1935, 82 pp., illustrations. 9½in.

Regimental Records, The Prince Albert's Somersetshire Light Infantry. Rawal Pindi: Regimental Press, 1st Battalion The P.A. Somerset L.I. 1898, 39 pp. and App. 9¾in.

The Somerset Light Infantry. By H. Popham. London: Hamish Hamilton, 1968, 151 pp., illustrations. 8½in.

Foreign Tour of duty of 1st Battalion The Somerset Light Infantry 1926–23. 250th Anniversary Souvenir 1685–1935. Aldershot: Gale and Polden, 1935. 20 pp., illustrations.

THE WEST YORKSHIRE REGIMENT
(THE PRINCE OF WALES'S OWN) [14]

The Record of the 4th Battalion West Yorkshire Regiment (Prince of Wales's Own) during the Boer War 1899–1902, 67 pp. J. Sampson, York, 1903.

A Peep over the Barleycorn; in the Firing Line with the P.W.O. 2nd West Yorkshire Regiment through the Relief of Ladysmith. Dublin, 1911. 214 pp., illustrations. 7½in.

The West Yorkshire Regiment. By A. J. Barker. London: Leo Cooper, 1974. 80 pp., illustrations. 8¼in.

In Iraq and Kurdistan with the 2nd Battalion The West Yorkshire Regiment (The Prince of Wales's Own). By C. Hinchcliffe. Aldershot: Gale and Polden, 1926. 55 pp., 4in.

1st Battalion Prince of Wales's Own. Mian-Mir and Dalhousie, Punjab 1906. Lahore: F. Bremner, 1906, 51 pp., illustrations. 8¾ × 10½in.

1st Battalion Prince of Wales's Own. Rawalpindi 1910. Lahore: F. Bremner, 1906. 51 pp., illustrations. 8¾ × 10½in.

2nd Battalion Prince of Wales's Own. Malta 1913. Paris; Evrard, 1913. 20 pp., illustrations. 8¼ × 10½in.

A Short History of the Prince of Wales's Own Regiment of Yorkshire (XIV and XV Foot) 1685–1966. By H. A. V. Spencer, privately published by the Regiment, 1967, vi, 36 pp. 8¼in.

The Prince of Wales's Own Regiment of Yorkshire. London: Malcolm Page, *n.d.* [*c.* 1960], 88 pp., illustrations. 8¾in.

Leeds Pals. By Laurie Milner. Leo Cooper Pen & Sword. 1991. 12½in. 280 pp. 250 photographs plus maps.

The Record of the 4th Battalion West Yorkshire Regiment (Prince of Wales Own) during the Boer War 1899–1902. By A. B. Ritchie. York: John Sampson, 1903.

A Short Historical Sketch of the 15th Battalion P.W.O. West Yorkshire Regiment, illustrated from Photographs, 180 pp. and index, many photographic illustrations and portraits, oblong small 4to, printed and published by R. Jackson, Leeds, 1917.

The Bradford Pals. The story of the 16th and 18th Bns. The West Yorkshire Regiment. By R. N. Hudson.

THE EAST YORKSHIRE REGIMENT
(THE DUKE OF YORK'S) [15]

A Short History of the East Yorkshire Regiment. *n.d.*, 8 pp. 8¼in.

2nd Battalion East Yorkshire Regiment. Fyzabad 1910. Paris: Evrard, 1910. 19 pp., illustrations. 8¼ × 10½in.

The East Yorkshire Regiment. By A. J. Barker. London: Leo Cooper, 1971. 152 pp., illustrations. 8¼in.

THE BEDFORDSHIRE AND HERTFORDSHIRE
REGIMENT [16]

The Bedfordshire and Hertfordshire Regiment. By G. W. H. Peters. London: Leo Cooper, 1970. 120 pp., illustrations. 8¼in.

A Short Account of the 1st (Hertfordshire) Volunteer Battalion the Bedfordshire Regiment in South Africa. By Capt. J. B. Wroughton, 27 pp., privately printed, Hertford, 1905.

History and Traditions of the 3rd Battalion The Royal Anglian Regiment. Aldershot: Forces Press (Naafi), *n.d.*, 8 pp., illustrations. 8¼in.

1st Battalion, The Bedfordshire and Hertfordshire Regiment (T.A.). Regimental History. Typescript 1953, 13 pp. 13in.

THE ROYAL LEICESTERSHIRE REGIMENT [17]

A pictorial history and souvenir of the 2nd Battalion Leicestershire Regiment. Belgium, India 1907. London Art Company, 1907. 31 pp., illustrations.

1/5 Battalion Leicestershire Regiment 'C' Wing 148 Pre-O.C.T.U. Training Establishment, Wrotham Camp. Souvenir Brochure. Aldershot: Gale & Polden, *n.d.*, 19 pp., illustrations.

Beyond Baghdad, with the Leicestershires. By E. J. Thompson. London: Epworth Press, 1919. 156 pp. 7¾in.

The Colours of the 17th or the Leicestershire Regiment of Foot (a brief regimental history). By P. D. S. Palmer. Aldershot: Gale & Polden, 1930. vii, 48 pp., illustrations.

THE GREEN HOWARDS
(ALEXANDRA, PRINCESS OF WALES'S OWN YORKSHIRE REGIMENT) [19]

Historical records of the 19th or the 1st Yorkshire North Riding Regiment of Foot, 1688–1848. By Richard Cannon. London: HMSO, 1848. 40 pp., illustrations.

The History of the 7th Battalion Green Howards [1914–1918]; a narrative extract from 'The Green Howards Gazette'. By Lt. Col. Ronald Fife. Richmond, Yorks, 1935, 56 pp. 9½in.

12th (Service) Battalion Princess of Wales' Own Yorkshire Regiment (Teeside Pioneers), no imprint, 50 pp., illustrations.

The Green Howards (The 19th Regiment of Foot). By G. Powell. London: Hamish Hamilton, 1968, 144 pp., illustrations. 8½in.

Story of One Green Howards in the Dunkirk Campaign by General Franklyn, 40 pp., portrait and maps, 1966.

THE LANCASHIRE FUSILIERS [20]

2nd Battalion Lancashire Fusiliers. Ferozopore 1934. Lahore: Bremner, 1934. 20 pp. 8¾ × 10½in.

Customs and Practices of XX, The Lancashire Fusiliers 1962. 44 pp., illustrations. 8¾in.

A Militia Unit in the Field, being a brief account of the Doings of the Sixth Battalion Lancashire Fusiliers in the South African War during the Years 1900 and 1901, Anon. 188 pp., printed for private circulation by Woodfall & Kinder, London, 1902.

THE ROYAL SCOTS FUSILIERS [21]

The Royal Scots Fusiliers, Recruiting Brochure, Aldershot: Gale & Polden, n.d., c. 1939. 48 pp., illustrations. 7in.

The 6th Battalion Royal Scots Fusiliers 1939–46. Ayrshire: D. C. Todd, c. 1947. 160 pp., illustrations, maps.

A Soldier's History. The Royal Highland Fusiliers. Glasgow: University Press, 1971, 72 pp., illustrations. 8¼in.

Pipe Music of the Royal Highland Fusiliers. 1967, 45 pp. 8¾in.

Regimental Standing Orders of the Royal Highland Fusiliers (Princess Margaret's Own Glasgow and Ayrshire Regiment). Glasgow: UniversityPress, *n.d.* [*c.* 1965] xii, 116 pp., illustrations. 9½in.

THE CHESHIRE REGIMENT [22]

A Short History of the 22nd or Cheshire Regiment. Two lectures given to the Cheshire Society of Natural Sciences, Literature and Art by the Colonel of the Regiment. Chester: printed by W. H. Evans & Co. Ltd., 1936, 56 pp. 7½in.

The First Battalion Cheshire Regiment, Illustrated with brief historical account of the Services of the Regiment, many photographic plates, photographs and publication by Frederick Bremner, photographer, Quetta, Baluchistan, oblong small folio, 1902.

22nd Regiment. Regimental Marches & Airs. P. Copy, 16p.

The Cheshire Regiment, or 22nd Regiment of Foot. By Frank Simpson. Reprinted from *'Chester Chronicle'*, 28th March 1914. 8 pp., illustrations.

Stockport Lads Together. By D. Kelsall. 1989. 45 pp.

THE ROYAL WELCH FUSILIERS [23]

Ar Orwel Pel; stgofion am y rhyfel-byd cyntaf 1914–1918. (15th Battn). By Gen. E. Beynon Davies. Llandysul, Llandysul, Gwasg Gomer, 1965. 85 pp., plates. 7in.

The Royal Welch Fusiliers, 23rd Foot. London: Pitkin Pictorials, 1969, 24 pp., illustrations. 9in.

Welsh Regiments in the Great War. Stirring deeds in France and Flanders. Cardiff: Western Mail. *n.d.* 40p, illustrations. 8¾in.

Medal Rolls 23rd Royal Welsh Fusiliers. Napoleonic Period. By N. Holme and E. C. Kirby. London: Spink, 1978. 207 pp. 8¼in.

The War the Infantry Knew 1914–19. By J. C. Dunn. li, 613 pp. A chronicle of the 2nd Bn Royal Welch Fusiliers on the Western Front based on the diaries of the author, and on personal contributions from 50 officers and men who served in the battalion as well as from a number of other units. Originally published in 1938. 1987 reprint with introduction Keith Simpson.

THE SOUTH WALES BORDERERS [24]

The South Wales Borderers. By J. Adams. London: Hamish Hamilton, 1968. 157 pp., illustrations. 8¼in.

Medal Roll (1793–1885) 24 Ft. By N. Holme. London: J. B. Hayward, 1971. 302 pp. 8¼in.

South Wales Borderers. India 1903–05.

Shoot to Kill (1st Battalion S. Wales Borderers, Malaya 1950–57). By Richard Miers. London: Faber, 1959. 216 pp., illustrations, maps.

South Wales Borderers. 2nd Battalion South Wales Borderers South African War 1899–1900. John Murray, 1902, for private circulation. viii, 119 pp., plates, map.

2nd Battalion South Wales Borderers, South African War 1899–1902, Anon. 125 pp., coloured illustration, Swiss, Devonport, *n.d. c.*1902.

War Diary of the 24th, South Wales Borderers. By Capt. C. J. Paterson. Printed for private circulation. London, 1915, 30 pp. 10in.

The Silver Wreath. Being the 24th Regt. at Isandhlwana and Rorke's Drift, 1879. By Norman Holme. 1979. 102 pp.

THE KING'S OWN SCOTTISH BORDERERS [25]

All the Blue Bonnets. The History of the King's Own Scottish Borderers. By Robert Woollcombe. London: Arms and Armour Press, 1980. 208 pp., maps, illustrations. 8¼in.

IV (Bn. K.O.S.B.) 1939–45, foreword by Lt-Col. E. D. Jackson, introduction by the War Committee, small oblong 8vo, illustrations, 216 pp., *c.*1946.

The Spirit of the Borders. 1956. 96 pp., illustrations.

The Borderers in Korea. By J. F. M. MacDonald. Berwick upon Tweed: Martins, *n.d.* 71 pp., maps, illustrations. 8¼in.

A Border Battalion: the history of the 7/8th (Service) Battalion King's Own Scottish Borderers. Edinburgh: 1920. 367 pp., illustrations, maps.

From Bordon to Loos with the 6th Service Battalion King's Own Scottish Borderers. By F. Claude Waller. Privately Printed. Winchester, 1917.

For King and Country and the Scottish Borderers. By Gavin Richardson. iv, 100 pp. and 10 pp. of adverts. The story of 1/4th (Border) Battalion, TF, K.O.S.B. on the Gallipoli Peninsula in 1915. Based on first hand accounts by survivors and on diaries, letters, newspapers, books and documents.

THE CAMERONIANS (SCOTTISH RIFLES) [26 and 90]

With the 4th Bn The Cameronians (Scottish Rifles) in South Africa 1900–1901. By Colonel A. H. Courtenay, vi, 95 pp., printed for the Author, Edinburgh: D. Brown. 1905.

Morale: a study of men and courage; the Second Scottish Rifles at the Battle of Neuve Chapelle, 1915. By John Baynes. London: Cassell, 1967, xiv, 286 pp., portraits, plates, map, 8vo.

The History of The Cameronians (Scottish Rifles). Volume 4. The Close of Empire 1948–1968. By John Baynes. London: Cassell, 1971. xvi, 303 pp., illustrations, maps. 8¾in.

Dress Regulations of The Cameronians (Scottish Rifles) (iii). Hamilton Advertiser, 1931. 61 pp., plates.

Some account of the 26th or Cameronian Regiment, from its formation to the present period. London: G. Mills, 1828. 107 pp.

With the 8th Scottish Rifles, 1914–19. J. M. Findlay. London: Blackie, 1926. xv, 240 pp., illustrations, map, 8¾in.

THE ROYAL INNISKILLING FUSILIERS [27 and 108]

The Royal Inniskilling Fusiliers. A Record of the Regiment's activities 1945–68. By J. Filmer-Bennett. London: Instance Printers, 1978. 112 pp., maps, illustrations. 8¼in.

An outline history of the Royal Irish Rangers (27th, 83rd and 87th) 1689–1969. By M. J. P. M. Corbally. Armagh: Trimble 1970 64 pp. 5½in.

THE GLOUCESTERSHIRE REGIMENT [28 and 61]

The Glorious Glosters. By T. Carew. London: Leo Cooper, 1970. 175 pp., maps, illustrations. 8¼in.

A New Short History of the Gloucestershire Regiment, 1694–1965. [Title on cover 'The Slashers']. Gloucester: Regimental Headquarters, 1965, 59 pp., portraits, plates (1 coloured). 8½in.

THE WORCESTERSHIRE REGIMENT [29 and 36]

1st Battalion The Worcestershire Regiment. Meerut: Official Press, 1926, 24 pp. 8¼in.

The Worcestershire Regiment in the Great War. By H. Stacke. London: Cheshire, 667 pp., illustrations.

The Amalgamation Parade of Worcestershire Regiment and Sherwood Foresters to form the Worcestershire and Sherwood Foresters Regiment (29th/45th Ft) 1970. Programme, 10 pp. 8¼in.

The Worcestershire Regiment. By R. Gale. London: Leo Cooper, 1970 122 pp., illustrations. 8¼in.

A History of 1st Battalion The Worcestershire Regiment in Malaya, 1950–1953. By Capt. B. A. Parker. In 'Firm' 1954–56. Worcester, 41 pp., sketch, maps. 9¼in.

THE EAST LANCASHIRE REGIMENT [30 and 59]

History of the East Lancashire Regiment, XXX and LIX. 1702–1902. Aldershot: Gale & Polden Ltd., 1919, vi, 56 pp. 6½in.

A short history of the Queen's Lancashire Regiment. Preston: Amblers, 1974. 16 pp. 5½in.

The Lilywhite 59th. By A. S. Lewis. Blackburn Recreation Services Department, 1985, 86p, illustrations. 8¾in.

Chorley Pals. By John M. Garwood. 56 pp. The Chorley Pals formed 'Y' Company, 11th (Accrington Pals) Battalion, East Lancashire Regiment. Many contemporary photographs.

Pals. The 11th (Service) Battalion (Accrington) East Lancashire Regiment. By William Turner. The Barnsley Chronicle. 10in. 256 pp. Well illustrated.

THE EAST SURREY REGIMENT [31 and 70]

East Surrey Regiment. Detailed bibliography by J. Paine in J.S.A.H.R. No. 56.

The East Surrey Regiment. Kingston-on-Thames: East Surrey Regiment [1938], 27 pp., illustrations. 12mo.

The East Surrey Regiment. By Michael Langley. London: Leo Cooper, 1972, 117 pp., illustrations. 8¼in.

History of the East Surrey Regiment 1920–1952, by D. S. Daniell. 1957, 283 pp., Honours & Awards.

The History of the 12th (Bermondsey) Battalion, The East Surrey Regiment, (1915–18). By John Aston and L. M. Duggan. London: The Union Press, 1936. 331 pp., illustrations, maps. 9¾in.

THE DUKE OF CORNWALL'S LIGHT INFANTRY
[32 and 46]

With 'The Thirty-Seconds' in the Peninsula and other Campaigns, edited by J. Wardell, 392 pp., Dublin, 1904.

A Short History of the Duke of Cornwall's Light Infantry Its Formation and Services 1702–1938. Plymouth: Underhill, 1945, 57 pp., illustrations. 6¾in.

The History of The Duke of Cornwall's Light Infantry, 1939–45. By Maj. Ernest George Godfrey and Maj.-Gen. Robert F. K. Goldsmith. 1966. Index, 34 maps, xiv, 437 pp. 8vo.

Duke of Cornwall's Light Infantry. By R. F. K. Goldsmith. London: Leo Cooper, 1970. 122 pp., illustrations. 8¼in.

The story of the 1st Battalion The Duke of Cornwall's Light Infantry (32nd Foot). By H. N. Newey. Aldershot: Gale & Polden, 1924. 46 pp., illustrations.

The Adventures of a Regiment; 46th during the Campaign in Egypt, July–October 1882; from the notes of a diary of One who was present. Alexandria: Printing Office V. Penasson, 1883, 67 pp. plans. 8¾in.

THE DUKE OF WELLINGTON'S REGIMENT
(WEST RIDING) [33 and 76]

Duke of Wellington's Regiment. History ... by Albert Lee. [Also remainder issue with frontispiece colour plate only]. Historical Record ... by Lt. Col. F. A. Hayden — variant issue. xix, 195 pp., 6 folding maps only.

The Duke of Wellington's Regiment. London: Malcolm Page, *n.d.* [*c.* 1956] 115 pp., illustrations. 8¼in.

Regimental Colours, 1st and 2nd Battalions the Duke of Wellington's Regiment. By A. C. S. Savory. London, *n.d.*, 23 pp., illustrations. 8¾in.

The Duke of Wellington's Regiment (West Riding). London: Malcolm Page, *c.* 1958. 96 pp., illustrations.

History of the Duke of Wellington's West Riding Regiment during the first 3 years of the Great War from August 1914 to December 1917. By J. J. Fisher. Halifax, 1917. 152 pp., illustrations.

THE BORDER REGIMENT [34 and 55]

A Short History of the Border Regiment. Aldershot: Gale & Polden, 1944, 31 pp., illustrations. 6¾in.

The Border Regiment [4 pp. section inserted in later impressions of Cannon's Record covering granting of battle honour 'Arroyo des Molinos' with coloured plate of revised regimental colour; also 8 pp. pamphlet carrying history to 1889].

2nd Battalion The Border Regiment (55th Westmorland Regiment). Photographic Record. Aldershot: Gale & Polden Ltd., *c.* 1910. 28 pp. 6¼in.

Tried and Valiant: The History of the Border Regiment, (The 34th and 55th Regiments of Foot), 1702–1959. By Douglas Sutherland. London: L. Cooper, 1972. 239 pp., illustrations, map. 8¾in.

A King's Own Border Bibliography. By J. E. G. Hodgson. In *'The Lion and Dragon'*, Vol. 5, No. 5, Spring 1974,pp. 217–218.

2nd Battalion The Border Regiment (55th Westmorland Regiment). Photographic Record. Aldershot: Gale and Polden 1924. 15 pp., illustrations. 7in.

THE ROYAL SUSSEX REGIMENT [35 and 107]

History of the War Service of the 1st Battalion Royal Sussex Regiment from 1701 to 1904. By F. St. D. Skinner. Ambala: Royal Sussex Regimental Press, 1906, 113 pp. 6¼in.

The Royal Sussex Regiment. The last 20 years 1948–67. Chichester: Regimental Association, 1974. 44 pp., illustrations. 8¾in.

The Shiny Ninth. By M. Gillings. The Pinwe Club, 1986. 176 pp., illustrations, maps. 8¼in.

Cinque Port Battalions, the Story of the 5th (Cinque Ports) Battalion the Royal Sussex Regiment, (T.A.) formerly 1st Cinque Port Rifle Volunteer Corps, its Antecedents, Traditions and Uniforms. By Colonel E. A. C. Fazan, 182 pp. and index, 18 illustrations and a map. Chichester: Royal Sussex Regimental Association, 1971. 8¼in.

THE ROYAL HAMPSHIRE REGIMENT [37 and 67]

An Account of the Part Taken by the 67th (South Hampshire Regiment In The Afghan Campaigns of 1878–80. n.pl: 2nd Battn. Hampshire Regiment, *n.d.* [*c.* 1880]. 52 pp. 9¾in. [Included in the Roberts papers].

The Royal Hampshire Regiment. By A. Wykes London: Leo Cooper, 1968; 127 pp., illustrations. 8¼in.

Some Account of the 10th and 12th Battalions, the Hampshire Regiment 1914–1918, 78 pp. Warren & Son, Winchester, 1930.

THE SOUTH STAFFORDSHIRE REGIMENT [38 and 80]

Extracts from the Records of the Services of the First Battalion South Staffordshire Regiment (Late 38th Regt.) as read by Lieut Colonel Eyre, Commanding the First Battalion, at a meeting of the Officers, past and present, held at the United Service Institute on the 3rd July 1883, to consider a proposition to place a Memorial of the Regiment in Lichfield Cathedral, with the Old Peninsula Colors lately restored to the Regiment by the Earl of Dartmouth. London: Army & Navy Society, 1883, 16 pp. 6¾in.

A Short History of the Staffordshire Regiment (The Prince of Wales's). By W. L. Vale. No imprint, *c.* 1960, 32 pp., illustrations. 8½in.

The South Staffordshire Regiment. London: Malcolm Page, *n.d.* [*c.* 1953], 204 pp., illustrations. 8¾in.

History of the South Staffordshire Regiment (1705–1959). By Col. W. L. Vale, xv, 489 pp. and index, 7 illustrations and 9 maps. Aldershot: Gale and Polden, 1969. 8¾in.

The Staffords 1881–1978 Badges and Uniforms. By G. Rosignoli and C. J. Whitehouse. Cannock: Rosignoli, 1978. 32 pp., illustrations. 8¾in.

Historical Records of the 1st King's Own Stafford Militia, now 3rd and 4th Battalions South Staffordshire Regiment. By C. H. Wylly *et al.* Lichfield: 'The Johnson's Head', 1902. 87 pp. 7in.

THE DORSET REGIMENT [39 and 54]

54th (West Norfolk) Regiment Succession Roll of Officers from Formation of the services of the Regiment in 1755, to June 30th, 1881, Lists of Colonels, Lt-Colonels ... and Medical Officers, with short record of the services of the Regiment, 26 pp., 4to, W. H. Charpentier, Military Printer, Portsmouth, 1887.

The 1st Battalion Dorsetshire Regiment in France and Belgium, August 1914 to June 1915, including a Roll of Honour, Honours and Awards, mentions in Despatches and summary of casualties 86 pp., 11 folding maps, privately printed, (preface signed A. L. R.). Mayflower Press, Plymouth, 1923. 8¾in.

Succession of Officers from the formation of the Regiment (54th) in 1755, to June 30th 1881. Portsmouth: W. H. Charpentier, 1887. 26 pp. 11in.

The Dorset Regiment. By H. Popham. London: Leo Cooper, 1970 126 pp., illustrations. 8¾in.

The Dorset Regiment. The 1st Battalion Dorsetshire Regiment illustrated with brief historical account of the sevices of the regiment. Ferozepore: 1906—photographic record by F. Bremner. 45 pp., illustrations.

Records of the 3rd Battalion Dorsetshire Regiment from 1757 to 1893, together with the names and dates of commissions of all officers who have entered the regiment from its formation down to the present time. London: Griffith Faran, *n.d.* [1893], 46 pp. 11in.

THE SOUTH LANCASHIRE REGIMENT
(THE PRINCE OF WALES'S VOLUNTEERS) [40 and 82]

The South Lancashire Regiment (Prince of Wales's Volunteers). London: Malcolm Page, *n.d.* (1965), 84 pp., illustrations. 8¾in.

From Preston to Ladysmith with the 1st Battalion, South Lancashire Regiment—by one of the Regiment. Preston: Platt & Co., 1900, 48 pp., illustrations. 7in.

The South Lancashire Regiment in the South African War 1899–1902. Warrington, Mackie, *n.d.*, illustrasions, 20 pp. 7¾in.

1st Battalion Prince of Wales's Volunteers. Lahore, 1910. Lahore: Bremner, 1910, 20 pp., illustrations. 7¾ × 10½in.

THE WELCH REGIMENT [41 and 69]

The Welch Regiment, 1719–1960. London: Malcolm Page, 1960, 76 pp., illustrations. 8¼in.

The Welch Regiment. Cardiff: Regimental Museum, 1978, 16 pp., illustrations. 5½ × 8¾in.

THE BLACK WATCH
(ROYAL HIGHLAND REGIMENT) [42 and 73]

The Black Watch, or 42nd Highlanders. By James Grant. London: George Routledge & Sons, n.d., [c. 1859], v, 391 pp. 6¾in.

Historical Record of the 42nd Royal Highlanders The Black Watch, 1729–1881. Extracts from the History of the Scottish Highlands, Highland Clans and Highland Regiments. Edinburgh: Jack, n.d., 809 pp., illustrations. 11in.

Jubilee Memorial—Historical Records of the 42nd Royal Highlanders The Black Watch, 1729–1887. Edinburgh: Jack, 1887, 322–445 pp. 11in.

With the Black Watch, the Story of the Marne. By Scout J. Cassells. London: Andrew Melrose, n.d., vii, 248 pp. 7½in.

The Black Watch. A brief story of the Regiment from 1725 to the present day. Revised by Brig. the Lord Ballantrae (from the original work by Lt. Col. John C. Stewart). Derby: The Pilgrim Press, 1974. 22 pp., illustrations. 5½in.

The Black Watch. By P. Howard. London: Hamish Hamilton, 1968, 141 pp., illustrations. 8¼in.

The Black Watch. By C. Grant. London: Osprey, Man at Arms, 1971, 40 pp., illustrations. 10¼in.

The Black Watch. 1910. Limerick, 1910. 26 pp., illustrations. 5½ × 8¾in.

The Black Watch. By Eric and Andro Linklater. London: Barne and Jenkins, 1977. 240 pp., illustrations. 10½in.

The 2/73rd At Waterloo. By Alan Lagden and John Sly. xvii, 236 pp.

Officers of the Black Watch 1725 to 1986 (second revised edition), by Maj. J. Samson, 1989, 110 pp.

THE OXFORDSHIRE AND BUCKINGHAMSHIRE
LIGHT INFANTRY [43 and 52]

The Oxfordshire and Buckinghamshire Light Infantry. By P. Booth. London: Leo Cooper, 1971. 156 pp., illustrations. 8¼in.

The Royal Green Jackets. By C. Wilkinson-Latham. London: Osprey Men at Arms, 1975, 40 pp., illustrations. 10¼in.

The 43rd Light Infantry in New Zealand. Ryde, NSW: New South Wales Military Historical Society, 19 pp., tables.

The 2nd Bucks. Battalion Oxfordshire and Buckinghamshire Light Infantry 1914–18. By J. C. Swann. 50 pp., map.

THE ESSEX REGIMENT [44 and 56]

With the 10th Essex in France. By T. M. Banks and R. A. Chell. London: 10th Essex Old Comrades Association, 1921. 302 pp., illustrations. 8¾in.

THE SHERWOOD FORESTERS
(NOTTINGHAMSHIRE AND DERBYSHIRE
REGIMENT) [45 and 95]

The 45th Regiment (Nottinghamshire) Sherwood Foresters. By P. H. Colomb. Derby: Bemrose, 1894, 12 pp. 7in.

The Sherwood Foresters. Karachi and Hyderabad 1929. Paris: Evrard, 1929, 24 pp. 8¼in.

8th Battalion, The Sherwood Foresters. The Colonels Book, 1750–1820 and 1859–1905. By E. H. Nicholson and E. G. C. Beckwith. Typescript, 1962, 2 vols in one. 13in.

THE LOYAL REGIMENT (NORTH LANCASHIRE)
[47 and 81]

The Battle Honours of the Loyal North Lancashire Regiment. By H. G. Purdon. No imprint. 1899. 27 pp., illustrations. 10¼in.

The Loyal Regiment, North Lancashire (47th/81st Regiment). London: Malcolm Page, *n.d.* [*c.* 1954], 60 pp., illustrations. 8¾in.

A Short Historical Record of the Loyal Regiment (North Lancashire). By R. E. Berkeley. Aldershot: Gale and Polden. 1922. 16 pp., illustrations. 9¾in.

1st Battalion Loyal North Lancashire Regiment. South African War 1899–1902. Devonport: Swiss and Co., 1903. 142 pp. 5½in.

The Loyal Regiment. Historical Record of the Loyal North Lancashire Regiment 2nd Battalion late 81st Foot 1793–1909. India, 1910? 43 pp., illustrated.

The Loyal Regiment. (North Lancashire). London: Leo Cooper, 1975 118 pp., illustrations. 8¼in.

THE NORTHAMPTONSHIRE REGIMENT [48 and 58]

The Northamptonshire Regiment 1st Battalion ... being reproductions of a series of photographs of the Battalion taken by a special artist and by Colour Sergeant J. Hull at Secunderabad, 1896. By Lt. Col. R. J. Chaytor. Philadelphia: 1896. 24 pp., illustrations.

Historical Souvenir and history of the Northamptonshire Regiment, Poona, India, 1908. British Historical and Art Publishing Co., 1908. 44 pp., illustrations. 11 × 15¾in.

The Northamptonshire Regiment. By Michael Barthorp. London: Leo Cooper, 1974. 89 pp., illustrations. 8¼in.

Northamptonshire and the Great War. By W. H. Holloway. Northampton: 'The Northampton Independent', *n.d.* 230 pp., illustrations. 11in.

Bicentenary 1st Battalion Northamptonshire Regiment (48th/58th). December 1955. 20 pp., illustrations. 7 × 10¼in.

THE ROYAL BERKSHIRE REGIMENT (THE PRINCESS CHARLOTTE OF WALES'S) [49 and 66]

The Royal Berkshire Regiment. By F. Myatt. London: Hamish Hamilton, 1968, 136 pp., illustrations. 8½in.

THE QUEEN'S OWN ROYAL WEST KENT REGIMENT [50 and 97]

The Silver Badge; [2nd Battalion Royal West Kent Regiment in the siege of Kut]. By Arthur G. Kingsmill. Ilfracombe, 1966. 96p. 12mo.

Royal West Kent Regiment (Medal Roll part 2 in 'Q.O. Gazette' 1933).

The 97th or Earl of Ulster's Regiment 1824–81. By H. D. Chaplin. Maidstone: Queen's Own Royal West Kent Regimental Museum, 1973. 72 pp., maps, illustrations. 9in.

The Queen's Own Royal West Kent Regiment. By R. Holloway. London: Leo Cooper, 1973 105 pp., illustrations. 8¼in.

2nd Battalion Queen's Own Royal West Kent Regiment Peshawar 1911. Paris: Evrard, 1911. 20 pp., illustrations. 6¼ × 10¼in.

THE KING'S OWN YORKSHIRE LIGHT INFANTRY [51 and 105]

A short history of K.O.Y.L.I. (51st and 105th) 1755–1965. Wakefield: Wakefield Express Series Ltd., 1965. 36 pp., maps; illustrations. 7in.

The King's Own Yorkshire Light Infantry. July 1968. 71 pp., illustrations. 8¾ × 11in.

The King's Own Yorkshire Light Infantry. By Leonard Cooper. London: Leo Cooper, 1970. 125 pp., illustrations. 8¾in.

THE KING'S SHROPSHIRE LIGHT INFANTRY [53 and 85]

The King's Shropshire Light Infantry. Trimulgherry. India, 1914. Paris: Evrard, 1914. 21 pp., illustrations. 8¼ × 11in.

The History of the Corps of The King's Shropshire Light Infantry. Shrewsbury, Regimental Secretary, Vol. 1. — The 53rd (Shropshire) Regiment 1755–1881. 1966, xv, 156 pp., portraits, plates. 6 coloured plates of uniform and colours. 13in. [Note: one of seven volumes projected; reproduced from typescript].

— Vol. 2. — The 85th (The King's Light Infantry) Regiment, 1759–1881. Shrewsbury, 1968. [Typescript]. x, 402 pp., portraits, plan, illustrations. Fo.

— Vol 3. 1881–1968. Shrewsbury, Regimental Secretary [Typescript], 363 pp., illustrations. 11¾in.

— Vol 4. The Shropshire Militia and Volunteers. By G. A. Parfitt. Shrewsbury, Regimental Secretary, 479 pp., frontispiece and 17 plates, roneo/cyclostyled, printed card covers, small folio, 11¾in. c.1969.

THE MIDDLESEX REGIMENT
(DUKE OF CAMBRIDGE'S OWN) [57 and 77]

The Middlesex Regiment. By G. Blaxland. London: Leo Cooper, 1977. 144 pp., illustrations. 8¼in.

The Diehards in Korea. By J. N. Shipster, no imprint, 1975. 78 pp., maps, illustrations, 9½in.

THE KING'S ROYAL RIFLE CORPS [60]

The King's Royal Rifle Corps (The 60th Regiment of Foot). By H. F. Wood. London: Hamish Hamilton, 1967, pp. 149, illustrations, 8½in.

THE WILTSHIRE REGIMENT
(DUKE OF EDINBURGH'S) [62 and 99]

Pictorial Record of the Duke of Edinburgh's 2nd Battalion the Wiltshire Regiment. Poona, India. 1915 Bombay: British Historical and Art Publishing Co., 1915, 36 pp., illustrations. 11 × 12½in.

1st Battalion Duke of Edinburgh's Wiltshire Regiment. Quetta, Baluchistan, 1899. Quetta: F. Bremner, 1899. 36 pp., illustrations. 8¼ × 11in.

The Wiltshire Regiment. By T. Gibston. London: Leo Cooper, 1969. 148 pp., illustrations. 8¾in

Historical retrospect of the Wiltshire Regiment, formerly the 62nd and 99th Foot and The Royal Wiltshire Milita; now styled The Duke of Edinburgh Wiltshire Regiment. Aldershot: Gale and Polden, 1899, 12 pp.

THE MANCHESTER REGIMENT [63 and 96]

To Manchester. A Tribute to 'The Fallen' and to 'The Spirit' of Her Great Regiment. By Brig. Gen. H. C. E. Westropp. Manchester: Sherratt & Hughes, 1920, 48 pp. 8½.in.

History of 3rd (Militia) Battalion, the Manchester Regiment. Typescript, 1937, 162 pp., maps. 10¼in.

Records of the Mounted Inf. Coy. 2nd Btn V.B. Manchester Regt., 1887–1908. Manchester: Baxter, *n.d.*, 59 pp. 8¾in.

THE NORTH STAFFORDSHIRE REGIMENT (THE PRINCE OF WALES'S) [64 and 98]

The Prince of Wales's North Staffordshire Regiment. Multan, Privately published, 1906, 10 pp. 6¾in.

The North Staffordshire Regiment. By H. C. Cook. London: Leo Cooper, 1970 136 pp., illustrations. 8¾in.

2nd Battalion North Staffordshire Regiment. Palestine, 25th Sept 1936—15th Jan 1938. Aldershot: Gale and Polden, 1938. 32 pp., maps, illustrations.

A short history of the North Staffordshire Regiment, 64th, 1756–1945. Hednesford, Staffs: A. D. Taylor, 1948. 20 pp., illustrations. 9in.

THE YORK AND LANCASTER REGIMENT [65 and 84]

A Short History of the York and Lancaster Regiment, 1758 to 1953. Published by the Regiment, 1953, 16 pp. 8¾in.

The York and Lancaster Regiment. By D. Creighton-Williamson. London: Leo Cooper. 1968, 136 pp., illustrations. 8¾in.

1st Battalion York and Lancaster Regiment. Quetta, Baluchistan, 1907. Lahore: Bremner, 1907. 60 pp., maps, illustrations. 8¼ × 11in.

History of the 12th Service Battalion York and Lancaster Regiment. By Richard A. Sparling. Sheffield, 1920. 143 pp., illustrations.

Sheffield City Battalion. The 12th (Service) Battalion York & Lancaster Regiment. By Ralph Gibson and Paul Oldfield. Barnsley Chronicle. 264 pp. Illustrations and maps. Diagrams of battalion, brigade and divisional organization.

The Centenary of the Hallamshires, 1859–1959. Privately published for the Regiment, 1959, 24 pp., illustrations. 8¾in.

Normandy to Arnhem; a Story of the Infantry. The Hallamshire Battalion, The York and Lancaster Regiment. By Brig. T. Hart Dyke. Sheffield: Greenup & Thompson Ltd., 1966. viii, 79 pp., portraits, plates, maps. 9½in.

Pals. The 13th and 14th Battalions York and Lancaster Regiment. By Jon Cooksey. 10in. 288 pp. Photographs and maps.

THE DURHAM LIGHT INFANTRY [68 and 106]

Standing Orders of the 1st Battalion The Durham Light Infantry. With a short Record of the Battalion. Aldershot: Gale & Polden, 1908, 85 pp. 7in.

Pictorial Souvenir and history of 2nd Battalion Durham Light Infantry. Ahmednagar, India 1923. British Historical and Art Publishing Co., 1923. 36 pp., illustrations. 9 × 12½in.

The Durhams in the Peninsula. By J. H. Rumsby. Derby: English Life Productions, 1975. 14 pp., illustrations. 5½ × 8¼in.

The Durhams in the Crimea. By A. Coates Klottrup. Derby: English Life Productions, 1975. 14 pp., illustrations. 5½ × 8¼in.

'The Durham Faithfuls' 1758–1968. Durham: D.L.I. Museum 1978. 20 pp., illustrations. 9½in.

Into Battle with the Durhams: 8 D.L.I. in World War II. Reprint of '8th Battalion The Durham Light Infantry, 1939–1945'. By Major P. J. Lewis and Major I. R. English, with authors' additions and amendments. London: The London Stamp Exchange, 1990. 9¾in.

Records of the 5th Battalion, The Durham Light Infantry, 1796 to 1914. Aldershot: Gale & Polden Ltd., 1914, 72 pp., illustrations. 7½in.

THE HIGHLAND LIGHT INFANTRY
(CITY OF GLASGOW REGIMENT) [71 and 74]

The Highland Light Infantry, (City of Glasgow Regiment). No imprint, *c*. 1939, 76 pp., illustrations. 7in.

Proud Heritage. Glasgow: Paramount Press, *n.d.* [*c*. 1951], 104 pp., illustrations. 8¾in.

Regimental Records of the First Battalion Highland Light Infantry formerly the 71st Highland Light Infantry 1777 to 1906, Reprinted from the Original Records 1906, 234 pp., Dinapore, The Watling Works, 1907. 9½in.

The Highland Light Infantry. By L. B. Oatts. London: Leo Cooper, 1969. 113 pp., illustrations. 8¾in.

The Highland Light Infantry. The Uniforms of the Regiment, 1891–1914. By J. B. Mackay and D. N. Anderson. Glasgow: Exacta Print Ltd., 1977. 90 pp., illustrations. 9in.

SEAFORTH HIGHLANDERS (ROSS-SHIRE BUFFS,
THE DUKE OF ALBANY'S) [72 and 78]

Seaforth Sketches (10th Battalion) Drawn by 'The Tout,' coloured plate and 20 monochrome plates, 4to, T. Allan & Sons, Edinburgh, *c*.1918.

A Short History of the Seaforth Highlanders. Dingwall: Ross-shire Printing & Publishing, 1928, 88 pp., illustrations. 5½in.

An introduction to the Queen's Own Highlanders (Seaforths and Camerons). 16 pp., illustrations. 11in.

Seaforth Songs, Ballads and Sketches. By G. W. Anderson. Dublin: Chapman, 1890. 238 pp., illustrations. 7in.

Queen's Own Highlanders (Seaforth and Cameron) A Short History. Inverness: printed by Highland Printers Ltd., 1961, 69 pp., illustrations. 6¼in.

Queen's Own Highlanders (Seaforth and Cameron). Lt. Col. A. Fairrie. Stirling: R.H.Q. Queen's Own Highlanders, 1983, 172 pp., illustrations. 11¾in.

THE GORDON HIGHLANDERS [75 and 92]

Glory of the Gordons. By Paul W. Pratt. Inverness: Highland Printers, 1966, 106 pp. 7in.

The Gordon Highlanders. By C. Sinclair-Stevenson. London: Hamish Hamilton, 1968, 133 pp., illustrations. 8½in.

The Life of a Regiment; the History of the Gordon Highlanders. Volume 6. 1945–1970. 1974.

1st Battalion The Gordon Highlanders. Haifa; Palestine, 1934. Aldershot: W. May, 1934. 60 pp., illustrations. 9 × 11in.

2nd Battalion The Gordon Highlanders. Peshawar, India 1907. Lahore: Bremner, 1907. 48 pp., illustrations. 9 × 11in.

2nd Battalion, the Gordon Highlanders 1914—Cairo, 24 pp. and printed cover; photographic illustrations by P. G. Evrard, Paris, c.1920.

The Gordon Highlanders in North Africa and Sicily August 1942—October 1943. By F. Barker. Sidcup, 1944. 32 pp., plans. [See also Bulloch (ed.) The House of Gordon Vol. III, Gordons under Arms].

THE QUEENS OWN CAMERON HIGHLANDERS [79]

The Queens Own Cameron Highlanders. Aldershot: Gale & Polden, n.d., c. 1939, 68 pp., illustrations. 7in.

THE ROYAL ULSTER RIFLES [83 and 86]

A Short History of the Royal Ulster Rifles. Belfast: Aiken, 1937. 122 pp., maps. 7in.

THE ROYAL IRISH FUSILIERS (PRINCESS VICTORIA'S) [87 and 89]

The Royal Irish Fusiliers. By Henry Harris. London: L. Cooper, 1972. vi, 171p, illustrations. 8¾in.

2nd Battalion Princess Victoria's Royal Irish Fusiliers, Ferozopore, India 1908. Lahore: Bremner, 1908. 68 pp., illustrations. 10¼ × 11¾in.

The Royal Irish Fusiliers. Agra 1930. 23 pp., illustrations. 8¼ × 11in.

The Wild Geese are Flighting (Tunisia, 1943). By J. Horsfall, 198 pp. including index, 12 illustrations and 3 maps, Kineton, 1976.

Say not the Struggle ... (Battle of France, 1940). By J. Horsfall, 198 pp. including index, 29 illustrations and 6 maps, Kineton, 1977.

Fling Our Banner to the Wind (Italy, 1944). By J. Horsfall, 242 pp. including index, 22 illustrations and 7 maps, Kineton, 1978.

Thirty Days to Dunkirk, the Royal Irish Fusiliers, May 1940. By Brigadier G. F. Gough, 194 pp., 3 maps, Wrexham, Clwyd, 1990.

THE CONNAUGHT RANGERS [88 and 94]

Adventures of the Connaught Rangers from 1808–1814, Vols. 1 – 11. By William Grattan. London: Colburn, 1847, 329 pp. 7¾in.

Regimental Album of the 2nd Batt. Connaght Rangers. Bombay: Bennett, Coleman & Co., 1908, 24 pp., illustrations. 8½in.

1st Battalion the Connaught Rangers, Ferozepore (India) 1914. Paris: P. G. Everard, 1914, 20 plates. 8¼in.

Regimental Records of 1st Battalion The Connaught Rangers. The Boer War, 1899–1901, c. 1902. No title page in copy seen. 70 pp., maps. 8in.

The Natal Campaign 1899–1900. By Lt.-Col. H. F. N. Jourdain, 36 pp., illustrations, wrappers, privately printed, no imprint, 1948.

The Connaught Rangers. By Alan Shepperd. Reading: Osprey Publishing, 1972. 40 pp., illustrations. 9¾in.

The Connaught Rangers. By T. P. Kilifeather. Tralee: Anvil Books, 1969. 211 pp. 8¼in.

Mutiny for the Cause. By S. Pollock. London: Leo Cooper, 1969. 106 pp., illustrations. 8¾in.

Record of the 5th (Service) Battalion The Connaught Rangers from 19th August 1914 to 17th January 1916. Privately published, c. 1916. 231 pp., maps.

The Devil to Pay. The Connaught Rangers Revolt in the Punjab, 1920. By Anthony Babington. Pen & Sword. 1991. 208 pp., 12 pp. illustrations.

THE ARGYLL AND SUTHERLAND HIGHLANDERS
(PRINCESS LOUISE'S) [91 and 93]

Historical Calendar of the Princess Louise's 91st (originally 98th) Highlanders. By Lieut. George M. L. Sceales. No imprint. 1908. 3, 70, 5 pp. 8½in.

The Argyll and Sutherland Highlanders. By L. Maclean Watt. Edinburgh: W. P. Nimmo, Hay & Miltchell [*n.d. c.* 1915]. 63p, illustrations. 4in.

The Historical Records of the 93rd Sutherland Highlanders now 2nd Battalion Princess Louise's Argyll and Sutherland Highlanders, from 1800 to 1890; from the Regimental Records, The War Office, and other original and authentic sources. By James MacVeigh. Dumfries, printed for the author by James Maxwell & Son, 1890, 134 pp., 3 portraits. 8½in.

Descriptive List of Plate, Pictures and Trophies belonging to the officers 91st Highlanders. By Capt. G. M. McSceales. Stirling, 1909, privately. 51 pp.

The Argyll and Sutherland Highlanders. By D. Sutherland. London: Leo Cooper, 1969, 127 pp., illustrations. 8¾in.

Honours List 10th Battalion (Princess Louise's) Argyll and Sutherland Highlanders, European War, 1914–1918. Record of the battalion's decorations, with accompanying citations. One of three copies? Typewritten, xii, 304 pp. 10½in.

THE PRINCE OF WALES'S LEINSTER REGIMENT
(ROYAL CANADIANS) [100 and 109]

Reminiscences of the North-West Rebellions, with a Record of the Raising of her Majesty's 100th Regiment in Canada … and political life. By Major Charles Arkell Boulton. 531 pp. including a list of officers and men (32 pp.), frontispiece, plate and 4 maps and plans. Toronto, Grip Printing & Publ. Co., 1886. 8vo.

Stand To. A Diary of the Trenches 1915–18, preface by Major-General Sir J. Capper, 358 pp. including index, photographs and maps, Hurst & Blackett, 1937.

THE ROYAL MUNSTER FUSILIERS [101 and 104]

A Postscript to History. By H. S. Jervis. Published by the Old Comrades Association, Royal Munster Fusiliers, 1957, 14 pp. 9in.

2nd Battalion, The Royal Munster Fusiliers (104th Foot)—A Pictorial Record. Cairo, privately printed, *n.d.* [*c.* 1920], 60 pp., illustrations. 6¾in.

THE ROYAL DUBLIN FUSILIERS [102 and 103]

The Royal Dublin Fusiliers Engagement Book, Aldershot, 1910.

THE PARACHUTE REGIMENT

Prelude to Glory, the Story of the Creation of Britain's Parachute Army, 368 pp., illustrations, 1948.

The Tenth; a record of service of The 10th Battalion, The Parachute Regiment, 1942–1945 and The 10th Battalion, The Parachute Regiment (T.A.) (County of London), 1947–1965. By Major R. Brammall. Ipswich: Eastgate Publications, 1965. xxx, 458, 28 pp., index, 8 maps and many portraits, illustrations. 8½in.

THE RIFLE BRIGADE (PRINCE CONSORT'S OWN)

A Rifle Brigade Register, 1905–1963. Compiled by Col. W. P. S. Curtis. Part I— A Roll of Regular Officers who have served in the Regiment from 1905–1963. Winchester: printed by Culverlands Press Ltd., 1964. 98 pp. 8½in.

Digest of Services of 1st Battalion Rifle Brigade (The Prince Consort's Own) from its formation in 1800 until its arrival in Bombay 1880. Belgaum, India, c. 1880. 129 pp. 9in.

Jackets of Green, a Study of the History, Philosophy, and Character of the Rifle Brigade. By A. Bryant. London: Collins, 1972. 478 pp., bibliography and index, 17 illustrations. 9in.

Rifle Green at Waterloo; An Account of the 95th Foot in the Netherlands Campaign of 1813–14, at Quatre Bras and Waterloo 16th–18th June 1815, and the Occupation of Paris. With a full Medal and Casualty Roll for the Fourteen Companies at Waterloo and Details of Weapons, Clothes and Equipment used in the campaign. By George Caldwell and Robert Cooper. 208 pp., 8 colour and 19 black & white plates, illustrations in the text and 9 maps. Leicester: Bugle Horn Publications, 1990. 9¼in.

SPECIAL AIR SERVICE REGIMENT

2nd Special Air Service Regiment. Missing Parachutists. By Major E. A. Barkworth, Intelligence Officer 2nd S.A.S. 94 pp., large folding map, portraits and illustrations, small folio, n.d. c.1945. Very limited series.

Special Air Service Regiment: Winged Dagger. By Roy Farran. 384 pp., illustrations. Collins, 1948.

The Artists and the S.A.S. by B. A. Young, 63 pp., illustrations, wrappers, published by 21st Special Air Service Regiment, Duke Road, 1960.

Who Dares Wins; The Story of the Special Air Service 1950–1980. By Tony Geraghty. London: Arms & Armour Press, 1980. 249 pp., maps, illustrations. 9¾in.

This is the S.A.S.: a pictorial history of the Special Air Service Regiment. By Tony Gerraghty. London: Arms & Armour Press, 1982. 156 pp., illustrations.

The Special Air Service. By Philip Warner. London: William Kimber, 1971. 285 pp., illustrations, maps.

SECTION III

DEPARTMENTS: CORPS

ROYAL ARMY CHAPLAINS' DEPARTMENT

In This Sign Conquer. The Story of the Army Chaplains. By Sir John Smyth. London: A. R. Mowbray, 1968, xxii, 362 pp., illustrations. 8¼in.

ROYAL ARMY SERVICE CORPS

The Army Service Corps. Volume I, 1760–1857, possibly by Brigadier Bullock. Volume II, Volume III. Reprinted by Sterling Publications, New Delhi, India.

Royal Army Service Corps, the Transport Corps of the British Army. Glasgow: Paramount Press, n.d. [c. 1960], 143 pp., illustrations. 8¼in.

The Royal Corps of Transport, 1794–1965. Compiled and edited by Major G. H. Edwards. Bidmouth Printing Works, 1966, 36 pp., illustrations, 12 coloured illustrations of uniform. 8¼in.

The Royal Corps of Transport Annual Book 1973. 120 pp., illustrations.

Ceremonial Parade to mark formation of R.C.T. 1965. 8 pp., illustrations.

The Story of 55 Company Royal Army Service Corps (Air Defence) By Capt. P. H. Houchin. Singapore: Jay Birch & Co. Ltd., 1965, 47 pp., portraits, illustrations, maps. 10in.

The R.A.S.C. By G. Crew. Famous Regiment Series. London: Leo Cooper, 1970. 320 pp., illustrations.

History of Transport Services of Egyptian Expeditionery Force 1916–18. By G. E. Badcock. London: Hugh Rees, 1925. 388 pp., illustrations.

The Story of the R.A.S.C. and R.C.T. 1945–1982, by Brig. D. J. Sutton. 1983, 801 pp.

THE ROYAL ARMY MEDICAL CORPS

With the R.A.M.C. in Egypt (1883–1917). By 'Serjeant Major, R.A.M.C.' London: Cassell, 1918, 315 pp., 32 illustrations. 7¾in.

R.A.M.C. By Anthony Cotterell. London: Hutchinson, 116 pp., 24 illustrations, c.1945. 8¼in.

Catalogue of contents of Muniment Room at R.A.M. College, Millbank.

History of the Army Medical Dept. By N. Cantlie. London: Churchill Livingstone, 1974. 2 vols.

The Royal Army Medical Corps. By Redmond McLaughlin. London: L. Cooper, 1972. viii, 121 pp. illustrations. 8¾in.

Commissioned Officers in the Medical Services of the British Army 1660–1960. By R. Drew. Two volumes (Incorporating 'Peterkin's Roll' and 'Johnston's Roll'). London: The Wellcome Historical Medical Library, 1968. 9½in.

With the R.A.M.C. at the Front. By C. Vivian. London: Hodder & Stoughton, 1914. 180p.

Surgeons in the Field. By J. Laffin. London: Dent, 1970. 306 pp., illustrations.

The Great War and the R.A.M.C. By Lt.-Col. F. S. Brereton. London: Constable, 1919. xiv, 299 pp., index, 9 maps, 1 plan and 2 appendices.

The Army Medical Services Campaigns, Vol. I, Vol. IV, Vol. V. By F. A. E. Crew. London: H.M.S.O, 1962, 687 pp., illustrations. 9½in.

Organisation, Strategy and Tactics of the Army Medical Services in War. By T. B. Nicholls. London: Bailliere, Tindall and Cox, 1937, 372 pp. 9in.

Medical Officers in the British Army 1660–1960. 2 vols. Vol 1 1660–1898 by A. Peterkin (1660–1727) and W. Johnston (1727–1898); Vol 2 (1898–1960) by Lt Gen Sir Robert Drew. Wellcome Historical Medical Library 1968. 1238 pp in all. A record of all commissioned officers in the medical services of the British army over a period of 300 years.

The Story of the Harton War Hospital Epsom. By J. R. Lord. London: Heinemann, 1920. 264 pp.

A Record of the 3rd East Anglian Field Ambulance (Four Lines) namely 1/3rd East Anglian Field Ambulance, Special Reserve, 2/2nd, and 3/3rd East Anglian Field Ambulance, during the Great War, 1914–1919, 125 pp., illustrations, c.1920.

With the 1/1st Lowland Field Ambulance in Gallipoli. By Col. G. H. Edington. Glasgow: Alex. Macdougall, 1920. 72 pp., plates, sketch maps. 9½in.

ROYAL ARMY ORDNANCE CORPS

A short history of the Royal Army Ordnance Corps. By A. H. Rushin. R.A.O.C. School of Instruction, 1931. 43 pp.

History of the Royal Army Ordnance Corps, 1920–1945. By Brig. Alan Henry Fernyhough and Maj. Henry E. D. Harris. Blackdown, [1967], xvi, 492 pp., portrait plates, maps and tables. 8vo.

The Royal Army Ordnance Corps. By M. J. Axford. Glasgow: Paramount Press, 1963, 140 pp., illustrations, map. 8¾in.

A Short History of the R.A.O.C. By Brig. A. H. Fernyhough. [Corps title in full on paper cover.] London: printed by C. B. Printers Ltd., 1966, 48 pp. 8½in.

History of 3 Base Ordnance Depot. By H. R. Alden, no imprint. October 1965, 116 pp., illustrations, maps. 9½in.

ROYAL ELECTRICAL AND MECHANICAL ENGINEERS

Craftsmen of the Army: The Story of the Royal Electrical and Mechanical Engineers. By Brigadier B. B. Kennett and Col. J. A. Tatman. London: L. Cooper, 1970. xiii, 425 pp., illustrations, maps. 9in.

CORPS OF ROYAL MILITARY POLICE

From the Beaches to the Baltic—Provost Company, 11th Armoured Div. By H. Mitchell. No imprint. 16 pp.

The Story of the Royal Military Police. By A. V. Lovell-Knight. London: Leo Cooper, 1977. 360p, maps, illustrations, 9¾in.

ROYAL ARMY VETERINARY CORPS

Army Veterinary Service in War, 191 pp., 1921.

The History of the Royal Army Veterinary Corps 1919–1961. By Brigadier J. Clabby. London: J. A. Allen, 1963. 244 pp., many text illustrations and photographs, maps.

QUEEN ALEXANDRA'S ROYAL ARMY NURSING CORPS

Grey touched with Scarlet. The War Experiences of the Army Nursing Sisters. By Jean Bowden. London: Robert Male Ltd., 1959, 189 pp., portraits, plates. 8½in.

SECTION IV

AUXILIARY FORCES

MILITIA: SPECIAL RESERVE

The Constitutional Force. By Col G. Jackson Hay. 1987 reprint of 1908 publication. Copy-numbered edition of 300. 447 pp. History of the Militia, which became the Special Reserve in Haldane's reforms. Order of precedence of every militia unit in existence in 1905 with periods of embodiment and details of active service.

A Short History of the Royal Buckinghamshire, King's Own, Militia and now 3rd Oxfordshire Light Infantry. Warwick: printed by R. Spennell, 1893, 11 pp. 6½in.

Record of the Royal Buckinghamshire King's Own Militia, raised in the reign of Charles IInd. Wycombe: R. Cowpe, printer, n.d., c. 188–, 20 pp. 6½in.

Some notes on The Royal Cardiganshire Militia and its heirs and successors, being the Auxiliary Forces of Cardiganshire. By G. Archer Parfitt. Shrewsbury: G. Archer Parfitt, 1981. viii, 75 pp., illustrations.

The Irish Militia 1793–1816: a Social and Military Study. By Sir Henry McAnally. viii, 338 pp. Coloured frontispiece. Dublin: Clonmore and Reynolds, and London: Eyre and Spottiswode, 1949. 8½in.

Historical Records of the West Kent Militia. With some account of the earlier defensive levies in Kent. By J. Bonhote. London: Hudson & Kearns, 1909. 490 pp., illustrations. 9¾in.

Northamptonshire Militia Lists 1777. By V. A. Hatley. Northamptonshire Record Society, 1973. 260 pp., illustrations. 10½in.

Militia, Yeomanry and Volunteer Forces of the East Riding, 1689–1908. By R. W. S. Norfolk. East Yorkshire Local History Society, 1965, 58 pp., illustrations. 8¾in.

YEOMANRY

ENGLAND AND WALES

The Berkshire Yeomanry: an interesting résumé of its history, status, and work ... Reprinted from 'The Whitehall Review'. 8 pp., illustrations.

The White Horse. A History of the Berkshire Yeomanry. Vol II (1921–1946) by W. H. Skrine. 87 pp. plus appendices (12 pp.), folio, 2 photocopies maps, roneo/ cyclostyled, *n.d.*, no imprint, *c.*1970.

The Cheshire (Earl of Chester's) Yeomanry 1898–1967: The Last Regiment to Fight on Horses. By Lt-Col. Sir Richard Verdin. London: Cavalry Club, 1971. xviii, 666 pp., frontispiece, illustrations, maps.

Order Book of the 26th (Dorset) Company I.Y. For About A Year in South Africa. By Capt. Sir E. Lees, 240 pp., illustration and map, printed for private circulation to members of the Corps by Henry Ling, Dorchester, 1903 Edition, limited to less than 200 copies.

The Essex Yeomanry, Records and Recollections, 1901–1914. Reprinted from the Essex Review, 1951, 19 pp., illustrations. 8½in.

A Short History of the Essex Yeomanry. By T. H. S. Story. No imprint [1969]. 5 pp. 8¾in.

An Outline History of the Yeomanry Forces of Glamorgan and Monmouthshire and Historical Records of Gunner Regiments of the Two Counties, Edited by Capt. A. R. Hazelrigg. Newport, Mon. 1965, ii, 37 pp. 4to.

The Yeomen of Yore. Glamorgan Yeomanry, 1794–1965. By D. Cowbridge. Brown & Sons, 1966, 63 pp., illustrations. 8¼in.

The Yeoman or Yore, Anecdotes and History of the Glamorgan Yeomanry 1794–1915. By J. Smith, 63 pp., Cambridge, 1966.

Glamorgan—Its Gentlemen and Yeomanry 1797–1980. By B. Owen. The Starling Press, 1983. 139 pp., illustrations. 8¾in.

Royal Gloucestershire Hussars, Coronation Year, 1953. Published by the Regiment, 1953, 48 pp., illustrations. 8¾in.

Hertfordshire Yeomanry and Artillery Uniforms, Arms and Equipment. Vol.1. By J. D. Sainsbury. Hertfordshire Yeomanry & Artillery Historical Trust, 1980. 83 pp., illustrations. 9¾in.

Kent Yeo. Sketches by a Kent Yeoman 1914–1918 (Gallipoli, Malta, Suez, Sollum, Palestine, France), 72 pp. many illustrations and sketches, 4to, wrappers, A. Melrose, *c.*1922.

With the 36th West Kent Squadron Imperial Yeomanry in South Africa, Jan. 9th 1900—July 19th, 1901. By Capt. H. Bertram Pott. Illustrated with photographs, 1901. 4to.

Trumpet Call. The Story of the Duke of Lancaster's Own Yeomanry (Boer War to W.W.II). By Lt.-Col. J. C. Bastick. 95 pp., illustrations and maps, 1973.

The Duke of Lancaster's Own Yeomanry. By Worsley. 1973. 84 pp., illustrations. 8¼in.

Records of the Rough Riders (XXth Battalion Imperial Yeomanry) Boer War 1899–1902. By Capt. H. G. McKenzie, 298 pp., illustrations and folding map, Brown & Wilson, Bedford, 1907.

The Sharpshooters. The 3rd County of London Yeomanry and successor units, 1900–61 and Kent and County of London Yeomanry 1969–70. By B. Mollo. London: Historical Research Unit 1970. 83 pp., illustrations. 8¾in.

Middlesex Duke of Cambridge's Hussars Yeomanry Cavalry. Historical Notes 1830–90. Published by Authority, 1890, 16 pp., illustrations. 6in.

Middlesex Yeomanry Magazine. Souvenir Number 1914–1919. No imprint. 1919. 72 pp., portraits, plates. 8½in.

The Norfolk Yeomanry in Peace and War. By J. Bastin. Norfolk: The Iceni Press, 1986. 309 pp., maps. 9in.

Northamptonshire Yeomanry 1794–1964. By H. de L. Cazenove. Northampton: H. de L. Cazenove, 1966. 19 pp., illustrations. 8¾in.

The Story of a Regiment, being a Short History of Northumberland Hussars Yeomanry 1819–1969. By H. Tegner. Index, coloured plates of uniform and guidons. Newcastle-upon-Tyne: Frank Graham, 1969. viii, 132 pp. illustrations. 9¼in.

A History of the Northumberland Hussars 1945–1983. By J. Bastin. Berwick: Northumberland Hussars, illustrations, 141 pp. 9in.

The Shropshire Yeomanry (6th) (Dragoons) R.A.C. (T.A.). By G. Archer Parfitt. Shrewsbury, Regimental Museum, n.d. [c. 1965], 28 pp., illustrations. 13in.

Rules and Orders to be observed by the South Shropshire Regiment of Yeomanry Cavalry; together with a List of Regimentals, part of the Sword-Exercise. Wellington, n.d., 1809, woodcuts.

Souvenir of The Queen's Own Royal Staffordshire Yeomanry, 1794–1894. The centenary celebration and visit of H.R.H. the Prince of Wales. Reprinted from the Lichfield 'Mercury' June 2nd 1894. Lichfield: Egginton & Brown, printers, 1894, 26 leaves and advertising pages, portraits, illustrations. 7 × 11¼in.

The Surrey and Sussex Yeomanry in the Second World War. By Lt. Col. T. B. Davis. Ditchling Press, 1980. 370 pp., illustrations, maps. 8¾in.

The historical journal of the Royal Wessex Yeomanry: with a Preface by The Secretary of State for Defence and a Foreword by Colonel The Duke of Beaufort, Honorary Colonel The Royal Wessex Yeomanry. Edited by J. D. Bastin. Royal Wessex Yeomanry, 1980. 118 pp., illustrations.

A History of the Westminster Dragoons 1901 to 1967, by Captains C. C. P. Lawson & N. Huw-Williams. 1969, 350 pp. Honours & Awards.

The Royal Wiltshire Yeomanry 1907–1967, by Brig. J. R. I. Platt. 1972, 272 pp.

The Queen's Own Worcestershire Hussars 1922–1956. By David Reginald Guttery. Stourbridge: Mark and Moody, 1958. 159 pp., illustrations, maps.

Militia, Yeomanry and Volunteer Forces of the East Riding, 1689–1908. By R. W. S. Norfolk. East Yorkshire Local History Society, 1965, 58 pp., illustrations. 8¾in.

Europe Revisited, the East Riding Yeomanry in the Liberation of Europe and the Defeat of Germany. By V. C. Ellison, 112 pp., 26 illustrations., Hull, c.1954.

SCOTLAND

Brief Historical Notes on the Ayrshire Yeomanry (Earl of Carricks Own) 152 Field Regiment, R.A, 1939–45. By Major B. M. Knox. Ayr: Stephen & Pollock, 1946, 80 pp., portraits, illustrations and maps, printed paper wrappers. 7½in.

Some Experiences with The Ayrshire Yeomanry in South Africa. By James Bell of Enterkine, Major. Introduction, initialled (James Edward Shaw) who saw the work published after Major Bell's death, is dated April 1916. No imprint, 1916, 63 pp., frontispiece. 8½in.

Historical Records of the Border Yeomanry Regiments by Engineer-Lieutenant Benson F. M. Freeman, T.N., 42 pp., 4to, (The four Eastern Corps of the Border Yeomanry), reprinted from the 'Kelso Mail' 1906.

From Gallipoli to Baghdad. By W. Ewing, [Edinburgh and Lothians]. 318 pp., 17 illustrations and a map. 1917.

The Muster Roll of the Forfarshire, or Lord Ogilby's Regiment raised on behalf of the Royal House of Stuart in 1745–6, with biographical sketches. By A. Mackintosh, xix, 189 pp., 20 illustrations, Inverness, 1914.

VOLUNTEERS: TERRITORIAL FORCE (LATER ARMY)

The Rifle Volunteers: the History of the Rifle Volunteers 1859–1908. By Roy Westlake. Chippenham: Picton Publishing, 1982. xviii, 173 pp., illustrations.

The Territorial Force 1914. By Ray Westlake. 1988. 138 pp. Detailed composition of the Territorial Force in 1914, showing headquarters and locations of every sub-unit, unit and formation and the Order of Battle of every division and brigade.

The Territorial Year Book. First Year of Issue. 1988 reprint by R. Westlake of 1908 publication. xiv, 295 pp.

A Short History of Units administered by the Bedfordshire Territorial and Auxiliary Forces Association. Published by the Association, 1955, 78 pp., illustrations. 7in.

With the Cambridgeshires at Singapore by W. Taylor, 129 pp. including index, illustrations and maps, 4to, March, Cambridgeshire, 1971.

Hertfordshire Soldiers from 1757, a Survey of the Auxiliary Forces raised in Hertfordshire. By Lt.-Col. J. D. Sainsbury, illustrations. Hitchen: Hertfordshire Local History Council, 1969. 103 pp. 9¾in.

An Inventory of Armour, Arms and Other Items of Military Interest in the Possession of the Honourable Artillery Company of London. By A. D. C. Le Sueur, no imprint, 1925, 38 pp., illustrations. 9½in.

Historical Records of the London Regiment. By A. R. Martin. No imprint, 1975. 96 pp., illustrations, maps. 8¼in.

London Men in Palestine, and how they marched to Jerusalem. By R. Coldicott, 243 pp., illustrations, 1919.

The Devil's Own Time. By Rell and Abel (Inns of Court O.T.C.). Phobus Press. 72 pp. 7in.

The C.I.V. and the War in South Africa 1900, the City Press Souvenir, 48 pp., illustrations, pictorial wrappers, City Press Office London, 1900.

The C.I.V., being the Story of the City Imperial Volunteers and Volunteer Regiments of the City of London, 1300–1900, The Inception, Organisation and Fighting Record of the Corps, with an Historical Introduction. Nearly sixty illustrations by well-known artists, from Descriptions by Members of the Corps. Contains Nominal Roll. 500 copies only. London: George Newnes Ltd., 1901, iv, 44 pp., portraits, illustrations. 14in.

An Historical Survey of The London Rifle Brigade Rangers. Produced by the Royal Masonic School, 1959, 8 pp. illustrations. 10in.

Terriers in the Trenches: The Post Office Rifles at War 1914–1918. By Charles Messenger. Picton Publishing, 1982. xii, 170 pp., illustrations, maps.

The 10th (County of London) Battalion The London Regiment, The Paddington Rifles 1908–1912. By J. P. Kelleher. London: J. P. Kelleher, 1982. 17 pp., illustrations.

2/15th Btn County of London Regiment: Prince of Wales Own Civil Service Rifles, London: Art Reproduction Co. June 1916. 24 pp., illustrations.

The Artists and the S.A.S. By B. A. Young. London: published by the Regiment, 1960. 63 pp., illustrations. 8¾in.

The Artists Rifles, 28th London Regiment. Published by the Regiment, n.d. [c. 1933]. 12 pp., illustrations. 7in.

The Lambeth & Southwark Volunteers a Century of Voluntary Service in the Volunteers and Territorials 1860–1960 (Queen's), by John M. A. Tamplin. 1965, 500 pp. Honours & Awards Roll of Honour. Chronological Roll of Officers, alphabetical Roll of Officers and other Ranks. Limited to 600 numbered copies.

The Volunteer Annual (Metropolitan Corps) 1903. Edited by A. E. Johnson. Reprint by Ray Westlake. 104 pp plus original adverts. Reference source on the organisation and work of the Metropolitan Volunteer and Yeomanry Corps.

The Early History of the 17th (North) Middlesex Volunteer Rifles, (Formerly 29th) 1859–1889. By Colour-Sergeant R. Rudd, 135 pp., illustrations, 4to, 1895.

History of the Volunteer Movement in Monmouthshire. By Col. Thomas Mitchell. Newport, 1913. v, 60 pp., portraits. 12mo.

Radnorshire Volunteers; a regimental history of Radnorshire, 1539–1968. By G. Archer Parfitt. Hay-on-Wye, 1968. 143 pp., portraits, illustrations. Fo.

The Book of the First Surrey Rifles; compiled from material gathered by Major Richards, illustrated with engravings made from photographs and edited by Lance-Corporal Henderson. Printed and published at St. Albans November 1914 for the battalion by Smith's Printing Co. Ltd., 48 pp., card covers. 9¾in.

The Territorials of Surrey, 1908–1958. By Lt. Col. Donovan Jackson. London: Owen Spyer & Co. Ltd., 1958, 28 pp., plates. 1 coloured plate of uniform and 1 of medals. 6½ × 8½in.

Sussex Sappers; A History of the Sussex Volunteer and Territorial Army Royal Engineer Units from 1890 to 1967, by Col. L. F. Morling, N.D., *c*.1970, 275 pp.

East York Volunteer Infantry 1859–1908. By R. Wilson and G. A. Collinson. Hull: Fineprint, 1982. 53 pp., illustrations.

West York Rifle Volunteers 1859–1887. By Dixon Pickup. Leicester: K. D. Pickup, 1981. 60 pp., illustrations.

SCOTLAND

In Kilt and Khaki, Glimpses of the Glasgow Highlanders in Training and in Foreign Service, 201 pp. Kilmarnock, 1916.

SECTION V

MISCELLANEOUS

WOMEN'S CORPS

F.A.N.Y. The Story of the Women's Transport Service, 1907–1984. By H. Popham. London: Leo Cooper, Secker & Warburg, 1984. 146 pp., illustrations. 8¾in.

A Short History of Queen Mary's Army Auxiliary Corps. By Col. Julia M. Cowper. [Guildford, 1966.] 68 pp., portrait, illustrations. 8vo.

DISBANDED REGIMENTS AND CORPS

SECTION 1—NUMBERED REGIMENTS

XXII Dragoons. 1760–1945. The Story of a Regiment. By R. Birt. Aldershot: Gale & Polden, 1950. xxix, 349 pp., illustrations, maps. 8½in.

78th Fighting Frasers in Canada. A Short History of the old 78th Regiment or Fraser's Highlanders, 1757–1763. By J. R. Harper. Chomedey, Canada: Dev-Sco Publications Ltd., 1966, xviii, 98 pp., illustrations. 7¾in.

SECTION 2 — NAMED REGIMENTS AND CORPS

A Narrative of the Campaigns of the Loyal Lusitanian Legion during the Years 1809, 1810 and 1811. By Lt Col W. Mayne and Capt Lillie (1812). Ken Trotman Military History Monographs. Limited edition reprint.1986. viii, 346 pp.

The Machine Gun Corps: a short history. By F. A. Stevens. Tonbridge: F. A Stevens, 1981, 46 pp.

An Informal Record of 26 Machine Gun Training Centre. (Formed of Royal Northumberland Fusiliers and Middlesex Regiment). Edited by Lieut. S. R. Barrey, assisted by Lieut. E. J. Frary. Chester: printed by W. H. Evans, Sons & Co. Ltd., 1946, xi, 249 pp., portraits, plates, illustrations. 9½in.

The Fighting Newfoundlander. A History of the Royal Newfoundland Regiment. Includes: Pringle's Newfoundland Volunteers 1778–80; Newfoundland Regt. of Foot, 1780–83; The Royal Newfoundland Volunteers, 1793–?; The Royal Newfoundland Regt., 1795–1802; The Loyal Volunteers of St. John's, 1805–12; St.

John's Volunteer Rangers, 1812–14; The Royal Newfoundland Fencible Infantry, 1803–16. Published by the Govt. of Newfoundland. Thos. Nelson (Printers) Ltd., London, 1965, xix, 614 pp., portraits, illustrations, maps, end-paper maps. 9½in.

The Queen's York Rangers. By S. H. Bull. Ontario: The Boston Mills Press, 1984. 248 pp., illustrations. 10¼in.

The Home Guard of Britain. By Charles Graves. London: Hutchinson, c. 1943. 364 pp., illustrations.

The Real Dad's Army: the story of the Home Guard. By Norman Longmate. London: Arrow 1974. 128 pp., illustrations.

ROYAL MARINES

Royal Marines Corps Album. By Captain J. J. Hicks. London: Whitehead Morris Ltd., n.d. [c. 1935], 42 pp., coloured and other illustrations. 6in, oblong.

1664–1964. An Account of the Royal Marines Tercentenary Celebrations, 1964. Ipswich: W. S. Cowell Ltd., n.d. [c. 1964], 88 pp., illustrations. 11in.

The Royal Marines. By Lord Latymer. London: Arthur L. Humphreys, 1915, 23 pp. 9¾in.

The Green Beret, the Story of the Commandos 1940–1945. By H. St.G. Saunders, 354 pp. and index, 35 illustrations and 6 maps, 1949.

The Royal Marines. By Maj.-Gen. J. L. Moulton. London: L. Cooper, 1972. x, 100 pp., illustrations. 8¾in.

Royal Marine Commando: the history of Britain's élite fighting force. By James D. Ladd. London: Hamlyn, 1982. 176 pp., illustrations.

Random Records of the Royal Marines, being a non-chronological collection of details from the diaries and letters of some of their past and present officers, non commissioned officers and men; from official documents, and from notes and accounts from various sources, of their character, history, uniform and colours, their barracks and other matters of interest. By Gen. Sir H. Blumberg and Col. C. Field. Based on Edye's collection, which came into Field's hands after publication of Britain's Sea Soldiers. 'Globe and Laurel' Journal, 1935, vi, 312 pp., illustrations. Large 4to.

A Ghost of a General and the R.M. Officer Corps of 1914. A Royal Marines Historical Society Booklet by Dr. Donald F. Bittner. 63 pp 18 photographs.

Swiftly they Struck, the Story of No 4 Commando. By M. McDougall, 208 pp., 23 illustrations and 3 maps, 1954.

Lower the Ramps! Action with the 43rd Royal Marine Commando in Yugoslavia. By E. G. Stokes. 136 pp., illustrations. London: printed and published by Brown, Watson, Ltd., 1955. 7½in.

History of 43 Commando Royal Marines. Printed by Group Printing Office, H.Q. R.M., Plymouth, 1962. 12 pp., portrait, 7¼in.

48 Royal Marine Commando; The Story, 1944–46. Printed by Tee & Whiten & J. Mead Ltd., 1946, plates, maps, end-paper maps. 8¼in.

ADDITIONAL INFORMATION

Page 14.
History of the Royal Dragoons, 1661–1934 by C. T. Atkinson. There is an edition limited to 125 copies on fine paper, bound in decorative half binding of light brown leather, gilt decorations.

Page 18.
The History of the Eighth King's Royal Irish Hussars, 1693–1927. By Robert H. Murray. Limited to 250 copies.

Page 42.
The Colours of the British Army ... by Robert French McNair, There is also an edition published in 1870 with xii, 64 pp., 20 coloured plates.

Page 130.
History of the Royal Munster Fusiliers. By Capt. S. McCance. There is a de luxe edition limited to 114 copies.

Page 190.
Historical Record of the Herefordshire Light Infantry and Its Predecessors, edited G. Archer Parfitt. Edition limited to 250 copies.

Page 213.
The Colours of the 4th Bn K.S.L.I. and its Predecessors. By G. Archer Parfitt, Edition limited to 250 copies.

Page 223.
Territorial Soldiering in the North-East of Scotland during 1759–1814. By John Malcolm Bulloch. Edition limited to 400 copies.

INDEX

Aberdeen University Coy. 224
Aberdeenshire Fencibles 147
Aberdeenshire Militia 156
Aberdeenshire Volunteers 223
African Colonial Corps, Royal 246
Ancient British Fencible Cavalry 146
Anglesey Militia 149
Anglesey 6th R. Welch Fus., T.A. 181
Anglian Regt., Royal, 1st Bn. (Norfolk &
  Suffolk) – see Appx
Anglian Regt., Royal, 2nd Bn. (Royal
  Lincs. & Northants.) – see Appx
Anglian Regt., Royal, 3rd Bn. (16th/44th
  Foot) – see Appx
Anglian Regt., Royal, 1st Bn. (Royal
  Leicestershire) – see Appx
Antrim Militia 158
Archers, Royal Coy. of 256
Argyll & Sutherland Highlanders 128,
  305
Argyll & Sutherland Highlanders 3rd
  Militia Bn. 158
Argyll & Sutherland Highlanders 5th, 6th
  Bns. T.A. 232
Argyll & Sutherland Highlanders 7th Bn.
  T.A. 233
Argyll & Sutherland Highlanders 8th Bn.
  T.A. 224
Argyll & Sutherland Highlanders 9th Bn.
  T.A. 226
Argyll & Sutherland Highlanders 7th Vol.
  Bn. 226
Argyll Fencibles 147
Argyll Mountain Bty. 224
Argyllshire Highlanders 224, 242
Argyllshire Militia 157
Armagh Volunteers 234
Armoured Corps, Royal 9, 267
Army Chaplains Dept., Royal – see
  Chaplains
Army Dental Corps, Royal – see Dental
Army Educational Corps, Royal – see
  Educational
Army Medical Corps, Royal – see
  Medical
Army Ordnance Corps, Royal – see
  Ordnance
Army Pay Corps, Royal, – see Pay
Army Physical Training Corps 143
Army Service Corps, Royal 138, 308
Army Service Corps, Highland Mounted
  Bde. T.A. 231
Army Service Corps, London, City of,
  M.T. (V.) 207

Artillery, Royal 27, 272
Artillery, Royal Field 32, 34, 273
Artillery, Royal Foreign 251
Artillery, Royal Garrison 32, 34, 273
Artillery, Royal Horse 30, 273
Artists Rifles 206, 317
Atholl's Troop of Horse 242
Auxiliary Territorial Service 236
Ayrshire Militia 157
Ayrshire T.A. Units 225
Ayrshire Yeomanry 175, 315

Banffshire Fencibles 147
Banffshire Militia 157
Banffshire Volunteers 225
Bedfordshire & Hertfordshire Regt. 69,
  316
Bedfordshire & Herts. T.A. 179, 316
Bedfordshire Militia 149
Bedfordshire T.A. Bns. 316
Bedfordshire Yeomanry 161
Belper Volunteers 183
Berkshire, R.H.A. 179
Berkshire, Militia, Royal 149
Berkshire Regt., Royal 105, 316
Berkshire Regt., T.A. Bns. 179
Berkshire Yeomanry 162, 312
Berwickshire Yeomanry 176
Birmingham Volunteers 217
Black Watch 95, 295
Black Watch, T.A. Bns. 227, 232
Black Watch, 14th (Yeomanry) Bn. 176
Bolton Artillery 272
Border Regt. 87, 292
Border Regt., King's Own Royal – see
  Appx
Borderers, King's Own Scottish – see
  Scottish
Breadalbane Fencibles 147-8
Brecknockshire Bn. S.W.B. 180
Brighton Volunteers 217
Bristol Volunteers 187
British German Legion 252
British Swiss Legion 253
Buckinghamshire Hussars Yeo. 162
Bucks Bn. Oxf. & Bucks L.I. 180
Buckinghamshire King's Own Militia,
  Royal 312
Buffs, The 53, 280
Buffs, 3rd Bn. 151
Buffs, T.A. Bns. 191
Buffs, Queen's Own – see Appx
Butler's Rangers 248

Caithness Fencibles 147
Caithness Bn., 5th Seaforth Highlanders 226
Camberley Cadets 216
Cambridge University R.V. 180
Cambridgeshire Militia 149
Cambridgeshire Regt., T.A. 180
Cameron Highlanders 79, 303
Cameron Highlanders, T.A. Bns. 230
Cameron Highrs., 3rd Militia Bn. 158
Cameronians 77, 289
Cameronians, T.A. Bns. Glasgow 229
Cameronians T.A. Bns. Lanark 231
Canadian Fencibles 249
Canadian Rifle Regt., Royal 246
Canadian Volunteers, Royal 249
Canadians, Royal – see Leinster Regt.
Cape Mounted Riflemen 246
Cape Regts. 246
Carabiniers, 3rd 11, 267
Cardiganshire Militia 312
Cardiganshire Yeomanry 171
Cardross's Dragoons 242
Carlow Militia 158
Carmarthenshire Yeomanry 171
Carnarvonshire Bn. R. Welch Fus. 181
Carnarvonshire Volunteers 181
Carnarvonshire Yeomanry 163
Ceylon Regts. 246
Ceylon Rifle Regt. 247
Channel Islands Militia 161
Chaplains Dept., Royal Army 138, 308
Cheshire Regt. 74, 287
Cheshire Regt. T.A. Bns. 181
Cheshire Royal Engineers 181
Cheshire Volunteers 181
Cheshire Yeomanry 162, 313
Chinese Regt. 247
Cinque Ports Bn. 217
City Imperial Volunteers 200, 316
Civil Service Rifles 203
Clackmannan Militia 158
Clackmannan Volunteers 226
Clan Alpine Fencibles 147-8
Claverhouse's Horse 243
Coldstream Guards 43, 277
Commisariat & Transport Corps 243
Connaught Rangers 127, 304
Connaught Milita Bn. 3rd 159
Connaught Milita Bn. 4th 160
Cork, North, Milita 158
Cork, South, Milita 158
Cork, Volunteers & Yeomanry 234
Cornwall Artillery Volunteers 182
Cornwall R.E., T.A. 182
Cornwall R.G.A. Militia 149

Cornwall's, Duke of, Light Inf. 85, 291
Cornwall's, Duke of, L.I., T.A. Bns. 182
Corsican Corps 250
Cromwell's Regts. 243
Cumberland R.G.A. Volunteers 182
Cumberland Sharpshooters 202
Cumberland Yeomanry 173

Denbighshire Bn. R. Welch Fus., T.A. 183
Denbighshire Yeomanry 163
Dental Corps, Royal Army 143
Derbyshire Bns. Sherwood Foresters, T.A. 183
Derbyshire Yeomanry 163
Devon & Dorset Regt. – see Appx
Devon Militia 150
Devon Yeomanry 163
Devonshire Regt. 63
Devonshire Regt. T.A. Bns. 184
Devonshire Volunteers 184
Doneraile Rangers 234
Dorset Militia 150
Dorset Regt. 92, 294
Dorset Regt. T.A. Bns. 185
Dorset Volunteers 184
Dorset Yeomanry 163, 313
Dorset & Hants Fd. Regt., 94th, R.A., T.A. 184
Downshire Militia 159
Dragoons, 1st Royal 14, 268, 322
Dragoons, 2nd (Scots Greys) 15, 268
Dragoons, 6th Inniskilling 13
Dragoons, 18th Light 237
Dragoons, 19th Light 237
Dragoons, 20th Light 238
Dragoons, 21st Light 238
Dragoons, 22nd Light 238, 319
Dragoons, 23rd Light 238
Dragoons, 27th Light 238
Dragoon Guards, 1st King's 10
Dragoon Guards, 1st Queen's – see Appx
Dragoon Guards, 2nd Queen's Bays 11
Dragoon Guards, 3rd Prince of Wales's 11, 267
Dragoon Guards, 4th Royal Irish 12, 267
Dragoon Guards, 5th Princess Charlotte of Wales's 13, 267
Dragoon Guards, 6th Carabiniers 11, 267
Dragoon Guards, 7th Princess Royal's 12, 267
Drummond's Troop of Horse 243
Dublin Fusiliers 306
Dumbarton Fencibles 147

Dumbartonshire Militia   158
Dumbartonshire Volunteers & T.A.   226
Dumfriesshire T.A. Bns.   227
Durham Fencibles   146
Durham Light Infantry   116, 301
Durham L.I., T.A. Bns.   185, 301
Durham Militia   150
Durham R.A. Volunteers & T.A.   185
Durham Yeomanry   170
Dutch Emigrant Artillery   251

Edinburgh Light Infantry Militia   157
Edinburgh T.A. Bns. & Artillery   227
Edinburgh Volunteers   227
Edinburgh's, Duke of, Royal Regt. – see
  Appx
Educational Corps, Royal Army   143
81st (Aberdeenshire) Foot   239
82nd, 1778-83   239
84th, 1758-63   239
84th, Royal Highland Emigrants   239
85th, 1759-63   240
85th, 1779-83   240
86th, Wall's African   240
87th, Keith's Highland   240
88th, Campbell's Highland   240
89th, Highland   240
Electrical & Mechanical Engineers, Royal
  141, 310
Engineers, Royal   36, 274
Engineers, T.A. units – see Section IV
Essex Militia   150
Essex Regt.   100
Essex Regt. T.A. Bns.   186, 296
Essex R.A., T.A.   186
Essex Yeomanry   164, 313

Fife Bn. T.A.., Black Watch   227
Fife & Forfar Yeomanry   176
First Aid Nursing Yeomanry   236, 319
Flintshire T.A. Bn., R. Welch Fus.   187
Flintshire Yeomanry   164
Foot Guards   41, 276
Foreign Artillery, Royal   251
Forfar Yeomanry   176
Frampton-on-Severn Volunteers   188
Fraser Fencibles   147
French Emigrant Artillery   251
Frimley Cadets   216
Furness Yeomanry   191
Fusiliers, Royal   58, 282
Fusiliers, Royal, 1st-4th London Regt.
  201, 317
Fusiliers, Royal, 1st Cadet Bn.   207

Fusiliers, Royal Dublin   131
Fusiliers, Royal Highland – see Appx
Fusiliers, Royal Inniskilling   80, 289
Fusiliers, Royal Irish   126, 303
Fusiliers, Royal Northumberland   54, 281
Fusiliers, Royal Northumberland, T.A.
  Bns.   212
Fusiliers, Royal Munster   130, 305
Fusiliers, Royal Tyrone   160

Galloway Artillery Volunteers   225
Galway Militia   159
Garrison Battalions   243
Gentlemen-at-Arms   255
German Legion, British   252
German Legion, King's   252
Glamorgan, T.A. Units   187
Glamorgan Yeomanry   301
Glasgow Highlanders   230, 318
Glasgow Militia   157
Glasgow T.A. Units   228
Glasgow Volunteers   230
Glasgow Yeomanry   176
Glengarry Fencibles   147
Glengarry Light Infantry   250
Glider Pilot Regt.   243
Gloucestershire Hussars Yeo.   165, 313
Gloucestershire Militia   150
Gloucestershire Regt.,   81, 289
Gloucestershire Regt., T.A. Bns.   188
Gloucestershire Volunteers   187
Gold Coast Artillery   247
Gooch's American Regt.   243
Gordon Fencibles   147-8
Gordon Highlanders   120, 303
Gordon Highlanders Militia Bn.   156
Gordon Highlanders T.A. Bns.   224
Grant Fencibles   147
Greek Light Infantry   251
Green Howards   71, 286
Green Howards T.A. Bns.   220
Green Jackets, 1st, 2nd, 3rd – see Appx
Grenadier Guards   41, 277
Guernsey Milita   161

Hampshire Regt., Royal   90, 293
Hampshire Regt. T.A. Bns.   188
Hampshire Milita   151
Hampshire Volunteers   189
Hampshire Yeomanry   165
Hants R.H.A., 1st   189
Haverfordwest Yeomanry   171
Herefordshire Regt., T.A.   190, 322
Hertfordshire Regt. T.A.   190

Hertfordshire Militia   151, 316
Hertfordshire Yeomanry   165, 313, 316
Hertfordshire, – see also Bedfordshire &
  Hertfordshire Regt.
Highland Fusiliers, Royal – see Appx
Highland Light Infantry   117, 302
Highland Light Infantry T.A. Bns.   229
Highland Regt., Royal – see Black Watch
Highlanders, Queen's Own (Cameron &
  Seaforth) – see Appx
Home Guard   320
Honourable Artillery Company   197, 200,
  316
Household Brigade   8, 266
Household Cavalry   8, 266
Horse Artillery, Royal   30
Horse Guards, Royal   9, 266
Huddersfield Volunteers   221
Huguenot Regts.   250
Hull Artillery   219
100th Regt., 1760-63   241
100th Regt., 1780-85   241
100th Regt., Pr. Regent's, Dublin   241
101st, 1760-63   241
102nd, New South Wales Corps   241
104th, New Brunswick Fencibles   241
105th, Queen's Own Highlanders   242
109th, 1761-63   242
109th Aberdeenshire   242
113rd, Royal Birmingham Vols.   242
116th, 1794-95   242
119th, 1762-63   242
Huntingdon Volunteers   190
Huntley Volunteers   226
Hussars, 3rd King's Own   16
Hussars, 4th Queen's Own   17, 268
Hussars, 7th Queen's Own   17, 269
Hussars, 8th Royal Irish   18, 269, 322
Hussars, 10th Royal   20, 269
Hussars, 11th   20, 269
Hussars, 13th   21
Hussars, 13th/18th Royal   21, 270
Hussars, 14th King's   22
Hussars, 14th/20th King's   22, 270
Hussars, 15th The King's   23
Hussars, 15th/19th The King's Royal   23,
  270
Hussars, 18th Queen Mary's Own Royal
  22
Hussars, 19th Royal   23
Hussars, 20th   23
Hussars, 23rd   238
Hussars, Queen's Own – see Appx
Hussars, Queen's Royal Irish – see Appx

Inniskilling Dragoons, 6th   13
Inniskilling Dragoon Guards, 5th Royal
  13, 267
Inniskilling Fusiliers, Royal   80, 289
Inns of Court O.T.C.   316
Inns of Court Regt.   198
Inverness Fencibles   147
Inverness-shire Militia   158
Inverness-shire T.A. Units   230
Irish Dragoon Guards, 4th Royal   12
Irish Fusiliers, Royal   126, 303
Irish Fusiliers, Royal Militia   160
Irish Guards   45, 278
Irish Horse, North   169
Irish Horse, South   245
Irish Hussars, Queen's Royal – see Appx
Irish Lancers, 5th Royal   24
Irish Regt., Royal   70
Irish Regt., R., Militia, Kilkenny   159
Irish Regt., R., Militia, Tipperary   160
Irish Rifles, Royal – see Ulster

Kensington Regt.   202
Kent Artillery Volunteers   190
Kent Militia   151, 312
Kent Regt., East – see Buffs
Kent Regt., West, Q.O. Royal   105, 298
Kent Regt., West, T.A. Bns.   191
Kent Regt., Royal – see Appx
Kent Volunteers   190
Kent Yeomanry   166, 313
Kilkenny Militia   159
Kincardine Volunteers   231
King Edward's Horse   243
King's Co. Militia   159
King's Dragoon Guards, 1st   10
King's German Legion   252
King's Hussars – see Hussars
King's Life Guard of Horse   244
King's Own Royal Regt. (Lancs.)   54,
  280
King's Own Royal Regt., Militia   151
King's Own Royal Regt., T.A. Bns.   192
King's Own Scottish Borderers – see
  Scottish
King's Own Yorkshire Light Infantry –
  see Yorkshire
King's Regt. (Liverpool)   60, 282
King's Regt. T.A. Bns.   193
King's Regt. (Manchester & Liverpool) –
  see Appx
King's Royal Regt. of New York   249
King's Royal Rifle Corps   110, 299

King's Royal Rifle Corps, 9th Bn. (N.
    Cork Militia) 158
King's Shropshire Light Infantry – see
    Shropshire
Kingston's, Duke of, Light Horse 244
Kinross Milita 158
Kinross Volunteers 226

Labour Corps 244
Lambeth and Southwark Volunteers 317
Lanarkshire Militia 158
Lanarkshire T.A. Units 231
Lanarkshire Yeomanry 177
    – see also under Glasgow
Lancashire Fusiliers 72, 286
Lancashire Fusiliers T.A. Bns. 193
Lancashire Regt. (Prince of Wales's
    Volunteers) – see Appx
Lancashire Militia 151
Lancashire Regt. East 83, 290
Lancashire Regt. East, T.A. Bns. 194
Lancashire, Loyal North – see Loyal Regt.
Lancashire Regt. South (Prince of Wales's
    Volunteers) 93, 294
Lancashire Regt. South, T.A. Bns. 194
Lancashire Yeomanry 166
Lancashire, East, R.E. 192
Lancashire, East, Fd. Amb., 2/3rd 195
Lancashire, West, Fd. Amb., 63rd 195
Lancashire, West, R.A. 191
Lancaster Regt., King's Own Royal – see
    King's
Lancaster's, Duke of, Own Yeomanry
    166, 314
Lancers, 5th Royal Irish 24
Lancers, 9th Queen's Royal 19
Lancers, 12th Royal 21, 270
Lancers, 16th Queen's 24, 270
Lancers, 17th 25, 271
Lancers, 21st 25, 271
Land Transport Corps 244
Leeds Rifles 222
Leeds Volunteers 222
Légion Britannique, 1760-62 250
Leicestershire Militia 152
Leicestershire Regt., Royal 69, 285
Leicestershire Regt., T.A. Bns. 195
Leicestershire Yeomanry 167
Leinster Regt. 130, 305
Leinster, Militia Bn., 3rd (King's Co.)
    159
Leinster, Militia Bn., 4th (Queen's Co.)
    160
Leinster, Militia Bns. 5th (Meath) 160
Life Guards 18, 266

Lincolnshire Regt., Royal 62, 283
Lincolnshire Regt., T.A. Bns. 196
Liverpool Regt. – see King's, The
Liverpool Scottish 193
Liverpool Volunteers 193
Lochaber Fencibles 147
London & Westminster Light Horse
    Volunteers 198
London C.I.V. 200, 316
London Cyclist Bn. 206
London, City & Co. of, Yeomanry 176
London Irish Rifles 204
London Field Ambulances 206
London General Hospital, 3rd 207
London Militia 152
London Regts 201, 317
London Rifle Brigade 201, 317
London R.A., T.A. 199, 272
London R.E., T.A. 200
London Scottish 203
London Trained Bands 152
London Volunteers 196
Longford Militia 159
Lothians & Border Horse 177
Loudon's Highlanders 244
Louis, Royal 250
Louth Militia 159
Lovat's Scouts 177
Loveden Volunteers 196
Lowland Field Ambulance 306
Loyal Regt., The (N. Lancs.) 103, 297
Loyal Regt., T.A. Bns. 193

Macclesfield Volunteers 181
Machine Gun Corps 244, 319
Malta Artillery, Royal 247
Maltese Corps 247
Manchester Regt. 113, 300
Manchester Regt., 3rd Bn. 300
Manchester Regt., T.A. Bns. 195, 300
Manchester Yeomanry 167
Manchester's, Duke of, Mtd. R.V. 190
Manx Fencibles 146
Manx Militia 151
Manx Volunteers & Yeomanry 190
Marines, Royal 253, 320
Maylor Yeomanry, Royal 163
Mayo Militia 159
Meath Militia 160
Medical Corps, Royal Army 139, 308
Medical Corps, Kent Vol. 191
Medical Corps, T.A. Birmingham 218
Medical Corps, T.A. Lancs. 195
Medical Corps, T.A. London 206
Medical Corps, T.A. Lowland 230

Medical Corps, T.A. Wessex 184
Medical Corps, W. Riding 223
Merioneth Militia 152
Merioneth T.A. Bn., R. Welch Fus. 208
Merioneth Volunteers 208
Meuron's Regt. 251
Middlesex Regt. 109, 299
Middlesex Regt. T.A. Bns. 208
Middlesex Volunteers 208
Middlesex Yeomanry 168, 314
Military Knights of Windsor 256
Military Police, Corps of Royal 142, 310
Military Train 244
Monaghan Militia 160
Monmouthshire Militia 152
Monmouthshire Regt., T.A. 209
Monmouthshire Volunteers 209, 317
Monmouthshire Yeomanry 165, 313
Montgomeryshire Militia 152
Montgomeryshire T.A. Bn. R.W.F. 210
Montgomeryshire Yeomanry 169
Morayshire T.A. Units 231
Mortlake Volunteers 215
Munster Fusiliers, Royal 130, 305, 322
Munster Fusiliers, 3rd Militia Bn. 158
Murray's, Lord John, Regt. 245

National Guard 207
New Brunswick Fencibles 241
New Brunswick Regt., King's 249
New Forest Yeomanry 165
Newfoundland Regt., Royal 249, 319
New Romney Fencible Cavalry 146
Newry Volunteers 234
New South Wales Corps 241
New York, King's Royal Regt. of 249
94th, Scotch Brigade 240
95th Regt., 1780-83 240
96th Regt., 1761-63, 1780-83, 1793-96
  241
97th Regt., 1794-95 241
97th Regt., Queen's Germans 241
Norfolk Fencible Cavalry 146
Norfolk Militia 153
Norfolk Regt., Royal 61, 282
Norfolk Regt. T.A. Bns. 210
Norfolk Yeomanry 169, 314
Northamptonshire Bty., R.F.A. 210
Northamptonshire Militia 153, 300
Northamptonshire Regt. 103, 297
Northamptonshire Regt. T.A. Bns. 210
Northamptonshire Yeomanry 169, 314
Northern Fencibles 147
Northumberland Fus., Royal 54, 281

Northumberland Fus., T.A. Bns. 212
Northumberland Militia 153
Northumberland Volunteers 211
Northumberland Yeo., Hussars 169, 314
Northumbrian Brigade R.A., T.A. 211
Northumbrian, 274th, Fd. Regt., R.A.,
  T.A. 185
Nottinghamshire Militia 153
Nottinghamshire Volunteers 212
Nottinghamshire Yeomanry 170
Nottinghamshire & Derbyshire Regt. – see
  Sherwood Foresters
Nova Scotia Regt., Royal 249
Nursing Corps, Royal Army 144, 311

Ordnance Corps, Royal Army 141, 310
Orkney Volunteers 232
Oxfordshire Hussars Yeomanry 171
Oxfordshire Militia 154
Oxfordshire & Buckinghamshire L.I. 98,
  296
Oxfordshire & Bucks. T.A. Bns. 213

Parachute Regt. 133, 306
Pay Corps, Royal Army 142
Peeblesshire Yeomanry 171
Pembrokeshire Militia 154
Pembrokeshire Yeomanry 176
Percy Artillery 211
Perthshire Fencibles 148
Perthshire Militia 158
Perthshire T.A. Units 232
Perthshire Volunteers 232
Perthshire Yeomanry 177
Pevensey, North, Legion 216
Physical Training Corps, Army 143
Pioneer Corps, Royal 143
Police, Corps of Royal Military 142, 310
Post Office Rifles 202
Prince of Wales's Volunteers – see
  Lancashire, South, Regt.
Prince of Wales's Regt. of Horse 245
Prince of Wales's Own Regt. of Yorkshire
  – see Appx
Provost Staff Corps, Military 142

Queen Alexandra's Imperial Military
  Nursing Service 144
Queen's Bays, 2nd Dragoon Guards 11
Queen's County Militia 160
Queen's Dragoon Guards 267
Queen's Light Infantry Militia 157

Queen Marys Army Auxiliary Corps   319
Queen's Own Highlanders (Cameron &
   Seaforth) – see Appx
Queen's Own Hussars – see Appx
Queen's Own Royal West Kent Regt. –
   see Kent
Queen's Royal Irish Hussars – see Appx
Queen's Rangers   248
Queen's Royal Regt. (West Surrey)   51,
   279
Queen's Royal Regt., T.A. Bns.   216
Queen's Royal Regt., T.A. 22nd & 24th
   London   205
Queen's Royal Surrey Regt. – see Appx
Queen's Westminster's   204

Radnorshire Military Hist.   213
Radnorshire Militia   154
Radnorshire Volunteers   317
Rangers, 12th London Regt.   202
Reay Fencibles   147-8
Reconnaissance Corps   245
Reconnaissance 5th Regt.   212
Reconnaissance 15th Scottish   245
Reconnaissance 3rd Regt. (N.F.)   212
Reconnaissance 43rd Regt. (Glos.)   189
Reconnaissance 52nd Div.   228
Renfrew Volunteers   232
Reserve Bns.   243
Richmond (Surrey) Volunteers   215
Rifle Brigade   133, 306
Rifle Bde. 6th Bn. (Longford Mil.)   159
Roger's Rangers   248
Roll's Regt.   251
Roscommon Militia   160
Rossall School Corps   195
Rothesay Fencibles   147
Roxburghshire Yeomanry   176
Royal – see main title
Rugby School Corps   218
Rutland Militia   153
Rye Volunteers   216

Scots Brigade   245
Scots Fusiliers, Royal   73, 286
Scots Fusiliers, T.A. Bns.   225
Scots Greys, Royal   15, 268
Scots Guards   44, 277
Scots, Royal   50, 279
Scots, Royal, Militia   157
Scots, Royal, T.A. Bns.   227
Scottish Borderers, King's Own   78, 288
Scottish Borderers, Militia   157
Scottish Borderers, T.A. Bns.   225, 227

Scottish Horse   177
Scottish Rifles – see Cameronians
Seaforth Highlanders   119, 302
Seaforth Highrs. T.A. Bns. 4th (Ross)
   233
Seaforth Highrs., 5th (Caithness)   226
Seaforth Highlanders, 6th (Moray)   231
Selkirkshire Yeomanry   176
Service Corps, Royal Army – see Army
71st (Fraser's)   238
72nd (Royal Manchester Vols.)   238
74th (Argyle)   239
76th (Macdonald's)   239
77th (Montgomery's)   239
77th (Atholl)   239
78th (Fraser's)   239, 319
Sharpshooters, 3rd & 4th London
   Yeomanry   168, 314
Sherwood Foresters   101, 296
Sherwood Foresters Militia   153
Sherwood Foresters T.A. Bns. (Derby)
   183
Sherwood Foresters T.A. Bns. (Notts.)
   212, 296
Sherwood Rangers Yeomanry   170
Shetland Volunteers   232
Shropshire Cadets   214
Shropshire Light Infantry, King's   108,
   298
Shropshire L.I., 4th Bn., T.A.   213, 322
Shropshire Volunteers   213
Shropshire Yeomanry   171, 314
Sidmouth Volunteers   184
Signals, Royal Corps of   40, 276
Signals, 47th London   200
Signals, 48th Div.   217
Signals, 49th W. Riding   221
Signals, 61st Div.   217
Skinner's Fencibles   249
Small Arms School Corps   142
Somerset Light Infantry   65, 283
Somerset Light Infantry, T.A. Bns.   214
Somerset Militia   154
Somerset Volunteers   214
Somerset Yeomanry   172
Somerset & Cornwall L.I. – see Appx
Special Air Service Regt.   133, 306
Spelthorne Legion, Royal   208
Staff Corps, Royal   246
Stafford Battery   214
Staffordshire, Militia   154, 294
Staffordshire Regt. – see Appx
Staffordshire Regt., North   113, 300
Staffordshire Regt., N., T.A. Bns.   214
Staffordshire Regt., South   91, 293
Staffordshire Regt., S., T.A. Bns.   214

Staffordshire Yeomanry   172, 314
Stirlingshire Militia   158
Stock Exchange Cadets   208
Strathspey Fencibles   147
Suffolk Militia   155
Suffolk Regt.   64, 283
Suffolk Regt. T.A. Bns.   215
Suffolk Regt., 15th (Yeo.) Bn.   172
Suffolk R.A., T.A.   215
Suffolk Volunteers   215
Suffolk Yeomanry   172
Surrey Cadets   216
Surrey Militia   155
Surrey Rifles, First   205, 317
Surrey Volunteers   215
Surrey Yeomanry   173, 315
Surrey, East, Regt.   84, 290
Surrey, East, Regt., T.A. Bns.   215, 291
Surrey, East, 57th, R.A., T.A.   215
Surrey, West, Q.O. Royal – see Queen's
Sussex R.A., T.A.   216
Sussex Regt., Royal   89, 292
Sussex Regt., T.A. Bns.   217, 292
Sussex Regt., 16th (Yeo.) Bn.   173
Sussex R.E.   318
Sussex Yeomanry   173, 315
Sutherland Fencibles   147
Sutherland T.A. Bn. 5th Seaforth   226
Swiss Legion, British   253

Tank Corps, Royal   25
Tank Regt., Royal   25, 271
Tank Regt., 2nd   271
Tank Regt., 4th   271
Tank Regt., 42nd   205, 271
Tank Regt., 44th   271
Tank Regt., 50th   271
Tank Regt., 51st Bn.   220
Tipperary, Militia   160
Tyne Electrical Engineers   211, 275
Tyneside Irish   160
Tyneside Scottish   160
Tyrone Militia   160

Ulster Rifles, Royal   124, 303
Ulster Rifles, Militia 4th Bn. (Antrim)
   158
Ulster Rifles, Militia 5th (Down)   159
Ulster Rifles, Militia 6th (Louth)   159
Ulster Volunteers   234
Ulveston Volunteers   191
United Arts Rifles   207

Vectis, Loyal, Yeomanry   165
Veteran Bns.   243
Veterinary Corps, Royal Army   142, 310
Victoria's Rifles, Queen   202

Waggon Train, Royal   246
Waggoners, Royal   246
Wales Borderers, South   77, 288
Wales Borderers, South, Brecknock Bn.,
   T.A.   179
Wales's, Prince of, Volunteers – see
   Lancashire Regt., South
Warrington Volunteers   194
Warwickshire Fencible Cavalry   146
Warwickshire Fusiliers, Royal – see Appx
Warwickshire Militia   155
Warwickshire R.A., T.A.   305
Warwickshire Regt., Royal   57, 281
Warwickshire Regt., T.A. Bns.   218
Warwickshire Volunteers   217
Warwickshire Yeomanry   173
Waterford Militia   160
Watteville's Regt.   251
Welch Fusiliers, Royal   75, 287
Welch Fus., T.A. Bns. 4th (Denb.)   183
Welch Fus., T.A. Bns. 5th (Flint)   187
Welch Fus., T.A. Bns. 6th (Car.)   181
Welch Fus., T.A. Bns. 7th (Montgom.)
   210
Welch Fus., T.A. Bns. 25th (Yeo.)   169
Welch Regt.   94, 295
Welch Regt., T.A. Bns.   187
Wellington's, Duke of, Regt.   86, 291
Wellington's, Duke of, 3rd Militia Bn.
   155
Wellington's, Duke of, T.A. Bns.   220
Welsh Guards   45, 278
Welsh Horse Yeomanry   169
Wessex Field Ambulance, 2/1st   184
West African Regt.   247
West India Regt.   247
West Indies Regt., British   247
West Riding Regt. – see Wellington's,
   Duke of
Westbury Volunteers, Loyal   188
Westminster Dragoons   167, 315
Westminster's, Queen's   204
Westmorland, T.A. Bn.   218
Westmorland Yeomanry   173
Wicklow Militia   161
Wight, Isle of, Rifles   189
Wiltshire Militia   155
Wiltshire Regt.   112, 299

Wiltshire Regt. T.A. Bns.   219
Wiltshire Volunteers   218
Wiltshire Yeomanry   174
Winchester College Corps   190
Windsor, Military Knights of   256
Women's Corps   236, 319
Women's Legion   236
Worcestershire Hussars   303
Worcestershire Milita   155
Worcestershire Regt.   82, 290
Worcestershire Regt. T.A. Bns.   219
Worcestershire Yeomanry   174

Yarmouth Battery, R.A., T.A.   210
Yeomen of the Guard   256
York Light Infantry Volunteers   251
York Rangers, Queen's   320
York & Lancaster Regt.   165, 300
York & Lancaster 3rd Militia Bn.   156
York & Lancaster T.A. Bns.   222, 300
Yorkshire Dragoons Yeo.   175, 315
Yorkshire Hussars Yeomanry   175

Yorkshire Light Infantry, King's Own
    107, 298
Yorkshire Light Inf., T.A. Bns.   220
Yorkshire Militia, E., N. & W.   155, 312,
    315
Yorkshire, Prince of Wales's Own Regt. –
    see Appx
Yorkshire Regt., Princess of Wales's Own
    – see Green Howards
Yorkshire Regt., East   68, 285
Yorkshire Regt., East, T.A. Bns.   219
Yorkshire Regt., West   67, 284
Yorkshire Regt., West, T.A. Bns.   221
Yorkshire, East Riding Vols.   220, 318
Yorkshire, North Riding Vols.   220
Yorkshire, North Riding T.A. Bns.   220
Yorkshire Volunteers   312, 315, 318
Yorkshire, West Riding Arty.   221
Yorkshire, West Riding Fd. Amb.   223
Yorkshire, West Riding R.V.   318
Yorkshire, West Riding Regt. – see
    Wellington's, Duke of